1

Sartre and Psychoanalysis

Sartre and Psychoanalysis

An Existentialist Challenge to Clinical Metatheory

Betty Cannon

 University Press of Kansas

For Hazel E. Barnes
Teacher and Friend

© 1991 by the University Press of Kansas
All rights reserved

Published by the University Press of Kansas (Lawrence, Kansas 66045), which was organized by the Kansas Board of Regents and is operated and funded by Emporia State University, Fort Hays State University, Kansas State University, Pittsburg State University, the University of Kansas, and Wichita State University

Library of Congress Cataloging-in-Publication Data

Cannon, Betty.
    Sartre and psychoanalysis : an existentialist challenge to
clinical metatheory / Betty Cannon.
        p. cm.
    Includes bibliographical references and index.
    ISBN 0-7006-0445-6
    1. Psychoanalysis. 2. Sartre, Jean Paul, 1905–1980.
3. Existential psychotherapy. I. Title.
RC506.C29 1991
616.89'17—dc20   90-12993
                                                                      CIP

British Library Cataloguing in Publication Data is available.

Printed in the United States of America
10 9 8 7 6 5 4 3 2 1

The paper used in this publication meets the minimum requirements of the American National Standard for Permanence of Paper for Printed Library Materials Z39.48-1984.

Contents

Preface

A preface seems to be the appropriate place to share with the reader my reasons for writing this book, together with my decisions about certain practical issues which necessarily arise from an interdisciplinary endeavor of this nature. The latter include choices about inclusion and exclusion of theorists, usage of philosophical and/or psychological terminology, inclusion of secondary sources, and determination of appropriate scope.

First of all, why did I write a book on Sartre and psychoanalysis? The book primarily derives from my own experience as a psychotherapist combined with my interest both in psychoanalysis and in Sartre. As a therapist originally trained in humanistic psychology, I found myself more and more interested both in Freud and in the post-Freudian theorists who discuss relational needs deriving from early childhood. It seemed to me that among contemporary psychological approaches, only psychoanalysis provided a comprehensive theory of the *origins* of human misery; but at the same time, traditional psychoanalytic metatheory was somehow always strangely disturbing to me. It appeared to me that it left out something important or that it ever so slightly distorted even its most accurate clinical insights.

Perhaps my prior interest in existentialist philosophy, especially the philosophy of Sartre, influenced my dislike of Freudian determinism and Freudian metatheory. In any case, I constantly found myself translating the writings of Freud and contemporary psychoanalysts into Sartrean terms. I especially remember listening to a lecture by Otto Kernberg in which he seemed to be doing his best to describe human actions and meanings with a psychoanalytic jargon which reduced them to things. To the extent that he did *not* succeed, I found that he presented some exciting ideas. Sartre's ideas about human reality, combined with psychoanalytic emphasis on the power of childhood experiences to influence present human interactions, have shaped my own approach to clinical practice. In fact, as time goes on, I find my clients more and more confirming my impression that though Freudian theory often deals well with the past as ground, it does not adequately address the significance of the future as meaning for all human endeavors. It is in the area of respect for individual freedom and desire to create meaning or value and of understanding how change occurs that Sartre has been most helpful to me as a therapist.

Thus I decided to write a book about psychotherapy and philosophy—specifically about how the ontological (being-oriented) metatheory of Sartre can more adequately elucidate certain critical contemporary issues in psychoanalysis than the psychobiological metatheory of Freud. Obviously, a metapsychology, or philosophy of mind or experience, based on the assumptions of existentialist ontology must be quite different from a metapsychology based on the assumptions of positivistic science. My hope was to pinpoint those differences with some exactitude and in doing so to suggest how Sartre's metatheory can provide solutions to certain contemporary issues which plague psychoanalysis itself—issues relating to the interpersonal nature of earliest experience and to the importance of the creation of a "self" noted by many contemporary psychoanalytic theorists. In other words, I wanted to produce a book which establishes a dialogue between psychoanalysis and existentialist ontology—a dialogue which might lead to a new way of thinking both about psychotherapy and about the human issues which are inextricably connected with therapeutic practice.

My first decision involved the inclusion and exclusion of theorists. Obviously, there must be a comparison of Freud with Sartre. It also seemed clear that it would be appropriate to exclude the Freudian theorists who established new approaches of their own—Carl Jung, Alfred Adler, and Wilhelm Reich, for instance—despite the intrinsic interest of their work. In addition, there are a number of radical revisionists whose views are closer to my own—George Klein, Roy Schaffer, Alice Miller, Harold Searles, and R. D. Laing, for instance. Laing, whom I will mention in passing at various points, has even attempted to revise Freud using Sartre's ontology. I decided for the most part to stay with the mainstream theorists for purposes of clarity.

The great wealth of mainstream post-Freudian psychoanalytic theory and theorists at first seemed both richly tempting and overwhelming. It also seemed virtually inevitable that I would have to exclude or minimize my discussion even of some of my own favorite theorists—for example, Erik Erikson and Edith Jacobson among the ego psychologists, Karen Horney and Frieda Fromm-Reichmann among the interpersonal theorists, and Harry Guntrip among the British object relations theorists. I have also discussed only in passing certain theorists who are very important to the history of psychoanalysis—Heinz Hartmann, René Spitz, and Anna Freud, for instance. And I have excluded certain very interesting contemporary approaches to psychoanalytic theory, such as Arnold Modell's attempt to integrate object relations and Freudian instinct theory or the work of J. Weiss, H. Sampson, and their colleagues at Mt. Zion Hospital in San Francisco.

I believe that I have chosen representative theorists from the best-known post-Freudian psychoanalytic "schools" to illustrate the issues I wish to address. The theorists discussed in the first four chapters of the book are for the most part mainstream psychoanalytic theorists whose own influence is considerable. The least orthodox of these is Harry Stack Sullivan, and his impact on mainstream psychoanalytic theory with respect to the treatment of psychotics has been enormous. Even Heinz Kohut, whose "self-psychology" has caused so much controversy in contemporary American psychoanalytic circles, is a past president of both the American Psychoanalytic Association (APA) and the International Psychoanalytic Association (IPA). The other theorists considered—Melanie Klein, Margaret Mahler, Otto Kernberg, and D. W. Winnicott—are generally accepted as mainstream post-Freudian theorists. What is interesting is the extent to which the views of these seemingly orthodox post-Freudians have taken them, as we shall see, in directions which ultimately seem more Sartrean than Freudian.

The notable exception which I make to this rule of choosing more or less mainstream theorists is Jacques Lacan, whose work I consider in Chapters 6 through 8. Although Lacan has often been considered a renegade by orthodox Freudians (Lacan himself considers his views to be the only orthodoxy), I believed it important to discuss his work in some detail—primarily because of his enormous influence as a metatheorist who presents an alternative (structuralist) view to both traditional psychoanalysis and existential psychoanalysis. Also, with the exceptions of R. D. Laing and Freud himself, Lacan is the only theorist mentioned in this book with whose views Sartre himself was familiar. And though Sartre admitted that he did not know Lacan's work well, he was nonetheless quite familiar with the structuralist challenge to existentialism through the work of his longtime friend and contributor to *Les Temps Modernes*, Claude Lévi-Strauss. As for Lacan, he certainly knew Sartre's early philosophy and may even have been influenced by it in certain respects. Lacan's structuralist challenge seems to me to be the only serious systematic metatheoretical challenge from within the psychoanalytic community to either Freudian or existentialist metatheory. In comparing Sartre with Lacan, I obviously do not accept the verdict of certain contemporary critics that existentialism has been rendered intellectually passé by structuralism—or the concomitant idea that Lacanian structuralist psychoanalysis is somehow more profound than Sartrean existential psychoanalysis. But I do take Lacan seriously enough to give his work a thorough reading.

My next decisions concerned terminology. I was well aware in making them that in attempting to bring together two writers as comprehensive as Freud and Sartre and two disciplines as different as psychoanalysis and phenomenological ontology, I ran the risk of entering a terminological morass from which there was no exit. My solution was to limit my discussion to the essential terms, thereby hoping to relieve the reader of undue strain. Nonetheless, certain philosophical terms, which are probably less familiar to the general reader than psychoanalytic terms, were inevitable to an understanding of my subject. I have used them while attempting to provide the reader with readily accessible definitions and explanations. This problem with philosophical terminology is further compounded by the fact that the later Sartre introduces a whole new set of terms for his discussions of group interactions and sociomaterial reality.

To avoid the confusion which might arise from a proliferation of terms, I have restricted myself in the first four chapters largely to the terminology of *Being and Nothingness* except where terms from the later philosophy provide further insight into the ideas being discussed. Then, in the fifth chapter, I provide a discussion of Sartre's later philosophy, as it adds a new sociomaterial dimension to existential psychoanalysis. Having thus introduced the terminology of the *Critique*, I continue to use it (together with terms from Sartre's earlier work) in the next three chapters to develop a comparison/contrast between existential psychoanalysis and Lacanian structuralist psychoanalysis. Throughout this discussion, I maintain that while Sartre's basic ontology does not change, his later social theory allows an understanding of an individual's relations with series, groups, and the whole world of worked matter which was not present in his earlier work.

The terminological difficulties arising from this proliferation of terms are still further compounded in the later chapters by the fact that Lacan uses terms previously identified as Sartrean with new meanings. For example, the "Other" (capitalized) for Sartre is my human counterpart, while for Lacan it is the linguistic unconscious; the other person in Lacan is the "other" (lower cased). Similarly, Sartre believes that the "Look" (*le regard*) which fixes me as an object originates in the Other (person), while Lacan insists that this same phenomenon (*le regard*) originates in the Other (linguistic unconscious). Sometimes the Lacanian Other (the linguistic unconscious) is written as the "Other(A)"—the grand Other (*le grande Autre*). To avoid confusion, I follow Lacan scholar Ellie Ragland-Sullivan in attempting to make consistent use of this form to designate the linguistic unconscious—except where I am quoting Lacan himself. Also, following Lacan translators, I refer to the Lacanian "Look" as the "gaze." Nonetheless, the realization that Lacan uses certain Sartrean terms with a twist leads to a discussion of the way in which Lacan may have appropriated—and twisted—Sartrean concepts to his own ends.

Other terminological difficulties arise from mixing two forms of discourse in an attempt to talk about psychoanalytic issues from a Sartrean perspective. For example, should I continue to use Freudian terms such as "transference" and "resistance" when they imply Freudian metatheory? What about the difference between the Freudian "psyche" and Sartrean "consciousness" as descriptions of human reality? Also, what about the "medical model" on which not only psychoanalysis but also much of psychotherapy in general is based?

In answer to the first question, I have decided to use Freudian terms when there is no comparable Sartrean term, simply because they are familiar to most readers. But I have been careful to re-explain them from a Sartrean perspective. Second, in discussing Freud's view of human reality I refer to the "psyche," whereas in discussing Sartre's view I refer to "consciousness." When I am discussing human reality in general, I write "psyche or consciousness" or use some more general term.

As for the medical model, my solution is mixed. I have used the Rogerian term "client" when I refer to an existentialist perspective and to my own work as a therapist mainly because that is the term I use in my practice and because I prefer its nonmedical implications. But I have used "patient" or "analysand" when I refer to the object of traditional psychoanalytic investigations. When I am referring to both, I have used both terms. I have not found comparable nonmedical terms for describing psychological distress or for referring to the successful outcome of therapy—and have therefore sparingly used "psychopathology" (and various Freudian and post-Freudian diagnostic categories) and "cure," usually in quotation marks. Sartre himself uses the latter, but then he also uses "subject" or "analysand" rather than "client."

I have encountered difficulties even with the terms "psychoanalysis" and "psychoanalyst" as they refer respectively to an existentialist and a Freudian perspective. These difficulties derive neither from Freud nor from Sartre but from my own perspective as the author of this book. Sartre said of himself that he was a "fellow traveller" who was sympathetic to but not fully convinced by psychoanalytic theory and practice (BEM, p. 199). Like many contemporary therapists influenced by psychoanalysis, I, too, consider myself to be a "fellow traveller." Hence while I often use interpretation as a technique, I also use techniques drawn from other therapeutic orientations—especially from Gestalt therapy and psychodrama, body-oriented psychotherapy, and Rogerian nondirectional therapy. All of my clinical work, however, is informed by psychoanalytic theory about the origins of psychological difficulties in childhood experience as modified by a Sartrean perspective. As a result of these contradictions, I feel more comfortable talking about "existentialist therapy" and the "existentialist therapist" than about "existential psychoanalysis" and the "existential psychoanalyst"—except where I am specifically referring to Sartre's own use of these terms. In using either term, I am, of course, referring to a Sartrean existentialist approach and not to a therapeutic approach derived from other existentialist philosophers. I believe these distinctions will be perfectly clear within context.

My third decision concerned secondary sources. There is a wealth of critical commentary on Sartre, Freud, Lacan, and the various mainstream post-Freudian psychoanalytic theorists. I thought that to include much of this material, together with the number of primary sources cited, would be to blur the lines of the argument with undue complexity. Thus, though I have learned a great deal from this material, I have limited myself to citing only those critics whose thinking has significantly influenced my own approach to a particular topic—for example, I have cited Frank J. Sulloway's (1979) intellectual biography of Freud in the first chapter, Jay R. Greenberg and Stephen A. Mitchell's (1983) division of post-Freudian theorists into "drive/structure" and "relational/structure" theorists in the second, and Ellie Ragland-Sullivan's (1986) excellent explication of Lacan in the sixth through the eighth. Otherwise, I have attempted to keep references to secondary sources to a minimum.

The exception to this rule is my liberal quoting from Sartre scholar and translator Hazel E. Barnes. I believe my use of her work is appropriate for several reasons. First, it was Hazel Barnes, as a translator and critic, who introduced Sartre *as a philosopher* to the English-speaking world. Second, Hazel Barnes's attempt to construct an ethics along Sartrean lines in *An Existentialist Ethics* (1967) is similar in some ways to my own attempt to expand

Sartre's comments on existential psychoanalysis to a full theory. And last and most important, Hazel Barnes, as a teacher and friend, has over a number of years had such a pervasive influence on my own work on Sartre that I am less concerned that I will quote her too frequently than that I will inadvertently consider some idea of hers, fully assimilated into my thinking, as my own. I would not, of course, make her responsible for any difficulties which the reader may have with this volume.

Finally, there was the issue of scope. I do not consider this book to be an exhaustive treatment of Sartre's potential influence on psychoanalytic metatheory, and it certainly is not a comprehensive treatment of the impact that a Sartrean perspective might have on clinical practice. Such a comprehensive treatment would have required a book at least several times the size of this one—and the reader probably considers it long enough as it is. Instead, I have limited myself to a Sartrean view of what I believe to be some critical issues in Freudian and post-Freudian metatheory. My intention is to present Sartre's ideas in such a way that therapists already convinced of the value of depth therapy might find Sartre's insights useful to their work with clients, as I myself have done. I would also expect that Sartreans would find this endeavor interesting. Although a phenomenological or existentialist perspective on psychotherapy or even occasional applications of Sartre's ideas to clinical practice are not new, what I believe is new in my approach is a systematic application of Sartre's ideas to contemporary psychoanalytic issues. My hope is that this will be the beginning of a serious treatment of Sartre as a psychoanalytic metatheorist, similar to the treatment of Heidegger by Ludwig Binswanger, Medard Boss, and others.

In concluding, I would like to thank the many friends and colleagues who have provided the support and encouragement that provoked me to complete this project amid many more pressing duties and commitments. First and most important is my friend and teacher Hazel E. Barnes, to whom this book is dedicated. Seldom has a book owed so much to one person. It was in working with Hazel Barnes as a graduate student at the University of Colorado that I began to see the relevance of Sartre's philosophy for clinical theory and practice. Those ideas, with Hazel's encouragement, eventually became the core of this book. Her careful reading of the manuscript in all its stages of completion, her advice on theoretical and practical matters, and her warm personal interest have proved simply invaluable. I am deeply grateful.

I would also like to thank my own therapist and teacher, Dr. Laurence Heller. Although Larry will probably disagree with a great deal of what I have said about metatheory, I can only reply that it is from him that I have learned by precept and example much of what I know about the practice of a humanistically oriented psychotherapy which I have come to regard as existentialist. In addition, I would like to thank my clients, whose struggles to be or to let go have engaged me deeply and who have generously agreed to allow me to tell portions of their stories (slightly altered to prevent identification) here. It is from their work with me that many of the insights of this book derive.

I want also to thank the many friends and colleagues who have read portions or all of this manuscript and who have discussed its ideas with me. They include (in alphabetical order) Jan Abu Shakrah, Valerie Broin, Ralph Buultjens, Mike Claussner, Mark Dubin, Marcus Edward, Paulette Feuer, Haim Gordon, Joanne and Albert Greenberg, Frances Harper, Graham Hereford, Julia Holloway, Judith Howell, Phyllis Kenevan, Sanford Krolick, Patricia and Luke Lea, Patrea Mah, Polly Mahoney, Steve Martinot, Bill Mattingly, Cynthia McLemore, Lee Morey, Bill Reinhardt, Annette Robinson, Ze'ev Sabar, Mary Schlesinger, Doris Schwalbe, Marc Weiss, and Elaine Yarbrough. In addition to dialogue about ideas and personal support, some of these people deserve thanks for special favors: Joanne Greenberg for her enthusiastic encouragement and for allowing me to quote our taped conversations in this book; Cindie McLemore and Pat Lea for final proofreading at a point where I could no longer see errors; and Phyllis Kenevan, Paulette Feuer, Mary Schlesinger, Cindie McLemore, and Pat Lea for being there in moments of existential anguish when I began to doubt the value of the whole enterprise.

I am grateful to Ernest Keen, Joseph Catalano, and Robert Stone for their very useful professional reviews of the manuscript and their encouraging written remarks. Robert Stone and Elizabeth Bowman also deserve thanks for pointing out to me manuscript materials which proved important to my argument in Chapter 5. I would like to thank my supervisor, Dr. William Philip, for patient listening and wise advice. Thanks also go to the Colorado School of Mines for much-needed sabbatical and leave time and to the waitpeople in the Harvest Restaurant, where I spent many hours writing, for the endless cup of tea. In addition, I would like to thank my son, Dylan Cannon, for his continuing enthusiasm and support for this project.

Finally, two other people deserve special thanks for facilitating the timely completion of this book. The first is my friend Gloria Riley, who not only spent long hours correcting and preparing the manuscript in its various stages but who also encouraged, (kindly) nagged, and otherwise provoked its author to complete it. The other is Michael Briggs, acquisitions editor at the University Press of Kansas, who is everything an editor should be—enthusiastic, supportive, demanding, and encouraging. In addition to carefully reading and commenting on the manuscript, checking on my progress, and sending me useful reviews on anything that related to my subject, it was Mike Briggs who encouraged me to include the chapters dealing with Jacques Lacan that I now believe are an integral part of my argument for the power of Sartre's metatheory over existing metapsychological approaches.

Abbreviations Used in Citing Sartre's Works

B   *Baudelaire*

BEM   *Between Existentialism and Marxism [Situations VIII and Situations IX]*

BN   *Being and Nothingness [L'Etre et le Néant]*

CA   *The Condemned of Altona [Les Sequéstrés d'Altona]*

CDR   *Critique of Dialectical Reason [Critique de la raison dialectique]*

DH   *Dirty Hands [Les Mains sales]*

E   *Existentialism [L'Existentialisme est un humanisme]*

EOT   *The Emotions: Outline of a Theory [Esquisse d'une théorie des émotions]*

FI   *The Family Idiot [L'Idiot de la famille] (vols. 1 and 2)*

FS   *The Freud Scenario [Le Scénario Freud]*

IF   *L'Idiot de la famille (vol. 3)*

L/S   *Life/Situations [Situations X]*

N   *Nausea [La Nausée]*

NE   *No Exit [Huit clos]*

SG   *Saint Genet: Actor and Martyr [Saint Genet, comédien et martyr]*

SM   *Search for a Method [Questions de méthode]*

TE   *The Transcendence of the Ego [La Transcendance de l'Ego]*

W   *The Words [Les Mots]*

1 · Introduction

This is a book about psychotherapy and philosophy. Specifically, it is an attempt to deal with what I see as a crisis in contemporary psychoanalytic metatheory by suggesting a change in metatheoretical models. This "crisis," which is often obscured by the propensity of psychoanalytic theorists to use Freudian terminology to gloss over difficulties, arises from the discovery by post-Freudian psychoanalytic theorists working with severely disturbed patients and with children of a whole new set of human needs which have nothing at all to do with Freudian drives. These needs may basically be described as consisting of two (interrelated) sets: relational needs for holding, mirroring, positive regard, and emotional responsiveness and needs for the development of a coherent and flexible sense of "self." Since the presence of these needs is not explained by Freudian drive theory and since they are mostly assumed to exist from earliest infancy, it seems obvious that contemporary psychoanalysis requires a more human approach to human reality—an approach which is not, I submit, provided by the counter position of Lacanian structuralist psychoanalysis. I believe that Sartre's ontology, enriched by the sociomaterial insights of his later philosophy, does provide that more human approach.

Before describing the structure of this book, however, I think it might be helpful to define "metatheory" and "ontology" as these terms will be used here and to discuss my choice of Sartre over other existentialist philosophers for developing a systematic metapsychology. I will also respond to a number of questions which people have asked me about the advisability of using Sartre's philosophy as a basis for this enterprise—questions which seem to reflect a skepticism which has echoes in critical commentaries as well. Let us begin with metapsychology. Clinical metatheory or metapsychology refers to those premises beyond validation by empirical observation which provide a philosophical framework for clinical hypotheses and constructs.

Freud himself considered metapsychology important, noting as late as 1937 that nothing could be achieved without consulting the "Witch Metapsychology." Indeed, Freud says, "without metapsychological speculation and theorizing—I had almost said 'phantasying'—we shall not get another step forward" (Freud, 1937, p. 225). The economic (drives, permutations of libido), topographical (conscious, preconscious, unconscious), and structural (ego, superego, id) hypotheses of Freud, together with his developmental theory, his ideas about psychodynamic conflicts, and his postulates concerning life and death instincts, are all metatheoretical constructs. Contemporary psychoanalysts have difficulty particularly with the economic hypothesis, so much so that some (see Guntrip, 1971; Schafer, 1976) have even proposed that drive theory should be superseded by more humanly understandable constructs. Psychoanalytic theorist George Klein (1976), noting that it is difficult to find empirical tests for Freudian metatheory, suggests eliminating metatheory altogether in favor of a purely clinical psychoanalytic theory, while G. Pribram and M. Gill (1976) argue that the metapsychological basis of psychoanalysis is a positive handicap.

What many of these theorists find difficult is the excessively mechanistic language of Freudian metatheory—a point Bruno Bettelheim (1982) has taken up by suggesting that the mechanicalness is the result of English translations and that Freud in the original German is much more humanistic. Roy Schaffer (1976) has even gone so far as to propose a new "action language" to replace the mechanistic terminology of traditional Freudian metapsychology—a language which would take into account human intentions, meanings, reasons, and subjective experience in a way that Freudian metatheory ignores. More orthodox Freudians, including many of those discussed in this volume, still speak the language of the drives, though they often either argue for specific modifications (see, for example, Modell, 1981) or use the old language with new meanings—a point to which I return in later chapters.

I do not propose to eliminate metatheory since I believe that metatheoretical assumptions are unavoidable in clinical practice. The question is not whether one has a metatheory but whether one has done some critical thinking about the nature of that metatheory and its effects on clinical practice. Even behaviorism, which purports to reject metapsychology altogether, is actually a "philosophy of mind" which denies the existence of "mind." As the materialist side of Cartesian dualism carried to an extreme, it is, as

Sartre says, "really only solipsism as a working hypothesis" (BN, p. 229). Freudian metatheory, by contrast, does not reject mind as such. Indeed, it glories in the discovery of new regions of the mind, such as the preconscious and unconscious and the ego, superego, and id.

Yet at the same time, classical psychoanalysis insists on reducing consciousness to an epiphenomenon of unconscious psychic forces guided by scientific laws of cause and effect. In doing so, Freudian metatheory looks behind human experience for explanations which lie outside that experience. For this reason, I suppose one could say that it is a kind of metaphysical metapsychology. And, indeed, J. Laplanche and J.-B. Pontalis comment on the connection between "metapsychology" and "metaphysics" in Freud's own mind (Laplanche and Pontalis, 1973, pp. 249–250). Freud himself defines metapsychology as a scientific endeavor to redress the constructions of metaphysics, which he sees as similar to superstitious beliefs or paranoiac delusions, by "transform[ing] *metaphysics* into *metapsychology*" (Freud, 1901, p. 259). One wonders whether Freud has replaced metaphysics with metapsychology or merely produced a metaphysical metapsychology which disguises its first principles as scientific positivism.

The alternative, as I see it, is an ontological metapsychology which is closer to the human experience it attempts to describe. The word "ontology," which means simply "philosophy of Being," has itself throughout most of the history of philosophy been considered synonymous with metaphysics or the study of first principles. Ontology, however, came to have a different meaning in the works of Martin Heidegger and Jean-Paul Sartre, both of whom were influenced by the phenomenology of Edmund Husserl. For Heidegger and even more for Sartre, ontology is a description of Being rather than a study of first principles.

The influence of Husserl on Sartre's phenomenological ontology is decisive. Indeed, a turning point in Sartre's career occurred when Raymond Aron introduced him to Husserl's philosophy in 1933. According to a well-known story, Sartre, Simone de Beauvoir, and Aron were drinking either apricot cocktails or beer (Beauvoir says it was the former, Aron the latter) at the Bec de Gaz in the Rue Montparnasse when Sartre attempted to sketch for Aron the outline of a novel he was writing. It would later become *Nausea* (1938). Aron related the theme of Sartre's novel to his own recent studies in German philosophy in Berlin, especially his study of Husserl's phenomenology. "You see, *mon petit comarade*," he said to Sartre, "if you're a phenomenologist, you can talk about this drink and that's philosophy" (Cohen-Solal, 1985, pp. 90–94; Hayman, 1987, pp. 97–101).

Sartre could not hide his enthusiasm for a philosophy which would bypass the familiar opposition between idealism and realism for a concrete relationship between consciousness and the world. For the next several years, he would make a thorough study first of Husserl and then of Heidegger—taking Aron's place at the French Institute in Berlin for the following year. Sartre would later say that "Husserl reinstituted the horror and the charm of things. He has restored to us the world of artists and prophets" (quoted by Collins, 1980, p. 12). The phenomenology which Sartre thereafter embraced assumes a partnership between consciousness and the world—a partnership in which consciousness is always "intentional" in the sense that it is always consciousness *of* some real, remembered, or imagined event. Indeed, Sartre would carry this idea further than Husserl, denying the existence even of a transcendental ego or of the possibility of withdrawal from the world or bracketing of one's intentionality (*epoché*) in order to study one's own subjective processes. For Sartre, one's "fundamental project" or choice of a way of being must be grasped in the midst of living and connecting with the world and not in some state apart—though, as we shall see in a later chapter, Sartre himself recommends a special state of mind (pure reflection) for a more accurate comprehension of one's own motives and actions.

Thus Sartre acknowledges his connection with the tradition of Husserl and Heidegger when, in the subtitle to *Being and Nothingness*, he refers to his own philosophy as "phenomenological ontology." Sartre's ontology differs from metaphysics in that it is an attempt not to describe the first principles behind Being, but Being itself, including those aspects of Being which are human being. As Joseph S. Catalano notes, Sartre, even more than Heidegger, "distinguishes ontology from metaphysics." For Sartre, metaphysics "is concerned with the question of *why* there is anything rather than nothing," whereas Sartre "claims that he is interested only in the fundamental descriptions of being, and not in speculations about its origins—although . . . he occasionally indulges in such speculations" (Catalano, 1974, p. 15).

Sartre's ontology would seem to be well suited to the demands of clinical metatheory since it opts for what psychologists refer to as "experience-near" descriptions rather than the "experience-distant" explanations of Freudian metatheory, which are making even contemporary psychoanalysts uncomfortable. At the same time that Sartre's ontology is more human, however, it is also a theory of Being and not mere empirical description—which means that it allows for an understanding of the meaning and significance of actions and symptoms rather than a simple cataloguing of events. It remains to be seen whether it elucidates the clinical facts of depth therapy better than Freudian metatheory, although I maintain that it does.

The question now arises as to why I chose Sartre as the basis for this study rather than another existentialist philosopher or a combination of existentialist philosophers, who might also be expected to produce experience-near descriptions of human dilemmas. After all, have I not already said that Sartre was heavily influenced by Husserl and Heidegger? And have Husserl and Heidegger, along with other existentialist philosophers, not already been richly mined for their psychological insights? Certainly, the Daseins-analysts (named for Heidegger's description of human reality as *Dasein*, or "being there"), especially Ludwig Binswanger (1963) and Medard Boss (1957, 1963), have already attempted a systematic rethinking of psychoanalysis along Heideggerian lines—a rethinking which first became influential in the English-speaking world through the wide dissemination of translations of Binswanger's work and the work of other European existential/phenomenological analysts in Rollo May, Ernest Angel, and Henri F. Ellenberger's epochal edition, *Existence* (1958). Certainly, there has also been a rich mining of Husserl for psychological insights, especially among the phenomenological psychologists at Duquesne University; a particularly ambitious work is Joseph Kockelmans's *Edmund Husserl's Phenomenological Psychology* (1967).

Furthermore, many existentially oriented psychologists and psychotherapists have been satisfied with a more eclectic approach, preferring to glean insights from a number of existentialist philosophers rather than to stay with the ideas of only one thinker. For example, J. H. Van den Berg's excellent (and somewhat neglected) book, *The Phenomenological Approach to Psychiatry* (1955), blends the ideas of Husserl, Sartre, and others in a sensitive application of existentialist ideas to clinical practice. Adrian Van Kaam's *Existential Foundations of Psychology* (1969) also blends sources in an existentialist reevaluation of psychological theory. J. H. Bugental's *The Search for Authenticity* (1965) applies existentialist insights to the contingencies of human existence as these relate to anxiety. Ernest Keen's *Three Faces of Being* (1970) presents an extremely interesting application of existentialist insights drawn from a number of sources to clinical issues centering around the Sartrean-Heideggerian themes of Being-in-the-world, Being-for-myself, and Being-for-others.

M. Guy Thompson's *The Death of Desire* (1985) presents a challenging discussion of the impact of phenomenology/existentialism on psychotherapy; he takes a more optimistic view than I do of the reconcilability of Lacanian structuralist psychoanalysis with phenomenological/existentialist approaches. Irvin D. Yalom's *Existential Psychotherapy* (1980) is likewise an excellent treatment of the impact of existentialist themes such as death, freedom, isolation, and the search for meaning on the conduct of psychotherapy, while his most recent book, *Love's Executioner* (1989), is a moving personal account of the existential dilemmas which face therapist and patient alike. In addition, there is the "logotherapy" of Viktor Frankl (1955, 1959, 1967, 1969), who considers the center of psychic life—and the source of psychopathology—to be the search for meaning (or its absence).

This array of theorists/practitioners would suggest that since Rollo May (1950, 1953; May, Angel, and Ellenberger, 1958) introduced existentialist psychology to the English-speaking world in the 1950s, existentially oriented psychotherapy has not lacked its adherents. May, who in his eclecticism tends to be less favorable to Sartre than to other existentialist philosophers, continues to have an enormous influence on the movement (see May, 1983). And the *Review of Existential Psychology and Psychiatry*, which recently produced volumes on Sartre and Heidegger, continues to provide a forum for writers on existentialist psychology and psychotherapy. This book obviously fits into that context. Indeed, I doubt that I would feel the need to justify it if so many people, hearing about the plan for the book, had not asked me the question, "Why Sartre?" Before addressing where I think these people's doubts are really coming from, I would like to counter with another question, "Why not Sartre?" For some time, I have considered a systematic application of Sartre's ideas to clinical theory and practice to be long overdue.

Let me explain. Evidence suggests that Sartre, more than any other existentialist philosopher (with the possible exception of Karl Jaspers), has demonstrated a deep and continuing interest both in psychological theory in general and in psychoanalysis in particular. Indeed, Sartre's student, journalistic colleague, and friend, the eminent French psychoanalyst J.-B. Pontalis, suggests that one day the "history of Sartre's thirty-year-long [forty-year long by the time of Sartre's death in 1980] relationship with psychoanalysis, an ambiguous mixture of *equally* deep attraction and repulsion, will have to be written and perhaps his work reinterpreted in the light of it" (Pontalis in BEM, p. 220). In this book, I propose instead to use Sartre as a basis for reinterpreting psychoanalysis. And although Sartre himself never underwent psychoanalysis, he became interested enough in the process during the period when he was writing his autobiography and trying to understand his dreams to suggest that Pontalis analyze him. In light of their long friendship, Pontalis very wisely refused (Pontalis in FS, p. xv; Hayman, 1987, pp. 393–94; Cohen-Solal, 1985, p. 443).

Sartre's own writing on psychological themes began with his thesis at the University of Paris in 1927, which was entitled *L'Image dans la vie psychologique, Role et nature*; it was later published in revised form as the first part of *Imagination* (1936). This was followed by two classical philosophical/psychological treatises, *The Emotions: Outline of a Theory* (1939) and *The Psychology of Imagination* (1940). In addition, Sartre's first major philosophical work, *The Transcendence of the Ego* (1937), is at least as significant psychologically as it is philosophically. Sartre also devotes a section of his philosophical masterpiece, *Being and Nothingness* (1943), to the development of major premises for an "existential psychoanalysis" (BN, pp. 557–75)—and, indeed, the whole work, as we shall see, has psychological as well as philosophical significance. Furthermore, Sartre was interested in applying his theoretical constructs to individual lives. In addition to the omnipresence of psychological dilemmas in Sartre's fiction and plays, there are the psychobiographies—subtle and increasingly penetrating studies of the lives of Baudelaire, Genet, and Flaubert, together with other less-lengthy pieces. Sartre's autobiography, *The Words* (1963), demonstrates the premises of existential psychoanalysis as applied to Sartre's own life.

Actually, not even death has silenced Sartre's voice as a psychobiographer who was deeply interested in psychoanalysis. In 1984, Pontalis brought out an edition of two versions (originally over eight hundred pages) of a screenplay on Freud's life which Sartre had written for John Huston in 1958 and 1959. Although the film starring Montgomery Clift contains little of Sartre's original dialogue and little of his brilliance, and although Sartre eventually had his name removed from the credits, *The Freud Scenario* may now be judged to contain some of Sartre's finest writing. It is also amazingly sympathetic to Freud. Despite Sartre's own assertion in an interview with Michel Rybalka that Huston had picked the wrong man for the job "because one shouldn't choose someone who doesn't believe in the unconscious to do a film to the glory of Freud" (Sartre in Schilpp, 1981, p. 12), there is no question that Sartre took the project seriously.

To prepare himself to write the screenplay, Sartre reread *Studies on Hysteria* and *The Interpretation of Dreams* and read Freud's *Autobiography*, the Freud-Fleiss correspondence (which had just been discovered two years earlier), commentaries on and critical works about Freud, and the newly translated first volume of Ernest Jones's biography of Freud. He also had Michelle Vian laboriously translate aloud, line by line, the other Jones volumes (Cohen-Solal, 1985, pp. 384–87; Hayman, 1987, pp. 351–61; Pontalis in preface to FS). This renewed interest in Freud, I believe, accounts in part for the depth of Sartre's own analysis of Flaubert's hysterico-epilepsy and for the strength of his insistence, in *Search for a Method*, that only psychoanalysis can provide the entrance into the world of childhood which is a necessary cornerstone for any viable social science theory.

I do not mean to imply, however, that Sartre was converted to orthodox Freudianism through writing *The Freud Scenario*—as Hayman wrongly contends in his biography (1987, pp. 352–53). As Hazel Barnes (1989) has pointed out, much of the action of Sartre's film script can be interpreted in two ways—according to Sartre's theory of bad faith and Freud's theory of the unconscious. Furthermore, Sartre himself says in the interview with Rybalka that although he had through the years gone "deeper into the doctrine of Freud," he was nonetheless "always separated from him . . . because of his idea of the unconscious" (Sartre in Schilpp, 1981, p. 12).

The truth is that Sartre's deep interest in psychological issues had led him to produce a philosophy that had always been pro as well as contra Freud. Those differences are perhaps encapsulated in the following passage:

> I must add [to Sartre's statement that Cartesian rationalism had mistakenly dampened his earlier enthusiasm for Freud] that I remain shocked by what was inevitable in Freud—the biological and physiological language with which he underpinned thoughts. . . . Right up to the time of Fleiss, as you know, he wrote physiological studies designed to provide an equivalent of the cathexes and equilibria he had found in psychoanalysis. The result is that the manner in which he describes the psychoanalytic object suffers from a kind of mechanistic cramp. This is not always true, for there are moments when he transcended this. But in general this language produces a *mythology* of the unconscious which I cannot accept. I am completely in agreement with the *facts* of disguise and repression, as facts. But the *words* 'repression,' 'censorship,' or 'drive'—words which express at one moment a sort of finalism and the next moment a sort of mechanism, these I reject. (BEM, p. 37)

Sartre, in other words, rejects Freudian metatheory.

Furthermore, Sartre believes that the mechanistic, authoritarian approach of psychoanalysis, in which the analyst is only subject and the analysand perpetual object, is mistaken. This idea of pushing for a more egalitarian model for psychoanalysis on one occasion led Sartre to create trouble on the editorial board of *Les Temps Modernes*. In 1969, an analysand presented Sartre with a tape-recorded version of a session with his analyst in which the presence of the tape recorder appeared to turn the tables in the subject-object dichotomy. Sartre insisted on publishing the transcript of this session, along with his own commentary and that of his dissenting board members, Pontalis and B. Pingaud. Although Pontalis (BEM, p. 220) may have been correct in thinking that Sartre's response indicates a failure to fully understand the clinical intricacies of psychoanalysis, I believe that it does illustrate an important difference between existential and Freudian psychoanalysis. Existential psychoanalysis finds that it must be alert to new interpersonal issues in the therapeutic relationship, issues deriving from the subject-object alternation which has been of key significance in Sartre's understanding of human relations—a point to which I return in later chapters.

Here, I suppose, it would be well to address directly the skepticism of the people who have questioned me about my choice of Sartre's philosophy as a basis for clinical metatheory. I believe these doubts spring from certain popular (and critical) misconceptions about Sartre's philosophy—misconceptions which are in some instances fueled by Sartre's own statements. Aside from the extent to which Sartre's interest in psychoanalysis and psychological issues in general is sometimes underrated, Sartre has often been regarded as a rationalist voluntarist (see, for example, Murdoch, 1953) whose rejection of the Freudian unconscious would make any depth therapy impossible. Perhaps it is for this reason that even a partially sympathetic critic such as Rollo May regards Sartre's philosophy as not being "the most useful introduction to the [existentialist] movement" because it represents "a subjectivist extreme" (1983, p. 49).

Furthermore, Sartre's views on human relations and the human condition in general have often been regarded as unduly pessimistic. The interpersonal relations described in *Being and Nothingness* are all conflictual, no-win situations, leading to the impression that Garcin's pronouncement toward the end of *No Exit* is indeed the view of the play's author. Garcin says, "Hell is other people" (NE, p. 41). As for the human condition, Roquentin's realizations in Sartre's novel *Nausea* that his fundamental response to his own bodily existence is one of nausea and that pure being without the addition of human meaning and purpose is senseless and absurd have been taken as indications that Sartre's brand of existentialism is unduly dark and nihilistic.

Indeed, some critics have gone even further to suggest that Sartre's philosophy itself is the production of a sick mind. Douglas Kirsner, for example, in *The Schizoid World of Jean-Paul Sartre and R. D. Laing* (1977), argues that the worldview shared by Sartre and Laing is best described as "schizoid," while

James Masterson, in his book *The Real Self*, labels Sartre a "narcissistic personality disorder" (1985, pp. 125–28). How, my critics want to know, can such a dark or even pathological philosophy have anything positive to contribute to the practice of psychotherapy? Furthermore, my more persistent questioners ask, what about Sartre's later conversion to Marxism? Does not the collective struggle advocated by Marxism invalidate an individualist discipline such as psychoanalysis? And what about the idea that existentialism is passé? Would it not be more valuable or at least more fashionable to investigate the views of structuralist psychoanalysis, as presented by Jacques Lacan?

I am not overwhelmed by these objections. First of all, it seems to me that the critics who label Sartre a rationalist voluntarist or a subjectivist demonstrate an intrinsic misunderstanding of his ontology. Although Sartre himself has suggested in later interviews that his earlier philosophy is too individualistic and too much under the domination of Cartesian rationalism, I believe that he is really talking about emphasis and examples. Clearly, the earlier Sartre did not understand as well as the later Sartre the significance of sociomaterial constraints and class struggle for the simple reason that he had yet to evolve the political awareness and intellectual tools for understanding these things. Nor, perhaps, did the earlier Sartre give enough credit to the elusiveness of what he came to refer to as *le vécu*, or lived experience, a concept which he later proposed as a substitute for the Freudian unconscious. Yet even though lived experience represents a "host of complex intentions" which are full of a richness they do not usually yield, Sartre continues to reject the idea that *le vécu* is either unconscious or on principle unavailable to reflective understanding. He merely concedes that it is not usually understood (Sartre in Schilpp, 1981, pp. 22–23).

This position is not a contradiction of Sartre's earlier philosophy, since Sartre had always maintained that there is an unsurpassable gulf between spontaneous lived experience and reflective understanding, between the consciousness reflecting and the (past) consciousness reflected on. It is this gulf, along with "bad faith" or lying to myself about the nature of reality, which helps to explain the strange phenomenon of my "willing" to do one thing on a reflective level while making another choice entirely on the nonreflective level. Obviously, this is not simplistic voluntarism, and, indeed, these two concepts of reflective/spontaneous consciousness and bad faith (as we shall see in the next chapter) will go a long way toward explaining many of the phenomena which Freud proposes as evidence of unconscious processes.

As for Sartre's own criticism of the overly rationalist strain in his earlier philosophy, I think that Sartre means that he had not earlier appreciated the extent to which an individual, in relating to the world, is impressed by early familial interactions and sociomaterial constraints. On the purely philosophical level, however, Sartre has never been a rationalist. Indeed, the choice of a rational, emotional, or imaginative relationship with the world has always been conceived by him to be prerational. Nor was Sartre ever the extreme subjectivist that May characterizes him as being. Consciousness, for Sartre, as I already said, is always consciousness *of* objects in the world.

The criticism that Sartre's earlier philosophy is unduly pessimistic, especially with respect to its description of human relationships, is perhaps more justified by Sartre's own statements. After all, what could be more pessimistic than Sartre's pronouncement, after describing the ontological purpose of human beings as the creation of an (impossible) substantive freedom, that "man is a useless passion" (BN, p. 615)? On the other hand, I think we should note that Sartre answers the charge that existentialism is nihilistic and pessimistic in his popular essay (originally presented as a public lecture), *Existentialism* (1946). There Sartre argues that although existentialism would embrace such negative terms as "anguish," "forlornness," and "despair," it would do so only to give them a new meaning in a philosophy which is not in the least pessimistic. Indeed, Sartre declares that "there is no doctrine more optimistic, since man's destiny is within himself" (E, p. 42).

Anguish, Sartre says, refers to the recognition that one is free without excuse—that one defines by one's own life what it means to be human. Forlornness refers to the realization that one is alone in a universe without divinely (or otherwise) ordained a priori values—a universe in which one is responsible for creating value and meaning. Despair refers to the realization that although one must continue to act, one cannot always control the consequences of one's actions, that the world will make of them what it will. All of this amounts to "an optimistic toughness" (E, p. 40) which places squarely on the shoulders of the individual the responsibility to make meaning and value while insisting that the individual is free to do so. Seen in this light, Roquentin's horrific ecstacy in *Nausea* loses its nihilistic implications. Roquentin simply has learned through a gut-level experience that pure contingent being (represented by his encounter with the chestnut tree) has no meaning which has not been placed there by the projection of a human future.

As for the pessimistic implications of Sartre's account of human relations, I must begin by saying that I think these descriptions are among Sartre's greatest contributions to existentialist psychological theory, provided they are not taken as the whole of what is possible in human relations. Indeed, it is the application of his ontology to the description of conflicted human relationships and his description of the nature and possibilities for such relating which, to my way of thinking, make Sartre's philosophy more immediately applicable to the consulting room than, say, the philosophy of Heidegger.

I am aware, of course, that apologists for Heidegger have criticized Sartre for this very thing—for the concreteness with which he spells out the implications of his ontology. The argument goes that whereas Heidegger is a true ontologist, or philosopher of Being, Sartre operates only on the ontic level, that of concrete beings. It seems to me that this criticism is unfair since, despite Sartre's indebtedness to Heidegger, he has far greater talents for spelling out the connections between ontological concepts and concrete applications than Heidegger. This difference is perhaps especially striking in Sartre's description of human relationships. Dissatisfied with Heidegger's vague designation of interpersonal relations as the *Mitsein* or "being with," Sartre sought to provide an ontological explanation of the perpetual presence of human conflicts—an explanation I present in detail in Chapter 3.

Yet although I believe that Sartre's description of human conflicts in the section of *Being and Nothingness* entitled "Concrete Relations with Others" (BN, pp. 361–430) is among his most brilliant contributions to psychology, I will acknowledge that Sartre does give the impression there that human relations are to be understood entirely in terms of a sadomasochistic power struggle which arises from a conflict over who gets to be subject and who object in a particular relationship. On the other hand, from an elusive footnote in which Sartre asserts the possibility of salvation from the sadomasochistic circle through a "radical conversion which we cannot discuss here" (BN, p. 412) and from the general implications of Sartre's ontology, one gets the impression that this is not the whole story about human relationships. But Sartre does not elaborate on this. Later, he would declare that all of the relations described in "Concrete Relations with Others" were in bad faith. And in his later work, he would strive more carefully to suggest that positive reciprocity and authentic love are genuine possibilities, a point to which I return in Chapter 3. I also explore there the very great significance which Sartre's ontological description of interpersonal relationships has for developmental theory—a significance which Sartre himself has begun to work out in the psychobiographies, but which this book is the first to propose as an answer to the metatheoretical dilemmas concerning the new "relational needs" discovered by post-Freudian psychoanalytic theorists.

As for the idea that Sartre in his later philosophy has abandoned his earlier belief in the free individual and converted to orthodox Marxism, a view which Hayman expresses in his biography, this is simply absurd. Yet it is part of a larger critical view (also expressed by Hayman) that Sartre constantly changed his philosophical perspective. Sartre, says Hayman, "had so much faith in his new theories that he forgot the old ones: rather than build higher on an old foundation he would start all over with a new one" (1987, p. 261). Sartre had already countered this line of thinking by asserting that he "never said that I changed every five years: On the contrary, I think that I underwent a continuous evolution beginning with *La Nausée* all the way up to the *Critique de la Raison Dialectique*" (Sartre in Schilpp, 1981, p. 12). This is not to say that new concepts fail to appear in Sartre's later philosophy. Raymond Aron (1969), for instance, is equally at fault in attempting to reduce Sartre's later ideas to his earlier ones. The truth is more complex than either of these critical views suggests. What Sartre actually does is to build on his earlier philosophy, sometimes changing his mind about details and often deepening an earlier concept but never abandoning his basic ontology.

Hence while the later ("Marxist") Sartre adds a new sociomaterial dimension to existential psychoanalysis, he does not abandon psychoanalytic individualism for Marxist collectivism. Indeed, the later Sartre is if anything more aware than the earlier Sartre of the significance of psychoanalysis for social science theory in general. His intention, he says very explicitly in *Search for a Method* (1960b), is to wed Marxism with psychoanalysis under the auspices of existentialism. The result, of course, is a "sea change" for Marxist determinism as well as psychoanalytic determinism since both will be undermined. Indeed, Sartre believes that the problem shared by traditional social science theory and traditional Marxism is in part their failure to recognize the insertion of the individual into the social scene in childhood—a failure which psychoanalysis, deprived of its metatheoretical "mythology" by existentialism, can be expected to correct. And at about the same time that he was theoretically discussing these issues in *Search for a Method*, Sartre was also attempting to apply the premises of (revised) existential psychoanalysis to his biography of Flaubert. In Chapter 5, I present a detailed investigation of the impact of these new ideas on existential psychoanalysis.

The final criticism—that existentialism is passé and has been superseded by new intellectual approaches such as structuralism and poststructuralism—is a topic I take up in Chapters 6 through 8 in my comparison/

contrast of Sartrean existential psychoanalysis with Lacanian structuralist psychoanalysis. I argue that structuralism is really a new scientific positivism, a synchronic rather than diachronic positivism, but one which is nonetheless as reductionistic as traditional Freudian metatheory in its failure to develop a fully human social science metatheory. Lacan does not solve the problem of the new relational needs and the desire to develop a coherent sense of self discovered by the post-Freudian theorists (whose work he mostly dismisses); indeed, he rarely even addresses those difficulties. Instead, he opts for a metapsychology based on structural linguistics which has some points of convergence with Sartre (by whom Lacan may have been influenced to some extent), but which is directly opposed to the ideas concerning intentionality and meaning production which are the cornerstones of Sartrean metatheory. As such, Lacanian structuralist metatheory is in reality much more nihilistic in its implications than Sartrean existentialist metatheory could ever purport to be. I conclude that not only has Sartrean existentialism not been rendered obsolete, but also that its rich potential for providing clinical precepts and insights has hardly been tapped.

By now, the reader probably has a sense of the structure of this book. In Chapter 2, I initiate the dialogue with psychoanalysis by developing a comparison/contrast between Freud and Sartre, suggesting some Sartrean answers to difficult Freudian questions. The chief challenge to Sartre will be to account in other ways for the phenomena which Freud uses to support his hypothesis of the unconscious, while the chief challenge to Freud will be to account for therapeutic change within a deterministic model. In Chapters 3 and 4, I develop the idea of a "crisis" in contemporary psychoanalytic metatheory, arguing for a Sartrean solution to problems relating to the discovery of new relational needs in earliest infancy (Chapter 3) and to the discovery of the need for development of a firm and coherent sense of self (Chapter 4). I also note in these chapters the differences in clinical implications for a Sartrean view of developmental theory over a traditional Freudian or post-Freudian perspective—differences which relate primarily to the idea of traditional psychoanalysts that the psyche has substance and structure as contrasted with the Sartrean view that consciousness is translucid and free.

Chapter 5 is a kind of transition piece in which I look back to the first four chapters and suggest additions which Sartre's later philosophy can make to existential psychoanalysis at the same time that I look ahead to the three chapters on Lacan. Those three (somewhat shorter) chapters discuss in turn Sartre's idea of the ego as contrasted with Lacan's; Sartre's idea of language as sociomaterial reality as contrasted with Lacan's idea of unconscious linguistic structure; and the impact of these ideas on existential as opposed to Lacanian psychoanalysis. The concepts I discuss in Chapter 5 prove important to developing a Sartrean answer to the challenge of structuralism, since it is in his later philosophy that Sartre takes into account the power of sociomaterial reality (including the part of sociomaterial reality which is language) while still maintaining the structuring significance of the individual project as that which creates and sustains everything. The final chapter summarizes the book's major points, providing a Sartrean case illustration and discussing possible paths for future inquiry.

Throughout this book, I attempt to relate Sartrean metatheory to clinical practice. The point which will be emphasized again and again in drawing those implications is that Sartrean metatheory differs from traditional Freudian and post-Freudian metatheory in suggesting that the aim of existential psychoanalysis is neither the reduction of unconscious conflicts (Freud) nor the repair of defective ego structure or the creation of a substantialized sense of self (post-Freudian psychoanalytic theorists). Nor is it a rapprochement with the linguistic unconscious, as Lacanian structuralist psychoanalysis seems to suggest. Rather, the (general) aim of existentialist therapy is to facilitate a client's letting go of the need to create a substantialized self—thereby effecting a radical reorientation which can lead to a release of spontaneity and a relinquishing of the need to use others to create a self which lies behind much interpersonal misery. The truth is that although Freudian and post-Freudian insights are in many respects useful to understanding the pain of a client's past, they are often less helpful than a Sartrean perspective in understanding the significance of the future as value, of interpersonal conflicts, and of those moments when a client—suspended between a past in which he or she no longer believes and a future which can only be known through living it—must make a new choice of a way of being in the world. It is with respect to this latter situation that I believe that a Sartrean perspective has most significantly aided me as a therapist in understanding and encouraging some of those important changes at which all depth therapy aims. And it is those moments of change, moments which admittedly take a great deal of groundwork, which are the most exciting and rewarding aspects of the practice of psychotherapy.

2 · Sartre versus Freud: Two Approaches to Metapsychology

The Nature of the Dispute

A juxtaposition of Freud's and Sartre's psychological metatheories may seem at first to be a matter only of contrasts, rather like comparing apples and oranges. Since they are fruits of different trees—namely, phenomenological ontology and positivistic science—they may seem to have nothing at all in common. Yet despite a fundamental disagreement with Freud about the nature of consciousness, or the psyche, Sartre acknowledges a great debt to him. Obviously, existential psychoanalysis would have been inconceivable without the prior invention of Freudian psychoanalysis. It could even be said that Sartre's earlier philosophical work is both *pro* and *contra* Freud just as his later work is *pro* and *contra* Marx.

Sartre objects to Freud and Marx for the same reason—their attempts to apply the philosophical tenets of nineteenth-century scientific materialism to the human sciences. In rejecting the mechanistic determinism of Freud and Marx, Sartre advocates instead the establishment of a *human* science of human beings. At the same time, however, he names his own metapsychology "existential psychoanalysis" just as he calls his later philosophy "Marxist." In this respect, it might be said that what Sartre accepts in both Freud and Marx is their talent as phenomenologists, which is sometimes deeply obscured by their attempts at establishing natural science credibility for their theories.

Existential psychoanalysis begins from a different set of premises and is the result of a different order of inquiry than Freudian psychoanalysis. Sartre attempts to discover the ontological structures of existence, declaring that "the final discoveries [of ontology are] the first principles of psychoanalysis" (BN, p. 575). Freud seeks to establish through empirical observation a natural science hypothesis about the workings of the human psyche. Even though this observation is of a scientifically suspect variety—that is, it concerns case studies and Freud's own self analysis—Freud nonetheless claims objective status for it. He believes it has led him to the discovery of an underlying psychobiological force, which, like gravity or electricity, explains the phenomena of psychic life. Thus Freud's "discovery" of the libido as the driving force in the psyche is a part of his general endeavor to establish the scientific credibility of psychoanalysis. If the natural sciences deal in physical forces, then psychoanalysis must base itself on a comparable psychobiological force. The problem is that such a force is really a metaphysical first principle based on scientistic metaphors rather than a scientific hypothesis. It is too broad, either explaining everything or nothing, and is therefore not subject to empirical validation.

Sartre, on the other hand, seeks to discover ontological structures. From reflective self-analysis and empathic comprehension of the internal lives of others, he wishes to discover within human experience the basic structures of *being human*. He does not seek to discover the scientific laws or metaphysical principles behind experience, nor does he wish to reduce psychology to biological or physical laws. Rather, he accepts the idea that consciousness is a different order of reality than the material world and that psychology therefore requires a different approach to its subject matter. Comprehension in the human sciences cannot be of the same order as comprehension in the natural sciences. It must include intentionality and meaning. Thus for Sartre the "force" in the human personality is not to be discovered *behind* consciously lived experience but rather *in* that very experience. From the beginning of his work to the end, Sartre objects to Freud's attempt to reduce human behavior to environmental and biological determinism, psychobiological forces, and unconscious urges.

At this point, the traditional Freudian psychoanalyst is probably asking why Sartre calls his revision of Freudian theory "psychoanalysis" at all. Obviously, if one makes the acceptance of unconscious mental functioning, psychic determinism, the psychosexual stages, mechanical defenses, and drive-based interpretations of experience the criteria for deciding whether or not an approach is psychoanalytic, then Sartre's approach is not psychoanalysis. In this book, I often use the term "existentialist therapy" rather than "existential psychoanalysis," for the reason just stated and because some of my clinical data derive from other approaches. On the other hand, Freud defines psychoanalysis as a technique or treatment which deals with transference and resistance (1914b, p. 16). If one defines "transference" as the repetition within the therapy situation and elsewhere of the patterns of childhood emotional attachments, and "resistance" as the refusal to face certain unpleasant truths about oneself and one's existence, then there is no reason why existential psychoanalysis would not be a possibility. In addition, Sartre has described some significant similarities between Freudian psychoanalysis and his own version of existential psychoanalysis. These are, of course, similarities in the midst of differences.

Similarities and Differences between Freudian
and Existential Psychoanalysis

As Sartre himself points out (BN, pp. 569–71), there are many points of comparison between existential and Freudian psychoanalysis. Similarities include the idea that the personality is unified, the idea that division can exist within this unity, and the idea that analysis is needed because of this division and because knowledge facilitates change. Both Freud and Sartre see meaning in the symptoms of mental illness which prior to Freud had been viewed as simply irrational or as indications of biological degeneration. And, in conjunction with this, both theorists interpret surface psychic manifestations (gestures, single actions, symptoms, tastes, the whole set of elements constituting concrete lived experience) in terms of a deeper aim. Sartre says, "A gesture refers to a *Weltanschauung* and we sense it" (BN, p. 457). Freud would agree—except that in Sartre's metapsychology the deeper aim is manifested *in* the concrete choices, whereas in Freud's it is to be discovered *behind* them in instinctual life and the unconscious.

Finally, neither Sartre nor Freud accepts the subject of the analysis as being in a privileged position with respect to his or her own subjective material. However, the reasons are different, leading to different treatment of patients or clients: For Freud, the analyst must wrestle with the analysand's resistance to making unconscious material conscious. For Sartre, there is a gulf between spontaneous experience (prereflective consciousness) and reflective awareness (reflective consciousness), but since the same person experiences both, the final intuition of the subject of an analysis can be taken as definitive. Also, the patient or client can be taken into partnership with the therapist in the mutual project of exploring and naming what Sartre refers to as the client's "fundamental project of being."

Existential psychoanalysis, like Freudian psychoanalysis, recognizes that the individual is all of a piece. The "fundamental project" in existential psychoanalysis takes on the same importance as the "complex" in Freudian psychoanalysis. It is also similarly subject to divisions within an overall unity, thereby making it an appropriate subject for "analysis." Just as the Freudian psychoanalyst attempts to discover the childhood events which led to the organized group of ideas and memories constituting the complex, so the existential psychoanalyst attempts to discover the "original choice of being" whereby a client has adopted this or that particular worldview. Both the fundamental project and the complex refer to the interpersonal world of childhood. And both forms of psychoanalysis seek to discover, as Sartre says, "the crucial event of infancy and the psychic crystallization around that event" (BN, p. 569). Yet the original other as libidinal object in Freudian psychoanalysis is quite different from the original Other as the first person who sees and names me in existential psychoanalysis. Also, the fundamental project differs from the complex in that the latter is unconscious and subject to the laws of nature, whereas the former is conscious and subject to continuing revision or even to radical transformation. It is a *pro-ject*, or a throwing of oneself forward from the past toward the future in a particular way.

Similarly, the division within unity of existential psychoanalysis differs from the division of Freudian psychoanalysis in that reflective consciousness and prereflective consciousness refer to the same conscious subject. Freud, on the other hand, depicts the psyche as a set of warring principalities—consciousness and the unconscious in the "topographical" hypothesis and the ego, superego, and id in the "structural" hypothesis. Finally, the knowledge which facilitates change, as discussed above, involves subjecting prereflective experience to reflective awareness in Sartre's formulation, whereas it involves making the unconscious conscious in Freud's. A therapeutic practice built on Sartre's metatheory, though it can include useful insights from Freudian psychoanalysis, will differ significantly in its approach to clients as being consciously aware of the experiences which they will reflectively need to confront in order to revise their fundamental projects of being.

In discussing similarities between the two versions of psychoanalysis, we keep encountering differences. There really are radical differences between the two approaches, as Sartre observes in his critique of "empirical" (Freudian) psychoanalysis in *Being and Nothingness* (pp. 557–75). Sartre objects to Freud's insistence on an unconscious area of psychic life behind consciousness, to Freudian determinism, to Freud's mechanical-biological explanations, to the idea that nature and nurture rather than an original choice of a

way of being in the world explain human behavior, to the idea of a psychobiological residue such as libido as an explanation of human motivation, to
the notion of universal symbols (for example, gold = feces or a pincushion
= the breast), and to the general nosology or diagnostic categories of Freudian psychoanalysis. Sartre proposes instead that the objective of existential
psychoanalysis would be to reveal in all its concrete richness an individual's
original choice of being, which, though grounded in the concrete world, is
not reducible to it. Such a choice is constantly changing and capable of radical transformation. Hence existential psychoanalysis must maintain a flexibility in interpreting symbols and symptoms not simply between individuals
but with a particular individual at different times in therapy.

Sartre says in *Search for a Method* that "a life develops in spirals; it passes
again and again by the same points but at different levels of integration and
complexity" (p. 106). Existential psychoanalysis is not reductionist in its attempts to explain such developments as permutations of the drives. Although psychosexuality is important in human development, it is not for
Sartre its motivating force. In place of pleasure as the goal of the human organism, Sartre proposes an attempt on the part of consciousness to establish
itself as value through concrete situations in the world. This is the "circuit of
selfness" through which Sartre says an individual uses a relationship with
objects and other people to attempt to create a solid sense of self. Although
this attempt is ultimately doomed because free consciousness is always
ahead of its attempts at self-definition, existential psychoanalysis aims at
grasping the meaning of an individual's concrete choices as part of a project
to create value. In this system, general nosology will not do. Sartre insists
that existential psychoanalysis must endeavor to grasp the particular rather
than the general structure of delusions or other symptoms—for example,
why an individual chooses to believe that he is Jesus Christ and not Moses
or Genghis Khan.

All this leads to a difference in methodology between existential psychoanalysis and Freudian psychoanalysis. Freud introduces only the first half of
the method—regressive analysis. He believes it is possible to discover the
sources of contemporary behavior in an analysand's childhood. Yet Freud
admits that his own method must always remain analytic rather than synthetic. It can reconstruct the past, but it cannot predict the future:

> So long as we trace the development [of a mental process] from its final
> outcome backwards, the chain of events appears continuous, and we
> feel we have gained an insight which is completely satisfactory or even

exhaustive. But if we proceed the reverse way, if we start from the premises inferred from the analysis and try to follow these up to the final
result, then we no longer get the impression of an inevitable sequence
of events which could not have been otherwise determined. We notice
at once that there might have been another result, and that we might
have been just as well able to understand and explain the latter. The
synthesis is thus not so satisfactory as the analysis; in other words, from
a knowledge of the premises we could not have foretold the nature of
the result. (Freud, 1920b, p. 167)

Freud believes that this failure of synthesis occurs because certain factors
in mental life must always remain unknown. Even if the psychoanalyst, for
example, understands the complete etiology of a psychological illness, he or
she cannot know the quality or strength or possible combinations of all the
etiological factors. Freud goes on to say that it is only after the fact that we
know which determining factors are weaker or stronger: The stronger factor
was the one that succeeded. "Hence," Freud concludes, "the chain of causation can always be recognized with certainty if we follow the line of analysis,
whereas to predict it along the line of synthesis is impossible" (1920b, p. 168).
Presumably, if the psychoanalyst had access to all the data, he or she would
be able to predict the future. It did not occur to Freud that the impossibility
of prediction in human affairs might result from something entirely different.

In *Being and Nothingness* (1943), Sartre first develops his idea that existential psychoanalysis must be based on synthesis as well as analysis. It must be
able to put together as well as to take apart. Sartre argues that the factor
which is missing in Freudian determinism is just the factor which would allow both synthesis and analysis,. This factor is freedom, intentionality,
choice. Since choices are always made in a situation, they *seem caused* in ret-
rospect. The truth is, however, that the material world cannot provide
causes for human behavior in the strictly scientific sense. It can only provide
motives. Or rather, to put the matter in Sartre's own terminology, I discover
causes in the nonscientific everyday sense as I approach the world as a
motivator for my actions; I discover *motives* when I reflectively look at my
own consciousness as grasping those causes (BN, pp. 445-50). "Thus,"
Sartre writes, "cause and motive are correlative—the one referring to the
world of things which consciousness grasps, the other to intentional consciousness" (BN, p. 449).

A rock, to use an example of Sartre's, appears "not scalable" only against the background of my project of climbing, including the expertise I bring and the daring I am willing to put forth. The truth is that "the environment can act on the subject only to the exact extent that he comprehends it; that is, transforms it into a situation" (BN, p. 572). For Sartre, the situation is "an ambiguous phenomenon in which it is impossible for the for-itself [consciousness] to distinguish the contribution of freedom from that of the brute existent" (BN, p. 488). Looking at the past, it may therefore seem that I could not have acted otherwise since, in fact, I chose to interpret the world and live my situation in this way and not in another. This mistaking of motive for causality in the scientific sense is exactly what the deterministic strain in Freudian psychoanalysis encourages.

In *Search for a Method* (1960b) and the *Critique of Dialectical Reason* (1960a), Sartre elaborates a methodology for the social sciences in general which is dialectical rather than analytical—which pays attention to analysis as only one moment in a "progressive-regressive method" (SM, pp. 85–166). This method, which Sartre adapted from Marxist sociologist Henri Lefebvre,[1] has three moments: (1) a moment of phenomenological description, or observation informed by experience and general theory; (2) an analytico-regressive moment—a regression back into the history of the individual or group to earlier stages; and (3) a synthetico-progressive moment which moves from past to present in an attempt to rediscover the present in all its particular complexity.

Freudian psychoanalysis recognizes the first two moments, although Freud's metatheory sometimes clouds the first. The third moment, the synthetico-progressive moment, is one which is not accounted for within the context of traditional Freudian analysis. In a cause-effect system, there is no intentionality to discover in past actions—no (past) future-directedness. Of course, Freudian analysts often do in practice recognize the intentionality of past actions—but this is not accounted for in strictly Freudian metatheory. And it seems to me a very important clinical matter for a therapist to have a theoretical basis for attempting to recapture past intentionality. Otherwise, the recovery of the past might become an excuse for stasis rather than an impetus to change. After all, to recognize the intentional nature of the past is to allow for present intentionality. If I *was* free, I *am* free. The future is liberated as well.

All this points to a primary difference between Sartre's and Freud's metatheories. As Gerald N. Izenberg (1976) rightly observes, the major difference between Freudian and existentialist metatheory is their respective characterization of meaning. For Freud, meaning is ultimately neurophysiological and evolutionary. In his early *Project for a Scientific Psychology* (not published until after his death), Freud writes that the intention of the project is to "furnish us with a psychology which shall be a natural science; its aim, that is, is to represent psychological processes as quantitatively determined states of specifiable material particles and so make them plain and void of contradictions" (1950, p. 355). As Frank J. Sulloway (1979) points out, the *Project* was an early attempt at physical (neurophysiological) reductionism.

In his later work, Freud, as a "biologist of the mind," leans more toward biological and evolutionary reductionism—though he never abandons the neurophysiological principle of constancy upon which all of his later work rests. As Sulloway's monumental intellectual biography convincingly argues, the *Project* is not, as some Freud scholars have insisted, merely an early neurological document which was abandoned by its author shortly after being written in favor of a theory of the mind which was purely psychological. Freud throughout his career remained influenced by the scientific ideas of his day. In *Beyond the Pleasure Principle*, he writes, "The deficiencies in our description [of the mind] would probably vanish if we were already in a position to replace the psychological terms by physiological or chemical ones" (1920a, p. 60). And as late as *Analysis Terminable and Interminable*, Freud insists that "for the psychical field, the biological field does in fact play the part of the underlying bedrock" (1937, p. 252).

Meaning, for Freud, is ultimately reducible to the play of physical forces within the human organism combined with biological propensities and laws. Behind conscious life lies unconscious fantasy, behind unconscious fantasy primary process, and behind primary process those instinctual forces which Freud conceives of as lying on the frontier "between the mental and the somatic" (1915a, p. 122). The pleasure principle, for Freud, is a mechanical principle involving the physical reduction of quantities of energy in the organism. The past is causally significant in the formation of symptoms because the energy surrounding uncatharted memories or fantasies disturbs the smooth working of the organism. Sexual pleasure has as its aim the preservation of the species, thereby serving the laws of evolution. Its opposite, the death instinct, is an involutionary principle which accounts for aggression as a turning outward of the inner physiological tendency to pursue a return to inorganic matter.

In place of both the pleasure principle and the death instinct, Sartre substitutes the human aim of creating value, which is a priori neither pleasurable nor painful and which can be aggressive or unaggressive. In place of

Freud's neurophysiological and evolutionary paradigms, Sartre substitutes an investigation of consciousness as intentional and meaning creating. He thus carries to its logical conclusion Freud's own idea that psychoanalysis should cleanse itself of everything but "psychological auxiliary ideas" (Freud, 1916–17, p. 21). Existential psychoanalysis, in its denial that the laws of scientific materialism apply to the world of consciousness and in its substitution of motives for scientific causality, frees itself entirely from such ideas. For the Freudian idea of the determining power of the past, existential psychoanalysis substitutes an understanding of both the past and the future as humanly meaningful in terms of choices and values. For the Freudian idea of desire as a biological instinct, Sartre proposes the idea first of *desire* (BN) and later of *need* (CDR) as a lack which is discovered not in the biological recesses of the self but on the face of the world as it responds to embodied consciousness. For the mechanistic universe of natural science, Sartre substitutes the human universe of phenomenological investigation and ontological categories as these are discovered within concrete lived experience.

Thus although Freud and Sartre would each say that a symptom is "meaningful," they indicate quite different things by this assertion. Both forms of psychoanalysis are a kind of hermeneutics—that is, the reading of the text of a life in its historical context on the basis of a subtext which explains what is going on. And each form of hermeneutics is, as Paul Ricoeur (1970) says of Freudian psychoanalysis, "a hermeneutics of suspicion." Neither accepts surface explanations or rationalizations. Here, however, the similarities end. I do not believe that Ricoeur's attempt to reconcile phenomenology and Freudian psychoanalysis really works because the kinds of meanings discovered by the hermeneutical processes of each system differ too greatly. The only reconciliation which seems really feasible to me is one which disregards the metapsychology of Freud and keeps what is valuable in his clinical analysis. As I will attempt to show throughout this book, I believe it is possible to reinterpret much of Freudian data along existentialist lines. Thus it might be possible for an existentialist approach to retain the highly valuable clinical insights of Freudian and post-Freudian psychoanalytic theory while giving up the cumbersome experience-distant metapsychology. Before deciding this, however, we must look in more detail at Freud's and Sartre's metatheories—at the ways in which each writer interprets the phenomenological data of human experience in terms of metaprinciples explaining what it means to be human.

Freudian Metapsychology:
Psychobiological and Neurophysiological Forces

According to Freud, the meaning of life is the pursuit of pleasure, which can be defined as an organismic return from excitation to equilibrium. All strong forces of excitation, external or internal, are perceived by the organism as pain; the return to zero energy charge is perceived as pleasure. This is the "principle of constancy" upon which all of Freud's psychological theories are based. Freud links it with the pleasure principle when he writes, in *Beyond the Pleasure Principle*, that the "pleasure principle follows from the principle of constancy: actually the latter principle was inferred from the facts which forced us to adopt the pleasure principle" (1920a, p. 9). Looked at in this way, the pleasure principle and the death instinct, as conceived by the later Freud, are really not so far apart after all since the ultimate absence of charge is death. For Freud, everything is part of a unified system. The economic hypothesis (energy flow, inhibition, and displacement in the psyche) is the most experience-distant part of Freud's theory; yet it lies behind the topographical hypothesis (conscious, unconscious, and preconscious areas of the psyche), the dynamic hypothesis (psyche explained by opposing mental forces), and the structural hypothesis (ego, superego, and id). The economic hypothesis is, in a sense, the engine that makes the Freudian machine go.

Although the economic hypothesis, with its charge and discharge metaphors borrowed from physics, is often disputed by contemporary psychoanalysts, there is no question that Freud takes it very seriously. An inheritance from his teachers in neurophysiology, Brucke and Meynert (Izenberg, 1976; Sulloway, 1979), it is never abandoned throughout the many permutations of his psychological theories. It explains, among other things, the connection between the psyche and its objects (cathexis) and the formation of neurotic symptoms (through displacement, condensation, and conversion). With libidinal energy, or generalized sexual instinct, as the main internal driving force of the organism, Freud can explain both normal development and pathology in terms of energetic permutations and displacements, conscious and unconscious. They have a meaning, but the meaning is ultimately to be found in the neurons and not in personal choice and creation. Even when Freud later pronounces that psychology and biology are separate sciences and must be treated as such, he never abandons the economic theory which had its origins in neurophysiology. And he persists in believing, as he states in the seventh chapter of *The Interpretation of Dreams* (1900), that the most fundamental explanations of psychological disturbances will one day be found to be neurophysiological. Part of the problem with the core of Freud's metatheory is that the neurophysiological theory on which it is based—the idea that the nervous system seeks to rid itself of all tension—is now outdated. The hydraulic metaphors, through which the mind is visualized as a machine driven by the flow of energy, also prove cumbersome.

Freud's theory of the connection between consciousness and its objects is thus mechanical rather than humanly meaningful. "Cathexis" is a concept implying the amount of psychical energy attached to an object, an idea or ideas, or a body part. Freud believes that this energy is at least theoretically measurable, that it can be condensed or displaced from its original objects to others, and that it explains such things as mourning or self-preoccupation. In mourning, the subject has withdrawn psychical energy from the outside world, hypercathecting the fantasied lost love object instead (Freud, 1917). In narcissism, the patient has hypercathected (a certain amount of ego cathexis is considered normal by Freud) his own ego to the exclusion of external objects (Freud, 1914a). As for hysteria, Freud believes that it is a clear case of the "conversion" of physical energy into "innervation" energy, thus producing such symptoms as hysterical blindness (Freud, 1896; 1905b). Even the state of being in love, unless returned by the love object, is seen as impoverishing the subject in terms of draining libidinal energy from the ego to the object (Freud, 1914a).

Obviously, for Freud, the most significant internal force is libido, or generalized sexual energy. Its many permutations in the psyche account both for neurotic symptoms and for growth and development. On the one hand, lack of immediate gratification promotes the development of the ego as a reality-oriented structure capable of assessing situations and postponing discharge. On the other hand, neurotic symptoms result from permanently binding or displacing energy which needs some route of discharge—that is, from repression or displacement. What is repressed from the conscious is, according to Freud's theory of equivalence, activated in the unconscious. Hence it becomes the source of unconscious complexes. Similarly, the energy displaced from one activity to a substitute activity, as in obsessional neuroses, retains its original intensity while being deprived of its original content. One washes one's hands with the same compulsive intensity that one wishes to engage in "dirty activities"—and the unconscious takes pleasure in the substitute activity as an equivalent for the repressed wish (Freud, 1909, 1913). Or, as in the case of Freud's patient Dora, one develops a hysterical cough as a substitute gratification for the unconscious wish for oral sex

(Freud, 1905b). In the first instance, the unconscious wish is satisfied through "reaction formation," in the second through "conversion."

This brings us to Freud's theory of the instincts, which forms a conjunction between his evolutionary theory and his neurophysiological theory. Actually, Freud's dual instinct theory undergoes a major revision in his later work. At first Freud conceives of sexual versus self-preservative or ego instincts (Freud, 1905a; 1915a) and later of life versus death (Eros versus Thanatos) instincts (Freud, 1920a; 1930; 1937). Although Freud sometimes refers to his instinct theory as a "mythology" (Freud, 1933, p. 95), he treats it seriously. For Freud, a drive or instinct has three components: a source, an aim, and an object. According to this point of view, it is the aim of the instinct, rather than the aim of the conscious subject, which is the real meaning of symptoms and of human activity in general.

There is, however, a difference in specificity of aim and object between the self-preservative instincts and the sexual instinct. Hunger and thirst can be satisfied only by eating food or drinking liquids (or, as Freud tells us, hallucinations of such fulfillment, as in the case of the frustrated infant who hallucinates the breast). The sexual instinct, on the other hand, chooses its objects and even its aims on the basis of personal history. There is no guarantee that biological maturity will constitute genital sexuality, for instance, or that the individual will choose intercourse with a member of the opposite sex. The object may be a fetish or the aim may be the fulfillment of some "component instinct" which is a throwback to polymorphous perversity. At any rate, Freud believes that in both mature genital sexuality and other more primitive forms, it is sexual arousal which leads the individual to seek an object. Biology is responsible for behavior in the world.

As forces on the border between the psychic and the somatic, instincts are made responsible for the variety of human responses to the world. The sexual instinct gives rise to primary process thinking which seeks immediate gratification through real or hallucinated objects. This mode, which is characteristic of the unconscious, is under the sway of the id. It is the source of unconscious fantasy and of dreams. Secondary process thinking, by contrast, is more under the influence of the self-preservative or ego instincts, which adhere to the reality principle as a means to individual survival. Freud later contends that the self-preservative instincts derive from libidinal cathexis to the ego, thereby postulating that all instincts originate in the id. According to Freud's first theory of the instincts, aggression is in the service of the self-preservative instincts. Later, he sees it as a manifestation of the death instinct.

The return to equilibrium, or zero energy charge, is one aim of sexual discharge; the other is the evolutionary aim of the preservation of the species. In either case, the meaning of human activity in the world is ultimately reducible to biological drives. Freud's fascination with evolutionary theory goes back to an interest in Darwin during his last years in the Gymnasium. He also took Carl Claus's "General Biology and Darwinism" as an elective his first year as a medical student at the University of Vienna (Sulloway, 1979, pp. 13–14). Darwinian and Lamarckian evolution subsequently had a tremendous influence on the development of psychoanalytic theory, providing a model for interpreting human activity in terms of the biological aims of survival and preservation of the species.

Thus Freud views instinctual behavior in terms of its biological function, which is not necessarily congruent with the conscious ideas of the individual. Using an ontogenetic model based on Darwinian principles, Freud explains psychopathology as a regression to earlier stages of sexual development or to "component instincts" which ought to have developed into the genital arrangement that best serves the continuation of the species. Normal progression, by contrast, involves an ontogenetic development through the psychosexual stages: oral, anal, phallic, and genital (Freud, 1905a).

The Oedipus complex and guilt are sometimes explained in terms of a Lamarckian inheritance of acquired characteristics. Freud (1912–13) thinks that the incest taboo gains part of its power from a phylogenetic memory: He hypothesizes that the primal brothers, jealous of the primal father's monopoly of women, had murdered the primal father, after which a sense of guilt had arisen on the human scene. Similarly, certain children's phobic fears of animals, Freud argues, are only in part a displacement of feelings toward their fathers. These fears also reproduce primitive totemism. That Freud was much influenced by this evolutionary paradigm is once again underscored by a statement he jotted down the year before his death: "With neurotics it is as though we were in a prehistoric landscape—for instance, in the Jurassic. The great saurians are still running about; the horsetails grow as high as palms" (quoted by Sulloway, 1979, p. 497). It was the categorization and treatment of these "prehistoric" states of mind which proved to be Freud's life work. He continued to view them in the light of the natural science paradigms of his day.

Even the late theory of the death instinct, which has provoked much disagreement among Freud's followers, derives from Freud's essentially biological paradigm: The forces of evolution are matched by forces of involution. Actually, as Sulloway (1979) points out, Freud's whole paradigm of mental illness requires a second force capable of reversing biogenetic achievements through regressions to previously abandoned stages of development. It is here, in fact, that Freud's neurophysiological paradigms and his evolutionary paradigms meet. The return to death is a cessation of all charge; it is also an impulse to return to earlier forms preserved in the (psycho-Lamarckian) phylogenetic memory of the race. Ultimately, this memory must include a memory of the emergence of life from undisturbed inorganic matter. Although Freud proposes the death instinct fairly tentatively in *Beyond the Pleasure Principle* (1920a), he has become quite convinced of this theory by the time of *Civilization and Its Discontents* (1930):

> To begin with, it was only tentatively that I put forward the views I have developed here [concerning the death instinct], but in the course of time they have gained such a hold upon me that I can no longer think in any other way. To my mind, they are far more serviceable from a theoretical standpoint than any other possible ones; they provide that simplification, without either ignoring or doing violence to the facts, for which we strive in scientific work. (Freud, 1930, p. 119)

As Sulloway so convincingly demonstrates, Freud's theory of the death instinct was neither subjectively determined (resulting from his unhappy experiences in Vienna during and after the First World War) nor a late and peripheral addition to psychoanalytic thinking, as many psychoanalysts would like to think. As Freud himself perceived, it was a concept in tune with the very heart of Freud's metabiological thinking. It explained, among other things, the presence of aggression throughout history, the pursuit of pain rather than pleasure (primary masochism), the repetition of painful patterns of experience (the repetition compulsion), and the existence of regressive tendencies in the psyche (Freud, 1920a, 1930).

Drive theory, or the economic hypothesis, is obviously the cornerstone of Freud's metatheory. The topographical, the dynamic, and the structural hypotheses are all inexplicable without it. Yet even Freud sees the difference in levels of abstraction between the hypothesis. Although he might concede on occasion that his drives or instincts are "mythical entities," he considers the existence of the unconscious to be a proven fact. The phenomena on which the topographical hypothesis (Freud, 1900, 1901, 1915c) is based (self-deception, memory lapses, symptom formation, parapraxes, and dreams) are as familiar to everyday life as to the consulting room—though they might, as we shall see, admit of other explanations than Freud's theory of the unconscious. Freud himself does not hesitate to make his more dubious idea of instinctual drives the force behind his "proven" concepts of unconscious mental life and conflicts.

According to Freud, the unconscious consists of two parts: the deep unconscious, which is the source of instinctual impulses and phylogenetic memories and which can never be brought into consciousness, and the dynamic unconscious, which is the habitat of wishes and memories which have been repressed. In addition, there is the preconscious, which can be brought into awareness without difficulty; it is simply not conscious at the moment. But since the unconscious is the location both of the primary drives and of repressed instinctual wishes, it is inexplicable except in terms of the economic hypothesis. The dynamic hypothesis (Freud, 1910, 1912a), which is closely related to the topographical hypothesis, explicitly formulates the conflicts between the psychic systems in terms of the repression and displacement of instinctual energy in the organism and the conflicts between opposing sets of instincts.

Drive theory is also made the cornerstone of the structural hypothesis (1923)—sometimes referred to as the second topographical hypothesis—which has been a main focus of interest among most modern psychoanalytic theorists. Yet whereas many of these theorists either ignore or merely pay lip service to Freudian drive theory, Freud himself postulates the formation of psychic structures by and for the purpose of managing the drives. The id, which is present at birth, is the dwelling place of the drives. It knows no sense of time and does not develop historically. The ego is, at least in Freud's early theory, conscious life adjusting to the demands of the outer world (Freud, 1895). Freud later conceives of the ego as mediating between the demands of the superego, the id, and the outer world and as having unconscious as well as conscious segments (Freud, 1923). Its origin is the id, and the ego develops out of the id because of frustration of immediate drive gratification by the infant's environment. The superego, the critical and judgmental part of the psyche, results from the resolution of the Oedipus complex due to the internalization of parental prohibitions against drive satisfaction. Because renunciation is involved in giving up one's original libidinal object (the mother), the young boy (girls, Freud [1930] says, do not develop adequate superegos because they lack castration anxiety) becomes capable of sublimation leading to cultural achievements.[2]

Interestingly, this theory of psychic structure leads to a conception of interpersonal relationships that views them as thoroughly instinctually oriented. It is as though the drives in some sense *create* their objects. Indeed, Freud himself says that, for the infant, "repeated situations of satisfaction have created an object out of the mother" (1926, p. 170). The object, Freud contends, is the "most variable part" of the instinctual apparatus. It "is not originally connected with [the instinct] but becomes assigned to it only in consequence of being peculiarly fitted to make satisfaction possible" (1915a, p. 122). There is obviously no reason why the libidinal object, according to Freud's conception, needs to be a person at all. In fact, a robot programmed for complete satisfaction might do better than a human love object from the viewpoint of the id. Love, according to such a view, "is nothing more than object-cathexis on the part of the sexual instincts with a view to directly sexual satisfaction" (Freud, 1921, p. 111).

As for friendships and social relations in general, they are sublimated homosexual longings or efforts to control unconscious hostility, incestuous strivings, and ambivalence in the interest of survival (Freud, 1912–13, 1921, 1930). Social relations are not fundamental and may be reduced to the transmutations of individual instinctual tendencies. Like the structure ego, they result from drive frustrations and permutations. Civilization itself, for Freud, is an ambiguous good—in return for safety and survival, human beings give up the most intense forms of primitive satisfaction (Freud, 1930).

Obviously, Freud is observing and describing phenomena in the human world and translating these into drive-related metatheory. Certainly, we all experience self-deception and the other phenomena which Freud uses in support of his hypothesis of the unconscious. We all also experience passion (id), reality orientation (ego), and pangs of conscience, guilt, and self-criticism (superego). I suppose there is no objection to calling these by their now familiar Freudian names if one does not mean to imply by this a meta-biological explanation of their origins. The real question is whether Freud's metatheory is the best conceptualization of the phenomena at hand. Although modern Freudians have sometimes de-emphasized the origins of Freud's metatheory in nineteenth-century natural science, especially its debt to now-outdated Lamarckian evolutionary theory, I think that there can be no doubt that Freud took his mechanical and biologistic metatheory seriously. It is in many ways an elegantly consistent system—not in every detail, as critics have often pointed out, but in overall design.

Freud's system is also appealing because of Freud's own obviously great clinical insights. Take, for example, Freud's insights into the phenomena he calls "transference" (Freud, 1912b, 1915b) and the "repetition compulsion" (Freud, 1914c, 1920a). I do not believe any depth psychology, that is, any therapeutic approach which explores past influences and nonbehavioral explanations of human functioning, can afford to do without these insights. Freud discovered that his analysands invariably responded to him as if he were a member of that person's family of origin—that he received first the positive and then the negative feelings which the analysand had for father, mother, sister, brother, or grandparents. If the analysand was a woman, she also frequently fell violently in love with her analyst without regard to any of his realistic personal qualities. The analyst's interpretation of this transference (the term refers to Freudian drive theory and indicates Freud's hypothesis that libidinal energy can be rerouted as if it obeyed hydraulic principles) of feelings from the original libidinal object to the analyst was made the primary technical focus of psychoanalysis. It was the vehicle for discovering the etiology of the analysand's neurosis.

Freud also notes that the analysand has usually spent years superimposing the family of origin onto many contemporary situations and relationships. Freud attributes this, together with the attempt at repetition within the analysis, to a compulsion to repeat the emotional experiences of the past. Here is an excellent descriptive piece linking the two concepts of transference and the repetition compulsion to everyday observation:

> What psycho-analysis reveals in the transference phenomena of neurotics can also be observed in the lives of some normal people. The impression they give is of being pursued by a malignant fate or possessed by some 'daemonic' power; but psycho-analysis has always taken the view that their fate is for the most part arranged by themselves and determined by early infantile influences. . . . Thus we have come across people all of whose human relationships have the same outcome: such as the benefactor who is abandoned in anger after a time by each of his *protégés*, however much they may otherwise differ from one another, and who thus seems doomed to taste all the bitterness of ingratitude; or the man whose friendships all end in betrayal by his friend, or the man who time after time in the course of his life raises someone else into a position of great public authority and then after a certain interval, himself upsets that authority and replaces him by a new one; or, again, the lover each of whose love affairs with a woman passes through the same phases and reaches the same conclusion. . . .

If we take into account observations such as these, based upon behavior in the transference and upon the life-histories of men and women, we shall find courage to assume that there really does exist in the mind a compulsion to repeat which overrides the pleasure principle. (Freud, 1920a, pp. 21–22)

So far, so good. But in the next section of *Beyond the Pleasure Principle*, Freud introduces a further permutation of his metatheory—the death instinct, or Thanatos. This late idea of Thanatos as an explanation of the need to repeat has often proven problematic to post-Freudian psychoanalytic theorists. Two notable exceptions to the general inclination to dismiss this concept are Melanie Klein, whose ideas on the subject are discussed in the next chapter, and Jacques Lacan, whose attempts to link the Freudian death instinct with psycho-linguistic theory are discussed in Chapter 7. Freud himself finds in the death instinct both a metabiological principle for explaining regression and aggression and a way of understanding the repetition of experiences which were obviously not pleasurable.

Despite all this, in an earlier section of *Beyond the Pleasure Principle*, Freud actually gives an insight into the origin of this need to repeat which does not accord with the hypothesis of the death instinct (Freud, 1920a, pp. 14–17). The two theories of repetition are, in fact, a good illustration of how Freud the talented observer can himself be at odds with Freud the metabiologist. Freud observed his eighteen-month-old grandson playing a game which Freud very cleverly identified as an attempt to master his mother's leaving him, which he permitted without crying. The child would fling away his toys into the far corners of the room with the long drawn-out expression, "o-o-o-oh," which Freud and the child's mother interpreted as meaning "go away" (*fort*). Later, Freud noticed that the child would occasionally with his significant "o-o-o-oh" fling away a wooden reel with a piece of string wound around it and then draw it back again with a joyful "*da*" (here). Yet the child much more frequently played at the *fort* part of the game than at the *da* part.

Freud interpreted this game as the child's technique for mastering his instinctive renunciation in allowing his mother to leave without making a fuss. The pleasure came from turning the passive situation of being left into an active one of controlling the leaving. Included in this mastery was the venting of hostility and defiance toward the mother, as if the child were saying, "All right, then, go away! I don't need you. I'm sending you away myself" (Freud, 1920a, p. 16). If one leaves aside the instinctual interpretation, it becomes clear that what Freud had observed was a reversal in play so that the child felt that he had the initiative in a painful situation. Freud observes that adults enjoy tragic drama for similar reasons. He also notes that this need for self-assertion does not require a separate (Adlerian) instinct toward mastery to explain it. Neither, I believe, does it need further interpretation in terms of Freudian metatheory, either with respect to the pleasure principle or the death instinct. The need to turn passive into active fits Sartre's ontology just as well as it fits Freud's metatheory.

Existentialist objections are not so much to Freud the clinical theorist as to Freud the metapsychologist, insofar as the two can be separated. Such objections are based on the observation that the experience-distant part of Freud's system is too mechanical and does not fit well with phenomenological analysis. For example, does experience show that human beings always seek reduction of tension, as the principle of constancy suggests, or is it sometimes true that they seek increasing excitement? Also, do Oedipal renunciation, sublimation, symptom formation based on unconscious displacement of libidinal energy, or the death instinct really explain why many human beings—both the psychologically healthy and the seriously ill—very obviously do not make pleasure the goal of their existence? In other words, it may be that Freudian metatheory does not account well for cultural achievement, much as Freud tried to reduce culture to the permutations of the drives.

Similarly, can the great repertoire of subtle emotional states discoverable in the healthy adult really be epiphenomena of the drives, resulting from the lack of immediate discharge? Perhaps human feeling is not ultimately reducible to the pursuit of pleasure or the avoidance of pain and human relationships to sublimations of libidinal energy. Because of this reductive strain, however, classical Freudian metatheory leaves many of the developments of post-Freudian psychoanalytic theory—ego psychology, object relations theory, interpersonal psychoanalysis, and self psychology—with a less than adequate metatheoretical grounding. Such developments require some appreciation of the Other as more than a libidinal object and as important in ways other than those leading to drive satisfaction—a matter I take up in detail in the next two chapters.

Finally and perhaps most importantly, existentialists object to Freud's theory because it draws upon mechanical explanations borrowed from the natural sciences—explanations which do not fit well with reflective analysis of one's own experience or empathic understanding of the experiences of others. Even if we accept Freud's occasional statements that psychology must establish itself as a separate discipline on the basis of purely psychical concepts, we would still have to say that Freud's metaphors about how the psyche works are drawn from nonpsychical sources—from physics and biology. As Sulloway (1979) so convincingly argues, Freud remains a "crypto-biologist." Such sources leave little room for understanding the human side of human relationships—oneself and the Other as subjects as opposed to oneself and others as objects. Although Freud expresses a desire to carve a separate realm for psychology as a specific science, he continues to describe human reality as if it were a thing subject to the laws of cause and effect which are discovered operating in the thing world. The chief objection to this model is that it inhibits the investigation of meaning in the exclusively human sense.

Sartrean Metapsychology: Consciousness as the Pursuit of Value

The initially most striking thing about Sartre's theory of human reality is his denial of the unconscious. The reader steeped in Freud will immediately wonder how one is to proceed with any depth therapy, much less psycho-analysis, without a theory of the unconscious. Without the unconscious, are we not thrown back into the world of rationalist voluntarism? Yet it is Sartre's denial of the unconscious which makes it possible for him to do without the instinctual forces and psychobiological explanations of Freud. A meaning which is unconscious is no meaning at all. Sartre's theory of consciousness, however, is not a voluntarist theory. He does not equate con-sciousness with the will. Nor does he deny the power of emotional, imagina-tive, and sexual consciousness as well as rational consciousness. Sartre's the-ory of consciousness also has a place for all those self-deceptions which are presented as phenomenological evidence for the unconscious in Freud's sys-tem. And perhaps most important, Sartre's theory of consciousness allows for an investigation of the future as meaning or value as well as the past as ground in human reality.

Sartre's own challenge in *Being and Nothingness* to Freud's theory of the unconscious revolves around a philosophical contradiction in Freud's think-ing. How, Sartre asks, does Freud's concept of the censor who stands be-tween consciousness and the unconscious in the topographical hypothesis make sense? There is also, though Sartre does not mention this, a second censor between the unconscious and the preconscious (Freud, 1915c). This proliferation of censors, however, only strengthens Sartre's argument. Sartre questions whether the censor is a viable concept. In other words, the censor, in order to perform the function of repression, would have to be knowledgeable of the unconscious material in order to repress it—that is, the censor would need to know it in order not to know it. The censor thus reintroduces the paradox of the dual unity of the deceiver and the deceived. We have returned to the original problem of self-deception which Freud's concept of the censor was intended to resolve: How can an individual (or a censor) lie to himself or herself about the nature of his or her wishes and desires? We might as well dispose of the censor and explain how a *consciousness* can be divided in this way.

Though Sartre does not discuss the later permutations of Freud's theory, this problem of the dual unity of the deceiver and the deceived is not solved by Freud's later introduction of the structural hypothesis. In *The Ego and the Id* (1923), Freud relegates the censorship function to the superego rather than to a censor between consciousness and the unconscious. In a sense, as we shall see, this conception is closer to Sartre's idea about how self-deception works in that the superego might be taken as a critical reflective voice which judges spontaneous experience. Yet to the extent that Freud conceives of the superego as a discrete principality within the psyche, the question still remains concerning *how* the superego as censor deceives itself about unconscious material it recognizes. The same objection applies to Freud's late (1940) attribution of the function of censorship to the ego as the home of the defenses. A psychological structure (the ego) has simultaneously to know and not to know itself in order to repress certain ideas, feelings, and impulses. One wonders if Freud's three revisions of the theory of censorship and his attribution of it to three different psychological structures indicate his own dissatisfaction with his attempts to understand how this function works.

In any case, Sartre further maintains that the "aha" experience of the analysand in psychoanalysis calls into question Freud's theory of the unconscious. All depth therapists are aware of this phenomenon in which the analysand or client suddenly lights up at the felt truth of a particular interpretation or insight: "Aha," the person says, "that is what has been happening all this time; I *see* it now." Freud would maintain that at this moment unconscious material is becoming conscious. Yet if the analysand recognizes a true picture of himself or herself in the analyst's interpretation, Sartre maintains, then this material could never have been unconscious in the first place. This sense of enlightenment is explicable only if "the subject has never ceased being conscious of his deep tendencies; better yet, only if these drives are not distinguished from his conscious self" (BN, p. 574). Otherwise, if the complex were truly unconscious, who would recognize it? The conscious subject could not, since it has always been out of reach of consciousness. Nor could the complex recognize itself, since Freud tells us that it lacks understanding. Only a subject who both knows and does not know his or her own tendencies and desires could recognize what had previously been hidden. In fact, only such a subject would be able to "resist" the analyst in bringing this material to light, since only such a subject would know that there is anything to resist or defend against.

Finally, Sartre claims that much of what Freudian psychology labels drives and instinctual forces of the deep unconscious is the result of a confusion of the essential structure of reflective acts with the essential structure of nonreflective acts—whether one is reflecting on oneself or on another person. Reification of consciousness occurs when "each time the observed consciousnesses are given as unreflected, one superimposes on them a structure, belonging to reflection, which one doggedly alleges to be unconscious" (TE, pp. 55-56). Thus one observes a young man falling in love with a young woman. Sartre would say that this particular young man discovers his desires for this particular young woman out there in the world rather than that the young man's libido drives him to find the young woman. Only a reflective act makes the Freudian psychoanalyst say that the young man found an outlet for his libido in courting the young woman or a substitute for it in writing a romantic novel or other activity. The young man's desire, Sartre would say, does not exist *prior to* living it but *in* living it. Reflection conceives of libido as an unconscious a priori when it is, in fact, a superimposition.

Thus Sartre believes that the analysand in psychoanalysis gains not consciousness of unconscious tendencies but knowledge of spontaneous experience. The problem is not that these tendencies are too dark, that they are hidden away in the unconscious, but rather that they are too light. Sartre writes,

> [Spontaneous consciousness] is penetrated by a great light without being able to express what this light is illuminating. We are not dealing with an unsolved riddle as the Freudians believe; all is there, luminous. . . . But this "mystery in broad daylight" is due to the fact that this possession is deprived of the means which would ordinarily permit *analysis* and *conceptualization*. It grasps everything, all at once, without shading, without relief, without connections of grandeur—not that these shades, these values, these reliefs exist somewhere and are hidden from it, but rather because they must be established by another

human attitude and because they can exist only *by means of* and *for*
knowledge. (BN, pp. 570–71)

What Sartre is describing here is the simple awareness of prereflective consciousness without the addition of reflective conceptualization. We must be
careful, however, not to conceive of "prereflective consciousness" and "reflective consciousness" as subdivisions of consciousness. Unlike Freud,
Sartre views consciousness as all of a piece, without compartments or
spheres. Reflective consciousness is simply prereflective consciousness turning and making an object of its own (past) actions, feelings, and gestures—
instead of being directed toward the world, consciousness is now directed toward the self. Yet it is in this very turning that self-deception becomes a
possibility, since a gap appears between the consciousness reflecting and the
consciousness reflected on. Before we can fully understand this, however, we
must first examine more carefully what Sartre means by "consciousness."

Consciousness for Sartre is not a thing with substance and structure, as
the psyche is for Freud. Nor is human reality motivated by underlying drives
pushing for instinctual gratification. Consciousness is translucid rather than
opaque. It is an openness toward Being, a *desire* or *lack* of a future fullness
rather than a self-contained, intrapsychic system. Because consciousness
brings into being a nothingness or gap between itself and its objects, it can
be aware of objects in the world. Otherwise, as a fullness, it could not be a
presence to other objects. Hence Sartre does not accept Freud's idea that the
infant is wrapped in a blanket of primary narcissism from which it is lured by
the discovery that objects in the world (particularly human beings) can provide gratification. Instead, Sartre's infant would be world-conscious from
the beginning. In fact, we might presume from Sartre's description of prereflective consciousness that the infant would be more world-conscious than
self-conscious—a view which might help to explain the finding of many
post-Freudian theorists that a young infant has difficulty distinguishing
himself or herself from the world.[3] The human being is not a bundle of
drives but rather the assumption of a position on Being. Consciousness implies its partner, the world. It is intentional in Husserl's sense of always being
consciousness of this or that object.

Sartrean consciousness is also always *consciousness for*. In other words, consciousness is temporalizing. It is aware of movement out of a past that has
been its only reality toward a future that is not yet. In this respect, Sartre
says that consciousness is doubly "nihilating," or doubly aware of itself as
not being its objects. Consciousness is aware that it is *not* its objects, and it is

aware that consciousness and its objects are *not* what they are going to be. This movement is perceived both in terms of objects in the world and of one's own project of being—or way of *pro-jecting*, or throwing oneself forward toward the future through those objects. Sartre gives the example of the crescent moon which is *going to be a full moon* (BN, pp. 86–87). The crescent moon is perceived by consciousness as the lack of a full moon. In itself, the moon does not recognize this future possibility; it is therefore brought into being *as possibility* by the presence of a human witness. Consciousness also actively attempts to bring into being its own possibilities. The Emperor Constantine, to use another of Sartre's examples, conceives of his empire in terms of a present lack of a Christian city in the east—a lack which leads him to found Constantinople (BN, pp. 433–34).

It is because consciousness inserts lack into the heart of Being that it can conceive of a future which is different from the present. For all of us, Sartre says, "being is revealed on the ground of the world as an instrumental thing, and the world rises as the undifferentiated ground of indicative complexes of instrumentality" (BN, p. 201). In other words, we perceive objects in the world in terms of our projects of being—not that we create the world, but that, for example, a mountain climber and a geologist might view a mountain as object quite differently. As Sartre puts the matter, using a concept borrowed from Gestalt psychologist Kurt Lewin, the world is "hodologically" organized (BN, p. 279, EOT, p. 57). In other words, it is organized in terms of the paths which I perceive toward and away from a variety of objects in the direction of a future which I intend to bring into being. This includes spatial as well as temporal relationships—my nearness or distance from objects and my way of conceiving them as furthering or obstructing my fundamental project in this way or that.

My fundamental project also includes all those tastes and habits by which I define myself in the world. On the level of prereflective consciousness, a person must be sought for in the concrete choices which clarify his or her fundamental project of being. This project is not to be found *behind* this concrete richness but *in* it. Sartre says,

> The value of things, their instrumental role, their proximity and real distance (which have no relation to their spatial proximity and distance) do nothing more than to outline my image—that is, my choice. My clothing (a uniform or a lounge suit, a soft or a starched shirt, whether neglected or cared for, carefully chosen or ordinary), my furniture, the street on which I live, the city in which I reside, the books with

which I surround myself, the recreation which I enjoy, everything
which is mine, that is, finally, the world of which I am perpetually conscious, at least by way of a meaning implied by the object which I look
at or use: all this informs me of my choice—that is, my being. (BN,
p. 463)

These prereflective choices, which include such things as my taste in food
and clothing as well as my way of relating to other people, may never have
been reflectively conceived. I may not be able to say, for instance, why it is
that I prefer my meat done medium-well rather than rare, or why I am more
comfortable being too hot than too cold. Yet according to Sartre, all of my
concrete choices, all of my various ways of being, doing, and having are
clues to my fundamental project of being—the meaning of my being in the
world.

Furthermore, these "cardinal categories" (BN, p. 431) of human reality—
being, doing, and having—by which I define myself in the world are not ontologically unrelated to each other. Doing, for example, is a mode of having,
and having is part of the attempt to *be*—to achieve a substantive sense of
self. The uniquely individual character of a person's fundamental project is
revealed through an examination of these cardinal categories. Indeed, Sartre
asserts, one might invent a "psychoanalysis of things" based on the qualities
of things and the relation of these qualities to an individual's choice of self
in the world. For example, as Sartre notes in a famous example, "slime" is a
quality which can be applied both to the human world (to a handshake, a
smile, a thought, a feeling) and to the physical world. The reason slime
strikes us as so horrible, Sartre maintains, is that it suggests a kind of "revenge of the In-itself" on the for-itself (BN, p. 609). Like a "liquid seen in a
nightmare" (BN, p. 609), slime possesses a leechlike softness which threatens
to possess me as I attempt to possess it.

The ontological significance of slime is therefore the discovery of the slimy
as "antivalue" (BN, p. 611). Slime suggests not substantive freedom (Being-in-
itself-for-itself) but a freedom sucked up and absorbed by matter (Being-for-
itself-in-itself). And it is for this reason that we tend to recoil from the slimy
substance or the slimy handshake. Unlike water, which provides a natural
symbol for the fluidity of consciousness, slime appears to be a kind of "agony of water" (BN, p. 607) which suggests just the opposite—a consciousness
not fluid and free, but sucked up by a material world within which it loses itself. Of course, Being-for-itself-in-itself is no more of a real possibility than
Being-in-itself-for-itself, but the "great ontological region of sliminess" (BN,

p. 6II) gives testimony to the horror which conceiving of such a state can evoke in the majority of people. Ontological investigations such as this one, Sartre proposes, might create a psychoanalysis of things to replace the universal symbology of Freudian psychoanalysis. Certainly a preference for slime (if one should have such a preference) would have a particular meaning in an individual's fundamental project of being. But because it would be discovered out there in the world rather than in the recesses of the psyche, it would represent a point of conjunction between consciousness and the world.

Such prereflective choices, on the other hand, would not necessarily be any better known in the reflective sense in existential psychoanalysis than they are in Freudian psychoanalysis. Indeed, the meaning of my various ways of doing, being, and having may be easily reflectively misconceived—especially if they are part of a project to deceive myself in this way or that. I may, for instance, conceive of myself as being a warm and generous person, when in actuality my warmth is hypocritical and my generosity a means to control others by ingratiating myself with them. Yet Sartre would maintain that my underlying aggressive motives are not unconscious. Rather, they are to be found *in* the way I perform my so-called warm and generous acts and probably also in my complaints when I do not receive the responses I desire. Yet Sartre says that to be is to act and to act is to intend to act. In fact, there is no difference between acting and intending to act, for "our acts will inform us of our intentions" (BN, p. 484). If I could attend to myself while performing these acts which I have reflectively designated as "warm and generous," I would discover their true nature. The problem is that I do not want to see this about myself. I want, instead, to perpetuate the myth that I am warm and generous. In fact, if others suspect my motives, I will probably remonstrate with a great deal of feeling—though my defensiveness will itself be a sign that I somehow recognize the truth of their statements. How, then, according to Sartre's concepts, is this self-deception possible?

Self-deception is possible because of the gap between prereflective and reflective consciousness. Although the same person spontaneously acts and reflectively conceives of those actions, these two acts of consciousness are separated by the same nothingness which separates consciousness from objects in the world. In other words, it is only by *not being* my past spontaneous self that I can reflectively conceive that self. Of course, I am not being it in the mode of reflectively designating it. Bad faith, or reflectively lying to oneself about the nature of reality, is possible largely because the "reflective attitude . . . involves a thousand possibilities of error . . . in so far as it aims at constituting across the reflected-on veritable psychic objects which are only probable objects . . . and which can even be false objects [depending on what I am trying to prove about myself in so reflecting]" (BN, p. 471). Thus the mother who calls her harshness love ("I'm only doing this because I love you") has reflectively created a false psychic object which may confuse her offspring for the rest of their lives. Her adult children may, for example, call their own harshness or that of others toward them "love." Fortunately, as Sartre points out, basic intentionality, unlike reflective awareness, "can never be deceived about itself" (BN, p. 471). It is therefore always possible to liberate oneself by returning to the prereflective level and renaming those objects.

This discussion brings up another question: What is consciousness trying to do in reflectively conceiving or misconceiving itself? That is, what is the meaning of all this naming and misnaming? In order to answer this question, we must first look at Sartre's idea of the aim of consciousness in both its reflective and prereflective modes. In contrast to Freud's reduction of meaning to psychophysiological drives, Sartre maintains that the creation of value is the primary human focus and aim. Sartre would not, of course, deny the existence of organismic needs or the grounding of consciousness in the body. In fact, Sartre believes that consciousness lives the world through its body. But this is the body for-itself, one's bodily experience of the world, rather than the body as an object of scientific and medical investigations or reflective analysis. He gives as an example the pain that I, upon reflection, say I feel in my eyes from reading. On the nonreflective level, this pain-consciousness is simply my way of reading. The lived body is not an object but a subject.

The body of scientific investigation, on the other hand, is an object. Sartre believes that it cannot be made to express meaning. "The nerve," he says, "is not *meaningful*; it is a colloidal substance which can be described in itself and which does not have the quality of transcendence; that is, it does not transcend itself in order to make known to itself by means of other realities what it is [as consciousness does]" (BN, p. 560). To read human meaning into physiological excitation is to switch levels of discourse. For Sartre, it is not psychobiological aims but the attempt at self/world transcendence, one's sense of becoming, which is basic human reality.

What interests Sartre is the fact that conscious experience, including bodily experience, is lived as a connection with the world through which we attempt to create value or meaning. One attempts to use the world to get a sense of self. Sartre refers to this attempt to create a self through objects in the world as the "circuit of selfness." This is the perception by consciousness of its "possibles" on the face of this particular world, as, for example, consciousness perceives its thirst concretely as this-glass-of-water-to-be-drunk or a project of writing as this-book-to-be-written. Instead of the Freudian reduction of human meaning to neurophysiological forces and evolutionary aims, Sartre would substitute a meaning which is inherent in each concrete human action and gesture. This meaning is teleological—it refers to future ends rather than to past causes, although the past may figure in its designation of future ends. On the nonreflective level, the world is revealed as the "plurality of tasks which are my image" (BN, p. 201). And as I find myself "sculpturing my figure in the world" (BN, pp. 463–64), it becomes impossible to distinguish what I bring from what the world discloses. My choice of myself in the world and my discovery of the world are identical. Sartre says, "Without the world there is no selfness, no person; without selfness, without the person, there is no world [in the sense of differentiated objects]" (BN, p. 104).

Thus, without denying the physiological givens of the human condition, it could never be said that there is first an instinct which then pushes for satisfaction through an object. Consciousness is desire or lack of a (future) fullness, but this desire discovers itself outside in the world rather than in the recesses of the self. Also, this desire is not primarily sexual in nature, though it can include sexuality as one of its modes of expression. It is a desire of Being rather than a desire for pleasure or cessation of tension. As an ontological desire, it is not a desire which consciousness *has* but a desire or lack which consciousness *is*. Since self/object discovery includes but goes beyond the satisfaction of elementary physical needs, Sartre does not require a reductionist system in which the higher activities of human beings must be explained as transmutations of elementary drives. If consciousness discovers itself in the world, it can do so in art or philosophy as well as in sexual fulfillment. Nor do the former need to be explained as a sublimation of the latter, as Freud believes.

But what is this desire or lack which consciousness is? In its concrete mode, the answer is as varied as the number of human beings in the world. Each fundamental project is different. But ontologically speaking, this desire is a desire for a future fullness, a desire to *be* a substantial self and yet to remain a free consciousness. This is the origin of Sartre's well-known statement that "man is the being whose project is to be God" (BN, p. 566). God, as the *ens causa sui* of Aristotelian and Thomist philosophy, is precisely this combination of a substantial being with a transcending consciousness.

Sartre calls this desire on the part of human beings to become the missing God "Being-in-itself-for-itself" because it would be a combination of the substantiality of an object (Being-in-itself, the material world) with human freedom (Being-for-itself). Unfortunately, this is an impossible goal. "Man," as Sartre puts it, "is a useless passion" (BN, p. 615). The goal is impossible because consciousness is always projecting itself toward the future—because it can never stop and be a static given.

Let us take Sartre's example of consciousness discovering its thirst in the glass of water which is to be drunk (BN, p. 101–2). Consciousness, Sartre says, conceives of a fulfillment of thirst, satisfied thirst, as a substantial thing. Such a fulfillment would be the *in-itself-for-itself* of thirst—that is, it would combine the two sides of reality, free consciousness with material being. The problem with this is that the moment the glass of water is drunk, it becomes the background for a new enterprise—say, continuing to write this chapter. This is the familiar movement between figure and ground of the Gestalt perceptual psychologists, whom Sartre admired. According to this view, consciousness can never coincide with itself. I can never be this kind of person as a table is a table. I must always face the anguish of my freedom, which means that I must face the truth that I can never establish myself in the world once and for all as *this kind of person.*

Actually, this philosophical perception receives implicit validation from everyday life. Take those endless personality quizzes or psychological tests which purport to help me discover "who I am" in the substantive sense. The truth is that the very existence of these tests indicates that the entity they claim to discover is in doubt. If consciousness were opaque, like the color of my hair, this fascination would make no sense. I do not need to *discover* that my hair is blond because I already know it. The facts about me as a person are of a different order from the facts about the physical world, including the physical contingencies of my own body. Or take the "serious man" (BN, p. 580) who identifies with his role in a way that Sartre would call "inauthentic." This man attempts to *be* a doctor or lawyer or clergyman or corporate executive (or café waiter, to include a well-known example of Sartre's) as a table is a table. We may say colloquially that he is "full of himself" in a derogatory sense because of the inflated nature of this stance. What is inflated about it is our recognition that there is a free consciousness behind this caricature of a profession. For this reason, we know—and suspect that he knows—that his pomposity is not justified.

On the other hand, all of us are trying to create a self by our every action and gesture in the world. As Sartre puts the matter, our fundamental project is always "the outline of a solution to the problem of being [the problem of creating a self in a world where one can never coincide with the self that one has created]" (BN, p. 463)—a solution which is not first conceived and then realized, but rather a solution that we continually live in all its concrete reality. So long as this aim is future-oriented, so long as we do not believe we have arrived at this destination, there is no lack of integrity in the pursuit. In fact, it is this pursuit, this plan, this stance toward Being, which Sartre regards as the "veritable irreducible" (BN, p. 560), which is the object of investigation in existential psychoanalysis. It is indistinguishable from one's way of living one's life in the world.

Part of this project will inevitably be reflective. The serious man who attempts to *be* a doctor in the substantive sense or the abusive mother who conceives of herself as loving are examples of the reflective side of this project. Probably all social roles are examples of it. So too, Sartre tells us, is the ego (which, for Sartre, is the "I" or "me" of ordinary experience and not the Freudian ego of the tripartite structure). In the inauthentic mode (possibilities for an authentic attitude toward one's ego are discussed in a later chapter), the ego is simply my reflective view of myself as having a particular character or nature. The difficulty with reflectivity, however, is that except as an attempt at simple presence to one's spontaneous self (a form which Sartre calls "pure reflection" and which I discuss in detail in a later chapter), reflectivity is likely to distort. While the distortions of reflective consciousness can take a variety of forms, their basic ontological aim is to create the illusion of substantive freedom, Being-in-itself-for-itself. As such, these distortions are an escape from freedom and responsibility.

"Bad faith" is Sartre's name for this evasion of reality. Although bad faith is strictly speaking an ontological rather than an ethical category, it often has ethical connotations as well—as, for example, when Sartre accuses the anti-Semite or the colonialist or the self-righteous person of bad faith. The notable exception is the bad faith which is manifested in mental illness. As Sartre says in a letter to R. D. Laing printed as the foreword to Laing and Cooper's book on Sartre's later philosophy, *Reason and Violence*,[4]

Like you, I believe that one cannot understand psychological illnesses *from the outside*, on the basis of a positivistic determinism, or reconstruct them with a combination of concepts that remain outside the illness as lived and experienced. I also believe that one cannot study, let alone cure, a neurosis without a fundamental respect for the person of the patient, without a constant effort to grasp the situation and relive it, without an attempt to rediscover the response of the patient to that situation and—like you, I think—I regard mental illness as the "way out" that the free organism, in its total unity, invents in order to live through an intolerable situation. (Laing and Cooper, 1964, p. 6)

I think this point is very important to a Sartrean perspective on psychotherapy since it implies that discovering the structures of bad faith in a client's fundamental project has nothing at all to do with judging one's client, which would obviously be inappropriate. In other words, whereas it is always possible to choose how one lives a particular situation, it is not always possible to have a *viable* choice.

The bad faith into which we all fall at one time or another may take two forms, based on the two sides of human reality. On the one hand, there is facticity—the contingent world which I did not create but which I must choose to live in some fashion or other. Facticity includes my own past as well as external circumstances. On the other hand, there is freedom—my choice of objects in the world as a way of realizing my own fundamental project of being. A full recognition of my freedom includes the recognition that nothing—neither myself nor traditional values nor God—has a priori status as value. Instead, I create value through valuing. I fall into bad faith if I take one or both of two dishonest positions about reality: If I pretend either to be free in a world without facts or to be a fact in a world without freedom.

If, for whatever reasons, I desire to escape my facticity, I may fall into the dishonest position of claiming that I am absolutely free in the sense of being able to do or be anything whatever or in the sense of having no connections with my past self. The dreamer who constantly expects a "new tomorrow" and the schizophrenic who completely ignores reality are examples of this form of bad faith. So too, Sartre tells us, is the man who denies his own past by claiming that, despite his preference for same-sex partners, he is *not* a homosexual just as a tree is *not* a rock. Certainly, he is not a homosexual as a tree is a tree since he has on some level chosen this route, but he cannot claim absolute disconnection with his past.[5] Similarly, the client in therapy who refuses to see past actions as past choices or who refuses to accept real present circumstances is attempting to deny facticity. We could, in fact, say that the "defense" of denial is exactly such an attempt at escape from facticity.

The other form of bad faith noted by Sartre—escape from freedom—involves a desire to make the world and my past or character determinative factors in my life. This is the form adopted by the serious man who wishes to

believe that the world has more reality than himself. Sartre says that "all serious thought is thickened by the world; it coagulates; it is a dismissal of human reality in favor of the world." It claims "the priority of the object over
the subject," and the serious man "takes himself for an object" (BN, p. 580).
Sartre contrasts the "spirit of seriousness" with the "spirit of play," which
involves a lightness and an acceptance of freedom. He comments that it
would "appear that when a man is playing, bent on discovering himself as
free in his very action, he could not be concerned with possessing a being in
the world" (BN, p. 581).

The playful person is not engaged in the serious but mistaken pursuit of
substantiality. Unlike the serious person, he or she does not attribute his or
her actions to nature, circumstances, or the past. "Play," Sartre says, "re-
leases subjectivity" (BN, p. 580). Thus the position of "seriousness," which is
essentially the position of Freud, is false because it denies one's presence to
the world as conscious choice. The client who in therapy dwells on the past
as caused rather than as chosen would be engaging in this form of bad faith.
So would the person who is afraid to change because change would imply a
betrayal of the past. From this discussion, we can see that Sartre's "reality
principle" is in diametric opposition to Freud's account of reality-
orientation as "serious" attention to the constraints of life. There are, of
course, constraints in life—but one *chooses* how to live them.

This idea that human beings are basically free within a situation does not,
however, imply a return to rationalist voluntarism. First of all, one may
choose oneself in an emotional, imaginative, or sexual mode, as well as a rational or irrational mode. Second, Sartre does not equate choice with
"will." Prereflective consciousness is basic intentionality. According to
Sartre, such intentionality is definitely not to be equated with the will,
which is reflective. In fact, even language can be deceptive since it comes
into existence (and may continue even in one's inner dialogue) "for others"
and is often reflective rather than prereflective. Sartre says that "a voluntary
deliberation is always a deception" (BN, p. 450). When I get to the point of
deliberating, the "chips are down" in the sense that I have already chosen
the values on which I will base my deliberations.

Thus Sartre agrees with Freud in dismissing much of what passes for
decision-making as the surface manifestation of a deeper motivation. The
difference is that Freud would see this deeper motivation as unconscious,
whereas Sartre would insist that basic intentionality is conscious even where
it has never been articulated—indeed, even where the articulation (which is
reflective) seems to contradict the basic choice. Hence Sartre maintains that

while I can seem to make "voluntary decisions which are opposed to the fundamental ends" I have chosen, I can really "attack these ends in appearance only" (BN, p. 475). In the end, I will have done what I intended to do. Sartre gives as an example the stutterer whose fundamental project is one of realizing his inferiority. The stutterer may make a concerted effort to overcome his stuttering and may even succeed, only to discover himself finding other means for realizing his fundamental project of proving that he is inferior.

This contradiction between prereflective intentionality and reflective statement is an everyday occurrence in psychotherapy. Over and over again, we meet people who say they want to do one thing but find themselves doing another or who give up one symptom only to replace it with another. Freud believes that these people are not in touch with their unconscious desires. Sartre would say instead that they are not able to reflect accurately on their basic intentions. I believe that Sartre is right since, if one asks these people to attend carefully to the prereflective act and to feel deeply what they are doing, they can usually come up with an accurate account of their motivation. In this sense, they are reflectively conceiving correctly what had previously been misconceived.

Take, for example, the alcoholic who says that he or she wishes to stop drinking but simply cannot do so. On a reflective level, this person believes that alcohol is ruining his or her life. On a prereflective level, the glass of whisky beckons in the form of a future state of intoxication which one desires. If we put aside the physical symptoms of withdrawal for the moment (the addiction could just as well be to a new lover for the Don Juan character or to a work project for the workaholic), we may find that on the prereflective level the state of intoxication represents an escape from an apprehension of ordinary life as an intolerable state of deprivation. Thus we come to understand that for this client to cease to reach for the glass of whisky (or the addictive relationship or the work project) will mean a willingness to face an intolerable longing. It will mean exchanging a known good (intoxication) for an unknown possibility of working through those feelings of deprivation which are revealed *in*, not *behind*, the reach for the glass of whisky. All of this is conscious, but it is not under the control of the reflective will.

There is one very significant way in which reflectivity can be contaminated. So far we have seen that Sartre has presented two ontological structures, which are to be contrasted with the purely psychological structures (ego, superego, and id) of Freud. The first of these is "Being-for-itself" (*l'être-pour-soi*), or human consciousness, which can be divided into reflective and prereflective modes depending on whether consciousness takes an object in the world or whether it takes its (past) self as an object. The second is *Being-in-itself* (*l'être-en-soi*), or the material world which is indifferent to consciousness, but which consciousness needs in order to make known to itself what it is. The third is *Being-for-others* (*l'être-pour-autrui*), or my awareness of myself as an object for another consciousness.

This third structure, which is extremely important to existential psychoanalysis, is not necessarily implied by consciousness in the same way that consciousness by its very condition as consciousness implies a world. Whereas a consciousness without objects is impossible according to a phenomenological definition, it is possible to imagine a consciousness in a world where there are no other consciousnesses—as sometimes happens in stories of human beings raised by animals. On the other hand, this would not be the human world as we know it. Sartre says that it is through an experience which he calls the "Look" that I come to be aware of the Other not simply as an object like other objects in the world but as a consciousness like my own. The Other's Look reveals another subject because it reveals to me my own object status beneath the gaze of that subject.

We shall explore the implications of the Other's presence in greater detail in the next chapter. What needs to be noted here is that my awareness of my Being-for-others—though it gives me the opportunity for conceiving of myself as a concrete being—leads to a contamination of reflective consciousness. Briefly speaking, the realization that I am an object for the Other gives me new hope of recovering substantive freedom. If I can incorporate the Other's view of me into my free project, then I imagine that I will become that impossible combination, Being-in-itself-for-itself. The problem is that in attempting to do so, I abandon the position of good faith, in which I accept the ontological failure implied in the value-making process, for a position of bad faith in which I attempt to make substantive freedom itself a thetic ideal.

Of course, I cannot really subvert the Other's freedom to this end, although my attempt to do so will lead me to engage in those interpersonal battles which Sartre describes as the "conflict of consciousnesses (BN, pp. 361–423). This is basically a conflict over my attempt to manipulate and use the Other to create substantive freedom. The attempt is doomed because the Other almost always wants to use me for the same ends and because the Other is a separate freedom—I cannot incorporate him or her into my consciousness. Sartre names this desire to incorporate the other person into oneself without in any way impairing his or her character as an external witness the "Jonah complex" (BN, p. 579)—thereby indicating the ultimately

pathological implications of the attempt to use the Other to create a substantive self.

On the other hand, even though I cannot in reality incorporate the Other
into my consciousness, I can mimic the Other's view of me in my own reflective consciousness—further alienating reflective awareness from prereflective
experience. If I am a child and the Other is one of my parents, I will inevitably engage in this reflective mimicry. To the extent that my parents refuse to
see and name me accurately, I will carry this reflective distortion forward as a
part of my project. In this sense, Freud's intuition about the censoring function of the superego was correct. But reflective awareness is not really a separate structure, and the motivations for incorporating the voices of the original others into reflective consciousness are different for Freud and for
Sartre. For Freud, the superego is an outcome of the successful resolution of
the Oedipus complex instead of a part of a project to achieve a substantive
sense of self. Through meta-reflection and a willingness to give up an inauthentic project, one can begin to purge reflective consciousness of these distortions. This too is a topic I take up in more detail in a later chapter.

It should be pointed out here that Sartre does not consider fundamental
change to be easy—any more than Freud does. Yet Sartre would not consider the reason for this to be the stubbornness of libidinal attachments or
the presence of unconscious conflicts. Rather, for Sartre, a change even in
the smallest significant detail of an individual's life means a challenge to
that person's fundamental project. Sartre gives the example of a man on a
hike with friends whose fatigue becomes very painful after several hours of
walking. He initially resists his fatigue but finally lets go, throwing his knap-
sack down beside the road and falling next to it. Sartre goes on,

> Someone will reproach me for my act [giving in to the tiredness] and
> will mean thereby that I was free—that is, not only was my act not de-
> termined by any thing or person, but also I could have succeeded in re-
> sisting my fatigue longer, I could have done as my companions did and
> reached the resting place before relaxing. I shall defend myself by saying
> that I was *too tired*. Who is right? Or rather is the debate not based on
> incorrect premises? There is no doubt that I could have done otherwise,
> but that is not the problem. It ought to be formulated like this: could I
> have done otherwise without perceptibly modifying the organic totality
> of the projects which I am; or is the fact of resisting my fatigue such that
> instead of remaining a purely local and accidental modification of my

behavior, it could be effected only by means of a radical transformation of my being-in-the-world—a transformation, moreover, which is possible? In other words: I could have done otherwise. Agreed. But *at what price?* (BN, pp. 453–54)

Obviously, the price would be a modification of my whole project of being— my way of living my body as fatigue to be succumbed to at such and such a point.

There are many other ways of living my body, including (Sartre tells us in his biography of Flaubert) psychosomatic illnesses which are intentional but not deliberate. The point is that changes even in what might seem like the insignificant details of living may involve a whole new way of "Being-in-the-world." To change the way I walk, for instance, is to change my orientation toward life. Thus when Sartre says that we are radically free, he does not mean that we are capriciously or willfully free. Fundamental change means facing one of those fearful psychological instants where self and world shift together. (This is also a point I discuss in greater detail in a later chapter.)

The Implications for Psychotherapy

Clearly, consciousness has a radically different relationship to its objects and to other people in Sartre's system than does the human psyche in Freud's system. The Freudian psyche is opaque, whereas Sartrean consciousness is translucid. Freud imagines a third substance, or psychic glue, which binds the psyche to its objects: the libido, or generalized sexual energy, which emanates from an unconscious realm of instinctual life beyond the reach of consciousness. Other people in Freud's system are important not as subjects but as need-gratifying objects. Motivation in interpersonal relations, as in everything else, emanates from the dark regions of the unconscious—from the drives and from unconscious wishes, conflicts, and complexes. The individual, according to Freud, emerges from the stages of psychosexual development as a fairly self-contained intrapsychic system. Without the intervention of psychoanalysis, the structural interplay between one's ego, superego, and id is likely to remain essentially the same, as are those repetitions of infantile experience which Freud refers to as "transference."

Sartre, on the other hand, describes the ontological structures of Being in such a way that consciousness is an openness to its objects. Although consciousness may divide itself into reflective and prereflective modes, it is really all of a piece since the same consciousness spontaneously acts and reflectively conceives those actions. Thus it is possible through close attentiveness to decipher one's own project of being and to change. Consciousness is both consciousness *of* and consciousness *toward* a particular future which one is attempting to bring into being. Sartrean consciousness is not circumscribed and determined by the past, as is the Freudian psyche. It therefore becomes as important in existential psychoanalysis to understand an individual's project in terms of the future which is its meaning as in terms of the past which is its ground. Furthermore, relations with others are not simply external and accidental. The Other affects me in my being, and I have with him "a reciprocal internal relationship of being to being." While this may be a source of much conflict, especially if I attempt to use the Other in the inauthentic project of achieving substantive freedom, it may also be a source of genuine positive reciprocity and intimacy (a topic I pursue in the following chapter).

In conclusion, we might say that the chief difference between Freud's psychobiological metatheory and Sartre's ontological metatheory is that although both initially rely on phenomenological analysis and description, Sartre attempts to discover the ontological structures of human existence which manifest themselves *in* experience, whereas Freud attempts to discover the metabiological (or metaphysical) forces which lie *behind* human experience. As an experience-near theory, Sartre's analysis is more in line even with many recent psychoanalytic approaches. Unlike most of these theorists, however, Sartre offers a metatheory—a philosophical inquiry that goes beyond phenomenological analysis to elucidate the general structures of human reality. This allows comprehension of psychological disturbances as variations on the human dilemma itself—that is, as manifestations of the various ways in which consciousness encounters the material world, other people, and the self of reflective analysis and either deals with or attempts to escape the anguish of responsible freedom.

The differences a Sartrean perspective might make to the practice of psychotherapy, based on insights discussed in this chapter, could be briefly described as follows:

1. A therapist working from a Sartrean orientation would substitute the idea of prereflective choice for Freudian determinism. Using the progressive-regressive method, he or she would not get stuck in regressive analysis; the future as meaning would become as significant as the past as ground for contemporary choices. Indeed, the past itself would be approached in a different way—as a past future-directedness with a significance that changes as one's

fundamental project changes. Past actions would be grasped as intentional and meaningful within the particular situations in which particular life choices were made and the directions of the fundamental project established. Such vivid reconstruction of the past can liberate the future as well, since the past now makes sense as emotional choice rather than as mere intellectual reconstruction. For example, if a client can recapture a past choice of shrinking from an overpowering parent and really feel what it was like as a child living that fearful situation, then he or she may begin to reflectively understand his or her choice of the future as one in which submission or defiance toward authority figures is prominent. And though this reconstruction might not be significantly different from similar reconstructions in Freudian analysis, the emphasis on the past moment of choice (a choice which is, of course, fully understandable within the situation) makes the choice of a different future seem more probable.

As for the future, the existentialist therapist would attempt to interpret present acts not only in terms of past choices but also in terms of future meanings. What future, the existentialist therapist would want to ask, is the client attempting to bring into being? Often the question, "What does [a particular way] of [doing, being, having] *do* for you?" will elicit this information. For example, suppressing a feeling may allow a client to believe that he or she will remain in control of an interpersonal situation. And while this supposition will undoubtedly have its antecedent in past experience, its meaning is a fear or an intention with respect to the future.

Similarly, the client who is erecting emotional barriers between himself or herself and others may understand quite well where this "wall" comes from in terms of past interpersonal relationships. It is nonetheless necessary to understand it as an intention toward the future as well. "This wall," as one client put it, "feels like a fortress. I don't know what's outside it since I haven't really let it down in years, but I suspect that what would happen to me would be awful. I don't want to look." This not wanting to look is a vote for future security over the awful anxiety that accompanies interpersonal vulnerability—but, of course, it is a security for which this client is paying a great price. Pointing this out leads to a dynamic conception of the wall as more than a mere static "result" of past interpersonal hurts; it is also a way of projecting oneself into the future, as a person walled in and unavailable for genuine intimacy.

Throughout all this, the existentialist therapist would not, of course, "blame" the client for such choices. He or she would instead try to understand them in all their complex significance within a client's particular situation. But this understanding would be an understanding of the motives rather than of the causes (in the deterministic sense) of a client's present actions. Such motives may well not be deliberate in the reflective sense; indeed, usually they are not or else they are reflectively distorted. But they *are* gut-level choices—and these gut-level choices must be elucidated in terms both of their origins in the past and of their meaning with respect to the future.

Throughout the process of therapy the existentialist therapist would approach the client not as a mere product of past (hereditary and environmental) forces, but as a free subject who deserves the respect of a free subject capable of creating meaning and of either resisting or allowing fundamental change to occur. Ultimately, the success or failure of therapy rests in the client's hands, not in the therapist's—though this does not, of course, excuse the therapist from helping the client to elucidate past and future-directed choices with the aim of alleviating misery by facilitating fundamental change.

2. The existentialist therapist would not only examine a client's project in terms of its three temporal *ekstases* (standing apart) of past, present, and future; he or she would also attempt to grasp that client's relationship to time and space as such—an ontological concern which has no corollary in Freudian analysis. Is a client stuck in the past, living in and ruminating on it while refusing to be aware of the future to any significant extent? For example, does this client go over and over a previous relationship, picking it apart to discover the client's or the relationship's defects? Does this person dwell excessively on the recent or distant past, looking for excuses for present failures or even regarding the past as a kind of paradise which is forever foreclosed? Or is a client at the opposite extreme—neglectful of all responsibility for past actions, living in a fantasy future or adopting a capricious attitude toward life? Or perhaps a client feels that he or she has no viable future at all? Has this person as a consequence become sunk into depression or even psychosis? How does a client's attitude toward the past change as his or her future-directed project changes? For example, a client who began to reflectively reassess the past harshness (which he had previously called love) of his parents suddenly felt an opening of sadness and tenderness which affected his approach to the future. He began to be less hard on himself and others and to ask for and offer more intimacy in his relations with others.

The existentialist therapist would also want to be aware of a particular client's way of living spatial relationships. Does a client feel closeness or distance from objects or other people? What is the quality of this closeness or distance and what does this say about the client's fundamental project? How much space or lack of space does a client feel that his or her body occupies? What is this person's hodological space like? What are the paths in the world that lead toward or away from which objects? For example, a client with whom I worked felt a sudden change in spatial perceptions resulting from a shift in his fundamental project which occurred in therapy. He was suddenly aware of feeling that he "had enough space to breathe" in a room full of people where previously he had felt crowded and even threatened by "teeming humanity." And he assured me that the room literally "looked different" as he experienced this crowd without the old (prereflective) intention of assessing their degree of threat to his personal integrity—a theme which, of course, had its roots in his childhood but which was also an intention toward the future which affected his spatial perceptions.

3. A therapist adopting Sartre's view of consciousness in place of Freud's view of the psyche would not regard therapy as a technique for making the unconscious conscious, but rather as a way to focus a healing reflection on a client's previously distorted or unidentified prereflective experience. As for the phenomena of self-deception which Freud regards as indications of unconscious forces and processes, the existentialist therapist would reinterpret these in the light of the gap between reflective and prereflective consciousness and the structures of bad faith.

Especially important here would be an investigation of the way in which prereflective choices have been reflectively distorted by attention to the voices of the original powerful others. For example, perhaps a client who is afraid to feel strongly identifies lack of feeling with "strength" and feeling with "weakness"—views which correspond to the views of his or her parents and which inhabit the client's project as a decision to *be* strong. Or perhaps there has been a failure of conceptualization. For example, a client who feels miserable over a lack of intimate contact with others may not have repressed his or her awareness of intimacy needs into the unconscious; instead, this person may simply have lived lack of intimacy as "the way things are" in a family which offered little emotional contact.

As for the structures of bad faith—the lie to myself about being free in a world without facts or a fact in a world without freedom—these may lead to a misunderstanding about reality in which I resist awareness in certain areas. From an existentialist perspective, such resistance does not amount to repression into the unconscious. For example, a person afflicted by the first form of bad faith might appear to have repressed a knowledge of past hurts, whereas a person living the second might appear to have repressed the capacity to act autonomously and effectively. The truth is that no repression in the sense of relegating something to the unconscious is going on at all here. Rather, there is a selective attention-inattention to the past or future based on a particular fundamental choice of being. There is reflective distortion, but no unconscious processes.

For example, I recall a client with a particularly painful and even abusive childhood who had resolved, as part of his fundamental project, to "put all that behind me." He remembered very little of his childhood by the time he entered therapy. But he also reported remembering very little of what happened last week or last month. He had, in effect, learned to forget as a way of surviving. Memories began to flood in as he changed his project of forgetting—memories which I would submit were never unconscious but which had been held at a distance in a project of forgetting.

Similarly, another client, afflicted with the second form of bad faith, came in week after week to tell me of the overwhelming circumstances which kept him from acting effectively in the world. He was not, as I discovered, afflicted with an unconscious motive to fail; however, he had made a fundamental choice of being in which he conceived of himself as exonerated from guilt (which was abundantly handed out in his childhood home) only so long as something outside made it impossible for him to act in any other way. This project was fully conscious—but it had never been reflectively examined.

The existentialist therapist, then, would not look for an unconscious complex to explain a client's "pathology." Instead, he or she would investigate the ontological structures of that client's project of being. Such a project would be assumed to be translucid and free. Its aim would not be pleasure (though pleasure could be included as a subsidiary aim), but rather the creation of meaning—a self as value. And because such a fundamental project is consciously, though not necessarily reflectively and certainly not accurately, known, the existentialist therapist would simultaneously refuse to consider the subject privileged in his or her *knowledge* of the fundamental project at the beginning of therapy while still respecting "the final intuition of the subject as decisive" (BN, p. 574). Because the consciousness reflecting and the consciousness reflected on are the same consciousness, there is no reason not to assume that it is possible for the client to understand the strategies of bad faith and reflective distortion which cloud the present reflective process and to see what is really going on (a point to which I return in a later chapter).

4. The existentialist therapist would regard relations with others as deriv-

ing not from a person's discovery of others as libidinal objects capable of gratifying/frustrating instinctual needs, but rather from a discovery of the other person as a subject who sees and names me. As such, others, especially the original powerful others, figure in my fundamental project as means to establishing a self as value. It is their reflected appraisals which must be purged through meta-reflection on a reflective process in which I have (badly) learned from them how to see myself. For example, many a child has learned to see his or her own needs as "bad" because parents unsuited to meet those needs have regarded the child as overly demanding or wrong. On the other hand, my sudden awareness of the Other as another subject through the experience of the Look also opens the way for a genuine intimacy and authentic relationship that do not appear possible from the Freudian perspective (a topic I discuss in a later chapter). The existentialist therapist, of course, hopes the therapeutic relationship will be such an authentic relationship.

5. The body in existentialist therapy would be regarded not as a source of psychobiological drives but rather as a way of living one's life in the world. The existentialist therapist would attempt to explore with the client all those modes of living the body as a subject and as an object for other consciousnesses which form a part of his or her fundamental project. The existentialist therapist would interpret bodily lived experience, including emotions, sexuality, and even psychosomatic symptoms, as choices. I do not, of course, mean that one chooses one's body as such, but rather that one chooses one's way of living one's body, including its limitations.

The existentialist therapist would be sensitive to these bodily ways of living one's project, both the therapist's and the client's, in the context of therapy. For example, he or she would be aware of closeness or distance, of eye contact or its opposite, of breathing or holding the breath, of muscular tightness, and so on as indications of the way a client is situating himself or herself in the world. Unlike Freudian analysis, existentialist therapy would not be regarded as a purely "talking cure." While bodily manifestations of difficulties might well need to be talked about in order to be reflectively apprehended, they would receive a focus in existentialist therapy that they do not have in classical Freudian analysis. After all, since the subject is always a body subject, the body itself may be regarded as signifying or indicating meaning.

6. Unlike the classical analyst, the existentialist therapist would not be satisfied either with general nosology or with general symptomatology or symbology. Consequently, the client's world would be interpreted not in

terms of abstract categories (either ontological or psychobiological), but rather as a concrete and uniquely rich individual world. The ontological categories are discovered *in* the client's experience, not *behind* it. For this reason, symbolism can never be universal. Dreams must refer to a person's way of living ontological structures and cultural experiences as part of his or her unique project.

As a deciphering of an individual's project, a hermeneutics or an interpretative enterprise, existentialist therapy must also be sensitive to the slightest change in the meaning of symbols or the client's overall project. These shifts signal the appearance of what Sartre calls a "psychological instant"—those moments when major life changes occur. These major changes are rare if for no other reason than that they remind us in the most direct way that the self we seek to create can never be a fixed entity. Thus resistance, according to this view, may be regarded as fear of facing the anguish of our freedom (a topic discussed more fully in a later chapter).

The existentialist therapist must be aware of the possibility of radical change and even cultivate it. Sartre describes the task of existential psychoanalysis in the following way:

> Thus existential psychoanalysis will have to be completely flexible and adapt itself to the slightest observable changes in the subject. Our concern here is to understand what is *individual* and often even instantaneous [in the sense of the emergence of radical change]. The method which has served for one subject will not necessarily be suitable for another subject or for the same subject at a later period. (BN, p. 573)

Existentialist therapy, at the same time that it seeks to understand the ontological structures of a client's fundamental project, is aware that that project is a *pro-ject*, or a throwing of oneself forward from the past to the future on the part of an intentional consciousness. As such, it is unique, individual, and ever changing—sometimes even radically.

7. Finally, the existentialist therapist would investigate with a client not the structures of the client's psyche (since consciousness lacks substance and structure) but the ways in which this person lives the three fundamental structures of being—Being-in-itself, Being-for-itself, and Being-for-others. In doing so, the existentialist therapist might want to ask himself or herself questions concerning a particular client's way of living the structures of Being—especially as these include attitudes of bad faith, or lying to oneself about the nature of reality.

Being-in-itself. What is this client's basic way of living his or her relationship with objects in the world? Does a client overemphasize the power of the environment or underemphasize it? In other words, which form of bad faith (overemphasis on freedom or overemphasis on facticity) is this client more inclined toward? Or is it a matter of some combination of the two? Or does this client, influenced by some early trauma, have a very tenuous connection with real objects, for which he or she substitutes imaginary objects? What are a client's concrete tastes, ways of regarding or disregarding objects, or other relationships with objects? For example, does a client cherish them, define himself or herself in terms of possessions, destroy objects, give objects away in a flourish of generosity, find the material world oppositional or malleable, and so on? And what does a particular attitude indicate about that person's attempt to use the material world to create a self?

Being-for-others. What is a client's way of living his or her life with others? Does a client constantly focus on himself or herself as an object for others, attempting to please or antagonize or placate or persuade or humiliate himself or herself before the Other? Or does a client constantly focus on maintaining power over others, on making himself or herself the subject and the Other the object? Or does a client attempt to ignore the Other, losing himself or herself in the thing world? How much can a client really allow others to know him or her or allow himself or herself to know others? In other words, what is a client's capacity for reciprocity and intimacy?

What is the history of a client's way of relating to others? Where did the client learn a particular pattern of relating to others, and why does he or she continue it? Did the original others fail to adequately see or acknowledge this client? Did they interfere, promising approval or threatening disapproval for particular kinds of behavior? Were they overwhelming or violent in their insistence that their wishes and needs be met at the expense of the client? And how did the client incorporate this into his or her reflective appraisal of self? Also, how does the client presently hope to manipulate the views of others, including the therapist, in the service of creating a particular sense of self? In other words, what are the particular structures of bad faith in a client's relationships?

Being-for-itself in the reflective and prereflective modes. What is a client's relationship with himself or herself? Is he or she overly reflective, irresponsibly nonreflective, or tormented by the (real or imagined) views of others which are constantly incorporated into reflective consciousness? How accurate is a client's reflective view of himself or herself? What is a client trying to prove or what kind of self is a client trying to create through reflectively rewriting the past? What are the bad faith elements in a client's reflective view of self? In other words, does a client attempt either to accept the idea of having a fixed nature (good or bad) or to flee all responsibility by denying that past actions have anything to do with their author? Does a client stifle all spontaneity by constant reflective self-observation? Or does a client refuse to take a look at himself or herself out of fear of what might be discovered? How tenaciously does a client cling to the view of himself or herself proposed by the original powerful others? What are his or her motives for doing so—that is, how does the client hope to use this reflective view to mold and have a self?

Obviously, there are significant differences between a Sartrean and a Freudian approach to psychotherapy—differences which I discuss in more detail in later chapters as they relate both to subsequent psychoanalytic theory and to the practice of psychotherapy. If Sartre's metatheory is to prove clinically viable, it must be able to account for the significance of other people other than as objects for instinctual gratification/frustration. A Sartrean perspective must also be able to account for failures in development without resorting to the structural hypothesis of Freud and for therapeutic change in some other way than making unconscious ideas and wishes conscious. And it must be able to accomplish its goal of achieving a more human approach to psychotherapy while maintaining a rigor similar to that of Freudian psychoanalysis at its best.

Actually, I believe that Sartre's metatheory accounts for the aim of psychotherapy, which is a radical shift in a person's way of being in the world, better than Freud's does. I also believe it is possible to gain a better understanding of many significant theoretical and clinical issues, including issues brought forward by post-Freudian psychoanalytic theorists which are difficult to incorporate into a traditional Freudian framework, through an understanding of the philosophy of Sartre. Obviously, no metatheory, including Freud's, can account for everything. It is enough if a metatheory proves clinically viable in dealing with difficulties which stand in the way of alleviating unnecessary human suffering and promoting authentic living and if it accords well with the majority of clinical data.

3 · Sartre and the Post-Freudian Drive Theorists: A Crisis in Psychoanalytic Metatheory

The Nature of the Crisis

We have seen in the preceding chapter that Freud does not conceptualize an internal and primary relationship between the psyche and its objects, either inanimate or human. Other people are valued not first and primarily for their human qualities, but rather for their capacities as objects for gratifying instinctual desires. Only a combination of frustration and gratification can lure the infant out of its blanket of primary narcissism. The ultimate origin of interpersonal relations is therefore the discovery that other people can aid in the reduction of tensions in the tissues of the organism, combined (Freud sometimes indicates) with phylogenetic racial memories. Although this kind of mechanistic view may be less than flattering to human relations, it fits quite consistently into Freud's metatheoretical system.

The psychoanalytic theorists who followed Freud have no such consistent system within which to place their versions of relations with others. For example, they notice, but do not provide a metatheoretical explanation for, the very significant role which the positive regard of the original others plays in the development of a sense of self-esteem. Thus the whole question of relations with others becomes critically important to psychoanalytic metatheory. If the Other is no longer simply an object for libidinal cathexis but has a more human role to play in the development of the psyche, then Freudian metatheory is no longer sufficient. The question becomes this: Can post-Freudian object (that is, human) relations theory accommodate itself to Freudian drive theory, or does the new wine burst the old bottles of Freudian metatheory? I think that the latter is the case and that the requirement is for the development of a new metatheory. Obviously, I believe that Sartre's metatheory can help to solve the crisis in post-Freudian theory which derives from the discovery of these new relational needs.

Psychoanalytic theory since Freud has made some enormous strides. It has provided an extension of psychoanalytic principles to allow for work with more disturbed personalities, including narcissistic, borderline, and psychotic patients whom Freud considered unanalyzable. It has advanced theories about human development, including the development of the ego from the earliest stages of infancy, based both on reconstruction of such stages from treatment of more severely disturbed adults and on direct observation of and work with children. Work with patients who seem to retain certain archaic personality structures (borderline, schizoid, narcissistic, and psychotic) has allowed a great deal of speculation on what the earliest stages of infancy and childhood must have been like. And though such speculations and even psychoanalytic infant studies have sometimes been accused of "adultomorphization" (Peterfreund, 1978), or attribution of adult qualities inappropriate to the infant, these theorists have nonetheless produced some fascinating evidence that the quality of earliest relations with others is of primary importance in developing a satisfying outlook on life.

At the same time, post-Freudian theorists have encountered a problem—the problem of accommodating Freudian drive theory, which states that drives are primary and human relationships secondary, to the new emphasis on relationships. In other words, post-Freudian theory has found itself without adequate metatheoretical grounding. Its two most significant metatheoretical issues are the problem of accounting for relational needs which indicate a desire for something other than instinctual satisfaction and the concomitant problem of accounting for the structuralization of the self or ego which results from the satisfaction/frustration of these noninstinctual needs.

Many writers on psychoanalytic theory have recognized these problems. For example, Jay R. Greenberg and Stephen A. Mitchell, in their book *Object Relations in Psychoanalytic Theory*, regard the problem of reconciling drive theory with the discovery of new relational needs as the central problem in post-Freudian psychoanalytic theory:

> Despite their differences, all contemporary [psychoanalytic] theorists are concerned with a common problem: how to account for the preeminent importance in all clinical work of relations with other people. Finding a role in theory for object relations has been the central con-

ceptual problem throughout the history of psychoanalysis because Freud's original drive theory takes the discharge of psychic energy as its fundamental conceptual building-block, assigning to relations with others a status which is neither central nor immediately apparent. Every major psychoanalytic theorist has had to address himself to this problem. (1983, p. 379)

The failure to solve this problem is the reason for the contemporary "crisis" in post-Freudian psychoanalytic metatheory.

Post-Freudian theorists have often attempted to avoid this crisis by emphasizing the structural over the economic hypothesis of Freud. In doing so, they propose to complete a task which is implicit in the later work of Freud—the task of describing how the ego develops out of the id or, as it is sometimes referred to in post-Freudian theory, the "undifferentiated matrix" of earliest infancy. Psychoanalytic structural theory has its origins in Freud's paper "On Narcissism: An Introduction" (1914a), which posited an ego ideal that is used as a standard for measuring actual performance, a concept later superseded by the superego. Structural theory is taken up again in "Mourning and Melancholia" (1917), where Freud explains depression as the result of the introjection of a harsh critic. And, finally, in *The Ego and the Id* (1923), the full theory of the division of the psyche into ego, id, and superego appears.

The notion of ego defenses, which has been so important to post-Freudian theory, was introduced by Freud in *Inhibitions, Symptoms, and Anxiety* (1926) and elaborated by Anna Freud in *The Ego and the Mechanisms of Defense* (1937). This latter work and Heinz Hartmann's *Ego Psychology and the Problem of Adaptation* (1939) firmly set the direction of post-Freudian psychoanalytic thought toward an investigation of the development of the ego through the stages of infancy and childhood. Anna Freud's idea that ego defenses can be externally directed toward the environment as well as internally directed toward instinctual impulses inspired further investigation of the effects of the environment on ego development. Hartmann's idea that the ego contains an amount of "neutralized libidinal energy" which can be used for ego functions such as thinking and evaluation and his concept of the "average expectable environment" within which the infant can grow into a healthy adult provided a starting point for those post-Freudian studies which have attempted to look at the development of the ego in relations with others. All of this has provided the impetus for a new direction in post-Freudian psychoanalytic theory.

Post-Freudian theorists are able to find much justification for this direction in Freud's later work. For example, the idea of ego splitting, which has been so important to post-Freudian understanding of the more severe psychological disorders, was first introduced by Freud. In "Splitting of the Ego in the Process of Defense" (1940), Freud discusses ego splitting with respect to both fetishism and defense mechanisms. For instance, he observes that the concomitant recognition and disavowal of the perceptual fact that girls do not have a penis can for fetishists persist side by side throughout their lives without influencing each other (1940, pp. 75–78). Statements such as this one paved the way for many discussions on ego splitting in pre-Oedipal conditions—for example, those emphasized by Melanie Klein, Otto Kernberg, and others. Similarly, Freud's idea that "the ego is a precipitate of abandoned object-cathexes and that it contains the history of those object-choices" (1923, p. 29) is a cornerstone for the development of the concept in object relations theory of "internal objects" and "partial objects" and their influence on psychological development—an idea first emphasized by Melanie Klein and later taken up by most object relations theorists.

On the other hand, Freud himself definitely regards the pre-Oedipal conditions which arouse so much interest among the post-Freudian theorists as unanalyzable because they are "narcissistic" in character. By this, Freud is referring not to Heinz Kohut's idea of "narcissism" as a natural line of development relating to the impact of others on self-esteem, but to narcissism as "self-love" or a pathological investment of the ego at the expense of an individual's ability to relate to objects. Freud believes that neurosis in part involves an opposite process—the pathological investment of objects leading to the depletion of the ego. Certainly, he would not agree with Otto Kernberg that interfused self and object investments are primary from the beginning of life and that the analysis of the "narcissistic" kernel of neurosis is a proper facet of psychoanalysis even with neurotics. In fact, when post-Freudian theorists reject Freud's concept of primary narcissism, they are doing more than slightly revising Freudian theory. They are challenging the very heart of Freudian drive theory—the idea that the desire for pleasure resulting from the cessation of tension motivates all human activity. By discarding primary narcissism, they make relations with others primary rather than secondary. For Freud, however, relations with others are a by-product of the principle of constancy.

Thus the economic hypothesis, like the ghost of Hamlet's father, remains to demand a reckoning of these new theoretical developments. How, we ask, is post-Freudian theory Freudian if it ignores or rejects the economic hypothesis? After all, the economic hypothesis is at the heart of Freud's metatheory—explaining the very need for object relations. In fact, the term "object relations" refers to the economic hypothesis. It means "libidinal object," and Freud is quite clear in stating that such an object is human only because the infant discovers that human beings are the most capable satisfiers of instinctual needs. Post-Freudian theorists are very sensitive to this issue, since it is the acid test of psychoanalytic orthodoxy. They have taken essentially two paths, which Greenberg and Mitchell (1983) refer to as "drive/structure" and "relational/structure" theories.

Although I think there is considerable overlap between the two groups, it is probably essentially correct to divide post-Freudian theorists into those who attempt to accommodate their ideas to Freudian drive theory and those who reject, ignore, or radically revise it. Melanie Klein, Heinz Hartmann, Erik Erikson, René Spitz, Edith Jacobson, Margaret Mahler, and Otto Kernberg fall within the first group. Harry Stack Sullivan, the British object relations theorists (W. R. D. Fairbairn, D. W. Winnicott, Harry Guntrip), and the later Heinz Kohut fall within the second group. There is also, as Greenberg and Mitchell point out, a third group—those who, like the early Kohut, attempt to combine relational theory with drive theory by assigning drive theory an explanatory function for one group of (neurotic) disorders and relational theory an explanatory function for another group of (pre-Oedipal) disorders. All of the post-Freudian theorists discussed in the next two chapters accept Freudian structural theory. A Sartrean position would discard both drive theory and structural theory while retaining and reconceptualizing some of the very useful insights of drive/structure and relational/structure theorists.

Thus a major metatheoretical problem for post-Freudian theorists lies in explaining the complexities of human relationships which even in the very earliest stages seem to suggest that the infant needs something other than cessation of the tensions associated with physiological needs. Particularly difficult to explain are the affective relationships and the uses of significant others to attain a sense of self discovered to be operating in earliest infancy. Post-Freudian drive theorists have generally explained affective commitments as developing out of initially vague and variable representations of self and others, which are based on pleasurable and unpleasurable experiences of instinctual gratification/frustration. Post-Freudian relational theorists have often dwelt instead on the structural hypothesis of Freud and the primarily object-seeking nature of the psyche, dismissing Freud's idea of primary narcissism and substituting for it an initial state of primary relatedness with the mother. Both groups of theorists run into difficulties when new relational needs for self-esteem, mirroring, positive regard, affection, and so on prove incompatible with orthodox Freudian metatheory. And neither seems to have satisfactorily solved the metatheoretical issues associated with the discovery of these new relational needs. After all, how can needs to use the Other as a source of affection and self-definition derive from needs to use the Other as a source of instinctual gratification? And if relational needs do not derive from drives, how are they to be explained?

In this chapter, I consider the failed attempts of three avowed "drive" theorists to accommodate their discoveries of new relational needs to traditional Freudian metatheory. Although this failure is largely unacknowledged or glossed over by drive theorists, I think it has grave implications for Freudian metapsychology. If the most orthodox of post-Freudian theorists cannot reconcile their own phenomenological data on relational needs with Freudian drive theory, what is to become of traditional psychoanalytic metatheory? I believe that Sartre's ontology answers the metatheoretical questions which are implicit in the phenomenological data—questions concerning who the Other is and how he or she can have such a profound impact on psychological development in ways which are unrelated to drive gratification/frustration. For Sartre, the Other is not a *libidinal object* at all, but rather another *subject* whose view of me profoundly affects my developing sense of who I am. Even as an object, the Other is not important to me primarily as a gratifier of libidinal needs. On the contrary, sexuality itself is a response to the subject-object alternation—although, of course, a response predicated on certain biological capacities. The post-Freudian drive theorists also implicitly recognize the significance of the Other as subject—but since they attempt to accommodate their insights to traditional Freudian metatheory, the results are often confusing.

The Discovery of New Relational Needs
by Post-Freudian Drive Theorists

Psychoanalytic theorists identifying themselves as traditional in accepting Freudian drive theory encounter difficulties when gratification/frustration fails to explain all of the interpersonal facts which they encounter and describe. Indeed, these theorists often fail to acknowledge the novelty in their discoveries of new relational needs. Instead they attempt to demonstrate their loyalty to traditional Freudian metatheory by continually referring to passages from Freud; by placing new concepts in the old bottles of Freudian terminology; by assuming drive causality where none is demonstrated; and by viewing their discoveries about earliest relations with others as extensions rather than revisions of basic Freudian theory, that is, exploring pre-Oedipal as opposed to Oedipal disorders. If Freud can be accused of mixing levels of discourse by combining psychobiological and physicalist metaphors with phenomenological description, post-Freudian drive theorists are even guiltier of this. This becomes especially evident when the assumed metatheoretical explanation is at odds with the phenomenological description, as when drive language is used to describe relational needs that serve the development of a firm and cohesive sense of self. Often, as soon as one gets beneath the obscurity of the drive language, the relational needs discovered by drive theorists appear as radical challenges to Freudian metatheory.

Psychoanalytic infant studies and developmental schemata frequently exemplify these challenges. Spitz's studies (1945; 1946; 1965) of institutionalized infants who were separated from their mothers are a case in point. Spitz himself was an orthodox Freudian who explained the devastating effects of maternal separation on infants as the loss of an object which allowed discharge of libidinal and aggressive drives. Yet many post-Freudians have viewed his work as an example of the devastating effects of lack of adequate mothering in the emotional sense, even when physical needs are met. Similarly, Erik Erikson's explorations (1959, 1968) into the social and cultural factors influencing the formation of the ego were intended to supplement Freud's theory, but have instead led to the possibility of substituting stages of identity formation based on social and relational issues for Freud's psychosexual stages.

Edith Jacobson's work (1964) also began as a traditional ego psychological extension of Hartmann's concept of the "average expectable environment." Yet when Jacobson actually gets down to discussing the negotiations between a phenomenologically conceived self and an object world composed of real human beings, she begins to encounter the shaping significance of "disappointment" as opposed to mere drive frustration in the derivation of psychological disorders. Despite Jacobson's own insistence on maintaining drive theory, her description of the evolution of the ego out of a shifting set of images of self and others introduces the possibility of a purely relational reading of psychological development.

Other post-Freudian drive theorists, whether their area of expertise is child development/therapy or severe emotional disorders emanating from disturbances in one's earliest relations with others, encounter similar difficulties with finding ways of accommodating relational needs for affective responsiveness and for the development of a secure sense of personal identity to traditional Freudian metatheory. Because of their significant impact on contemporary psychoanalytic theory, I shall discuss three of these theorists—Melanie Klein, Margaret Mahler, and Otto Kernberg—in somewhat greater detail. Although an overview cannot hope to do justice to the full complexity of their insights, I believe that the theoretical difficulties we shall discover in their work are shared by most seemingly orthodox contemporary psychoanalytic theorists whose work is similarly based on psychotherapy with children or severely disturbed adults. Klein's and Mahler's insights derive from their work with children, whereas Kernberg is a specialist in treating the pre-Oedipal disturbances known as borderline and narcissistic personality disorders. All three theorists obscure the implications of their discoveries of purely relational needs by using drive terms and pseudocausal explanations.

Melanie Klein in many ways represents a crossroads between contemporary drive theory and relational theory. Indeed, she has in one way or another influenced most subsequent drive and relational theorists—despite certain theoretical disagreements they may have with her. Although Klein at first reading would appear to be a drive theorist par excellence, her work clearly demonstrates the contradictions inherent in the attempt to reconcile relational needs with drive theory. As a children's analyst interested in early developmental issues, Klein seems to view the whole world first in terms of the pleasure principle and later in terms of the death instinct as well. According to the early Klein (1923, 1928), a child's very curiosity and desire to learn can be attributed to libidinal impulses. For example, letters and numbers entice because strokes and circles unconsciously recall the penis and the vagina; geography fascinates because it promises a map of the interior of the mother's body. Or, according to the later Klein (1930, 1948, 1957, 1964), the infant projects cataclysmic fantasies of destruction, born of the death instinct, onto its earliest caretakers. The only real divergence from orthodox Freudian theory would appear to be that Klein places the Oedipal struggle and superego formation further back into infancy.

Yet despite this apparent allegiance to drive theory, Klein's thinking is deceptively unorthodox on two counts: She rejects Freud's concept of primary narcissism, and she proposes the existence of developed affects in infancy which can hardly be attributable to transmutations of drives. In these respects, Klein foreshadows many subsequent drive and relational theorists—though their explanations about why these things are so may differ from hers. For Klein, the human infant is object-related from the very beginning through a priori images of the gratifying breast, penis, babies, and so on. While this concept of a priori images derives from an attempt to enlarge Freud's idea of phylogenetic memories as explicated in such works as *Totem and Taboo* (1912–13), Klein is actually calling into question not only Freud's concept of primary narcissism but also his idea of the subordination of objects to the drives. In doing so, she makes room for the purely relational view of the psyche espoused by the British object relations theorists (Fairbairn, Winnicott, Balint, and Guntrip) who followed her. These theorists simply discard the a priori images and retain the idea that relational needs are primary.

Similarly, Klein does not appear to recognize the antidrive implications of her proposition that very young infants (second quarter of the first year of life) experience the developed affects of "envy and gratitude" and that they have an urge to "repair" the mother they had previously aggressively attacked (at least in fantasy) as a "bad" partial object. Thus the infant entering what Klein calls the "depressive position"—where the bad/frustrating, good/gratifying images of the mother come together as one person—does not simply seek gratification from the mother. The infant actually loves the mother and mourns her fantasied destruction not merely as a libidinal object but as a person. If this reparative effort fails, the world will forever seem split into all-good and all-bad ego states and people, with no possibility for a fully human appreciation of another whole person in all of his or her complexity—a psychological state characteristic of many borderline and narcissistic patients.

The problem with Klein's formulation is that the achievement of the depressive position is not explicable on the basis of drive gratification. As Harry Guntrip points out, "There could hardly be a more fully personal object-relational concept than reparation made for hurt of the loved person." Hence, despite Klein's "verbal play with ideas of instincts, she was really concerned with good and bad object-relations, love and hate, and guilt and reparation, not with ideas of quantitative gratifications of instinctive drives" (Guntrip, 1971, p. 64). Klein's "paranoid-schizoid" and "depressive" positions are not psychosexual but relational stages based on affects rather than drives. As Greenberg and Mitchell put the matter, "Drives, for Klein, are relationships" (1983, p. 146).

If Melanie Klein's discovery of relational needs and developed affects in earliest infancy calls into question traditional psychoanalytic metatheory, Margaret Mahler's extensive observation of normal children in various developmental phases (together with her work with severely disturbed children) provides even more convincing evidence that earliest relational needs go beyond optimal drive gratification/frustration. Unlike Klein, who is often described as an id psychologist, Mahler has found a place within traditional American ego psychology.[1] She is quite interested in the structural formation of the ego in the earliest stages of infancy and childhood. And though her work has generated much less controversy in orthodox psychoanalytic circles than Klein's, it seems to me that it is potentially even more threatening to traditional Freudian metatheory. This is because Mahler documents complex relational needs and developmental stages only hinted at in Klein's theory, describing in great detail the process through which a child becomes "the child of this particular mother" (an oft-repeated phrase in Mahler, Pine, and Bergman, 1975, and Mahler, 1979). Yet like Klein, Mahler considers herself an orthodox drive theorist and reports her findings using drive terminology. Unlike Klein, she accepts Freud's idea of a primary objectless state, which she designates as "normal autism." If we really look closely at what Mahler is saying, however, she appears to have discovered a whole set of relational needs which can hardly be accounted for by Freudian drive theory. These are largely needs for responsiveness which allows the flowering of a firm and unique individuality.

The primary issue of earliest childhood, according to Mahler, is the problem of negotiating a strong, separate sense of self in a context in which one feels related, loved, and loving. Mahler contends that the "psychological birth of the human infant" is not coincident with physiological birth. It involves a "hatching" first from normal autism (at about three or four weeks) and second from mother-infant symbiosis (at about five months). The "separation-individuation" process, which Mahler describes in terms of four subphases lasting from five months to two and a half or three years, is one of achieving both an intrapsychic awareness of separateness (separation) and a unique sense of individuality (individuation).

Mahler views the child as an active rather than a passive participant in this process. Indeed, she continually marvels at "the extent to which the normal infant-toddler is intent upon, and usually is also able to extract, contact supplies and participation from the mother, sometimes against considerable odds; how he tries to incorporate every bit of these supplies into libidinal channels for progressive personality organization" (Mahler, Pine, and Bergman, 1975, p. 198). Although Mahler phrases this in drive language, her observations strongly imply that what the child needs from mother is not so much drive satisfaction as human relatedness. It is the success of "mutual cuing," the duet between mother and baby, which determines the happy or unhappy outcome of the child's development of a strong sense of personal identity. Thus though Mahler attempts to relate the various subphases from normal autism to consolidation of individuality and object constancy (end of the second year onward) to the psychosexual stages of Freud, what is really striking in her descriptions are the nondrive-oriented relational needs and existential crises which characterize the process.

Mahler is most orthodox in her discussion of the stage about which she has the least observational data. Since most mothers did not bring their children to the laboratory nursery where Mahler and her co-workers observed them until they were several months old, she has little direct data on the "normal autistic" subphase. Many infant observers, including Mahler's coauthor Fred Pine (1985), have questioned the existence of an objectless stage of primary narcissism. And some (Eagle, 1984; Stern, 1985) have also questioned whether there is actually a symbiotic stage in which the infant experiences lack of differentiation from the mother. Furthermore, despite Mahler's failure to acknowledge heterodoxy and despite the concept's widespread acceptance in contemporary psychoanalytic circles, normal symbiosis actually diverges from traditional Freudian metatheory. Freud believes that narcissistic libido and object libido are always clearly differentiated. Thus Mahler is already not so orthodox as she would have us believe.

For our purposes, however, the significant heterodoxy lies in Mahler's demonstration of the existence in infancy and earliest childhood of relational needs which have nothing at all to do with Freud's idea of libidinal cathexis. These relational needs center around the development of self-esteem and a firm sense of self through touching, mirroring, and other forms of emotional and physical responsiveness from the first caregivers. Mahler claims that such responsiveness leads to the neutralization of libidinal and aggressive drive energy, thereby allowing the establishment of a "conflict-free" ego sphere such as that described by Hartmann. Unfortunately, this ego psychological explanation does not necessarily fit with the phenomenological data which Mahler presents. The causal link between instinctual gratification and the need to be recognized as a person is missing.

While touch is important to a developing sense of self, one is struck by the key importance of needs for visual "mirroring" (a term Mahler borrows from British object relations theorist D. W. Winnicott), especially the need to be seen and appreciated, as these manifest themselves throughout Mahler's subphases. Whereas touch might be associated with drive gratification, it is hard to see how the need to be seen can be related to anything other than ontological recognition of oneself as a person. Even touch, as Mahler and others have observed, must be emotionally sensitive rather than mechanical to promote optimal development. And Mahler notes that touch is also important to defining body boundaries, which would hardly seem to be a directly drive-related need.

It is still more difficult to see how the need to be visually mirrored can be related to instinctual tension reduction. Mahler notes that this need for acceptance in the mother's eyes is of primary significance to identity formation in most of the stages of early infancy and childhood. It is present as early as the symbiotic phase (four weeks to five months), where "all other conditions being equal, symbiosis was optimal when the mother naturally permitted the young infant to face her—that is, permitted and promoted eye contact, especially while nursing (or bottle-feeding) the infant, or talking or singing to him" (Mahler, Pine, and Bergman, 1975, p. 45). Among other things, the early or late appearance of the smiling response is related to such interactions.

Seeing and being seen, as well as expanded exploration of the world predicated on developing locomotor functions, seem to be even more important to infants at the differentiation stage (five to nine months). For example, a baby of this age will spend much time exploring his or her mother's face, is likely to experience anxiety beneath the gaze of a stranger, and is much delighted by peekaboo games. Mahler explains the latter by commenting, "To be found by mother, to be seen by her (that is to say, mirrored by her) seems to build body-self awareness" (Mahler, Pine, and Bergman, 1975, pp. 221–22). Mahler further notes that the infant's awareness of his or her own bodily movements is intensified through the mirroring the infant receives from an "admiring onlooking adult (especially the mother)" (Mahler, Pine, and Bergman, 1975, p. 205). It is as though the mother's gaze is required to build a bodily sense of self.

Nor do mirroring needs disappear at later stages. Mahler observes that the "practicing" subphase child (nine to fourteen or fifteen months), despite greater locomotor independence and the grandiloquent feeling (especially in the later practicing subphase, when upright locomotion is possible) that the "world is his oyster," still needs the mother's positive regard to successfully negotiate this phase. Mahler notes that the mother's "admiration, when it is forthcoming, augments the practicing toddler's sound narcissism, his love of himself" (Mahler, 1979, 2:159). Self-love, it appears, is not primary, but rather is mediated through the love of others. Even the child's confidence in his or her locomotor abilities is mediated through the mother's belief in the child's ability to "make it out there [in the world]" (Mahler, Pine, and Bergman, 1975, p. 74). It is also true that "maternal unavailability" at this time is likely to make the practicing subphase "rather brief and subdued" (Mahler, Pine, and Bergman, 1975, p. 81) and to deprive the child of the elation over locomotor accomplishments and an upright view of the world which is characteristic of this age.

For the child in the "rapprochement" subphase (fifteen to twenty-four months), the mother, as a witness to the child's expanding sense of self, is important in an even more complex way than she was in the preceding subphase. Mahler notes that what is now required for the development of a firm identity is not mere drive gratification or even the cuddling, physical/emotional availability or applause of earlier ages, but rather higher level "dialogue" and developed "emotional understanding" of the child's mood swings (Mahler, 1979, 2:68–69). The mother must encourage independence while not rejecting the child's dependency needs. A child of this age has an even hungrier need for mirroring than the practicing subphase child. The toddler needs mother to "*share with him* every new acquisition on his part of skill and experience" (Mahler, 1979, 2:128), and the toddler is continually "filling her lap with objects that he found in his expanding world" (Mahler, Pine, and Bergman, 1975, p. 90).

This is an ambivalent age, characterized by shadowing mother on the one hand and darting or running away on the other. Mahler describes the existential crisis faced by the rapprochement child in this way:

> On the one hand is the toddler's feeling of helplessness in his realization of separateness, and on the other hand is his valiant defense of what he cherishes as the emerging autonomy of his body. . . . This is the time of the rapprochement struggle, from which the toddler may emerge through transmuting internalization . . . and other identificatory mechanisms with a measure of integration of his self representation, or he may get caught up in uncertainty about his own identity as a viable separate being. (Mahler, Pine, and Bergman, 1975, pp. 222–23)

A child in the rapprochement stage is very sensitive to verbal rebuke (as an extension of nonverbal acceptance or rejection) and woos the mother's participation in his or her world. At the same time, however, the toddler resents any intrusions into his or her autonomy. He or she resents being "handled" as a passive object and particularly resists "being kept or held in a passive position while being dressed or diapered." Nor does the rapprochement child like "to be hugged and kissed, unless he is ready for it" (Mahler, Pine, and Bergman, 1975, p. 91). The successful negotiation of the rapprochement crisis leads to a firm internalization of loved objects (especially mother but also father to some extent) together with a firm sense of self. The one is mediated through the other, as the toddler emerges into a state of self and object constancy simultaneously.

Mahler's discussions of child and adolescent psychoses illuminate the drastic consequences of ignoring the relational needs of infancy and early childhood. Interestingly, Mahler proposes that such psychoses refer to failure at the symbiotic stage, which she defines as a "dual unity" lacking differentiation between subject and object. Yet what she actually describes is a deprivation of mirroring (which implies a rudimentary subject-object differentiation) leading to the lack of a sound sense of self. In fact, she comments that the "primary method of identity formation consists of mutual reflection during the symbiotic phase" (Mahler, 1979, 2:87). One case history demonstrating the effects of a lack of adequate mirroring involves an adolescent suffering from a "symbiotic psychosis." As the son of an extremely narcissistic and seductive mother who had no real interest in him as a person, Mahler tells us that "Charlie" is left searching for "the 'good' symbiotic mother—whom he can reflect and whose eyes will reflect love for him" (Mahler, 1979, 2:97). Hence, when dancing with a girl, this young man reported maneuvering "around by the mirror-glass door where I can look at my own face—see what I look like *from the point of view of the others*" (Mahler, 1979, 2:96).

Similarly, a hospitalized fourteen-year-old patient, "Alma," spent much time "looking into the mirror and said that the whole ward (world?) was a mirror image of herself" (Mahler, 1979, 1:148). Alma believed that she was her mother's mirror image or that the world was her own mirror image and felt that her friends did not like her because something was wrong with her face. Clearly, Alma's "symbiotic psychosis" related to a failure of self-identity based on inadequate mirroring. Or take the plea of seven-year-old "Betty," who expected her therapist's pronouncements to impart feelings to her: "Do I look sad today? Please say I look happy" (Mahler, 1979, 1:189). These instances of psychoses deriving from inadequate recognition as a person are multiplied many times in Mahler's examples, suggesting that they reflect purely relational difficulties rather than difficulties in the structuralization of drives. This would reinforce my contention that what Mahler has actually described in her account of the separation-individuation process is not an orthodox addition to Freudian developmental theory but an alternative to the psychosexual stages.

Mahler does not acknowledge this, claiming that there is no clash between "anal stage oppositionalism" and the delicate issues of the rapprochement crisis as she describes it. Her drive language often obscures the problem, as when she writes, "The principal conditions for mental health, so far as pre-Oedipal development is concerned, hinge on the attained and continuing ability of the child to retain or restore his self-esteem in the context of relative libidinal object constancy" (Mahler, Pine, and Bergman, 1975, p. 118).[2] Yet we have seen that it is not as a libidinal object in the Freudian sense but as a mirroring object that the mother helps the child to develop self-esteem. Heinz Kohut, recognizing the contradiction, refers to these relational needs as "selfobject" needs to differentiate them from "libidinal object" needs; but, as we shall see, there is some question as to whether the mother as witness to the child's developing sense of self is an object at all. Instead, it would seem that she is a subject and that the child perceives himself or herself as the object of her attention. Furthermore, considering the prevalence of mirroring needs and needs for emotional relatedness in the pre-Oedipal phases described by Mahler, one cannot help wondering how the drives could become important at a later stage. If one finds emotional relatedness and human needs in earliest infancy, where is there room for drive theory? This, indeed, is a primary problem for most psychoanalytic theorists looking into the relational needs of infancy and early childhood: They find not drives but affective attachments and needs for self-esteem based on fully human interactions. This brings into question as well Freud's account of the Oedipal struggle.

This dilemma is particularly evident in the work of contemporary American ego psychologist Otto Kernberg. Kernberg, whose theory derives from work with severely disturbed borderline and narcissistic patients rather than from work with children, strongly identifies himself as a traditional theorist. Yet he in effect rejects three cardinal tenets of Freudian drive theory. Kernberg implicitly or explicitly takes issue with Freud's concept of primary narcissism, with Freud's view that instinctual needs rather than affects are primary, and with Freud's theory that pathological narcissism results from libidinal overinvestment of the ego rather than from thwarted needs for self-esteem. Even though Kernberg insists on speaking the language of the drives, one wonders what is left of the economic hypothesis once he is finished with it.

Kernberg, like Melanie Klein and unlike Margaret Mahler, categorically rejects Freud's concept of primary narcissism. He believes that "the concept of primary narcissism no longer seems warranted because, metapsychologically, 'primary narcissism' and 'primary object investment' are in effect coincidental" (1975, p. 341). One's relationship with self is mediated through one's relations with others from the very beginning of life. Freud, as we have seen, would disagree. According to Freud (1914c), primary narcissism is an objectless state in which the newborn infant is libidinally invested in himself or herself and totally uninterested in the external world; secondary narcissism is the narcissistic investment of the ego at the expense of withdrawal of libidinal energy from the external world. Thus it is impossible to have coincidental and mutually reinforcing self and object investment.

Yet Kernberg writes that in normal development there is "an optimal mixture of 'object libidinal' and 'narcissistic' ties, in that the investment of objects and the investment of self go hand in hand" (1975, p. 323). Thus "when there is an increase of narcissistic investment [self-love], there is a parallel increase in the capacity to love and to give, to experience and express gratitude, to have concern for others, and for an increase in sexual love, sublimation, and creativity" (Kernberg, 1975, p. 320)—or, conversely, in the case of loss of love or other losses, there is a decrease in concern for others. In other words, love by others, love of self, and love of others are mutually reinforcing. What this means is that Kernberg has redefined the drives so that they no longer maintain any vestiges of the quantitative energy permutations which are crucial to Freud's metatheory. They clearly are no longer drives but human emotions.

Kernberg, in fact, rejects Freud's idea of the primacy of drives over emotions. Despite his devoted use of drive language, Kernberg claims that affects, not drives, are the primary organizers of early infantile experience. He argues that " 'cathexes' are, first of all, 'affective cathexes,' . . . which are activated in the context of primitive units of internalized object relations; affects are actually the organizers of such primitive units." Gradually, affects become "linked with the organization of motivational systems, or drives, into the 'libido' series and the 'aggression' series" (Kernberg, 1975, pp. 339–40). Perhaps Kernberg's quotation marks should make us suspect that he is not really talking about the economic hypothesis at all. In fact, Kernberg has reversed Freud's postulate: For Kernberg, drives derive from feelings rather than feelings from drives.

What then, one wonders, are "drives," and how can they be equated with "motivational systems"? Is this not an example of the worst kind of mixing of levels of discourse? Also, when Kernberg insists that the source of difficulty for borderline and narcissistic patients is primitive, untamed drives, especially oral rage, envy, and paranoid fears, held rather precariously in check by primitive defenses, what is he really saying? Is he talking about drives or is he talking about human emotions? Kernberg himself says that for such patients it is the "loss of the world of loving and loved internal objects [which] brings about the loss of meaning of the self and of the world" (1975, p. 313), thereby leading to a sense of emptiness and meaninglessness accompanied by states of primitive envy and rage. It would seem that Kernberg is talking about emotions and about the human need for a meaningful life with others rather than about drives.

Perhaps the heart of these metatheoretical difficulties lies in Kernberg's view of severe psychological disorders. Kernberg's view is quite different from Freud's and much closer to that of relational theorist Heinz Kohut. In fact, despite much-publicized differences between the two theorists, Kernberg, like Kohut, uses his work with borderline and narcissistic patients as a basis for discovering new relational needs which are important to normal as well as pathological development. Kernberg's view is very different from that of Freud, who considers "narcissistic neuroses" (psychoses) to be unanalyzable because there is not enough object-directed libidinal energy available to form a transference. Kernberg disagrees, commenting that psychotic patients reveal not a lack of object relations but the presence of "primitive, pathological object relations" which are activated in "psychotic, in contrast to neurotic, transferences" (1975, p. 342).

Thus Kernberg, like Kohut, believes that at least some of the narcissistic disturbances on the border between neurosis and psychosis are analyzable. This is possible because, according to Kernberg, pathological narcissism is caused not by an extreme withdrawal of libidinal energy from objects, but rather by an attempt to defend against damaging internalized objects resulting in "an aggressive investment of the self" (1975, p. 321). Therefore, Kernberg believes that the basic function of narcissism in all pathology is "the protection of self-esteem" (1975, p. 330). And although he makes certain bows in the direction of innate aggression, what Kernberg actually seems to be saying is that the deeply disturbed patient makes other people less real because they have previously been all too real and threaten to become so again.

Following Melanie Klein, Kernberg views the maintenance of conflicting (split) ego states by borderline and narcissistic patients as resulting from the failure of the very young child to integrate "good" and "bad" partial images of the mother—a failure which is actually an attempt to protect the good images from engulfment by the bad. The good images are needed to maintain some vestiges of self-esteem and meaningfulness. The borderline personality achieves this through contradictory ego states which, though consciously known by the patient, are never integrated with each other. The narcissist does it by activating a grandiose self-image which makes of others, except for those who are taken into the circle of narcissism as extensions of the self, mere shadows who can no longer attack and hurt; for the narcissist, others are important as resources for self-aggrandizement. The narcissist's grandiosity serves to guard against reactivation of the "sadistically perceived mother image" and with it the "sense of empty loneliness in a world devoid of personal meaning" against which the narcissist is protecting himself or herself (Kernberg, 1975, p. 287).

Kernberg believes that this lack of ego integration in narcissistic and borderline patients may derive from a failure to resolve the rapprochement crisis, as described by Mahler. He does not, however, relegate narcissistic disturbances solely to the arena of pre-Oedipal disorders. Again like Kohut, Kernberg indicates that narcissistic injury is significant even in neurosis—commenting that dealing with a "narcissistic lesion" is always a "part of analytic efforts to modify a neurotic character structure" (1975, p. 330). In other words, the need for self-esteem, as derived from positive (loving, not instinctually gratifying) relations with others, is a primary human need. Thus one cannot help questioning Kernberg's quarrel with Kohut's discovery of a separate line of narcissistic development which is nondrive motivated. Is this not exactly what Kernberg himself has discovered? After all, what has the need for self-esteem based on loving relations with others to do with drive gratification? One simply cannot predicate the former on the latter. There is an unbridgeable gap between the two.

With Kernberg, we see the implicit metatheoretical difficulties in the work of earlier theorists made quite explicit. Even more strikingly than in Melanie Klein's work, the "drives" in Kernberg's work turn out to be human emotions. Hence, as with Mahler, one must be constantly on the alert to translate Kernberg's drive language into affective terms. Unlike Mahler, however, Kernberg resembles Klein in his rejection of a state of primary objectless narcissism, though he is even more radical than Klein in that he does not try to bolster this rejection with a priori images drawn from phylogenetic memories. Like Klein, Kernberg believes that the split ego states of severely disturbed patients derive from punitive superego forerunners. Yet unlike Klein, Kernberg is well aware that punitive real relations with the earliest caregivers, as opposed to mere projection of aggressive drive energy, may have set the stage for these punitive superego forerunners.

In this respect, Kernberg may be linked with Edith Jacobson, who deeply influenced his work, and with Margaret Mahler, whose idea of the rapprochement crisis he found useful. Like Jacobson, Kernberg does not accept Klein's failure to recognize the impact of real parental failures on the development of negative introjects. And like Jacobson, Kernberg contends that the shaping of drives out of the undifferentiated matrix of primal energy derives from real interactions with others—from the partnership of the self and the object world. Like Mahler, Kernberg relates the narcissistic lesion at the base of severe psychological disorders to early disturbances in the mother-infant relationship as well as to constitutional proclivities. And like Mahler, Kernberg is aware that self-esteem needs are at the base of narcissistic and borderline disturbances. In fact, he is even more explicit than Mahler in conceiving of a narcissistic element—in Kernberg's sense rather than Freud's—in all psychological disturbances.

It is this breakdown of the distinction between the sources of Oedipal disturbances (where Freud was correct) and pre-Oedipal disturbances (where there is room for discovery of new needs in the formation of the ego) that most severely challenges Freudian metatheory. If relational needs for self-esteem rather than drive gratification are at the base of psychological development, and the denial of relational needs at the base of psychopathology, why retain Freud's drive model? Thus with Kernberg we reach the culmination of a trend in post-Freudian drive theory. This trend perhaps began with Melanie Klein's recognition of complex affective interactions between mother and infant, gained impetus with Margaret Mahler's description of the mirroring needs critical to the separation-individuation process by which an infant develops an identity, and culminated in the views of Kernberg, who, despite heavy use of traditional terminology, hardly retains any vestiges of orthodox metatheory.

The questions which naturally arise out of this discussion of the developmental significance of relations with others are these: Who is this Other who is required for the acquisition of self-esteem in post-Freudian drive theory, and is he or she a libidinal object in Freud's sense at all? It would seem that we would have to answer the latter question in the negative, since, for Freud, fear of the loss of the gratifying object precedes fear of the loss of love. Nor is affective attachment primary for Freud, as it is for Kernberg; rather, affective attachment derives from underlying instinctual energy and its permutations and fluctuations. The new formulation, particularly as it is expressed by Kernberg, makes recognition as a person at least as important as gratification from earliest infancy ón. Even when a theorist such as Mahler accepts Freud's idea of primary narcissism, she does not explain how the new relational needs evolve out of it. The relational theorists I consider in the next chapter insist even more strongly on regarding relatedness as primary from the beginning of life. Since there appears to be no way to explain the new relational needs as transmutations of the drives, even among the more orthodox post-Freudian theorists, it would seem that we need a new approach to explain them. I believe that Sartre's ontology can provide this new approach.

Sartre's View of the Other as Subject and Object

There is a philosophical problem embedded in the question of why the infant needs empathic responsiveness and mirroring in order to develop self-esteem. This is the ancient philosophical problem of the existence of others. Sometimes referred to as the problem of solipsism, it involves the question of how I know that there are other consciousnesses—that I am not alone in the universe. This question requires an answer because the new relational needs discovered by post-Freudian theorists imply the significance of the Other as another consciousness, as a witness who can see and name the infant. Although in earliest infancy this other consciousness may be only dimly perceived through the touching and mutual gazing which Mahler and others describe, there is no doubt that by the time of the rapprochement crisis, the mother's attitude toward the toddler, both verbal and nonverbal, is of primary importance. How then does the Other become important in this way? We can begin to answer this question by contrasting Sartre's solution to the problem of solipsism with that of Freud.

Freud's solution to the problem of solipsism is a curious wedding of scientific empiricism and critical idealism. As a materialist, Freud argues that the other person is important as another body—as a need-satisfying material object. The stuff that binds us to others as material objects is libidinal energy, and libidinal cathexis explains the investment of others with direct or sublimated value as gratifiers/frustrators of instinctual needs. Gratification is required to lure the infant out of his or her blanket of primary narcissism; frustration is required to provoke ego development. More developed affects, including those experienced in friendships and comradely relations as well as in love relationships, are transmutations of primitive instinctual urges.

Aggression, for example, is sometimes characterized as a response to frustration and sometimes as a transmutation of primary masochism associated with the death instinct.

According to this view, we have no direct intuitive awareness of the Other as another consciousness. As Freud says, the notion that other people "possess a consciousness is an inference which we draw by analogy from their utterances and actions in order to make this behavior of theirs intelligible to us. . . . [Like the assumption of consciousness in animals,] the assumption of a consciousness in them rests upon an inference and cannot share the immediate certainty which we have of our own consciousness" (Freud, 1915c, p. 169). Our very interest in others as other consciousnesses has its origins in their significance as "libidinal objects." Presumably, as we have noted, a cleverly programmed robot might be able to provide optimal drive gratification as well or better than another human being.

The idealist side of Freud's theory follows Immanuel Kant's philosophical distinction between appearance and reality—the thing as perceived and the thing itself. As Ilham Dilman (1984) points out, Freud compares his own idea that mental processes are not directly knowable to Kant's idea that the outside world is never directly perceivable "by means of the sense-organs." Freud goes on to say, "Just as Kant warned us not to overlook the fact that our perceptions are subjectively conditioned and must not be regarded as identical with what is perceived though unknowable, so psychoanalysis warns us not to equate perceptions by means of consciousness with the unconscious mental processes which are their object. Like the physical, the psychical is not necessarily in reality what it appears to be" (Freud, 1915c, p. 171). In fact, Freud seems to provide some relational categories through which all experience is filtered, similar to Kant's regulative categories for experiencing the external world. Instead of quantity, quality, relations, and modality, Freud's a priori relational categories include the Oedipus complex, castration anxiety (in boys) or penis envy (in girls), incest taboos, superego development, transference of childhood experiences to adult relationships, and so on. Everyone will experience relations with others as mediated by these categories, and part of this experience will be governed by (unknowable) unconscious forces. According to this view, I "create" the other as a libidinal object through the mediation of these categories.

What is striking about both of Freud's approaches to relations with others is that they deny direct intuitive experience of the Other as another consciousness whose value in relationships is based on this experience. Freud, like behaviorist B. F. Skinner, regards the existence of other consciousnesses as an inference. Such a view fails to solve the problem of solipsism in its more sophisticated form. Thus although Freud's combined materialist-idealist solution works fairly well within the context of his own system, it cannot account for the relational needs, operating since earliest infancy, which have been reported by the majority of post-Freudian psychoanalytic theorists.

Sartre attempts to solve the problem of solipsism by providing a description of an experience of "apodictic certainty" similar to the certainty about one's own existence as a consciousness which Descartes attributes to the thinking subject. Contrary to Freud, Sartre asserts that I know that the Other exists as a consciousness not by mere inference but by direct experience. In order for the Other's existence to be certain rather than probable, the Other "can not *at first* be an object" (BN, p. 252). Nor can I deduce the Other's subjectivity from my own. Sartre says that we "*encounter* the Other: we do not constitute him" (BN, p. 250). He calls the experience through which this encounter occurs the Look (BN, pp. 252–302). The French term, *le regard*, means notice or attention as well as a physical gaze.

According to Sartre, it is not my experience of the Other as an object, not even as a mirroring object, which establishes my certainty about the Other's existence as a consciousness. Rather, it is my experience of myself as an object beneath the Other's gaze (or other form of presence since even a blind person can be the source of the Look) which gives me this certainty. Such certainty arrives not as a logical deduction but as a shudder in my being—a shudder which points undeniably to the Other's existence as a subject. Thus although Sartre takes the viewpoint of a number of psychoanalytic theorists, including Freud, that there can never be a merging of consciousnesses or a way of directly experiencing the Other's subjectivity as the Other experiences it, he at the same time denies that this means that I can have no direct intuitive experience of the Other as another consciousness. In fact, it is my experience of the Other's Look on my flesh which largely motivates all those inferences by which I attempt to understand the Other's actions and gestures as emanating from a subjectivity like my own.

Sartre's example of the experience of the Look is a man who, with his eye glued to a keyhole out of curiosity or jealousy or vice, suddenly hears footsteps. Where before the keyhole was a simple instrument through which he was attending to the scene inside, he suddenly becomes aware that he has an outside. He becomes aware of his Being-for-others—that is, of his being a man looking through a keyhole. He experiences shame. The other two basic reactions to the discovery of my Being-for-others are pride, which is a derivative of shame in that through pride I attempt to assume and bask in the object status which I have for the Other, and fear, which arises from my knowledge that I am in danger before the Other—that the Other may use me as an object for ends which are not my own. In fact, the Other might even use his or her own knowledge of my subjectivity against me—to manipulate me, defeat me, or use or abuse me in some other way. And though I might attempt to assume an attitude of pride as an antidote to shame or fear, the truth is that despite certain illusions to the contrary, pride, like the other two attitudes, is a testimony to the Other's power over my status as an object in the world. It is the Other, and not myself, who sees and names me as a real object. For myself, I am forever only a "pseudo-object" created by a reflective attitude which can never fully grasp that which it attempts to contemplate since I cannot simultaneously *see* and *be* the object of contemplation.

Possibly Sartre's keyhole example, though emotionally convincing, is somewhat misleading. Sartre is very clear that the feeling of shame does not originate in any particular version of being made an object—from being caught at a shameful act such as spying or voyeurism, for example. The reason the threat of being shamed for a particular action is so effective a mode of control is that it refers to an ontological experience of shame which occurs not because I am this or that particular object before the Other, but because the Other makes me an object at all.

The Other's Look is a dethronement—an original fall which degrades me as a sovereign subject and makes me a mere object in the Other's world. This is why, in the Adam and Eve story of Genesis, the Other appears as God looking on man's nakedness. Extreme shyness is a perpetual feeling of shame beneath the real or imagined gaze of others. The ontological truth behind my recoil from others, if I am shy, is that I feel the Other's Look as a penetration of my being—the naming of an object which I cannot cease to be but which I can never fully grasp or understand as it appears *to the Other*. Everything happens as though the Other's reactions point mysteriously toward an object I cannot see—and this object is me.

This experience of the Look gains ontological significance as it connects with Sartre's larger philosophy. We have already seen in Chapter 2 that the basic human aim is to create a self which is an object like other objects in the world while still remaining free. This goal of achieving substantive freedom is the significance of all human enterprises. It does not involve bad faith so long as it remains a simple value-making process on the nonthetic level. But the inevitable human temptation seems to be to turn and try to reflectively make the process of self-creation refer to a created self. This is the point where bad faith arises. The Sartrean paradox is that an approach in good faith to the problem of living involves accepting the impossibility of achieving substantive freedom while remaining committed to the process of self-creation.

As we have seen, the Other provides a particular lure into bad faith, or lying to myself about the possibility of achieving the missing God, in that it is the Other who provides me with the experience of knowing that I have an outside. Without the Other, I might have a kind of rudimentary reflective consciousness based on my perception of my own body and my awareness of past events. But I can never actually have an outside, can never actually be another for myself as I am another for the Other. I therefore imagine that if I could only grasp this object which I am for the Other, I would be in possession of the secret of my being as an object in the world. The truth is that if this were possible, I would indeed be in possession of such a secret: I would know my being outside in the world as it is for this particular Other. If I could then merge the Other's knowledge of me with my free living of my project, I would be a free being with a substantive nature—Being-in-itself-for-itself. That is, this would be so until I met a new Other, who would then objectify me or the relationship between me and the first Other with whom I had originally merged.[3]

Because of this fantasy that the Other can provide the key to my nature, relationships pose a special temptation—the temptation either to try to submerge myself in the Other's consciousness (love/masochism) or to lure, coerce, or manipulate the Other into submerging himself or herself in me (desire/sadism). A third attitude, indifference, involves the pretense that the Other does not exist as another subject, but rather as a mere object like other objects in the world. Indifference results from the failure of other forms of relating. If I do engage with the Other, I quickly discover that the Other has his or her own plans for the relationship—and hence arises the "conflict of consciousnesses" which Sartre describes in the section of *Being and Nothingness* entitled "Concrete Relations with Others" (pp. 361–430).

The urge toward symbiosis, seen in the light of this attempt to use the Other to achieve a self, is not retrospective but prospective. It is part of the attempt to invent the missing God. Lovers, especially, tend to feel with particular poignancy this "urge to merge," and it is often the source of their endless quarrels over whether each "loves" the other enough. The problem is that the gulf between consciousnesses is impassable. However accurate and sensitive my guesses, I can never experience the Other's experience, feel his or her feelings, live his or her possibilities. I can directly experience the

Other's Look, but I can never directly grasp the object which I am for the Other as it (I) exists for the Other. In fact, as Sartre puts the matter, the moment I turn to look at the Other's Look, "I no longer see anything but eyes" (BN, p. 380). The Other has ceased to be a subject and has become an object. Although I may gain much information about how the Other sees me from this object Other, I can never directly apprehend and possess the Other as a perceiving subject.

It is my experience of the Other as a subject which provokes my interest in the Other as an object, regardless of which I discover first.[4] Even as the object of my attention, the Other is a different kind of object than other objects in the world. It is not the Other's mere physical presence or gifts for gratification/frustration of physical needs which absorb me, but rather his or her intentions, aims, and attitudes toward me and the world at large as these are perceived through actions, gestures, and words. Even as an object, the Other interests me as a transcendence—as someone who, like myself, is involved in the process of making a future for himself or herself, whose actions have meanings as well as physical parameters and effects. In this respect, Sartre says that the Other has "stolen the world from me" (BN, p. 255). In discovering the Other, I suddenly find "that the world has a kind of drain hole in the middle of its being and that it is perpetually flowing off through this hole" (BN, p. 256). This hole is the Other as a center of reference for a set of meanings, perceptions, and actions which are not my meanings, perceptions, and actions. The world is a different world for a different consciousness than my own, and the Other is bringing into being a different future than my own future.

Sartre says that the Other as an object is unlike the simple things I use as instruments in fulfilling my project of being. The Other is instead "an explosive instrument" which constantly has the possibility of making me "experience the flight of the world away from me and the alienation of my being" (BN, p. 297). In other words, the Other as an object is constantly threatening to become a subject who will make me an object. For this reason, my relations with the Other as an object may be made up of "ruses designed to make him remain an object" (BN, p. 297). Thus the attempt on the part of certain people to make others into mere objects like other objects in the world, to deprive them of humanness, is a reaction to the discovery of the Other as another consciousness—a reaction of denial.

This reification is possible precisely because people are *not* things, though one may attempt to treat them as things in order to deprive them of their objectifying power over oneself. Yet even the position of indifference is unstable. Because I remain dimly aware of the Other's transcendence, it haunts me as an unseen danger at the edges of my consciousness. And except for this reaction of indifference, my interest in the Other is the opposite of that described by Freud: I am not interested in the Other as a subject because the Other has proved to be a sensually gratifying object; rather, I am interested in the Other as a (transcendent) object because I know that he or she is a subject.

Yet this realization that the Other is a subject who makes me an object, in any attitude except the avoidant one of denial of the Other's subjecthood, leads to a conflict which profoundly affects me. And, indeed, Sartre maintains that the two primitive attitudes which I may take toward the Other imply such conflict. In the first of these, which Sartre associates with desire/sadism, I attempt to transcend the Other's transcendence, thereby subsuming the Other's freedom in my own. In the second, which Sartre associates with love/masochism, I attempt to incorporate the Other's transcendence within me without removing from it its character as transcendence (BN, p. 363). In the first position, I concentrate on the power of my own subjectivity to banish the Other's power as a subject by transforming the Other into an object, whereas in the second I concentrate on myself as an object beneath the Other's gaze.

Neither of the two positions is primary chronologically. Rather, they form a circle in which, because each attitude is unstable and contains within it the other as the seed of its destruction, the failure of one may easily lead to the adoption of the other. The problem is that I can never be satisfied with either position toward the Other because each position (Other-as-subject or Other-as-object) refers to its opposite and this reference leads to its own collapse. Our unstable relations with the Other forever include being tossed between the two poles—being a Look and being looked at—with no hope for a resolution.

There is no way out for the simple reason that we cannot simultaneously apprehend the Other's freedom and the Other's facticity—or the Other ours. We cannot place ourselves on a plane of equality "where the recognition of the Other's freedom would involve the Other's recognition of our freedom" (BN, p. 408). Hence if I attempt to recover my sovereignty as a subject by making the Other an object, I soon find that without the Other I have lost the means to founding my objective being. But if I then turn and attempt to recover that objective being by identifying with the Other's freedom as its foundation, I discover that the inevitable separation of consciousnesses prevents me from accomplishing this feat. The Other remains an alien freedom which I cannot absorb into my objectness, and I remain a freedom without substance for myself. If I then turn and attempt to absorb the Other as a subject, I again discover that this is impossible because the Other, even at the extreme limits of sadism, may recover subjecthood simply by looking at me. Since neither of these two positions can be held without contradiction, Sartre notes, the one will always remain present at the very core of the other as the possibility of its death. At least on the plane of bad faith, where our project is one of using the Other to achieve substantive freedom, there is no escape from this conflictual circle.

Since the circle of love/masochism–desire/sadism is so much at the heart of most neurotic projects, I think it will be useful to describe these positions in more detail. Although a person may easily get stuck at one or the other side of the circle, it is often true that people alternate between the two in different relationships or in the same relationship at different times. An individual, depending usually on life experience, may enter the circle at any point. Sartre himself begins with love/masochism, though he points out that this attitude is in no way prior to the other position.

According to Sartre, what usually passes for love in the world is at bottom a desire to *be loved*—a point with which object relations theorist Michael Balint (1969) would agree. What the lover wants from the beloved is *justification* for his or her existence. In order to achieve this, the lover wishes to assimilate the beloved's freedom as the lover's foundation. This does not mean, however, that the lover wishes simply to be freely loved by a beloved who does as he or she pleases. On the contrary, the lover wishes to be the "object limit" of the beloved's freedom. The lover does not wish to be one object among others in the world, but rather to be the beloved's "whole world" or else to be that by which there is a world for the beloved. The lover wishes to be an untranscendable object which cannot be used instrumentally for the beloved's own ends. The lover wishes to be the beloved's whole "reason for living," as popular songs are fond of saying.

Such "love" is, of course, a way of attempting to overcome the danger which I am otherwise in with respect to the Other's freedom—the danger of being for the Other an object over which I have no control and which (though I am responsible for it) I did not found as an object. In the original situation with the Other, as Sartre points out, my being remains over there at a distance from me—"like the dinner of Tantalus" (BN, p. 364). In love, on the contrary, I imagine that I can recover myself as an object by absorbing the Other's freedom and thereby realizing the missing God, Being-in-itself-for-itself. In pursuing this project, I am not interested in the Other's enterprises as they relate solely to the Other; such pure transcendence threatens me. Instead, I want to assimilate the Other as the "Other-looking-at-me" (BN, p. 365).

One wonders if this desire to attain a secure being within the consciousness of an Other who is always attending to me is the source of those seemingly irrational feelings of jealousy which pervade some love relationships, wherein the lover is threatened by *anything* (work, friends, leisure activities) which seems to absorb any of the beloved's time or attention. Feeling possessed by the Other's freedom, I want to absorb that which possesses me. I want to reduce the Other's freedom to a freedom which is subject to my freedom. In attempting to do so, I may make myself ever so seductive—holding out to the Other the promise of a whole world which is supposedly contained within me as an object.

At the same time, however, I will not be satisfied with my lover's attending to me out of duty. I do not want to possess the Other as an enslaved freedom; rather, I want to possess the Other's freedom as freedom. I am therefore not after power. Instead, I want the Other to *want* me. I want the Other to voluntarily make me his or her ultimate value. That is, I want my beloved to *will* his or her captivity. And this voluntary enslavement must not be simply to an unchanging me-object. Instead, I want assurance that my beloved will love me no matter what I become, that his or her love is not based on this or that characteristic for which my beloved loves me. Like the lover in a poem by W. B. Yeats, I want to know that my beloved will "love me for myself alone and not my yellow hair" (1956, p. 240). I want to be for my beloved an "object-transcendence" which can never be devalued (BN, p. 369). As absolute value, I also want to know that my beloved would do anything for me—steal, kill, betray his or her friends. In other words, I want the Other's freedom to found my essence as its ultimate value.

This is an impossible goal, first because in reality I am one object among others for my beloved and never simply the sole object of his or her attention. Even if my beloved seems to be totally absorbed in me for a time, his or her awakening from the dream of love is always possible. And because my beloved can at any moment make me appear as an object among other objects or as a different object than I had expected, I am perpetually insecure. Second, the goal of using the Other to create substantive freedom is impossible because my beloved, if he or she loves me, will want the same thing from me. My beloved will want to *be loved* as a means to justifying his or her right to *be* through my subjective absorption in him or her as an object. This will create conflict since each of us wants from the other a love which is not reducible to the project of being loved. We each want a "pure engage-ment without reciprocity," without demands—an "unselfish" love which is impossible if for no other reason than that each of us wants it and in want-ing it wants to make use of the Other to get it. The Other, we each find, can never be a pure subjectivity founding my objectivity.

Finally, even if the two lovers manage to achieve a kind of *folie à deux* in which each pretends to stand as justification for the other's existence, there is always the possibility that a third person will look on the duo and destroy their love as an absolute axis of reference. It is for this reason, Sartre points out, that lovers seek solitude. They wish to escape this alienation as an us object in the look of a third who can destroy the power of each to justify the other's existence. Perhaps the loss of a love is often so poignant because one feels that one has lost this justification for one's own existence. The terrible thing has happened: The Other has turned and made of me something other than the object limit of his or her freedom; indeed, he or she may even have made of me a disagreeable object over which I now have no control. That is why, I think, dispossessed lovers are prone to go over and over again in their heads and with their friends the reasons why their former lovers are "wrong" in their assessments of them.

The inevitable failure of the project of love may lead to the adoption of a debasement of this project in the attitude of masochism. In masochism, I give up the project of justifying myself by assimilating the Other as a witness to my free project as object. Having been thrown back on my subjectivity without justification, I adopt a position of despair which leads to a new ma-nipulation. Instead of attempting to induce the Other to make me *be* as an objective freedom, I attempt to rid myself of that subjectivity which I now perceive as an obstacle to the Other's founding me in my being. I attempt to make myself into a mere object, a pure in-itself, rather than a transcendent object. In shame, I assume the position of instrumentality which I had previ-ously rejected. In doing so, I desire to be used by an Other who is radically free so that through identification with this freedom I can become fascinated with my self-as-an-object.

Unhappily, masochism, too, is a failure since I cannot on principle appre-hend for myself the object which I am for the Other. The obscene postures which I assume, for example, are there in the world for the Other in a way that they can never be there for me. Not only this, I have to recognize that it is I *as a subject* who assume the stances which are intended to reduce me to a mere object for the Other. Hence the more I try to taste my objectification, the more I become aware of my subjectivity. The man who pays a prostitute to whip him, for instance, discovers that he is treating the woman as an instrument and is therefore taking the position of a transcendent subject in relation to her. This discovery of her objectivity thus frees the masochist's subjectivity, leading to a collapse of the whole project of masochism (BN, pp. 278–79).

With this failure of love/masochism, the person may move to the other side of the circle, assuming the position of desire/sadism—though the assumption of the attitude of desire/sadism may be taken on its own as an original reaction to my Being-for-others without my having first assumed the attitude of love/masochism. Nonetheless, the realization that I cannot assimilate the Other's freedom either by becoming its object limit or by becoming a mere object may lead me to attempt to co-opt the Other's freedom from another angle. After all, as we have seen, the failure of masochism leaves me with an awareness of an unjustified subjectivity from which I cannot escape. Thus freed from identifying with the Other's consciousness of me as an object, I may turn toward the Other and look at him or her. But since a Look cannot be looked at, the Other-as-subject disappears to be replaced by the Other-as-object. A new enterprise may be born of this experience. Since I cannot absorb the Other's pure freedom into myself as (transcendent or mere) object, I may attempt to catch the Other's freedom (and hence the Other's objectification of me) in the Other as object.

In order to do this, I must first induce the Other to incarnate himself or herself—to subsume his or her consciousness in the body so that I may skim it off as a person skims cream off milk (BN, p. 394). What I want thereby to possess is not, of course, simply the Other's body as a body. Rather, I want to possess the Other's body as it is possessed by that consciousness which in turn possesses me as an object (BN, p. 394). I do not desire the Other as body but the Other as flesh. But in order to desire the Other as flesh, I must first make myself flesh. If, like a client with whom I once worked, I cannot put myself into a state of sexual desire in the presence of the Other, if I cannot make myself flesh, then the Other will also be unable to feel desire (at least under normal circumstances). Indeed, this client, much to his dismay, always achieved only friendships with the women who figured so strongly in his solitary imagination as the objects of amorous adventures. He could not understand why they did not desire him until he realized that, when they were present at least, he did not allow himself to desire them.

What then does it mean to make oneself flesh and to enter the world of desire? Sartre distinguishes the body-as-flesh from the body-in-action by noting that in making myself flesh, I consent to being "absorbed by my body as ink is by a blotter" (BN, p. 395). In a state of desire, I give up my body as an instrumental synthetic organization of my acts and replace it with a body which aims at pure "being there" (BN, p. 395). The for-itself ensnared in the body has as its ultimate project a "Being-in-the-midst-of-the-world," an infection with facticity which helps explain why in world literature sensual pleasure is so often linked with death—which is also a metamorphosis into Being-in-the-midst-of-the-world as opposed to Being-in-the-world. Desire has therefore a heaviness which signals the "non-thetically lived project of being swallowed up in the body" (BN, p. 389). It is a "clogging" of consciousness with facticity, a "troubled" consciousness in the same sense that we speak of "troubled water" as water which seems to be clogged with itself. In reality, of course, the water is troubled by fine solid particles suspended in the liquid, but we are talking here about a nonscientific impression. Desiring consciousness presents a similar appearance because it seems to be clogged with a "yeasty tumescence of fact" (BN, p. 388). Of course, this inertia which appears to be characteristic of desiring consciousness is itself an illusion in the sense that consciousness does not simply succumb to desire; rather, it "chooses itself as desire" (BN, p. 391).

The meaning of this choice is not pleasure (though it is often accompanied by pleasure), but rather the attempt to realize the incarnation of the Other through one's own incarnation. Thus desire experienced alone has a suffocating quality, a vertigo which gives me the impression that I am going to drown in my own facticity. This is because sexual desire, from a Sartrean perspective, always has interpersonal implications. As such, desire also has a language—the language of the "caress." The caress—which can be accomplished with the eyes as well as with the body—is, in fact, equivalent to desire itself since I must first put myself into the attitude of being flesh in order to caress. What is desired in the caress is, of course, not simple bodily contact, the meeting of "two epidermises," but rather a shaping of the Other's body by mine and mine by the Other's (BN, p. 390). In caressing the Other, I cause the Other's flesh as embodied consciousness to be born beneath my touch—a touch which has itself been metamorphosed by desire into a kind of passivity.

In caressing the Other, I do not so much instrumentally take hold of a part of the Other's body (which would undoubtedly cause the Other in a state of desire to recoil) as place my own body against the Other in an almost studied fashion. As Sartre puts it, "It seems that I lift my arm as an inanimate object and that I place it over against the flank of the desired woman, that my fingers which I run over her arm are inert at the end of my hand" (BN, p. 391). Infected with inertia, I affect the Other with inertia—causing the Other to be born as flesh. And, indeed, Sartre notes that the "true caress" is not even a matter of caressing the Other with my hand. It is instead a contact between the more fleshly parts of our bodies—those parts (breasts, buttocks, thighs, and stomachs) which form more of an image of pure facticity because they are incapable of spontaneous movement (BN, p. 396).

Furthermore, it is not only my orientation to the Other which changes in a state of desire but my whole world orientation. The world itself is metamorphosed into a world of desire, which reveals to me the "fleshy" side of objects. Normally, in living my body instrumentally as a synthetic organization of acts, I approach objects as means to my own ends. They are there to be utilized or ignored. In a state of desire, however, objects reveal to me a whole different side of themselves. They caress me or assault me, revealing to me their depth and their texture. I feel, for instance, the caress of warm air, sunshine, silk sheets, even the clothes against my body. Or I feel rudely assaulted by the harshness of a cold draft or a rough surface. This caress (or anti-caress) of objects is similar to the caresses I exchange with my lover and, indeed, is born of my placing myself in a state of desire with respect to him or her.

Thus sexual desire for Sartre is not, as it is for Freud, a lonely enterprise of instinctual stirring which requires an outlet. Rather, it is a *"double reciprocal incarnation"* which can only happen reciprocally (BN, p. 391). Although desire, as we shall see, also has its failure, it is in this sense perhaps more satisfying than (inauthentic) love, in which the only mutuality is the antagonistic mutual desire of each partner to be loved. Although the Sartrean description of desire is very different from sexual desire as described by orthodox psychoanalysis, there are nonetheless some points of convergence. For example, Sartre agrees with Freud that sexuality is a preoccupation for the life span. Sexual desire, Sartre tells us, "appears with birth and disappears only with death" (BN, p. 384). Children, eunuchs, and old people feel desire, not just adults who are capable of completing the sexual act. Sartre also agrees with Freud that sexuality pervades all of our relations with others and not simply those with the opposite sex; indeed, Sartre points out that even sexual disgust (for example, the disgust often felt by heterosexuals at the thought of taking a same-sex partner) testifies to a fleshly recognition of the Other as flesh. As for other seemingly nonsexual attitudes—for example, pity, admiration, envy, or gratitude—they also have their sexual components. Furthermore, Sartre agrees with Freud that sexuality is different in kind from other bodily "appetites."

Here, however, the similarities end. Since Sartre rejects the economic hypothesis in favor of an interpersonal hypothesis, he considers the significance of sexuality to be its ontological meaning as related to my Being-for-others rather than its instinctual aim. This meaning is not the pleasure of instinctual release, the return to zero energy charge; rather, it is the use of the Other to create a self by means of the mutual reciprocal incarnation. Pleasure, where it happens, is a by-product and, as we shall see, often spells the death of desire. This does not mean that Sartre would deny the biological facts of sexuality, including orgasm and secondary sexual characteristics, but he does not consider these contingent facts to be its primary significance.

Indeed, Sartre suggests rather whimsically that the usual way of thinking about these things may be backward: "Man, it is said, is a sexual being because he possesses a sex. And if the reverse were true? If sex were only the instrument and, so to speak, the *image* of a fundamental sexuality? If man possessed a sex only because he is originally and fundamentally a sexual being as a being who exists in the world in relation with other men?" (BN, p. 383). Obviously, this is a metaphysical speculation which Sartre cannot prove. But this seemingly whimsical statement testifies to where he thinks the emphasis ought to be placed—on ontological rather than biological significance. In a sense, post-Freudian psychoanalytic theorist George Klein agrees with this assessment when he notes that the sexual aim represents "some more encompassing need [than mere instinctual gratification] in which self-conception and self-status are at issue" (1976, p. 97).[5]

This account is obviously different from sexual desire as described by Freud, which, though it lacks specificity with respect to objects and even with respect to aim in the sense of the kind of sexual practice desired, does not lack specificity with respect to the energetic release which is its goal. Hence when Sartre says that sexual desire differs from mere bodily appetites, he has in mind something different from Freudian lability of aim and object as these relate to a fundamentally polymorphously perverse sexual instinct. What Sartre means is that in sexual desire, unlike simple hunger or thirst, I must change my fundamental orientation toward the world. I must enter the world of desire, which is an interpersonal world, and in doing so I must clog my consciousness with facticity as I desire the Other to clog his or her consciousness with facticity. Thus it is impossible, much as I might like things to be this simple, to follow the old adage, "Make love to a pretty woman when you want her just as you drink a glass of cold water when you are thirsty" (BN, p. 388). I cannot *not* be changed in the process, nor can I fail to take note of the Other as transcendence.

Therefore, even though Sartre can see how psychoanalysts might view sexuality as a kind of tabula rasa deriving all its determinations from individual history, he nonetheless believes that, although one's individual history will certainly fix the particular type of relationship one seeks with the Other, sexuality itself is determined not by biological instincts but by one's original "upsurge . . . into a world where 'there are' Others" (BN, p. 407). Sexuality, for Sartre but not for Freud, is originally and inescapably interpersonal—even where one attempts to escape its interpersonal significance in onanism (as Jean Genet did in Sartre's biography). For this reason alone, we might say that Sartre's version of sexuality squares better with the post-Freudian theorists' discovery of the primacy of interpersonal needs in infancy than does a Freudian theory of an instinct which must thereafter attach itself to objects. According to Sartre's view, the infant's interpersonal needs are not at variance with its developing sexuality.

Sartrean sexual desire, however, is, like Sartrean love, an unstable position, since the mutuality arrived at in the "double reciprocal incarnation" cannot last. The discovery that I must incarnate myself to induce the Other to incarnate himself of herself leads in two ways to the failure of desire to achieve its goal of capturing the Other's freedom in his or her body. In the first place, my own pleasure subverts this goal. Because pleasure motivates the appearance of a reflective consciousness of corporeality which is "attention to pleasure" (BN, p. 397), I become forgetful of the Other's incarnation and hence lose my object. The pleasure of caressing is replaced by the pleasure of being caressed as I become absorbed in my own incarnation.

This failure can lead to a passage to masochism if I then seek to become absorbed as an object into the Other as consciousness, thereby becoming a flesh swooning beneath the Other's Look. Or it can lead to a passage to sadism if I break the reciprocity of incarnation by attempting to take hold of and appropriate the Other's flesh—which to some extent I must do in the active side of sexual intercourse. At this point, however, the Other as incarnated consciousness will disappear as the Other as object takes his or her place. Although the Other may remain flesh for himself or herself and I may understand this, this is no longer a flesh which I understand through my flesh. Instead, I am a body, an instrumental organization, confronting a flesh. The mutuality has been broken.

The "sado-masochistic strain" in normal sexuality which results from this inevitable instability of the positions of love and desire (BN, p. 404), however, must not be equated with masochism and sadism proper. We have already seen how the perversion of masochism leads me to try to make myself into a mere object. Sadism is similarly an embellishment and a perversion of this sadistic seed in normal sexuality. The sadist reacts to the rupture in reciprocal incarnation by attempting an instrumental appropriation of the incarnated Other. As a transcendent subject, the sadist attempts a nonreciprocity in which he or she "enjoys being a free appropriating power confronting a freedom captured by flesh" (BN, p. 399). Desire, for the sadist, is either a humiliating state or else one which simply is beyond the sadist's power to achieve.

Hence the sadist's mode of attempting to capture the Other's consciousness is to produce pain rather than to induce pleasure since pain can cause facticity to invade consciousness in the same way that pleasure can—producing a reflective consciousness which is attention to pain. What the sadist wishes is to enslave the Other's freedom—to make the Other beg for mercy, humiliate himself or herself, or betray his or her most cherished values. The sadist wishes to create in the heaving body of the Other "a broken and enslaved freedom" which is subject to the sadist's will (BN, p. 404).

Sadism, however, is also an unstable position which bears within it the seeds of its own destruction. On the one hand, at the moment when the sadist seems to have succeeded in reducing the Other as a pain-consciousness to an enslaved freedom, the complex "flesh-as-instrument" which the sadist had attempted to create disappears and the body of the Other reappears. The sadist, at this moment, does not know what to do with the submissive body which appears before him or her. The only way to keep it flesh would be for the sadist to enter a state of desire and become flesh himself or herself. But if the sadist at this moment incarnates himself or herself, the project of sadism will have failed in the emergence of desire just as desire had previously foundered in sadism.

Even if the sadist does not become sexually aroused, the project is likely to fail from another direction. This is so because the project of the sadist—to appropriate the transcendent freedom of the victim—is on principle out of reach. One Look from the victim, at the extreme limits of torture, can apprise the sadist of this fact. This Look, like the look of the dying black Joe Christmas at his white castrators in Sartre's example from Faulkner's *Light in August*, dethrones the sadist from the position of only subject and reestablishes the victim in the position of a subject confronting the sadist as object.

The passage Sartre quotes from the novel certainly does provide a graphic illustration of this point:

"But the man on the floor had not moved. He just lay there, with his eyes open and empty of everything save consciousness, and with something, a shadow, about his mouth. For a long moment he looked up at them with peaceful and unfathomable and unbearable eyes. Then his face, body, all, seemed to collapse, to fall in upon itself and from out of the slashed garments about his hips and loins the pent black blood seemed to rush like a released breath. It seemed to rush out of his pale body like the rush of sparks from a rising rocket; upon that black blast the man seemed to rise soaring into their memories for ever and ever. They are not to lose it, in whatever peaceful valleys, beside whatever placid and reassuring streams of old age, in the mirroring face of whatever children they will contemplate old disasters and newer hopes. *It will be there, musing, quiet, steadfast, not fading and not particularly threatful, but of itself alone serene, of itself alone triumphant.* Again from the town deadened a little by the walls, the scream of a siren mounted toward its unbelievable crescendo, passing out of hearing." (BN, p. 406)

Sartre goes on to remark that "this explosion of the Other's look in the world of the sadist causes the meaning and goal of sadism to collapse" (BN, p. 406). The sadist, at the point where his victim turns to look at him, "experiences the absolute alienation of his being in the Other's freedom" (BN, p. 405)—and his project of sadism, as we might have predicted, founders on the reef of the Other's subjectivity.

These, then, are the unstable positions one may take with respect to the Other in Sartre's description of "Concrete Relations with Others." Even the position of hate, or desire for the Other's death, will not save me from this sadomasochistic circle since I cannot, by annihilating the Other, reestablish myself as pure transcendence. If out of despair over my inability to escape the circle, I kill the Other, I will discover that the Other, "by slipping into the past[,] becomes an irremediable dimension of myself" in the form of "having-been" (BN, p. 412). I will then, like the lynch gang in *Light in August*, be contaminated by the Look of an Other which is unchangeable, since the destroyed Other will carry the key to my being with him or her to the grave. What I was for the Other is fixed by the Other's death, a fact which may help to explain why dead parents are often more difficult to deal with in therapy than live ones.

Obviously, these are good descriptions of neurotic relationships, descriptions which can be very useful to a therapist in understanding clients' dilemmas. But the question which now arises is this: Does Sartre provide any way out of the sadomasochistic circle, or are all relationship possibilities as dismal as the ones described here? Is it really true, as Garcin says at the end of Sartre's *No Exit*, that "Hell is other people" (NE, p. 47) and that there is no remedy for this situation? Although Sartre has often been accused of having a pessimistic attitude toward human relations and although he himself insists in "Concrete Relations with Others" that relating to Others necessarily involves conflict, I do not think that Sartre's ontology requires us to take a negative view of interpersonal relations. For one thing, Sartre later admitted that all the interactions described in "Concrete Relations with Others" were in bad faith. For another, as Hazel Barnes notes, there is at least a shade of hope for mutuality in the "double reciprocal incarnation" of Sartrean desire. And, finally, Sartre himself suggests in a provocative footnote that the preceding argument does not preclude "the possibility of an ethics of deliverance and salvation" from the sadomasochistic circle—a possibility predicated on a "radical conversion" to what we later learn is a valuing of freedom itself (BN, p. 412 and 625–28). In *Search for a Method*, Sartre refers to this as a "philosophy of freedom" (p. 34), but there he considers ethical/psychological deliverance to be practically impossible in a world dominated by scarcity.

Still, many passages in *Being and Nothingness* give us an idea of what this radical conversion might be like—and the later Sartre insists, even more than the earlier Sartre, that positive reciprocity is a genuine human possibility. The radical conversation would mean a renunciation, concomitant with a renunciation of the belief that substantive freedom is possible, of all those attempts to coerce, manipulate, plead with, or degrade the Other so that he or she might provide me with a substantive sense of self. This renunciation would not, however, lead to the position of hate based on despair which Sartre describes as one possible outcome of the discovery that one cannot get out of the sadomasochistic circle. Despair, as Sartre points out toward the end of *Being and Nothingness*, is a position in which one is still committed to one's mission of effecting the in-itself-for-itself at the same time that one realizes that this enterprise is doomed to failure. One is still caught up in the "serious world." The radical conversion goes beyond this position by valuing the value-making process itself while renouncing the aim of creating a substantive self (BN, pp. 626–27).

Rather than leading to hate or despair, the radical conversion leads to a situation in which I freely respect the Other as another subject like myself, whose desires, views, and life project may be different from and at times even antagonistic to my own, but which I nonetheless do not attempt to subvert to my own ends. This does not mean, however, that I delude myself into thinking that I do not affect the Other or the Other me. Instead, I remain open to the Other, and in doing so I realize that we cannot *not* affect each other. As Sartre points out, even if I take a position of laissez-faire and tolerance toward the Other, I cannot thereby escape establishing myself as a "factual limit to the Other's freedom" (BN, p. 409). In this case, for example, I throw the Other into a tolerant world and thereby "remove from him on principle those free possibilities of courageous resistance, of perseverance, of self-assertion which he would have had the opportunity to develop in a world of intolerance" (BN, p. 409). The same, of course, is true of the Other as a factual limit to my freedom. And the radical conversion would not erase this truth. It would, however, go a long way toward releasing me from the struggle that is a result of my believing I can use the Other to create substantive freedom.

Perhaps we can recognize even more of the positive potential of the Look if we understand that, as Hazel Barnes points out, there are two other possible Looks which Sartre does not emphasize in *Being and Nothingness* but which are not contradicted by his observations there. The first is two people looking at the world together, the "we" of the "common project" which Sartre does mention in *Being and Nothingness* (pp. 423–30) but on which he does not elaborate. It is the basis for comradeship, whether this occurs in the work world or in an intimate relationship.

The second is the experience which Barnes designates as the "Look-as-exchange." She regards such a Look not as "a union of subjects but a mutual affirmation of respect for the Other as subject," resembling Sartre's enterprise of "love" as described in *Being and Nothingness* but lacking the "attempt to assimilate the Other's freedom" (Barnes, 1974, p. 64). The Look-as-exchange involves the usual subject-object alternation, but with the added intention of positively understanding the Other's world and using this understanding to enhance both self and Other (Barnes, 1967, pp. 333–34). Perhaps the primordial prototype of the Look-as-exchange is the contented mutual gazing of the normal mother-infant pair described by Mahler and other infant observers. The Look-as-exchange is marked not by hostility or fear but by mutual receptiveness. We can easily see it as lying at the heart of what Sartre in his later works referred to as positive reciprocity—and authentic love.

The fact remains, however, that the Sartre of *Being and Nothingness* does not describe human relations in good faith. On the other hand, the later Sartre of *Search for a Method*, the *Critique of Dialectical Reason*, the psychobiographies, and other works repeatedly suggests that positive reciprocity is possible. It is possible partially because even negative reciprocity (which arises in part because the Other in a world dominated by scarcity poses both an economic and a psychological danger to oneself) involves a comprehension of the Other as a subject like oneself (CDR, pp. 131–34). Yet positive regard, genuine love, and "care" (a term Sartre uses in his posthumously published *Ethics* [*Cahiers pour une morale*; 1983]) can also arise from such comprehension. Nor are people in the later works perceived so much as isolated individuals. Although Sartre hates the "terror" which arises as groups on the way to institutional ossification attempt to force their members to comply with group norms, he is much enamored of the energy and sense of common aim and purpose which can arise in a "group-in-fusion" (*group-en-fusion*) (CDR, pp. 345–404).

Thus we should not be totally surprised to find Sartre at seventy years old, in an interview with Michel Contat, suggesting that absolute transparency between people is desirable:

> I think transparency should always be substituted for secrecy. I can imagine the day when two men will no longer have secrets from each other, because no one will have any more secrets from anyone, because subjective life, as well as objective life, will be completely offered up, given. It is impossible to accept the fact that we yield our bodies as we do and yet keep our thoughts hidden, since for me there is no basic difference between the body and the consciousness. (L/S, p. 11)

What Sartre means, of course, is that the body is not simply a physical object but an indicator of consciously lived life; as such, it can be seen, touched, and interpreted by others.

Despite the dangers to oneself which self-revelation might pose, secrecy provides another kind of danger. Consequently, Sartre points out that "this dark region that we have within ourselves, which is at once dark for us and dark for others, can only be illuminated for ourselves in trying to illuminate it for others" (L/S, p. 12). This becomes clear when one understands that for Sartre, the beginning of self-reflection lies to a great extent in the reflection of others on the self to which one can now add disclosure to others who see and (one hopes) comprehend oneself. One can probably do this only if one has previously undergone a "radical conversion" to a philosophy of freedom—that is, if one can bear to have the Other see oneself differently from the way one would have wished. Actually, Sartre had himself pursued a pact of absolute transparency with Simone de Beauvoir since the early days of their relationship—a pact which apparently gave to both a great advantage in developing self-understanding. His later view is an extension of that early commitment to transparency in his most significant relationship.[6]

The later Sartre even attempts to present a different view of "love" than the inauthentic project of incorporating the self into the Other which he had designated by that name in *Being and Nothingness*. He says in an interview in 1975 that beginning with *Saint Genet* he had "changed my position a bit, and I now see more positivity in love." He even goes so far as to give this as his reason for writing the book: "I wrote *Saint Genet* to try to present a love that goes beyond the sadism in which Genet is steeped and the masochism that he suffered" (Sartre in Schilpp, 1981, p. 13). In other words, Sartre wished to suggest the possibility of a love which transcends the sadomasochistic circle of *Being and Nothingness*.

Contrasting Genet's solipsism with real love, Sartre says,

It is the appeal of the Other that makes the reality of love. We are drawn, then held, by the promise of parted lips, by the expectation that we read in the Other's eyes. In order to be able to love a voice, a face, we must feel that they are calling out for love; hence, the beauty that we ascribe to them is not likely to be a lie: it is a real gift, and the beloved, who feeds on it, draws new confidence from it, is beautified by joy. In order to be completely true, a love must be shared; it is a joint undertaking in which the feeling of each is the substance of that of the Other. Each of the two freedoms addresses the other, captivates it, tempts it, it is the Other's love of me that is the truth of my love: if my passion is solitary it becomes a cult or a phantasmagoria. (SG, pp. 327–28)

I quote this passage at length both because the mutuality described is so different from the conflictual inauthentic love described in *Being and Nothingness* and because I think it is an equally logical outcome of Sartre's ontology. Also, it seems to me that many of the cases of unrequited or nonreciprocal love which clients present in therapy can be understood as solipsistic projects to *make the Other love me* so that I can feel that I have value. Not so extreme as Genet, these clients are nonetheless unhappy because they have similarly failed to develop a capacity for genuinely mutual caring.

The truth is that Sartre does believe that is possible to understand another person, both in a love relationship and in the professional relationship of the social scientist to his or her subject or subjects. As early as *Being and Nothingness* (1943), Sartre had suggested that an empathic human comprehension is the primary tool of existential psychoanalysis. In *Search for a Method* (1960b) and the *Critique of Dialectical Reason* (1960a), he went further to elevate comprehension to an essential way in which dialectical reason can grasp human truth in all of the social sciences (CDR, pp. 74–76). There Sartre defines "comprehension" as the ability to understand the actions of another person or persons (in our own or another historical age) in terms of human intentions or purposes. In order to achieve comprehension, the social scientist must be willing to give up his or her attempt at being the godlike objective observer and perceive other people as meaning-engendering like himself or herself.

Comprehension is contrasted with "intellection," which Sartre does not accept as an effective method in the social sciences so long as it is the purely intellectual analysis of analytical reason. Only when intellection is wedded to comprehension does it become useful. Comprehension without intellection might yield an understanding of people in a given situation while failing to grasp the intersection of historical processes that are initiated but not understood by people in a sometimes unforgiving physical world. But intellection without comprehension has produced an approach to the social sciences which is a reified parody of the social world which it seeks to understand in that it leaves out the one thing which makes social and historical processes intelligible—human intentionality and meaning.

Sartre's demonstration of the dialectical process which he proposes for the social sciences in *Search for a Method* and the *Critique of Dialectical Reason* does not occur so much in the unfinished second volume of the *Critique* as in the psychobiographies—especially the later biographies of Flaubert and Genet.[7] There Sartre's biographical method is identical to the empathic method which he sets for the social scientist in the *Critique*: It involves comprehension in the sense of an empathic giving of oneself to the Other. What had been a task for the existential psychoanalyst in *Being and Nothingness* has become a task for Sartre the psychobiographer.

A Sartrean Perspective on Developmental Theory

It is in the biographies that Sartre spells out most concretely what the Look can mean, positively or negatively, to human development. I believe his discussions of the process of "valorization" in childhood and of three different forms of the Look (which I have designated the look, the touch, and the word) will aid us in understanding the developmental insights of the post-Freudian theorists discussed earlier—especially their discovery of needs for mirroring and positive regard from the original powerful others. At the same time, I believe that a Sartrean perspective on developmental theory will change our understanding of those insights and how they can be used in therapy.

In the first volume of the Flaubert biography, Sartre discusses the child's need for validation by the original powerful others and laments the devastating effects of lack of such validation. Not only negative regard but lack of regard can result in what R. D. Laing calls "ontological insecurity" about one's right to be in the world (Laing, 1959a). Sartre attributes Flaubert's passivity to such early lack of positive regard, or "valorization":

> [Flaubert's malaise] will be easier to discuss now that we know the fundamental reason for it: *nonvalorization.* This is not a matter of conjecture: a child must have a *mandate to live,* the parents are the authorities who issue the mandate. A grant of love enjoins him to cross the barrier of the moment—the next moment is awaited, he is already adored there, everything is prepared for his joyful reception; the future appears to him as a vague and gilded cloud, as his mission. . . . If later on with a little luck he can say: "My life has a purpose, I have found purpose in my life," it is because the parent's love, their creation and expectation, creation for future delight, has revealed his existence to him as a movement toward an end; he is the conscious arrow that is awakened in midflight and discovers, simultaneously, the distant archer, the target, and the intoxication of flight. . . . [If this happens] living will be the *passion*—in the religious sense—that will transform self-centeredness into a gift; experience will be felt as the *free exercise of generosity.* (FI, 1:133–34)

The love of the parents guarantees the valorized child's value and mission—a mission which "becomes a sovereign choice, permitted and evoked in the subjective person by the presence of self-worth" (FI, 1:135). Without this mandate to live, which Sartre acknowledges is more often than not missing in children's interactions with their parents, a child will be left afloat in a meaningless universe where physical laws perhaps point to a sense of a future but where one's own existence appears senseless or wrong. Time, for such children, becomes "a slack succession of present moments that slip back into past" (FI, 1:134), leaving them unable to cross the "barrier of the moment" (FI, 1:133) to create a meaningful existence. In this way, unvalorized children, such as Flaubert, are discouraged from experiencing themselves as agents. Because the past holds no empathic nourishment, the future holds no promise.

The reader familiar only with Sartre's early work may be wondering at this juncture if this sense of a meaningless universe, upon which the individual must impose meaning, is not exactly what Sartre declares to be the case in *Being and Nothingness* and elsewhere. In other words, is the valorized child's sense of a mission not an expression of bad faith because it rests on the a priori mandate of the parents? And is the "teleological urgency" (FI, 1:133) of the loved child not based on an illusion? Sartre's reply in *The Family Idiot* is curious for anyone familiar with Sartre's early work, but it does not contradict his earlier hypothesis. Sartre says that the mandate to live is, in fact, a necessary deception which makes possible a later encounter with the truth of existence. The senseless existence which the unloved child discovers in himself or herself is therefore a lying truth, whereas the meaningfulness which the loved child has conferred on him or her is a true lie. The unloved child—though he or she can discover orderly connections, means and ends, in the world—can discover no reason for his or her own being. In other words, the unloved child is unable to form an authentic project of being— though such a child may make a project of trying to get the love that was missing in infancy and early childhood.

Sartre therefore believes that the "ethical-ontological" truth that one must create one's own value "must be revealed slowly" at the "end of a long vagabond delusion" (FI, 1:136). To reveal it earlier through lack of valorization is to subject the child to the delusion not simply of being unjustified but of being "unjustifiable"—that is, unable to make a meaningful life— which is "a hundred times farther from his real condition" than the lying truth which convinces the loved child that he or she is justified in advance (FI, 1:136). The lie of the parental mandate leads to the truth of discovering one's existence as a temporal being who creates meaning. The truth of a too early confrontation with the meaninglessness of contingent existence-in-itself, based on the experience of parental neglect or hostility, leads to the lie of disregarding one's temporalizing destiny. Thus the lack of a real future combined with a sense of meaninglessness and emptiness is characteristic of the borderline and narcissistic patients noted by Kernberg and others, whereas neurotics (who have probably had some degree of valorization) are more likely to seek this experience again where it is inappropriate—in the desire for "perfect understanding" and complete involvement from an adult partner. The "conflict of consciousnesses," in this latter situation, most often becomes a quite accurate description of interpersonal relations within the duo.

We can further conclude from the psychobiographies that the Look, as an ontological category, includes all of the ways in which one directly experiences oneself as an object for others—touching and verbal responses, as well as actual looking. In fact, Sartre specifically tells us in *Being and Nothingness* that it is not "eyes" but rather the feeling of the regard of another consciousness which produces the Look. We might consider the three subcategories of the Look—which Sartre discusses in various places without ever specifically spelling them out—to be the (physical) look, the touch, and the word.

The touch is especially important in earliest infancy. In *The Family Idiot*, Sartre comments on the importance of touch to the infant's developing rudimentary awareness of self:

> When a mother nurses or cleans an infant, she expresses, like everyone, her integrity of *self*, which naturally sums up her entire life from birth; at the same time, she achieves a relationship that is variable according to circumstances and individuals—of which she is the *subject* and which can be called maternal love. . . . [B]y this love and through it, through the very person of the mother—skillful or clumsy, brutal or tender, such as her history has made her—the child is made manifest to himself. That is, he does not discover himself only through his own self-exploration and through his "double-sensations," but he learns his flesh through the pressures, the foreign contacts, the grazings, the bruisings that jostle him, or through a skillful gentleness. He will know his bodily parts, violent, gentle, beaten, constrained or free through the violence or gentleness of the hands that awaken them. Through his flesh he also knows another flesh, but a bit later. To begin with, he internalizes the maternal rhythms and labors as qualities lived with his own body. (FI, 1:47)

The mother's touch, according to this passage, is that through which the infant comes to know himself or herself as an object. One's sense of one's body for-others is thus intimately connected with spontaneous awareness of or pleasure in one's body as lived for-oneself. In fact, the two are only dimly differentiated in earliest infancy. This fleshly knowing of self/mother is also the beginning of a relationship with mother which will later develop into a full subject-object relationship—in which the infant will come to know "another flesh" and still later another person in the fully human sense.

Without this experience, the growing child can hardly come to have a bodily sense of self—as is perhaps evident in psychoanalytic descriptions of severe personality disorders where differentiation of one's various bodily appetites and functions, including a sense of inside and outside, are severely disturbed. Peter Giovacchini, for example, describes a patient who had difficulties distinguishing his appetites one from another (1984, pp. 155–56). Eating, for him, was a mechanical response to an indiscriminate feeling of hunger. He had no appetite for any particular food—oatmeal and caviar were the same to him. He also had no fantasies while masturbating, describing it as relieving himself of some ill-defined tension. In fact, he found it difficult to define his sensations—responding to a vague uneasiness by having to "decide" whether he was hungry, needed to defecate, or was sexually aroused. He also had difficulty distinguishing what was a part of him from what was not. During the first week of analysis, for instance, he pounded on the wall in order to determine where his body (fist) ended and the world (wall) began. Although Giovacchini attributes these difficulties to lack of adequate ego development, I think we might well see them from a Sartrean perspective as deriving from the failure of the first others to present the child with a viable future which would have allowed him to project the discernment and fulfillment of his own needs and desires within it.

According to this view, the more severe disorders reflect not a lack of ego development in the Freudian sense, but rather a lack of experience of oneself as a particular kind of (valued) object for the earliest others. At the most primitive level, this will of course relate to one's bodily sense of self. And one suspects that even in less severely disturbed people, certain dimly recognized though deep feelings about one's own body—as active, passive, disgusting, appealing, and so on—derive from this period. One client graphically put such a feeling into words in the following manner, "Sometimes I feel that my body is totally icky—that I have little bumps all over me, like alligator skin or leprosy—and that although I can't see them other people can and turn away from me because of it." Her mother, she remembered, was squeamish about bodily functions and reluctant about touching.

As for the word, Sartre gives it particular attention in his biography of Jean Genet (1952). Genet, Sartre says, first lives his childhood thefts as prereflective acts devoid of judgment. Because the child Genet is a foundling in the custody of an institution, he has no legitimate access to the property which, for the Morvan peasants into whose care he is given, defines one's being a person. Genet acquires from them an absolute respect for property, which becomes the genesis of his need to steal. Genet, unlike the legitimate children with whom he associates, is deprived by birth of a right to the property which otherwise might define him and give him a sense of self-respect at the same time that he is subjected to the humiliation of being dependent on the generosity of his caregivers—a "generosity" which Genet depicted with vitriolic sarcasm in *The Maids* (1952 [1947]). His response is to "play at possession" through theft (SG, p. 13). In the quiet of his solitary existence, this playing acquires a trancelike quality in which a hand somehow reaches out to take something from a drawer.

At some point, however, Genet will be "caught in the act"; someone will enter the room and direct a Look at him. He feels the Look, but is still ignorant of its meaning. Soon he and the whole village will hear the "dizzying word" (Sartre is quoting Genet here): "You're a thief." This word transforms Genet's life. He now has an identity. He is a thief. This word might not have become decisive for another child who stole, but who was by birthright a legitimate member of the human community through inclusion in his or her family. The young Sartre himself at one point became such a "legitimate" thief when he stole money from his mother's purse in order to buy treats for his friends (Hayman, 1987, pp. 43-44).

Genet, however, can only regain his agency by a rather spiteful decision: He will decide to be the thief they said he was—"to be what crime made of me," as he himself has said (SG, p. 49). In doing so, he will no longer be a passive victim, but he will nonetheless be forever alienated from the spontaneous child he was. By enshrining the look and word of the Other forever in his consciousness, Genet will discover that "I is another" (SG, p. 138). Sartre is quite clear that the dizzying word which pillories Genet forever in the so-called right-thinking man's conception is a rape—not a metaphorical rape but an actual assault on his being which "took a child and made a monster of him for reasons of social utility" (SG, p. 23).

In reality, although Genet's case is extreme, it is not in its milder forms that far removed from what many children from more "normal" situations experience. Sartre is quite aware that families can impose identities on children by verbally presenting them with prefabricated lives. These can, of course, be positive destinies, in contrast to the negative destiny that had been prepared for Genet. Sartre opposes the imposition of all such prefabricated destinies on children. In his introduction to André Gorz's autobiography, Sartre writes, "It seems that one can still find on earth savages stupid enough to discover reincarnated ancestors in their newborn children. . . . What barbarism! They take a kid who is very much alive and sew him into the skin of a dead man. He will suffocate in this senile childhood without other hope than to poison future childhoods after his death" (quoted by Collins, 1980, pp. 111–12). Or, as Franz says in *The Condemned of Altona*, "Nine months before my birth they had chosen my name, my career, my character and my fate" (p. 75). I cannot help thinking of clients, in the process of becoming parents, who had already identified their unborn child with a particular relative—mother, father, grandfather, dead brother, or even one of the parents. They seemed fully prepared to react to this child as if he or she were that person.

Even where naming does not involve the revelation of a prefabricated destiny, the word can present itself as a rape when it condemns a child to look at a particular spontaneous action—this can be anything from sexual exploration to exuberance—as bad, shameful, wrong, without redemption. A child's reaction can be everything from repressing the feeling or action in order to be "good" in the parent's eyes to deciding, like Genet, to spitefully take on the "bad" identity as one's own. In either case, the word which designates the child as this or that object becomes a form of violation—thereafter alienating the child from his or her own spontaneous being.

Interestingly, this sense of violation occurs even if the inaccurate naming is praise, where the praise involves a distortion of one's real feelings. For example, "What a good little girl you are," can be an injunction to stifle one's spontaneity. Sartre tells us in *The Words* that he had himself as a child experienced the applause of adults which transformed him into a "fake child" whose playacting "robbed me of the world and of human beings" (p. 84). The truth is that even in its mildest forms where accurate naming is intended, the words of the original others have the power to distort experience ever so slightly or, simply by naming, to make one aware of having an outside for others that is different from one's own spontaneous experience. Recognition, or accurate verbal reflection, therefore becomes a critical factor in allowing the child to survive his or her earliest years and still be "very much alive." Although the living death which Sartre describes as Genet's destiny is perhaps relatively rare, very few if any of us make it through those years with our spontaneity fully intact. As with Genet, the "melodious child" in us is usually "dead" long before we reach adulthood (SG, p. 1).[8]

As for the actual physical look, it is too pervasive and fundamental in Sartre's writing to need much explication. From the agonizing look of the third in *No Exit* to the blaming look of the general who married Baudelaire's mother and excluded him from her narcissistic admiration to the look of the "righteous" man on the child-thief Genet to the humiliating and disappointed look of Achille-Cléophas Flaubert on his superfluous son Gustave to the judging look of the future represented by a jury of crabs in *The Condemned of Altona*, this has been a motif in Sartre's fiction and biographies throughout his career. Although it is the prototype of my awareness of the Other's presence as a subject who judges and names me, it is not its only form.

Throughout his writing, through the three forms of the Look, Sartre explores the power which the Other as subject has, on the one hand, to alienate me from myself and, on the other (though this is less often discussed), to make me acquainted with myself. Where a person experiences his or her parents' Look as a narcissistic wound, this is likely to lead to repression of spontaneity—leaving that person, as Sartre says of Genet and Baudelaire, with the predilection to "see himself as another." And as with Baudelaire, his or her life is likely to be "but the story of this failure"—since, of course, the failure of solipsism is that one can never actually be oneself and another (B, p. 32). One must learn to accept and respect the otherness of the Other.

I think we are now in a position to find an ontological grounding for the new relational needs discovered by many post-Freudian drive theorists. The "mirroring" needs discovered by Mahler under the influence of Winnicott, the "good internalized objects" and needs for "self-respect" discussed by Kernberg, and the basically object-seeking libido of Melanie Klein all make sense within a context in which the Other first appears to me not as an object but as a subject. The child is not instinctually and accidentally related to others. He or she is fundamentally related to the Other not as an instinctually gratifying "object" but as another consciousness like his or her own. It is not the Other as an object, not even as a mirroring object, who figures so significantly in one's developing sense of self. Rather, this importance is accorded to the Other as a subject for whom one is oneself an object. We may, from a Sartrean perspective, discover stages in the child's dawning recognition of the full implications of the presence of the Other. But some kind of dim recognition of the Other as another consciousness must have been present almost from the beginning. Relational needs can therefore be understood as a part of the attempt to create a reflective view of self out of the reactions one gets from the earliest significant others.

Of course, such a view is different from Mahler's account of the separation-individuation process as a movement from symbiosis to object constancy. In fact, both Mahler's beginning and ending stages would be discounted for two reasons: First, there can never be an actual merging or symbiosis with the mother—though, according to Sartre's account, the infant's purely prereflective consciousness, which is only dimly aware of its differentiation from the world, might *seem* much more "merged" than the later reflective view of self and world. Sartre's account of the impact of touching in infancy indicates how earliest relations with others prepare the way for a rudimentary reflective sense of body-self. Second, there can never be a stage of internalized object constancy because representations of objects are not actually incorporated into the psyche—as Mahler, Klein, and Kernberg seem to believe. What appear to be introjects or internalized objects are really fantasies in which one attempts to take the reflective view of the Other on oneself as a means to achieving the impossible goal of substantive freedom (a topic I take up in greater detail in the next chapter when I discuss post-Freudian views of the formation of a self).

If, however, Mahler's metatheoretical explanations are at variance with Sartre's, her phenomenological observations of the various stages of infancy and early childhood fit very well with Sartre's concept of the Look. When Mahler talks about the "libidinization of the body," for instance, she is really talking about the bodily sense of self which is gained from the mother's touches and looks. Or when she discusses the way in which the exuberance of the practicing subphase child can be muted by nonvalidating parents, she might almost be quoting Sartre on the nonvalorized infant: Flaubert, Sartre tells us, "has never felt his needs as sovereign demands, the external world has never been his oyster, his larder; the environment is revealed to him little by little in the dreary and cold consistency which Heidegger has named *nur-Vorbeilagen*" (FI, 1:130). Sartre, of course, implies that the "healthy" condition would be for an infant, as Mahler says of the practicing subphase infant, to feel that the world *is* his or her oyster.

The truth is that Sartre's metatheory can, more easily than Freud's, help us to understand the infantile needs which Mahler discovered. Sartre's idea of the significance of the Look allows us to appreciate, for example, why feeding or holding an infant in the "symbiotic" stage in a face to face position that promotes eye contact facilitates psychological growth; why lack of adequate "mirroring" promotes a "symbiotic child psychosis"; why peekaboo games involving seeing and being seen are so important to infants in the differentiation stage; why being looked at increases the differentiating infant's awareness of his or her own body and promotes pleasurable movement; why differentiating infants are less anxious and more curious about a stranger when the stranger averts his or her gaze; why the child in the practicing subphase needs admiration and applause; and why the child in the rapprochement phase woos the mother to participate in his or her every new discovery and experience at the same time that he or she is excessively sensitive to censure or rebuke. Since the Other's Look helps to fix the child's identity from the outside, the Look can be a source of anxiety, as when the child shrinks from the stranger's gaze or the mother's reproof; or it can be a source of security, which happens when the child is valued, enjoyed, and applauded.

If we regard the ontological issues as primary, we might view the child's dawning reflective sense of self as it develops in the presence of others as leading to an existential crisis. In doing so, we would reinterpret Mahler's account of the rapprochement crisis. Mahler explains this crisis as emanating from a realization on the part of the child in the practicing subphase that he or she is, in fact, not all powerful—that the child is still small and dependent after all, and that he or she cannot partake of an omnipotent dual unity with the parent. Thus the elation of the practicing subphase gives way to the somberness of the rapprochement subphase. Yet Mahler also notes that even the child in the practicing subphase is likely to be subdued if the parents' admiration is not forthcoming. I can believe that Mahler is correct in assuming that the child in the practicing subphase is elated over achieving upright locomotion and that this is accompanied by a wonderful elevation in self-esteem—especially if the parents are there to applaud the new achievement. But I think there is something more in the toddler's somberness and moodiness than Mahler suggests.

The rapprochement subphase is not simply a crisis in dependence-independence issues, though it is partially that. Since this is the time of the acquisition of language, it is also, as Daniel Stern suggests, a time which involves a crisis in self-comprehension. According to Stern, "The crisis in self-comprehension occurs because for the first time the infant experiences the self as divided, and rightly senses that no one else can rebind the division. The infant has not lost omnipotence but rather has lost experiential wholeness" (Stern, 1985, pp. 272–73). Verbal representation always causes a division in experience because it is from a reflective rather than a nonreflective position. Of course, reflective awareness had been developing in a rudimentary form before this as a result of the child's awareness of others' looks and touches. Stranger anxiety in the differentiation and rapprochement stages probably emanates from the feeling that the child has an outside beneath the stranger's gaze. And the elation of the child in the practicing subphase is obviously at least in part an elation over having a positively perceived self who can stand and act in the world.

At the same time, the child in the rapprochement stage encounters the reflective power of the word, which makes it more difficult to see the Other simply as an audience. The Other is becoming another person with perceptions of oneself which are foreign to one's actual experience. These empathic failures occur even for the most sensitive parents because words are necessarily a reflective designation of experience rather than spontaneous experience itself. In fact, these failures are probably necessary to draw the child out of his or her sense of being the "object limit" of the parents' freedom—out of the positive narcissism experienced by the normal child in the practicing subphase. However, if the empathic failures are grave—if the parent is indifferent, harshly critical, or verbally or physically abusive—then the movement away from narcissistic needs for total acceptance and appreciation will probably not occur. Having never had the necessary acceptance, the child will not feel that he or she can live without it.

Thus we might view the rapprochement crisis as the beginning of a long process through which an individual, if he or she is to experience genuine reciprocity in relationships, must turn away from simply using the Other to give a sense of self and begin to appreciate the Other as a person in his or her own right. I am not saying that the successful resolution of the rapprochement crisis represents a final solution to this problem, that it is the radical conversion to the philosophy of freedom which Sartre mentions in *Being and Nothingness*. In fact, it may be that the achievement of genuine reciprocity is a problem for the life span. Certainly, the child throughout his or her early years, and even through adolescence in a different way, needs to continue to feel that the parents are basically capable of positive mirroring. But the resolution of the rapprochement crisis may represent the beginning of a renunciation of the demand of the child in the practicing subphase that the Other be all audience, all attention to self. If this is so, the resolution of the rapprochement crisis might, like Klein's depressive position, mark the beginning of a comprehension of the Other as another subject in the fully human sense—not another self, but a separate Other with whom one is able to empathize as well as to disagree.[9] But first comes the crisis, in which one protests not the loss of an omnipotent union which never existed, but the loss of the hope of the union of one's free self with the Other's perfectly harmonious view—that is, the loss of the hope for substantive freedom, or Being-in-itself-for-itself. The delicate "egos" of many borderline, narcissistic, or even neurotic clients may emanate from this inability to renounce the hope of getting a total absorption, understanding, and regard from others which is only appropriately available in early infancy and childhood. They want what they never had or had and lost too soon, the delighted applause of the parents of the child in the practicing subphase: "Look what the baby can do!"

The Implications for Psychotherapy

What difference, then, does a Sartrean perspective make to the practice of psychotherapy? Although I believe that the very discovery and formal recognition of new relational needs make contemporary psychoanalysis more sensitive to important interpersonal and developmental issues, I also think that there are certain significant differences which a Sartrean reinterpretation of clinical data could make to the way therapists work with their patients or clients.

1. The therapist using a Sartrean perspective can once and for all lay to rest the tendency to think about relational issues in drive language—that is, libidinal and aggressive drives, anal stage oppositionalism, oral rage and envy—and thus avoid the tendency to cloud therapeutic interpretations with such thinking. Although an existentialist perspective would not deny the existence and importance of spontaneous desires and feelings, the question becomes one of determining how these are filtered through and affected by one's earliest relations with others. In other words, it is not the Oedipal struggle which is so much at issue as my way of defining myself as a sensual/sexual person on the basis of my earliest relations with others. In fact, the child's struggle could just as easily refer to acceptance or rejection of himself or herself as a joyful person or a sad or angry person—in other words, to any relationship between spontaneous feelings and actions and reflective perceptions as these are influenced by the original others.

For example, I think of a client who, the minute he starts to feel happy, begins to look for problems within or outside himself. His mother's reaction to his feeling good was something like this: "You can't be happy when X is wrong with you/me/the world." He now truncates his joy with a reflective view that anticipates difficulties. From a Sartrean perspective, one need not necessarily look beneath this scenario for sexual implications and meanings. The reflective suppression of joy is just as much a possibility as the reflective suppression of sexual urges.

2. The existentialist therapist can zero in on particular categories of expe-

riences of the Look which might not otherwise be available without Sartre's concepts. Does the negative self-representation which a client has adopted or against which he or she is guarding emanate from a particular kind of look, touch, or word? In this regard, I have had clients become aware of the origins of whole sets of negative self-appraisals and/or interpersonal fears by asking, at appropriate junctures, questions such as these: What was your mother/father's touch like? How would you imagine the look in your mother/father's eye when you did/said that? What, in particular, did your mother/father say when you acted exuberant/expressed anger/refused to obey, and so on?

Obviously, the relevant memories are sometimes less accessible to direct questioning or accessible only through contemporary transference situations. For example, the woman mentioned earlier who felt as if she had leprosy or alligator skin had no memory of her mother's feelings about touching her as an infant. But she did have a "skin" feeling about how contemporary others might respond to her. In this instance, her block to positive reciprocity lay in a negative anticipation of bodily rejection—not in critical words or looks. On the other hand, people who are pathologically shy are almost always supersensitive to the negative looks of others—as though judging eyes follow their every movement or gesture. Or sometimes the problem is with critical words, in which case the client finds himself or herself hyper-reacting to the slightest hint of negative evaluation or else discounting others in advance as a defense against such evaluations. There is also the person who was neglected and who hungers for any look, touch, or word of acknowledgment—and feels empty and lost when this is not forthcoming. Perhaps one category of response was missing and not others: For example, a parent may have offered words of encouragement but withheld touching or eye contact. It is, in fact, important to discover which category of the Look wounded the child or which kind of response was denied to him or her. When such experiences are uncovered in all their concrete reality, therapy becomes less intellectual and more affecting on a "gut level."

3. The therapist with a Sartrean orientation can more accurately understand and interpret motives for the continuation of painful relations with others and/or self. He or she can attempt to locate the point on the sado-masochistic circle from which the client is currently conducting his or her unhappy relationships. Obviously, this may be different with different people or at different times in a client's history, making a historical perspective on relationship issues important. The objective is to uncover the ontological motives, past or present, for a client's taking various positions in his

or her attempts to create a substantive self and to expose the impossible nature of this quixotic quest.

Of course, in working with these issues, existentialist therapists would seldom use theoretical terms such as "Being-in-itself-for-itself" in talking with clients, any more than classical analysts would use the technical terms of Freudian metatheory. But these philosophical concepts would nonetheless inform their clinical interpretations and questions. For example, I might, remembering Sartre's reconstruction of the life of Genet, guess that a particular client's insistence on failing occurs because he or she is determined to "*be* the failure they said I was.*" In fact, I frequently discover this kind of motive in people: It is often both a means to revenge and an active assumption of a previously passive destiny.

Perhaps I might come to understand that a particular women client, who is going over the details of her very painful divorce for the thousandth time two years later, is still working with the loss of the impossible goal of being the "object limit" of her ex-husband's freedom. She wishes to nullify his judgments in her own mind. Or I might guess that another client's need to dominate in his relationships—and his dropping the women as soon as dominance is achieved—is an attempt to incorporate the Other's freedom from the position of desire/sadism. This latter situation may further indicate an avoidance of an earlier failure, thereby representing a mode of escape from the masochistic merging demanded by a mother (or father) who wished to use the child either as a mirror or as a narcissistic extension of self.

Furthermore, with respect to using other people to gain an identity, I may find myself working with a client who attempts to force a warm relationship with a cold and distant partner. I may ask, "What would it *do* for you to have this person respond in the way you want?" The answer is likely to be, "It would make me feel more alive/loved/lovable/valuable and so on." Mind you, not just any relationship will perform this miracle—only one which resembles the negative relationship with an original other. An existentialist interpretation of this situation is different from Freud's idea of "transference" and the "repetition compulsion" in that it does not use the mechanical nature of the libido and death instinct as explanatory principles. Instead, one understands that this client is actively seeking to use the Other to become a certain kind of self by gaining a certain kind of response from a certain kind of Other—as though someone resembling the magician who cast the original spell over one's capacity to *be* this or that must remove it.

Once the illusory nature of this quest is revealed (both the fact that the questing person is not so much desiring to *love*, as he or she thinks, but to *be loved* in a particular way and the fact that it is no longer possible to gain in this way the sense of confident being one might have had as a child from one's parents), it becomes possible to give up a quest which is contradictory in terms. In other words, I will by definition not be able to have warmth and love from a person who prefers to remain cold and distant—unless, of course, that person changes, in which case he or she will no longer resemble the cold and distant parent.

Giving up the impossible quest is not, however, an easy task, since it amounts to a conversion to a philosophy of freedom on the part of a person who has never had his or her fill of secure contingency. Also, the ways in which a client uses others to fulfill his or her original project of being are never simple. The mystifying connections between reflective views of self, relations with contemporary and original others, and the conundrums formed out of the attempt to achieve the in-itself-for-itself are often as intricate as Sartre's psychobiographies indicate.

4. The existentialist therapist can gain a clear view of the kinds of relationships which might be the goal of therapy—relationships involving genuine positive reciprocity—and hence of the false expectations and actions which can block the development of such relationships. For example, attention can be drawn to the way in which a client, in his or her heart of hearts, cannot brook the slightest disagreement on the part of a lover, demands perfect understanding and constant attention, and gets (secretly or openly) enraged and accusatory if these are not forthcoming. Obviously, the client will not present the situation in this light, but will instead, sometimes simultaneously or in succession, either blame the other person for resisting his or her legitimate requests or blame himself or herself for not being more independent. These reactions must be explored without judgment, and therapist and client should try to understand their aim—which is usually some version of the attempt to attain substantive freedom.

In the end, the trick is to feel the emotions (rather than to repress them), to trace them to their origins in the distant past, and to refuse to act them out in current relationships—a refusal which tends to intensify them and therefore to make their origins more apparent. Ultimately, the demand that the Other should make oneself whole must be renounced in favor of a more genuinely reciprocal acceptance of the other person as different from oneself and as having needs which have nothing to do with one's own needs to be constantly adored and accepted. But this is a difficult and tricky process, one which is, needless to say, not under the control of reflective resolution or will.

This scenario is not, of course, the only possible one in which genuine reciprocity is lacking. With a different kind of client, the therapist might work to discover the feelings of powerlessness at the hands of original others which have led to a passion for manipulating and controlling others. Or one might explore the fear of the Look which lies behind submission, indifference, or avoidance of genuine intimacy.

5. Finally, adopting a Sartrean perspective can make a great difference in the client-therapist relationship. Even traditional transference issues in which a client projects onto a therapist childhood conflicts with mother, father, sister, brother, and so on might be understood differently. For example, the existentialist therapist might ask what particular kind of subject/object conflict the projected relationship points to? Also, what permutations have there been in a client's original way of relating to others? Do a client's attempts to relate to the therapist indicate a desire to submerge the self in the Other (masochism), to submerge the Other in the self (sadism), or to manipulate the Other as an object which can never become a subject or can only become a subject under the control and domination of oneself (narcissism, psychopathy, and sociopathy)? Or has the client withdrawn into an attitude of indifference (schizoid withdrawal) as a result of previous hurts and/or irresolvable conflicts?

Interpretations of these various positions might stress the wound which the client received in terms of the Looks—or indifference—of the original others and the ways in which the client expects this situation to be repeated with the therapist. The therapist can also be aware that approval, therapeutic or parental, can be damaging when it encourages inauthenticity. The existentialist therapist can be attentive to possible ways in which the therapeutic relationship can heal through accurate reflection and genuine relatedness. And he or she can attempt to avoid situations in which the therapeutic relationship leads to further distortions—as might happen, for example, if a therapist is unwilling to abandon the position of witness (technical neutrality) when what the client needs is not neutrality but rather an experience of positive reciprocity.

From the preceding discussion, we can see that a Sartrean perspective both answers some intrinsic difficulties in post-Freudian psychoanalytic theory, as represented by the discovery of nondrive-related relational needs, and suggests new therapeutic insights that are unavailable from a traditional

Freudian viewpoint. In the next chapter, we shall see how a Sartrean perspective on the self can clear the way to a fuller understanding of the impact of relational issues on human development and psychopathology.

4 · Sartre and the Post-Freudian Relational Theorists: Toward a Psychoanalytic Theory of the Self

What Is the Self?

One of the interesting developments in recent psychoanalytic theory is the introduction of the phenomenological term "self" in place of the structural term "ego." The popularity of concepts of the "self" in psychoanalytic circles is evident from the number of recent books that contain the term in their titles—even if one excludes from the list books dealing with the so-called self psychology of Heinz Kohut. I believe that this reintroduction of a subject at the heart of experience is a concomitant of the discovery by post-Freudian relational theorists of others as people rather than as mere gratifiers of instinctual needs. Despite certain theoretical confusions in the work of these theorists, I agree with Roy Schafer that "the popularity of concepts of self and identity is symptomatic of a fundamental shift toward a modern conception of theory making and a modern psychological concern with specifically human phenomenology. . . . Freudian analysis can only benefit from such a shift" (1976, p. 192).

On the other hand, I believe that the lack of grounding in metatheory of psychoanalytic concepts of the self leads to many different and confused interpretations of the term, as well as to a kind of reification of the self, similar to Freud's reification of the ego, which is not helpful to therapeutic insights. I believe that Sartre's ontology can help to create a metatheoretical understanding of the self[1] which can clarify both the need to create a substantial self which is discovered by these theorists and the need to transcend the idea that one can *have* a substantial self—a topic not addressed by most relational theorists.

The discovery of the significance of the need to create a self by post-

Freudian relational theorists is, as I have noted, a concomitant of their discovery that purely relational needs—rather than drives—lie at the heart of human development. If post-Freudian drive theorists cannot avoid the discovery of new relational needs which call into question the economic hypothesis of Freud, relational theorists are even more emphatic in their insistence on the primacy of relational needs from the beginning of life. No relational theorist, for instance, accepts Freud's concept of primary narcissism, as Margaret Mahler does. Instead, relational theorists concentrate on the significance of relations with others from earliest infancy. Nor does any relational theorist accept Freud's view of the death instinct or the primacy of aggression, as Melanie Klein does.

As for the economic hypothesis, most relational theorists are more straightforward than the drive theorists in facing the implications of the new relational discoveries for traditional metatheory. Thus they are more likely than drive theorists to disregard or to ignore drive theory completely. As Harry Guntrip, who is perhaps the most radical of the British object relations theorists, puts the matter, it is time to discard outmoded Freudian drive theory altogether in favor of a "consistently psychodynamic theory of the unique individual in his personal relations" (Guntrip, 1969, p. 382). Other relational theorists, such as D. W. Winnicott, are more circumspect in their departures from Freudian orthodoxy, although most pay little heed to the drives. Perhaps that is why relational theorists are less likely than drive theorists to obscure new discoveries by using traditional economic terms and concepts.

Instead, these theorists characteristically either change the meaning of traditional Freudian terms or invent new terms for new discoveries. Thus W. R. D. Fairbairn states unequivocally that "libido is not primarily pleasure-seeking but object-seeking" (1952, p. 137)—thereby radically changing the meaning of "libido" to indicate the pursuit of relationships rather than the pursuit of pleasure. Or Michael Balint (1969) replaces primary narcissism with "primary object love"—which he defines as the desire to *be loved*. Or D. W. Winnicott (1965a, 1965b, 1971) rejects primary narcissism and autoeroticism in favor of a concept of the "nursing couple" (mother and baby) for whom purely relational needs are primary. Similarly, Harry Stack Sullivan's "tenderness theorem" (1940, 1953) indicates relational needs for giving and receiving love on the part of the mother and baby from birth. And John Bowlby (1969, 1980) proposes a new relational drive which is evolutionarily based. As for the meaning of these relational needs, their aim is clearly something other than the tension reduction of Freudian drive theory. In fact, their aim is the creation of a self rather than the pursuit of plea-sure. Thus it is that Heinz Kohut (1977, 1984) renames them "selfobject" needs to distinguish them from the "libidinal object" needs of Freud. Actu-ally, as we shall see, these needs have nothing to do with the Other as ob-ject, but rather refer to the child's experience of himself or herself as an ob-ject for another subject.

The significance of earliest relations with others to the formation of a self is not, of course, an exclusive concern of post-Freudian relational theorists. As we saw in the preceding chapter, the development of a self or identity is also an important issue in the work of drive theorists such as Erikson, Mahler, Jacobson, and Kernberg. Yet though these theorists sometimes slip into a more active use of the term "self" (Mahler, Jacobson, and Kernberg) or "identity" (Erikson), they basically accept Hartmann's traditional defini-tion of the self, or rather the "self-representation,"[2] as a phenomenological concept referring to a set of images similar to the set of images of objects formed by the ego. As we have seen in the work of Mahler, drive theorists are often unaware that the pursuit of a self or sense of identity as a superor-dinate aim is incompatible with Freudian drive theory—with which they try to reconcile it. The self of relational theorists, on the other hand, is clearly not simply the set of passive images of Hartmann; it is also an active, orga-nizing center of behavior. The self of relational theorists is a subject rather than an object—or it is a combination of subject and object.

Theoretical confusion concerning the term "self" arises in part because of a philosophical confusion about the nature of consciousness or the psyche which is inherited from Freud. Although relational theorists have often felt a need to speak of a personal self rather than an impersonal ego, they have not altogether left behind Freud's idea that the psyche is a *thing* which has substance and structure. Thus in the work of relational theorists such as Heinz Kohut, discussions of the "structuralization of the self" replace discus-sions of the "structuralization of the ego." Or, in a formulation which seems to me much closer to the truth, Harry Stack Sullivan extends the economic hypothesis of Freud to develop a view of the self not as a thing per se but as a set of energy transformations. Or, in the work of D. W. Winnicott, Harry Guntrip, and James Masterson (1985), the discovery of a "true self" becomes not a matter of simple authentic living but of uncovering such a self beneath the conformist shell of a "false self," both of which are regarded as entities.

In post-Freudian theory, there is often a great deal of confusion about the nature of the self as subject and as object—a confusion inherited from Freud's own discussions of the ego. This is perhaps nowhere better illustrated than in Masterson's book *The Real Self*, which provides a kind of summary of contemporary psychoanalytic perspectives on the self. This is particularly evident when Masterson mixes drive terms with relational terms, as in the following statement: "Simultaneously and in parallel with the maturation of ego functions, and with self and object representations becoming whole, the now whole, separate real self becomes autonomous and takes on its capacities" (1985, p. 26). How, we ask, does this self differ from the ego with which it matures "in parallel"? How does it differ from the false self with which it is compared? And how do whole self-representations, which imply the self as an object of reflection, lead to an autonomous self with the "capacities" of a subject? The list of capacities of the self which Masterson provides to support the preceding assertion does not at all clarify matters. In a discussion that summarizes a good deal of post-Freudian literature on the self, he lumps together under the rubric of "self" a number of functions which Sartre would label as either "reflective" or "prereflective." The resulting confusion is one that often pervades ordinary discourse—but psychological description should be more precise.[3]

I believe that Sartre's view of the self can help to resolve some of this theoretical confusion. As Hazel Barnes (1983) notes, Sartre uses the term "self" in three different, sharply defined ways. There is the spontaneous self of prereflective consciousness, which is the center of action and conscious life. We might also, if we do not introduce implications of substance, refer to this self as the agent or doer. There is the self of reflective awareness, designated by Sartre as the "ego," which is an object rather than a subject. And there is the self as aim or value—the self which is the future goal and meaning of human activity, of one's "project of being." This is the self as a pursuit rather than as an actual entity. Although it can be reflected on, it is not necessarily an object of reflection; in fact, it is frequently reflectively misconceived. The ultimate aim of the self as value is the pursuit of Being-in-itself-for-itself, substantive freedom.

Such a pursuit of self or meaning is never isolated or autonomous. It is always made on the face of a particular world and it is bodily oriented. Sartre asserts, "Without the world there is no selfness, no person; without selfness, without the person, there is no world" (BN, p. 104). According to this view, the enclosed psyche of traditional Freudian theory is not a possibility. Interestingly, it is only the reflective glance backward or the prospective glance forward which gives one a sense of having a (pseudo) self in the substantive sense. In the present, one is all translucidity, all movement toward or away from the objects which compose one's experience—including the reflective experience of self as an object which so concerns and occupies each of us. Although Sartre never spells out these three usages of self, they are quite clear in context.

The post-Freudian relational theorists, on the other hand, run into many theoretical difficulties when they confuse the self as agent with the self as object. I believe this happens partly because they fail to recognize the full significance of the self as value. Obviously, post-Freudian relational theorists could hardly be expected to clarify these issues without first shifting metatheoretical premises—without, for example, substituting the ontology of Sartre for Freudian metatheory. Without some such ontological perspective, they have no way of understanding why the creation of an adequate self becomes so important to human development. Because of this, these theorists, like their patients, may fall into the inauthentic position of reifying the psyche and thereby conceive the aim of therapy to be the provision of the missing "substance" and "structure" which the patient thinks he or she needs.

Although the terrible "identity diffusion" syndrome described by Erikson (1959, 1968) and the "disintegration anxiety" described by Kohut (1984) are certainly very real experiences for some clients, they do not point to the need for psychological structure in the substantive sense but rather to a need on the part of the client to learn to structure experience in the existential sense. If this is so, then a recognition and acceptance of the radical freedom of the individual may have much more to do with psychological "healing," especially in the later stages of therapy, than has hitherto been recognized.

In pointing out these difficulties, I do not mean to ignore the very real theoretical advances that post-Freudian relational theorists have made. These theorists generally recognize the organizing nature of the human psyche ("consciousness" in Sartre's terminology), and they realize that the attempt to create a particular kind of self in the world is a primary human motivation. They also emphasize the significance of relations with others in the formation of such a self. If we look at the work of the American interpersonal psychoanalysts, the British object relations theorists, and the American self psychologists who follow Heinz Kohut, we cannot help being struck by the emphasis on the significance of human relations rather than drive gratification to personality formation. While I believe such a shift is salutary, I think it needs a metatheoretical grounding which will allow both a clarification of confusions and an understanding of the superordinate desire to create a self or to experience oneself as *being* this or that.

In this chapter, I provide a Sartrean critique of theories of the self as they are presented in the work of three influential post-Freudian relational theorists from three different "schools": Harry Stack Sullivan, D. W. Winnicott, and Heinz Kohut. Like the drive theorists discussed in the preceding chapter, these theorists derive their ideas about relational needs from work with more severely disturbed adults or from work with children. Sullivan was one of the first psychiatrists to successfully treat schizophrenics with a form of psychoanalysis. Along with fellow interpersonal theorists Clara Thompson, Karen Horney, Frieda Fromm-Reichmann, and Erich Fromm, he emphasizes the sociocultural as well as the individual origins of psychological disorders. Of the three relational theorists I discuss, Sullivan is probably the most forward-looking in his awareness of nondrive-oriented relational needs and his refusal to reify the self.

D. W. Winnicott, who derives his theory from work with children rather than psychotic adults, is similar to Sullivan in noting the effects of earliest family relations—especially that of the mother and infant—on personality development and pathology. Yet like fellow British object relations theorists W. R. D. Fairbairn, Michael Balint, and Harry Guntrip, Winnicott is less interested in sociocultural influences than Sullivan and more inclined to reify the self. This tendency toward reification is perhaps an inheritance from Melanie Klein, whose view of internal "objects" and "partial objects" heavily influenced the British theorists. Heinz Kohut, who is a specialist in treating narcissistic personality disorders, presents a still more reified view of the self as an entity in need of structure and organization. On the other hand, he is the most precise of all the relational theorists in characterizing the various relational needs that facilitate the formation of a firm and flexible self.

Hence while the post-Freudian relational theorists provide some significant insights into the formation of a personal sense of self, they do not for the most part avoid the tendencies toward reification in psychoanalytic theory in general. Nor do they clarify the metatheoretical premises on which their own discoveries would have to be based. I believe that Sartre's ontology does answer the question of why a firm sense of self as object seems so important at the same time that it allows us to understand that the establishment of such a substantive self is not the final aim of psychotherapy. That aim is instead a full and responsible acceptance of the spontaneity and freedom of the prereflective self as agent—an aim which is understandable from a Sartrean but not from a traditional Freudian perspective.

Relations with Others and the Creation of a "Self":
Three Post-Freudian Views

In the preceding chapter, we discovered that the drives of post-Freudian drive theorists usually turned out to be emotions and that the discovery of new relational needs for mirroring, self-esteem, attachment, and so on tended to undermine orthodox Freudian metatheory. Furthermore, drive theorists such as Erik Erikson, Edith Jacobson, Margaret Mahler, and Otto Kernberg found themselves interested in the way in which the meeting of relational needs leads to the development of a sense of identity or self. Yet these theorists were also reluctant to stray too far from traditional Freudian terminology and explanatory principles. Thus they continued to speak of drives, mechanisms, psychosexual stages, libido, and aggression, seemingly without noticing that their orthodox language was undermined by their discoveries of new relational needs.

The relational theorists I have selected for discussion here are generally less constrained by traditional Freudian concepts and terminology (though D. W. Winnicott does make bows in the direction of accommodation) and more open to new terminology and new ways of conceptualizing psychological development. They seem to take for granted, for instance, that relational needs are primary, and they move from there to a discussion of how the meeting or frustration of relational needs leads to the formation of a "self"—a term they generally prefer to the traditional Freudian term ego. Yet in doing so, they carry with them some of the traditional Freudian baggage, particularly the tendency to view the psyche as an entity with substance and structure.

The degree of reification, however, varies with the theorist. Harry Stack Sullivan is the least guilty of reifying the self. Heinz Kohut, whose views in this respect have greatly influenced contemporary American relational theory, is the most guilty. And D. W. Winnicott is somewhere in between. All three contribute valuable insights into the way in which earliest relations with others influence the development of a self. Yet none fully understands the self in its three Sartrean forms—as prereflective consciousness or agent, as object or ego, and as aim or value. I believe that a Sartrean perspective on post-Freudian relational theory can clarify theoretical confusions, thereby making the contribution of these theorists even more clinically useful.

Let us begin with Sullivan, who, although one of the first, is at the same time perhaps the most radical of relational theorists. Sullivan is seldom given credit as the originator of ideas which many subsequent relational theorists have developed, perhaps independently of Sullivan. Yet, as Greenberg and Mitchell note, the fact that Sullivan's concerns and formulations were often derided by classical Freudians during his lifetime has not precluded his having had an enormous influence on contemporary psychoanalytic thinking: "It has been suggested that Sullivan 'secretly dominates' much of modern clinical psychiatry in the United States . . . and that he has been 'America's most important and unique contributor to dynamic psychiatry' " (1983, pp. 80–81). In contrast to many post-Freudian theorists, Sullivan appears not to have agonized over departures from traditional Freudian theory. Instead, he simply offered substitute concepts where these seemed correct.

Hence Sullivan's view of the psyche differs radically from Freud's. Rejecting the idea of primary narcissism, Sullivan believes that the infant is relationally oriented from the beginning of life and that this relational orientation continues throughout a person's development. Sullivan's tenderness theorem states that need in the infant is inclined to evoke tender responsiveness in the "mothering one."[4] Where this does not occur, difficulties arise in the formation of what Sullivan calls the "self," or "self-system," of the child. While these relational needs vary according to the age of the child (a view with which Mahler and Winnicott would agree), reciprocity is viewed as a natural occurrence rather than as a graft onto the root of primary narcissism or secondary experiences of gratification/frustration.

Sullivan's self-system is a complex concept, incorporating both the more conservative view of the self of ego psychology (the self as a set of representations) and the more radical view of many relational theorists (the self as a center of personality organization) within an overview which (unlike many more recent formulations) refuses to see the self as a static entity at all. Sullivan's self, or self-system, is not a structure but a "dynamism"—which he defines as "a relatively enduring pattern of energy transformations" (1953, p. 103). As a system of representations, the self is organized around the "reflected appraisals" of the original caregivers (Sullivan, 1940, p. 22) in a manner similar to the mirroring experiences noted by Winnicott and Mahler. These reflected appraisals lead to "good-me," "bad-me," and "not-me" definitions of areas of experience which are predicated on parental approval or disapproval. Anxiety arises not as the result of a superfluity of undischarged libidinal energy, as Freud believes, but as a response to the threat posed by disowned experiences to one's conception of self.

Sullivan is quite adamant in rejecting Freud's physicalist view of anxiety, commenting that anxiety has "nothing whatever to do with the physico-chemical needs of the living young" but rather is related to the "*personal* [and interpersonal] environment" (1953, p. 42). Mother's anxiety about certain behavior induces a similar anxiety in the child through "empathic resonance"; the child subsequently defines the anxiety-provoking behavior as "bad me" or, if the anxiety is more extreme, as "not me," thereby achieving security at the sacrifice of diminished possibilities for satisfaction. The aim of the self-system is to secure "necessary satisfaction without incurring much anxiety" (Sullivan, 1953, p. 169). Conflicts arise when security and satisfaction are at odds—when reflected appraisals necessary for security demand the sacrifice of spontaneous satisfactions. The self-system is therefore not the whole personality, since the disowned experiences may resurface in other forms. Indeed, it is not a real entity at all but rather a "quasi-entity" or set of "security operations." This is the active side of Sullivan's self-system—the organization of experience so that it will not contradict one's self-definition (whether this is based primarily on "good-me" or "bad-me" experiences) and hence threaten the security which is necessary to ward off unbearable anxiety.

Sullivan's concept of the conflict between security and satisfaction is not simply a new version of Freud's idea of the structural conflict between ego, superego, and id or between unconscious wishes and conscious restrictions. First of all, the security operations of Sullivan's self-system are not based on fear of punishment; instead, they derive from ontological anxiety about the kind of person one *is* in the eyes of others. Second, in Sullivan's system, there are no internalized others, or "internal objects." There are merely the various operations designed to avoid anxiety-arousing threats to one's sense of self. Although Sullivan recognizes that this anxiety is predicated on memories of earlier interpersonal situations which cause unpleasant anticipation of similar situations, he is suspicious of the usual structural conceptualization of this process. Thus he comments that "if you wish, you can talk about the significant person having been introjected and becoming the superego, but I think you are apt to have mental indigestion" (Sullivan, 1956, p. 232).

As for unconscious motivations, Sullivan does not usually speak of the exclusion of conflicting tendencies as unconscious, though he provisionally accepts Freud's notion of unconscious mental life. Still, Sullivan's concept of the unconscious, in passages such as the following one, appears to be quite different from Freud's:

The unconscious, from the way I have actually presented the thing, is quite clearly that which cannot be experienced directly, which fills all the gaps in the mental life. In that rather broad sense, the postulate of the unconscious has, as far as I know, nothing in the world the matter with it. As soon as you begin to arrange the furniture in something that cannot be directly experienced, you are engaged in a work that requires more than parlor magic and you are apt to be embarrassed by some skeptic. (1964, p. 204)

Sullivan himself prefers terms such as "covert operations," "selective inattention," and "parataxic [mapping childhood interpersonal situations onto the present] distortions"[5] to describe lack of awareness. He comments, "Much of that which is ordinarily said to be *repressed* is merely unformulated" (1940, p. 185). It is lived but not reflectively understood. Certainly, for Sullivan, the exclusion of experience from awareness is an operation rather than a mechanism.

Such exclusion points to the paradoxical nature of the self-system as a means to stability on the one hand and a source of stagnation on the other. Sullivan concludes that the self-system is simultaneously "the principal stumbling block to favorable changes in the personality" and the "principal influence that stands in the way of unfavorable changes in the personality [that is, disintegration resulting from intolerable anxiety]" (1953, p. 169). The self-system aims to create the illusion of substance. Change, on the other hand, requires the willingness to face the anxiety which arises in the face of shifts even in negative self-appraisals. Such shifts are always interpersonal and not merely intrapsychic, and the unbearable anxiety associated with them arises precisely *because* psyches are not things, as we might like to believe.

Sullivan writes of the fear of change on the part even of schizophrenic patients, who might on the surface seem of all psychiatric patients to have the most motivation to want to change:

You may be wondering why the schizophrenic person goes on suffering the terrifying experiences when everything would be resolved by accepting the dissociated tendencies into the self. This is a rather natural question, if one has lost hold of the interpersonal principle, and instead is thinking of the self as a thing and the dissociated as another thing, the two being the units which make up a personality. To "accept a dissociated tendency system into the self" is tantamount to undergoing an extensive change in personality, implying a marked change in the sorts of interpersonal situations in which one will have one's being. Not only is there this element of great change, but also there is no possibility of foresight as to the direction and extent of the change. (1940, pp. 142–43)

Sullivan is one of a very small number of post-Freudian theorists to recognize that the fear of change as such is an inhibiting factor in therapy, a motive for what is usually referred to as "resistance." In fact, he occasionally suggests that in a culture which is not repressive an individual might find no need to develop a self-system at all because there would be no forbidden areas against which to defend oneself.

Sullivan is able to so clearly see the paradoxically useful and inhibiting aspects of the self-system partially because he avoids thinking of psychological reality in terms of stagnant structures; he prefers instead a "dynamic" (in Sullivan's, not Freud's, sense of the term) orientation which is future as well as past oriented. Sullivan insists that "experience functions in both recall and foresight" (1953, p. 170). The therapist's task is to "determine what the patient is trying to do" (Sullivan, quoting William Alanson White, 1940, p. 177) in terms of what might have been done to him or her. Thus therapists must center their endeavors around discovering how patients are avoiding the anticipated reliving of past anxiety-provoking interpersonal situations in the present relational context. It is the duty of the therapist to call attention to this repetition based on "unpleasant anticipation" and to work with the patient in a healing process which is necessarily interpersonal.

Unlike traditional ego psychology, interpersonal psychoanalysis concentrates not on building structure *in* the personality, but rather on the way in which a particular patient *structures* reality (including that important part of reality in which one defines and maintains a sense of self). Sullivan calls the final view of the patient's experience at which patient and therapist arrive together "consensual validation." It signals the arrival of the patient at a "syntaxic," or interpersonally verifiable, view of reality, as opposed to the private meanings and defended (good or bad) fantasies about the self with which the patient entered therapy. In other words, the patient does not strive to make the unconscious conscious in the usual Freudian sense, but rather to give up "parataxic" distortions of reality—that is, distortions based on purely personal connections, associations, and anticipations of interactions and their impact on self-esteem deriving from childhood experiences which are no longer interpersonally valid.

The relational theorists who succeeded Sullivan repeat his insights in many ways but with certain additions; most of them do not credit him as a source. Where these theorists do not follow Sullivan, it is often in what I consider to be an adverse direction—that of reifying the self as Freud reifies the tripartite psyche and as the ego psychologists reify the ego. D. W. Winnicott is the British object relations theorist whose insights most closely resemble those of Sullivan. Winnicott, as a pediatrician turned child psychiatrist, is as aware as Sullivan that mere gratification of physical needs does not promote optimal development. In fact, Winnicott notes that "it is possible to gratify an oral drive and by doing so to *violate* the infant's ego-function, or that which will later on be jealously guarded as the self, the core of the personality" if the feeding becomes a seduction away from more significant interpersonal satisfactions (1965b, p. 57). It is definitely not "instinctual satisfaction that makes a baby begin to be, to feel that life is real, to find life worth living" (Winnicott, 1971, p. 116); rather, it is the development of a sense of meaning and purpose, a sense of an authentic self derived from accurate mirroring and holding by the original caregivers.

Like Sullivan, Winnicott therefore discards Freud's concept of primary narcissism, though he occasionally retains the term while giving it a new meaning. According to Winnicott, there is no such thing as a baby—there is only the "nursing couple." And like Sullivan, Winnicott views the mother's need to respond as the natural complement to the child's need for responsiveness. Winnicott names his version of Sullivan's tenderness theorem "primary maternal preoccupation," and, like Sullivan, he observes that it normally lessens as the child's needs for separation-individuation come to the forefront.

Even Winnicott's notation of the "mirroring" needs of the infant and young child has its antecedent in Sullivan's "reflected appraisals." As is the case with negative and damaging reflected appraisals, negative mirroring can lead to the suppression of spontaneous needs and desires. The ontological basis of mirroring needs is even more strongly indicated by Winnicott than by Sullivan, since for Winnicott it is not only negative appraisals that can cause difficulties but also neglect, or lack of mirroring. The child needs a witness in order to develop, to gain a sense of being. Neglect, or absence of adequate mirroring, leads to the feelings of disintegration, emptiness, and lack of a core personality which characterize schizoid personality disorders. Such emptiness may be covered over by the development of a false self, which goes through the motions of living but can never be touched in its core. Negative mirroring also leads to the development of a false self on a compliance basis, as contrasted with the development of a true self—which occurs when the parents mostly accept, encourage, and positively channel the expression of spontaneous needs.

Thus the self-system of Sullivan is divided in two by Winnicott and provided with a kind of reificatory hue. If Winnicott means by a true self only authentic, spontaneous living and by a false self only compliant, overly adaptational living, then the terms need not imply reification. They are simply designations for two different modes of living, with the self for Winnicott implying a center of personality organization. While Winnicott often uses the terms in this way, he moves in the direction of reification when, for example, he maintains that one purpose of the false self is to safeguard the true self—as though the true self were a homunculus in the personality to be uncovered and triumphantly brought forward by therapy.

I do not dispute the fact that Winnicott's description of the situation is a persistent fantasy on the part of patients or clients. But I have to agree with Sullivan that there is, in fact, no hidden true self to be discovered in the course of therapy; there is merely a different orientation toward reality which must be achieved by dispelling the "negative anticipations" which characterize distortions of interpersonal reality. In some ways, Winnicott's conceptualization may be more comforting to patients than Sullivan's—since they could use it to minimize the unspeakable anxiety associated with fundamental change in the direction of the unknown interpersonal future of which Sullivan writes so well. But that does not make Winnicott's ideas more true or more useful to therapists, who need to recognize and deal honestly with the ontologically based anxiety associated with such moments of change.

Part of the difficulty with Winnicott seems to be his allegiance to Freudian terminology. This difficulty with accommodating traditional Freudian terms to his own new relational concepts is perhaps nowhere better exemplified than in the many passages in which Winnicott appears to give lip service to orthodox concepts while in reality either ignoring or reinterpreting them. A familiar pattern of Winnicott's is to begin a talk or a chapter with a nod toward a traditional Freudian concept, followed by much discordant material, or to conclude with a bow toward Freudian orthodoxy which does not follow from the preceding argument. For example, Winnicott begins one such talk with a summary of Freud's concept of the psychosexual stages, expressing his hope that the audience will agree that anything he says about growth from dependence to independence "does not in any way invalidate the statement I might have [just] made of growth in terms of erotogenic zones, or of object relating" (1965b, p. 83). The truth, however, is that Winnicott's concept of primary dependency or relatedness, which he proceeds to describe, is antithetical to Freud's concept of primary objectless narcissism.

Similarly, in another piece, Winnicott takes great pains to distinguish the happy normal play of children from play which is complicated by bodily excitement, pointing out that this not simply a difference in degree but in kind. He then concludes the chapter with the perplexing statement, "We may pay tribute to the importance of ego-relatedness *per se* without giving up the ideas that underlie the concept of sublimation" (1965b, p. 35). One wonders how this is possible, since Winnicott has just proceeded to divest normal play of its libidinal roots. Again, Winnicott, following a chapter on the true self and the false self which has hardly any connection with orthodox Freudian concepts, concludes by saying, "As far as I can see it [Winnicott's own approach] involves no important change in basic [Freudian] theory" (1965b, p. 152). How, one is left wondering, is authenticity connected with drive gratification/frustration?

The matter becomes even more confusing when Winnicott uses traditional Freudian terms with altered (relational) meanings. For instance, Winnicott attempts to equate his own idea of infantile dependence with Freud's idea of primary narcissism (Winnicott, 1965b, p. 44). The truth is that Winnicott's mother-child couple and Freud's objectless libidinal state are fundamentally incompatible. Or Winnicott claims an affinity between his own notion of a true self and a false self and Freud's "division of the self into a part that is central and powered by the instincts (or by what Freud called sexuality, pregenital and genital) and a part that is turned outward and is related to the world" (1965b, p. 140). Freud clearly does not intend to equate id impulses with a true self and ego development with a false self. Nor is this what Winnicott means by the true self and the false self, since Winnicott makes it clear that the true self is capable of "concern" for others and value development as well as spontaneous desire.

The characteristics of Winnicott's true self are spontaneity, integrity, and creativity, including the capacity to "play" and to participate in cultural activities. The true self develops adequately not because it has been allowed channels for direct and sublimated instinctual satisfaction, as is the case with the Freudian id, but because the child has received adequate holding and mirroring and because he or she has found an object (mother) who reliably and empathically meets needs, remains constant despite aggressive excitement, and encourages continuity of being by her quiet, nonintrusive presence. In other words, the concerns of the true self are ontological concerns rather than drive concerns. The only uses Winnicott sees for the false self, unlike the enormous usefulness Freud accords to the ego as the center of mature psychic life, are the management of social situations where intimacy is not appropriate (in normal individuals) and the protection of the true self (in those disturbed individuals where intrusion and/or indifference have threatened the core of the personality and encouraged a retreat). All this is quite un-Freudian.

Another way in which Winnicott attempts to achieve continuity with orthodox psychoanalytic principles is by restricting his own contributions to pre-self disorders (psychosis, schizoid and borderline cases, and false self disorders) while maintaining that Freud was right concerning the neuroses and Oedipal disorders. Yet Winnicott's account of the Oedipus complex is itself unorthodox. He sees it through Kleinian glasses as a conflict between a boy's love and hate for his father in a context in which the boy's "in-love relationship" with his mother has been activated. This conceptualization deviates from Freud's account of the Oedipus complex as a conflict between incestuous and murderous instincts on the one hand and the fear of retaliation combined with constitutional bisexuality and phylogenetic memories of primordial father murder on the other. Winnicott's Oedipus complex, by contrast, is a purely relational affair—a "three-body" conflict versus the "two-body" conflicts of early infancy, as Winnicott likes to put the matter.

Moreover, after redefining areas of concern—Freud's as neuroses defined by castration anxiety and his own as self disorders defined by "annihilation anxiety" (Winnicott, 1965b, p. 130)—Winnicott goes on to redefine regression. Whereas for Freud, regression to earlier psychosexual stages was to be discouraged in analysis, Winnicott maintains that regression to the point where the true self was abandoned is necessary for cure. In this, he agrees with Ferenzi, Balint, and Laing. Furthermore, Winnicott's division of the territory between himself and Freud does not remain constant. Early on, he maintained that the majority of cases were amenable to orthodox psychoanalysis. Later, like many other post-Freudian theorists, he came to see self disorders as the rule rather than the exception and to view neuroses as deriving from "the strain of ambivalence in relationships between relatively normal 'whole' persons" (Winnicott, 1965b, p. 116). Surely, as Greenberg and Mitchell point out, Freud would not agree to equate the "common unhappiness" of normal persons with neurosis; nor would he agree that most psychological distress consists of disorders of the self. At this point, as Greenberg and Mitchell note, Winnicott is proposing "not an extension, but an alternative to Freud's approach" (1983, p. 209).

Yet despite these bows toward orthodoxy, Winnicott presents a very sensitive characterization of the interactions between mother and child. Of all the post-Freudian theorists, Winnicott alone insists on the importance not only of high points, traumas, and overt responses, but also of the quiet moments of "going on being" that one hopes the young child will experience in the mother's presence. In fact, Winnicott names the mother of these moments the "environment mother" to distinguish her from the "object mother" who is the target of the child's imperious desires. The environment mother is optimally a quiet presence, neither intrusive nor neglectful, who allows the child to develop a sense of self-continuity. This experience is also the basis for the adult's later ability to enjoy being alone. It is as though the mother's presence imposes on the child's ongoing experience a meaning which fends off disintegration into discrete unintegrated instants. If this quiet experience of "being with" is ruptured by a mother who ignores or intrudes upon her infant, the infant experiences an "annihilation" of the self—a feeling of fragmentation which is covered over by the development of a false self. Actually, despite his own claims to the contrary, Winnicott's descriptions both of mirroring needs and of the environment mother are severely at odds with traditional Freudian theory, which views relational needs as deriving from repeated experiences of drive gratification/frustration and not from a basic need for a witness to one's development of an ongoing sense of self.

Winnicott's ideas are also at odds with those of his teacher Melanie Klein. Although his account of the child's attempt to "repair" the object mother who is the goal of striving for drive gratification appears to be derived from Klein's ideas about innate aggression and the achievement of the "depressive position," Winnicott actually translates Klein's ideas into more strictly relational concepts. He says that in moments of excitement the object mother becomes the target of the infant's aggressive exploitation. But in order to develop properly, the infant needs to see the environment mother survive these hungry attacks. This is because there will come a time when the growing child will realize in an emotional sense that the object mother and the environment mother are the same person. The result, in Kleinian terms, is a sense of guilt—though Winnicott prefers the term "concern" to characterize the depressive position. The truth, however, is that Klein's good-gratifying versus bad-frustrating breast dichotomy is not equivalent to Winnicott's juxtaposition of the object mother and the environment mother. In Klein's system, both experiences relate to the satisfaction of drives. In Winnicott's the environment mother is a provider for relational not instinctual needs.

Furthermore, in Klein's system, the reparation which the baby attempts is a fantasy activity; Winnicott, by contrast, believes the young child needs to feel that he or she can actually make a difference to the mother, that the amends are real. Hence the chronically depressed mother, as Harold Searles (1979) also notes, deprives her child of this experience of reparation, of making a difference by expressing concern. Similarly, the unreliable or blaming mother fails to assure her child that she has successfully survived the child's aggressive attacks. Winnicott's emphasis is on the initial actual relationship rather than on the initial fantasy relationship as described by Klein; however, for Winnicott, these actual relationships become the basis for later fantasies.

Although Winnicott seems to believe otherwise, his idea of the importance of the transitional object and of the concomitant development of a capacity to play to the development of a true self also find no grounding in traditional psychoanalytic metatheory—which regards play as an attempt at mastery or as a kind of sublimatory activity. According to Winnicott, the transitional object provides a bridge between the world of earliest infancy, where the infant experiences the mother as a "subjective object" whom the infant has "created," and that of later childhood, where the mother has become an "objective object" with her own center of subjectivity and control. The manipulation of transitional objects (blanket, teddy bear, favorite toy, and so on) provides an avenue of connection between the inner and the outer worlds through the presence of an object which is experienced neither as truly subjective nor as truly objective. It exists, as Winnicott says, in "*the potential space* between the baby and the mother" (1971, p. 107). Such an object is neither completely under the control of the self (as is the case with mere fantasies) nor completely under the control of the external world.

The manipulation of transitional objects leads to an ability to play. Only the ability to play can give an individual a sense of possibilities as opposed to mere facts. Thus Winnicott defines psychotherapy as "two people playing together" (1971, p. 38). In fact, the recovery of the ability to play is the essence of cure, since "it is only in being creative that the individual discovers the [true] self" (Winnicott, 1971, p. 54). What Winnicott seems to be saying is that the transitional object provides an invitation to imaginative activity, to departing from the world of *is* to the world of *may* or *might be*, which is the basis for artistic and cultural activity/participation, creative scientific discovery, and creative living. Such a world, which is future as well as past oriented, escapes the causal mechanism of traditional Freudian metatheory.

Kohut, like Winnicott, values not only the development of a self, but the development of a firm, flexible, and creative self. Like Winnicott, Kohut uses the term "self" as an active organizing center of experience rather than as a set of reflected appraisals—although Kohut's self is quite clearly a personality "structure," whereas Winnicott's is more ambiguously so. The term "self psychology" indicates the primary importance which this active, organizing self is accorded in Kohut's theory. And just as Winnicott's environment mother is distinguished from Freud's object mother, so Kohut's "selfobject" needs are distinguished from Freud's "libidinal object" needs. In fact, in Kohut we have finally arrived at a theorist who clearly recognizes and names the new category of relational needs discussed by so many of the post-Freudian theorists. According to Kohut's final formulation (1984), there are three categories of selfobject needs which are critical to the development of an adequately structured self. To develop such a self, the child needs to experience adequate "mirroring," a sense of "twinship" with another who is like himself or herself, and the calm presence of an "idealizable" other.

It is only by internalizing experiences of reflective support, as opposed to mere drive gratification, that the self can acquire firmness, cohesion, and flexibility. Although a certain amount of empathic failure is inevitable and even necessary to growth, the child who has largely and persistently had his or her selfobject needs denied will fail to develop a "nuclear self" (borderline and psychotic patients) or will develop a severely disturbed self (narcissistic patients). Even the castration anxiety experienced by the Oedipal child and reexperienced by the analysand usually masks a deeper anxiety—"disintegration anxiety," the fear not of physical death but of "loss of humanness: psychological death" (Kohut, 1984, p. 16). Thus for Kohut, unlike Freud, lust and destructiveness are not primary reactions and affection and assertiveness secondary. Rather, lust and destructiveness are reactions to empathic failure—a sentiment with which Sullivan and Winnicott would agree.

Kohut's account of the disintegration anxiety which accompanies such failures echoes Erikson's description of the "identity diffusion syndrome"; Sullivan's account of the disintegrative effects of anxiety caused by repeated attacks on the self-system; and Winnicott's description of the "annihilation" of the self experienced by the young child who is usurped or ignored. Kohut believes that not only the more severely disturbed patients who provided the sources for his theory but also neurotics need to investigate narcissistic (in Kohut's sense of attacks on one's sense of self-esteem rather than in Freud's sense of the investment of libido in the ego at the expense of objects) disturbances of the self.

Analysis in self psychology therefore takes the form of uncovering and filling in (through a process which Kohut calls "transmuting internalization") the selfobject needs that were not met in earliest childhood. It is important to the therapeutic process to recognize which of the three forms of selfobject needs a particular patient has had the most difficulty getting met. Mirroring needs refer to the child's requirements for an other who is able to accept and accurately mirror his or her basic vitality and assertiveness. Lack of adequate mirroring leads to a feeling of unreality similar to Winnicott's (1965a, 1965b, 1971) and Guntrip's (1969) accounts of the feeling of unreality reported by schizoid patients or to R. D. Laing's (1959) account of "ontological insecurity." Idealizing needs refer to the child's craving for a calm, uplifting adult who is able to present goals and projects and with whom the child can identify. The lack of an idealizable other may lead to a sense of aimlessness, or lack of direction, or to a feeling of anxiety similar to the anxiety which Sullivan describes in his patients. Twinship needs refer to the child's desire for an alter ego—a sense of the presence of others who are *like* oneself and who can confirm one's essential humanness. The absence of a "twinning" other can lead to a failure to learn tasks or to feel at home in the human community. The meeting of mirroring needs leads to the confirmation of ambitions; the meeting of idealizing needs to the acquisition of goals; and the meeting of twinship needs to the acquisition of skills and talents. Throughout all of this, the other person is the mediator of the development of a firm, flexible, and creative self.

Therapeutically, such distinctions are very useful. For example, I think of a client who at the beginning of therapy dreamed of monsters from outer space who pathetically expired beneath the gaze of an uncomprehending crowd (an old theme in his dreams). Our investigation of this dream showed the presence of a hunger to be accurately mirrored rather than ignored by an unempathic mother and a frequently absent father. As therapy progressed, this client began to have dreams of funerals, in which someone shared his grief. These dreams proved more satisfying than the earlier ones because they reflected the fulfillment of a wish for a "twin" (the therapist?) who would share his grief over childhood losses—including the loss of the original self who failed to be mirrored. This client repeatedly expressed the wish that people close to him should not only understand but "*feel* what I feel." It was a prerequisite, he seemed to say, to his being able to stop feeling alienated from others. At other times, he expressed the desire for a calm parent who might have lifted him out of the endless anxieties and night terrors he had experienced as a child. His chief complaint was that he frequently felt, even with the people he loved most, "all alone." The origin of this feeling was not the frustration of instinctual needs; rather, it was the lack of resonant empathy and commonality with his aloof parents.

Thus it seemed particularly important to this client that I accurately reflect the nuances of his feelings, that I let him know that his feelings were not "alien" (that I myself might have felt the same under similar circumstances), and that I empathize with his loneliness. He wished to know most of all, in the language of his dreams, that he was not a "creature from outer space." Part of this client's solution to these dilemmas lay in his increasing ability to use my presence to fill in the gaps in his experience of self as an object for an interested, calm, and caring other who was also like himself in many ways—in other words, in the provision of mirroring, twinship, and idealizing needs within the context of therapy. No doubt, Kohut would refer to this as "transmuting internalization."

Despite their clinical usefulness, however, there are several problems with Kohut's formulations. First, Kohut's selfobject needs do not seem to refer to objects at all, but rather to the child's experiences as an object for others who as subjects see and affirm (or, conversely, negatively judge and/or ignore) the child. Yet what is the metatheoretical basis for the child's understanding that others can be subjects? Second, Kohut's ideas concerning the structuralization of the self are somewhat contradictory because they seem to confuse the self as subject with the self as object or aim. If the self is a subjective center of reference, how can it have structure or content, firm or otherwise? And if it is an object, how can it be resilient and creative?

Finally, what is the metatheoretical basis for Kohut's concept of the "transmuting internalization" of the therapist and the therapeutic milieu? Does the analysand metaphorically "eat" the therapist as the child metaphorically "eats" the selfobjects? Following this gastronomical metaphor, Kohut asserts that if therapy has proceeded properly the analysand, like the properly parented child, will thoroughly assimilate the analytic experience. No bits and pieces of the analyst will be left to cause intrapsychic indigestion. Could we not, then, get along without this idea of transmuting internalization—replacing it with Sullivan's idea that, having had a different interpersonal experience with the therapist, the patient will be able to let go of his or her "negative anticipations" that future interpersonal relations will pose the same threat as past ones to the self-system?

The implications of these two views for treatment of more severely disturbed patients make these seemingly minor distinctions between Sullivan and Kohut appear significant. Thus it is that Sullivan, who believes that the psyche is a fluid and changeable energy configuration rather than a thing, approaches the treatment of schizophrenia with optimism. Schizophrenics simply have more anxiety than other patients about threats to an already shaky self-system, but they are not bereft of the psychological structure that other patients have. All of us, Sullivan seems to imply, are dealing with illusory notions of the self as a stable entity.

Kohut, on the other hand, although he believes that narcissistic personality disorders are treatable because the core of a "nuclear self" begins to form in infancy and early childhood, does not hold the same hope for more deeply disturbed borderline and psychotic patients. While Kohut thinks that it is theoretically possible to confront the persisting sense of hollowness at the center of the borderline patient's personality, he believes that, practically speaking, the therapeutic relationship with such patients should aim at allowing them to manage their defensive structures to their best advantage rather than try for a genuine cure. For the narcissistic patient, by contrast, psychoanalysis attempts to provide "a matrix in which the defects in the structure of the self—even more severe defects that lead to the temporary appearance of serious, quasi-psychotic symptoms—are filled in via reactivation of the needs for narcissistic sustenance (i.e., the need for mirroring and the need to merge with an ideal) that had not been provided in childhood" (Kohut, 1984, pp. 8–9). As for the borderline or psychotic patient, since the foundation has not been laid, the house cannot be built. The more radical post-Freudian theorists who have worked successfully with borderline, schizophrenic, and schizoid patients—including Sullivan, Fromm-Reichmann, Guntrip, Laing, and Searles—would certainly disagree.

Although all of the theorists discussed in this section have some grasp of the significance of relational needs to the formation of a self, none seems to fully understand the significance of the self as a goal of being as well as a source of action and an object of reflection. Why, we ask, does the individual need the security of a clearly defined self-system (Sullivan), the mirroring of a true self (Winnicott), or the cohesiveness of a self that has had narcissistic needs for mirroring, idealization and twinship met (Kohut)? Nothing in Freud's metatheory can explain the overpowering need for the sense of self-continuity which these theorists recognize. It is especially difficult to see how the pursuit of pleasure could provide this motivation.

If, on the other hand, as I suggested earlier, the defensive operations designed to preserve the status quo are in the service of a desire to bring into being substantive freedom, then post-Freudian relational theorists would be acting in bad faith to the extent that they endorse structure building as a therapeutic goal. And if such structure is illusory, the "cures" effected by self psychologists and others ascribing to this goal must be explained in some other way. I believe that Sartre's ontology provides this explanation at the same time that it promotes a positive going beyond the pursuit of stability in the direction of a pursuit of meaning as freely constituted by the individual.

Sartre's Concept of the Self

In discussing Sartre's concept of the self, we must be careful to distinguish it from more common psychological usages. We must also be clear about what Sartre means by the term "self" when he uses it in three different ways—as prereflective consciousness, as ego or personality, or as the aim or value which consciousness is attempting to bring into being. Although these three usages are clear in context, Sartre never formally differentiates among them—perhaps because they are inextricably interlinked anyway. Although the French word for self (*soi*) translates into English with the same connotations, Sartre's three usages point to a quite different view of human reality than that of most psychoanalytic theorists. The shift from what is basically an essentialist to an existentialist view of human reality has, I believe, implications for the practice of psychotherapy which are both subtle and significant.

Contemporary psychoanalytic theorists are working within a philosophical tradition which ultimately derives from Aristotle. According to Aristotle, every being is composed of matter and form or structure. Each entity also contains within itself a potentiality (not yet actual) which it is its nature to realize. Sometimes referred to as the "acorn theory" (an oak tree is the realization of the potentiality of an acorn), this view of human development secretly permeates much psychological discourse from psychoanalysis to humanistic psychology. Now outdated as a philosophy of nature with respect to physics if not to biology, Aristotle's solution to the problem of change has been much embraced as a solution to the problem of human change. When I change, say the humanistic therapist and client, I "realize my potential." Many psychoanalytic theorists similarly believe that I find and free my true self while dissolving the false self which adverse environmental influences have caused me to form.

Sartre disagrees. The self as prereflective agent has neither structure nor substance. Prereflective choice, not the realization of an a priori potentiality, lies at the heart of human reality: "Existence precedes essence." As for the self as ego or character, it is given form and substance by the self as agent—

but as this happens, it becomes a pseudo-object similar to other objects in the world. It is no longer a living consciousness but an image or impression of that consciousness. Much of the confusion among psychologists, Sartre contends, derives from their treating the self as object as though it were a real experiencing self rather than a construct of reflective consciousness. As for the self as value, it is this self which haunts the self as agent in the form of that substantial freedom, that self-correspondence, which is to be achieved down there in the future. But Being-in-itself-for-itself is an illusion. The self as value can never actually exist. It can only exist as the future-directed meaning of my present actions, feelings, thoughts, and gestures—a point which should become increasingly clear as we investigate the three forms of the self in Sartre.

Let us begin with the self as prereflective consciousness. This self is the source of the other two selves. As an agent, I am concerned with the project of bringing into being the self as value, whereas as a person with a past who lives among other people, I always do end up creating some kind of version of myself as an object or personality. Despite these interconnections, I think we can isolate some of the ontological characteristics of the self as prereflective consciousness. What defines the self as prereflective consciousness is not *potentiality* as an inner essence to be realized, but *possibility* as discovered on the face of a particular world.

Possibility may have to do with the world, as when I look out at gray clouds and remark, "It is possible that it may rain this afternoon" (Aristotle would say instead that the potentiality of the clouds is fulfilled in rain). Or it may have to do with my activities in the world, as when I say, "It is possible that I may finish this book this summer" (the humanistic psychologist would say that I am "fulfilling my potential" as a writer). In both instances, however, the *possible* is neither an inner potency waiting to be realized nor a mere indifferent *might*; it is that which I view myself or the world as *going to be*. In the first instance, possibility has to do with my awareness of the future of the world, and in the second, with my awareness of my own future within it. According to Sartre, both kinds of possibility are wholly and fundamentally human. Material objects have no awareness of a future. The self of prereflective consciousness, on the other hand, has no substance in the sense of fullness of being.

This brings us to Sartre's famous definition of human reality as a *desire* or *lack*. As desire or lack of Being, consciousness is aware of a gap between itself and its objects. Sartre calls this awareness of distance between self and (present and future) world "nothingness," and he considers the act of being aware a "nihilating act" in the sense that it by definition involves an awareness of distances. Although this idea is often viewed pessimistically—even Sartre has much to say about the "anguish of our freedom" or the "unhappy" state of human consciousness—it is really the only possible outlook which allows for human freedom and responsibility. The philosophical term "nihilation" is therefore not to be equated with negativity in the usual sense; instead, it must be understood as the distantiation which allows the world to come into existence *for me*. It is through a dim awareness of my distinctness from the objects of my consciousness, both as they are and as I expect them to become, that I maintain the character of an intentional being—that I become *consciousness of*. According to Sartre, a consciousness stuffed with itself could not encounter the world. Perhaps, one is tempted to think, this is why the Freudian psyche so often appears to be a closed intrapsychic system: Its substantiality leaves no room for the world.

In any case, Sartre maintains just the opposite position. Since prereflective consciousness is translucid, it contains none of the psychological content or structural properties which psychological investigations like to attribute to the human subject. Although Sartre says that such a consciousness is "personal" in the sense of being aware that it is aware (*conscience [de] soi de l'objet*), it has none of the character traits and qualities usually associated with the personality. It is personal only in the sense of existing "for itself as a presence to itself" (BN, p. 103). The self (*soi*) of prereflective consciousness comes into being simultaneously with my awareness of the world (*de l'objet*); this prereflective self is, in fact, purely and simply my awareness of the gap between self and world with the parentheses indicating that such self-awareness is not a real awareness of self as object. Rather, it is more like the taste of self which goes along with each of my acts of world formulation. Dimly aware of myself as not being the material world or even as not coinciding with a particular view or attitude toward the world, I am "all lightness, all translucence" (TE, p. 42). I am all openness to being. In fact, to use the term "I" is a misnomer, though I have retained it for linguistic convenience. The truth is that when I am deeply immersed in an activity, I am not even aware of an "I"—though if you stopped to ask me who is doing a particular action, I would reply that "I" am doing it. Prereflective consciousness is, in other words, aware of individual continuity as a temporal being.

Actually, it is only when I reflectively turn and make an object of my (past) self that the "I" and "me" of ordinary discourse appear. Sartre maintains in *The Transcendence of the Ego* that the "I" and the "me" are objects rather than subjects. The consciousness which characterizes them is beyond the object being characterized in the very act of linguistic formulation. In the formula for reflective consciousness, the self of prereflective consciousness is never equivalent to the self of reflective consciousness: There is an impassable gulf between the first and the second *soi* in *conscience (de) soi de soi*. Even in a simple statement such as, "I like this," the "I" who speaks the sentence is reflectively beyond the "I" who does the liking. This becomes even clearer with statements such as, "I am a good/bad/exciting/depressed/angry person," which involve reflective characterizations extending far beyond the immediate past into the distant past and by implication into the future as well.

Such reflective judgments coalesce into what Sartre refers to as the "ego," by which he means not the Freudian ego as part of a tripartite structure but the whole psyche. Yet the Sartrean ego or psyche, as an object both apprehended and created by consciousness, is opaque, whereas prereflective consciousness is translucid. The ego, according to Sartre, "is neither formally nor materially *in* consciousness: it is outside, *in the world*" (TE, p. 31). The act of regarding one's own past as an object is similar to the act of apprehending other objects in the world—and equally (in some ways more so) open to error. It is for this reason that Sartre agrees with Freud that the subject of a psychoanalysis does not have "a privileged position to proceed in these inquiries concerning himself" (BN, p. 570)—and not because Sartre accepts the Freudian unconscious.

This shift in the usual perspective reverses many of the accepted ideas both of psychology and of everyday life. Psychologists most often view personality traits as lying *behind* actions, which are said to emanate from them. Sartre reverses this: Personality traits are not a source but a *product* of one's reflective view of self. The center of the ego is not a living consciousness but a "nucleus of opacity" (BN, p. 103). As an object of reflective consciousness (which is the name Sartre gives to prereflective consciousness when it turns and attempts to take a position on itself), the ego is "the transcendent unity of states and of actions" (TE, p. 70). What Sartre means is that consciousness, as a transcendence or going beyond its objects, creates an ideal (not a real) whole out of its past actions and states (which it may further unify into personality qualities or traits).

Actions include not only physical actions but "psychical actions like doubting, reasoning, meditating, making a hypothesis" (TE, p. 69). In positing the "I" pole of the ego, consciousness sees itself as the transcendent unity of these past actions. I am the person who acts/acted in such and such a fashion. Similarly, I may make my past feelings (which are also actions) into a "me" pole of the ego. For example, my hatreds and loves come to define me. Yet hatred and love are states which can only appear to reflective consciousness. Prereflectively, I may feel repugnance, anger, or joy in someone's presence. But hatred and love imply a permanence which simple momentary emotions do not have. Thus when I say that I have a hatred for someone or that I have done a particular act out of hatred, I have gone beyond merely descriptive reflection to state more than I can know. I have made of my hatred an object *in* consciousness, which it can never really be, or a motive for behavior, which it is not.

In fact, I may even be mistaken about a state: I may believe that I hate when I love or that I love when I hate. If I go one step further, having observed several or many such "hatreds" or "loves," I may decide that I have a disposition toward hatred or love or some other state. When I do this, I attribute to myself the quality or personality trait of being spiteful, loving, or something else. As Sartre points out, the "faults, virtues, tastes, talents, tendencies, instincts, etc." which we attribute to ourselves and others are such hypothetical qualities (TE, p. 71). We view them as "potentialities" or forces within ourselves when they are really reifications of repeated feelings or actions. They do not exist a priori but a posteriori; so, in fact, does the ego, although it is popularly thought to be the source of the qualities, actions, and states which define it.

The ego as conceived by popular imagination appears to have claims on the future as well as the past. If I *am* this kind of person, then I *will be* this kind of person. It is here that the self as ego connects with the self as aim or value—at least to the extent that such a self is conceived in bad faith. In fact, the point of constructing an ego may be exactly this: It gives a sense of substantiality or security concerning the future. Sartre says that consciousness "is frightened by its own spontaneity because it senses this spontaneity as *beyond* freedom" in the sense that the prereflective self I am down there in the future could make a different choice than I might wish to make right now. My future self could betray my present self. For this reason, Sartre considers that "perhaps the essential role of the ego is to mask from consciousness its very spontaneity" (TE, p. 100).

Many irrational fears spring from exactly this source. Sartre gives the example of a young bride described by Pierre Janet who lived in terror of sitting at a window and summoning passers-by as if she were a prostitute. Nothing in her past served as an explanation for this fear, yet she could not shake it. Sartre tells us that this young woman was experiencing "a vertigo of possibility"—that her feeling "monstrously free" took the form of fear of this shameful action (TE, p. 100). Fears about doing shameful things in a crowd or of getting too near the edge of a cliff may have a similar source. The person I will be down there in the future might stand up in a crowded restaurant and shout or undress or my future self might choose to jump off a cliff. Such things, in fact, often happen in dreams. Indeed, if consciousness is pure spontaneity, what is to prevent me from making a future choice which will go against all that I have ever considered important? The ego offers itself as a comfort against this recognition that I am and will be pure freedom.

To the extent that consciousness constitutes the ego as a substantial self which provides an escape from its freedom, the ego provides a "a false representation of itself" (TE, p. 101). As a product of "accessory reflection," which differs from "pure reflection" in this very attempt to reify living consciousness as a potentiality for certain actions and states, the ego can be allied with bad faith. I will discuss pure reflection—or the simple presence of the consciousness reflecting to the consciousness reflected on—in greater detail below. Here it should be noted that the ego is inclined toward bad faith because in creating an ego I usually engage in the inauthentic attempt to substantialize consciousness. As a part of an effort to realize a self that is substantively free (Being-in-itself-for-itself), the ego represents at least a slightly skewed vision of myself. This vision is a lie because it denies my freedom or imbues it with an impossible substantiality, regardless of how accurate a picture of myself I may draw in other respects.

Sartre does not suggest that it is possible to live without an ego. In fact, in *The Transcendence of the Ego*, he states that even though the ego is not the "owner" but the "object" of consciousness, it nonetheless "appears *on the horizon* of a spontaneity" in the sense that one has a sense of the ego as a reflective unification of one's project (TE, p. 97). In *The Family Idiot*, Sartre deplores the fact that as a child Flaubert's "ego," or sense of himself as an object, is so alienated from prereflective experience that "he knows it only by hearsay" rather than as an "immediate structure [which is] . . . the spontaneous affirmation at the heart of concrete intuition." For the young Gustave, his ego is not simply elusive, confused, or blurred; rather, like the false self of Winnicott, it exists only in the significations of others. It is part of Gustave's acquiescence to the "magical power of grown-ups"—which he himself is unable to understand by making it his own (FI, 1:154–155). In other words, Sartre understands as well as the relational theorists discussed in this chapter the tragedy of a child's failure, through lack of adequate mirroring and positive regard, to develop a sound sense of self (ego) as object.

Although Flaubert's case is extreme, it is understandable from a Sartrean perspective why a person might substitute the distortions of others for his or her own direct reflections on self. For one thing, one's own view of oneself as an object is vulnerable to error in a way that is not true of one's view of other objects in the world. This vulnerability is inescapable because the object of reflective consciousness is always a pseudo-object for the simple reason that prereflective consciousness cannot be present to my view as are other objects in the world. I cannot simultaneously *see* and *be* the consciousness reflected on, though in pure reflection I may approach some approximation of this. I can, however, be truly present as a real object beneath the Other's gaze. For this and other reasons discussed in the preceding chapter, I may be tempted to adopt the Other's view of me in place of my own. Much human misery, as we have seen, begins exactly here—in the many variations of this attempt to use the Other to bring into existence substantive freedom.

This leads us to a discussion of the self as value. This is the future self which I am attempting to bring into being. Sartre calls it a value because it is that which consciousness desires or lacks down there in the future. Ultimately, this lack is a lack of self, and the ultimate pursuit is the impossible pursuit of Being-in-itself-for-itself, or substantive freedom. The *nothingness* which separates prereflective consciousness from its objects is not just a simple awareness that *I am not this table*; it is also an awareness of a present lack which imagines itself as a future fullness. Sartre says that the "for-itself is itself *down there*, beyond its grasp, in the far reaches of its possibilities" (BN, pp. 103–4). The "circuit of selfness," as we saw in Chapter 2, is intimately connected with the world. Sartre uses "circuit of selfness (*Circuit de ipséite*) for the relation of the for-itself with the possible which it is, and 'world' for the totality of being in so far as it is traversed by the circuit of selfness" (BN, p. 102). One is always in the process of creating a future self in terms of the "possibles" one encounters on the face of this particular world. In this respect, the self as value is a pursuit, a self-making process, rather than an actual entity.

Interestingly enough, reflection is not a necessary component of this pursuit of a self as value, though in reality the self as value always contains reflective elements. A mundane example of how this operates on a nonreflective level was given in Chapter 2: One experiences thirst out there in the world in one's apprehension of this glass of water as desirable. What one desires is a satisfied thirst, which Sartre calls the in-itself-for-itself-of-thirst. What one gets is the disappearance of thirst and the appearance of a new desire or lack. All this could happen on a purely nonreflective level, though it is always possible to turn and grasp the situation reflectively: I am thirsty. It is conceivable that much of one's life project could be lived on a totally non-reflective level, though in actuality this would probably only be possible for a person deprived of human society and language. Nonetheless, there is much that goes on for each of us that is never reflectively scrutinized. Indeed, much of what Freudian analysis regards as "unconscious" may fall within this category. It is lived as a future-directed project, but this project is never named or else it is misnamed. In fact, it may be a part of one's project to refuse to name it or to name it incorrectly.

Reflection, and with it the voices of others which one has reflectively adopted, enter into the value-making process when one attempts to characterize the self as value as a *this* or a *that*. To the extent that one realizes that the self one is making, the value one is projecting oneself toward, will never be *made* (except at the moment of death, when one's life becomes a value *for others*), the self-making process can be undertaken in relatively good faith. But the temptation toward bad faith—toward believing either that one *is not* the self one has been because one has no connection with those past choices or that one *is* or *will become* the self one is pursuing—is definitely strong. We have seen that belief in the substantive ego is one manifestation of bad faith which is well nigh universal. One reflectively creates an ego, which is a pure in-itself or "nucleus of opacity" (BN, p. 103), and then imagines it as the source of one's states and actions. The only possible release from this propensity toward self-deception is facing the reality that human consciousness is an "unhappy consciousness" (BN, p. 90) to the extent that its fundamental project—bringing into being substantive freedom or a substantial self as value—is impossible.

I believe, however, that this unhappiness looms larger to a consciousness that has not yet performed on itself the radical "katharsis" of recognizing and validating its freedom. Sartre himself says much about the anguish of freedom and very little about its joys—though his descriptions of the "lightness" of the person who recognizes his or her freedom or the playfulness of the person who has been converted to such a position presage a recognition of the pleasures which such a shift can bring. Certainly, his description of the "conflict of consciousnesses" vividly displays the miseries of human relations lived in bad faith—or in holding fast to a project which involves using others to create the illusion of substance.

On the other hand, Sartre concludes *Being and Nothingness* with a set of questions which were to be the basis for a book on ethics that he never finished. These questions concern the possibility of transcending the trap of believing that one can achieve substantive freedom:

> What will become of freedom if it turns its back upon this value [of bringing into being the in-itself-for-itself as a real possibility]? Will freedom carry this value along with it whatever it does and even in its very turning back upon the in-itself-for-itself? Will freedom be reapprehended from behind by the value which it wishes to contemplate? Or will freedom by the very fact that it apprehends itself as a freedom in relation to itself, be able to put an end to the reign of this value? In particular is it possible for freedom to take itself for a value as the source of all value, or must it necessarily be defined in relation to a transcendent value which haunts it? And in case it could will itself as its own possible and its determining value, what would this mean? A freedom which wills itself freedom is in fact a being-which-is-not-what-it-is and which-is-what-it-is-not, and which chooses as the ideal of being, being-what-it-is-not and not-being-what-it-is. (BN, p. 627)

Sartre, toward the beginning of *Being and Nothingness*, defines human reality as that being "which is what it is not and which is not what it is" (BN, p. 63). In the passage above, he suggests that it may be possible to choose this same paradoxical human reality as value—and thereby to escape the trap of bad faith.

Sartre allies the goals of existential psychoanalysis to this ethical enterprise of recognizing that one *creates* value rather than *finds* it. The aim of existential psychoanalysis, he says, is to repudiate the "spirit of seriousness"— by which he means the propensity to look at oneself as a product of environmental demands, past and present. In its place, existential psychoanalysis would presumably place the "spirit of play" (BN, p. 580), of recognizing the lightness of one's freedom. One is reminded of Winnicott's definition of psychoanalysis as "two people playing together." In any case, existential psychoanalysis "is going to reveal to man the real goal of his pursuit, which is being as a synthetic fusion of the in-itself with the for-itself; existential psychoanalysis is going to acquaint man with his passion" (BN, p. 626). Sartre, of course, means neither the sexual passion of Freud nor passion defined as self-interest (which, Sartre says, is "only one way freely chosen among others to realize this passion" [BN, p. 626]); he means instead the passion for creating a self down there in the future.

In order to be a "means of deliverance and salvation" rather than an invitation to despair, however, existential psychoanalysis must reveal to the "moral agent that he is *the being by whom values exist*" (BN, p. 627). In other words, it must release the analysand from the illusion of substance into a feeling of responsibility for a life which one is always making, but which is never made. From such a viewpoint alone, surprises about who one has been and who one might become would be welcome. I believe that this enterprise of validating one's freedom involves a kind of therapeutic "transcendence of the ego" in that one recognizes that the ego one identifies with is an illusion of substance. And this insight that the ego or the self as object must in some respect be repudiated is, I believe, a major contribution which existential psychoanalysis can make to contemporary psychoanalytic discussions of the self.

"Pure Reflection": A Sartrean Approach
to the Self in Psychotherapy

As we have seen, many contemporary psychoanalytic relational theorists recognize that it is the pursuit of a self, rather than the pursuit of pleasure, which is the chief human concern. Most follow Sullivan, Winnicott, and Kohut in recognizing the significance of relations with others, especially with respect to allowing the development of an adequate sense of self. Some, such as Kohut and (to a lesser extent) Winnicott, regard this self as having actual substance and structure. A few, such as Sullivan, view the self as activity or energy rather than substance. The truth is that much theoretical confusion surrounds contemporary psychoanalytic discussions of the self. Certainly, there is no metatheoretical principle which would account for the need to create or establish a firm sense of self.

I believe that Sartre's ontological insight that the pursuit of Being-in-itself-for-itself is a description of being human provides such a metatheoretical grounding for the significance of the development of a self. Yet Sartre's ideas take us beyond contemporary psychoanalytic insights to an understanding that only the paradoxical acceptance of human reality as a plan without a blueprint can release us from the many forms of distress which are the province of psychopathology. It is not the development of a substantial self which is the final aim of existential psychoanalysis, but rather the transcendence of the need to develop such a self.

For the most part, the establishment of a firm identity, self, or ego has been the goal of psychoanalytic theory from the ego psychologists to the self psychologists (as Kohut's theory is styled). Even Sullivan, who recognizes that the pursuit of a substantive self can in some instances lead to stultification, fails to follow the full implications of his discovery of the fluidity of consciousness. Although Sullivan does not regard the experiencing subject as a *thing*, he does consider the ultimate human aim to be the attainment of a maximum of satisfaction within a context which allows for a maximum of security or lack of dissonance. Sartre, by contrast, would consider this search for a secure self to be a sign that one is living in bad faith. As for the more mainstream theorists, they are similar to Kohut in that they view the self the same way they view the ego—as an entity with substance and structure (or lack thereof). Or they see the self as a potentiality to be realized, as Winnicott does.

Sartrean consciousness, on the other hand, is anything but a substantial entity or an identity or potentiality to be realized. Consciousness desires solidity, it aims at substantiality, and it would like to see itself as having character or potential. But in this regard consciousness is always frustrated. As for identity, the very word in its philosophical meaning of coincidence with what one *is* is anathema to existential psychoanalysis as a description of consciousness. The theorem "$x = x$" never works with respect to consciousness. As applied to prereflective consciousness, one can never coincide with oneself because one is always at a distance from oneself. A human being is, after all, that being who "is what he is not and is not what he is." For example, if one believes, one is dimly aware that one believes by *making oneself believe*—that this belief is a prereflective choice of a way of relating to the world. Or one is aware that one defines oneself in terms of objects which one is not. On the reflective level, the consciousness reflecting can never be equated with the consciousness reflected on. The moment I turn to look at my spontaneous actions, I am no longer the spontaneous choice of myself which I previously was—as, for example, when I reflectively look at myself as a person who is writing. Pursuit of a substantial true self, as discussed by Winnicott and others, is another variation on this attempt to establish one's identity as a *this*. The existentialist therapist does not attempt to provoke the emergence of a true self or substantial ego identity, but rather tries to encourage the development of an authentic way of living.

How does one achieve this goal? Probably, it will not be achieved completely,[6] but it will not even become a focus if client and therapist continue to expect the emergence of a substantive structured self. It may be necessary, especially with more severely disturbed people, to work for a long time at providing an approximation of the reflection which was missing or severely distorting in early childhood. Here the therapeutic approach suggested by Kohut can be quite useful, though existentialist therapy will provide a different theoretical understanding of why accurate mirroring in therapy is so important. This is not because mirroring provides missing structure *in* the psyche, but rather because it facilitates a different reflective orientation toward one's prereflective experience. It is the relationship between the self as agent and the self as object which is at issue.

Eventually, even in working with very disturbed clients and perhaps even more so in working with people who are usually considered neurotic, it will be necessary to confront the fact that one can never become a fixed, always reliable self. This, too, involves developing a particular relationship between reflective consciousness and prereflective consciousness. If Sartre is correct in saying that the aim of existential psychoanalysis is "to acquaint man with his passion" (BN, p. 626), then there must be a reflective confrontation with the self of prereflective consciousness—which is at bottom *no thing*, sheer translucidity and temporalizing movement. Such a confrontation changes one's basic way of conceiving of self/world. It is also the only possible avenue for mitigating the human misery which Sartre describes as the "conflict of consciousnesses" by exposing the illusory nature of the attempt to use the Other to create a self. Interestingly, what the client must do is first use another (the therapist) to counteract the original distortions and neglect and then realize that this very enterprise of using others to create a self is part of a mistaken effort to bring into being the missing God.

What, then, is the approach by which existentialist theory attempts to facilitate a confrontation with oneself as responsible freedom? I believe it is something close to Sartre's somewhat problematic concept of "pure reflection." Sartre later admitted that he had never really given a full account of pure reflection, but had instead shown "only the facts of accessory reflection" (quoted by Barnes, 1983, p. 46). Hazel Barnes points out that as an actual mode of reflection, pure reflection is an impossibility. The operation, *conscience (de) soi de conscience (de) soi*, is not possible if the second consciousness is to be equated with the first (Barnes, 1983, p. 44–45). The consciousness reflecting is always separated from the consciousness reflected on. Barnes wonders if Sartre had in mind "some technique which he lacked the capacity, ability, or will to spell out" (1983, p. 46).

Since Sartre was not a psychotherapist, I think this might well be the case. But since pure reflection, which Sartre defines as the simple presence of the consciousness reflecting to the consciousness reflected on, has great importance in Sartre's theory of psychoanalysis, I think he must have conceived that something *like* pure reflection—if not actual pure reflection—was a possibility. He himself says that pure reflection "keeps to the given without setting up claims for the future" (TE, p. 64). Such reflection lacks the usual motivation of manipulating events in the direction of achieving Being-in-itself-for-itself. Because Sartre maintains that "reflective apprehension of spontaneous consciousness as non-personal spontaneity would have to be accomplished *without any antecedent motivation*" (TE, p. 92), pure reflection would have to be the cornerstone of discovering oneself as prereflective spontaneity which is the goal of existential psychoanalysis. Only such a reflection could accomplish this goal, since any impure reflection would already be contaminated with the goal of creating an ego or self as object. Although Sartre admits that such reflection is extremely rare, he maintains that it "is always possible in principle" (TE, p. 92). I think we might more realistically say that the movement *toward* pure reflection is a human possibility.

Actually, pure reflection, though not always identified by name, is a critical concept for both *The Transcendence of the Ego* and *Being and Nothingness*. In the first place, without something approximating pure reflection, it would have been impossible to arrive at the philosophical truths of either work. It must be possible for Sartre as reflective consciousness to apprehend his own free spontaneity as prereflective consciousness in order to write about this. Once he has done this, Sartre finds himself, at the end of *Being and Nothingness*, on the verge of an ethics or an existential psychoanalysis which takes as its first premise the possibility of embracing a "philosophy of freedom" which might make it possible to live one's life, including one's relations with others, in relatively good faith. Such a conversion, which is the aim of existential psychoanalysis, is based on the possibility of pure reflection.

The radical conversion is also a likely outcome of adequate parental love in childhood, as we have seen from the passage quoted from Sartre's biography of Flaubert in the preceding chapter. In that passage, Sartre discusses the importance of accurate positive reflection, noting that the child who has experienced the "true lie" of parental love will escape the despair over future possibilities which is the lot of the unloved child. This will make it easier later to face the truth that one is oneself the source of all value—that this is guaranteed neither by parental love nor by any character or personal potential given beforehand. But such a coming of age is predicated on pure reflection, since only pure reflection can reveal one to oneself as responsible freedom. Where parental love was lacking in making such reflection likely, existential psychoanalysis can take up the task.

Pure reflection is important to the process of existential psychoanalysis partially because only pure reflection will reveal the immediate past as a spontaneous choice rather than an emanation of the ego. As Sartre puts the matter, "We see here two reflections: the one, impure and conniving, which effects then and there a passage to the infinite [in terms of conceiving of the self as a static object which one was, is, and will be] . . . ; the other, pure, merely descriptive, which disarms the unreflected consciousness by granting its instantaneousness" (TE, pp. 64–65). Sartre gives as an example of the difference between the two an everyday occurrence where someone says in anger, "I detest you," and then catches himself and says, "It is not true, I do not detest you, I said that in anger" (TE, p. 64). Hatred or detestation is a state attributed to the ego. Anger is an immediate prereflective response. An interesting phenomenon which one often meets in therapy is the client who resists feeling something (anger, sadness, fear) out of concern that this feeling will last forever or that it will define him or her as a person. Often a response on the part of the therapist such as "That's what you're feeling *right now*—it's not who you *are*," will disarm this fear.

Pure reflection is, in fact, the source of those moments of radical change which Sartre designates as "psychological instants" to distinguish them from temporal instants (which do not exist because time is a continuous flow). These instants—in which an individual, suspended over an abyss, grasps in order to let go and lets go in order to grasp a new way of being in the world—are extremely critical to psychotherapy. They occur when prereflective consciousness takes its own immediate past as an object, evaluates it, and makes a new choice of being based on this evaluation. Sartre says that the "act of objectivizing the immediate past is the same as the new choice of other ends; it contributes to causing the instant to spring forth as the nihilating rupture of the temporalization" (BN, p. 467). Obviously, it is not always necessary to make a new choice of being at those moments, but Sartre conceives that it is *possible* to do so.

Part of the process of allowing such instants to arise also involves focusing pure reflection on situations in the distant past which have never been reflectively conceived or, one might assume, have been reflectively misconceived. Here the possibility of error is greater than with closer situations—as Sartre shows in making his character Hugo choose the meaning of the past in terms of his present project in *Dirty Hands*. On the other hand, Sartre points out that "every unreflective consciousness, being non-thetic [non-thinglike] consciousness of itself, leaves a non-thetic memory that one can consult" (TE, p. 46). The process of psychoanalysis, in fact, rests on attempting a more or less accurate reconstruction of the past in terms of a present project which one is attempting to change. Reevaluating the distant past—especially those emotional situations in the past which have been contaminated by the demands and evaluations of others and which continue to influence the present—is a central part of the task of depth psychotherapy.

When one attempts this reevaluation process, I believe it is important, insofar as this is possible, to approach the past through pure reflection, since accessory reflection will reveal states and qualities rather than choices. If one then makes a radically new choice of being, the past, including one's childhood, will take on a different meaning. This is not to say that the "facts" of the past will change *per se*—these, Sartre tells us, are "irremediable"—only that their significance may be radically altered. In beginning to project a different future, I come to "have" a different past. My past, according to Sartre, comes to meet me out of the future. It is for this reason that the past can take on such different colorings at various phases in a life or at various stages in the course of psychotherapy.

It is also important to understand that while the psychological instant may be hoped for, it is also feared. Sartre says that consciousness is "perpetually threatened by the instant" (BN, p. 466). This is so because the existence of the psychological instant demonstrates that a "radical modification of our fundamental project" is always possible—a radical modification which, however much we may imagine that we want it, is the surest possible demonstration that substantive freedom, Being-in-itself-for-itself, is an illusion. As a moment of "double nothingness" (BN, p. 466), the psychological instant shows me beyond a shadow of a doubt that I can never *be somebody* in the substantive sense.

It is for this reason that we often prefer familiar pain to the chance for an alien happiness. Radical change involves abandoning the whole weight of a past project, including the knowledge of all the various paths in the world for realizing that project, for an unknown future—an act which certainly requires considerable courage. In fact, as we have seen in a passage quoted earlier from Sullivan, it is this venture into the unknown which keeps even the schizophrenic embedded in his or her familiar delusions. Joanne Greenberg, in her autobiographical novel, *I Never Promised You a Rose Garden*, similarly validates this idea that part of the problem is that the schizophrenic patient must exchange a known miserable world for an unknown possibility of living differently. As Dr. Fried (who is modeled on Frieda Fromm-Reichmann) says to the young patient's mother in the novel: "Believe it or not, her sickness is the only solid ground she has. She and I are hacking away at that ground, on which she stands. That there will be another, firmer ground for her after this is destroyed she can only take on faith" (1964, p. 109). Of course, such fundamental shifts in a client's project usually take place over time and not all at once. Still, in therapy there is usually a point at which a client realizes exactly what is happening. The question, "Who will I *be* if I [make this or that fundamental change]?" can only be answered with, "You'll only really know by making it." And, forever after, such a client will understand something else as well—that the self is not the substantial *thing* which he or she once took it to be.

Since the self is not a thing or a set of qualities, the goal of inquiry in existential psychoanalysis "must be to discover a *choice* and not a *state*" (BN, p. 573). Sartre says that the existential psychoanalyst "must recall on every occasion that his object is not a datum buried in the darkness of the unconscious but a free, conscious determination—which is not even resident in consciousness, but which is one with this consciousness itself" (BN, p. 573). At the same time, he or she must recognize that even where the subject and object of existential psychoanalysis are the same person, the project revealed will be "*from the point of view of the Other*"—that is, it will be reflective rather than prereflective (BN, p. 571). This second statement would seem to invalidate the claims of some critics that Sartre had abandoned the translucidity of consciousness in his later work when he claimed that "lived experience" (*le vécu*) was not completely accessible to reflective awareness. Actually, although the later Sartre may have become more humble in his conception of the degree of self-knowledge which is actually possible, the early Sartre had never believed that prereflective consciousness can be reflectively conceived exactly *as it is*. The very act of reflection provides a view of the object reflected on from the outside.

On the other hand, unless something approximating pure reflection is possible, the critical point of existential psychoanalysis in which "the resistance of the subject collapses suddenly and he *recognizes* the image of himself which is presented to him as if he were seeing himself in a mirror" will never be reached (BN, p. 573). Yet Sartre insists that this "enlightenment of the subject is a fact. . . . The subject guided by the psychoanalyst does more and better than give his agreement to an hypothesis; he touches it, he sees what it is" (BN, p. 574). It is for this reason that "the final intuition of the subject" must be recognized as "decisive" in existential psychoanalysis (BN, p. 574).

We appear to have reached a theoretical impasse here. Sartre seems to take as the basis both of his philosophy and of the existentialist approach to psychotherapy an action which is impossible. The consciousness reflecting can never be exactly present to the consciousness reflected on. The nonparenthetic *de* in *conscience (de) soi de conscience (de) soi* forever divides them. Nor, one presumes, can the consciousness reflecting ever leave behind its own project since it *is* this very project. In other words, it can never be the purely descriptive consciousness which Sartre defines as pure reflection. Is this not at least as problematic as the theoretical difficulty which Sartre himself notes in the Freudian project of making the unconscious conscious? To attempt to make the prereflective reflective, to move from consciousness to knowledge, would seem to be as flawed an enterprise as the attempt to make the unconscious conscious. The self as agent and the self as object would seem to be unalterably alienated.

Actually, I think this difficulty is more apparent than real. Strictly speaking, it is probably true that knowledge can never reveal everything about consciousness, as Sartre seems to say in an interview late in his career (Sartre in Schilpp, 1981, pp. 22–23). On the other hand, because consciousness is translucid, because it has no content, it is possible to grasp one's past translucidity. For example, I can reflectively understand that as a consciousness totally absorbed in the process of writing, the ego-I did not exist—that nonreflective self-consciousness was simply *this* absorption in the work. Partially, I can do this because prereflective consciousness itself is a kind of reflexive (not reflective) self-awareness. This, indeed, is the meaning of the parenthetic *de* in *conscience (de) soi*. Hence it is only one slight step from this reflexive self-awareness to a (pure) reflective looking over my shoulder as I write.

Similarly, I can overtake myself in the process of accessory reflection: I can catch myself in the lie of trying to create a substantive self. Thus it is that the radical katharsis of deciding to give up the process of self-reification, which leads me in the direction of pure reflection even if I can never exactly achieve it, becomes a possibility. For this reason, I (as reflective consciousness) become more and more able to give up some of the maneuvers of accessory reflection and to attempt a simple understanding (pure reflection) of my prereflective self. It is this which leads to the "aha" experience of the mirror recognition, which Sartre describes as the end of the analysis and the beginning of "cure."

I believe that most so-called depth therapy relies on this process, even where it has no theoretical explanation for doing so. The concept of the "observing ego" and the therapeutic alliance in traditional Freudian analysis is a recognition along this line. As Sartre points out, "Empirical [Freudian] psychoanalysis, to the extent that its method is better than its principles, is often in sight of an existential discovery, but it always stops part way" (BN,

p. 573). I believe that this stopping part way is something which post-Freudian relational theorists for the most part share in common with traditional Freudian analysts. They go further than Freud in understanding that it is not the pursuit of pleasure but the pursuit of a self which is the primary human motivation. But most stop short of recognizing that one can never create a substantial self or identity—and that the process of therapy should eventually involve giving up this enterprise.

Perhaps this failure is understandable, considering the fact that much post-Freudian relational theory, like most post-Freudian drive theory, derives from work with severely disturbed adults (who seem to lack the "structure" which could have been provided by accurate reflection) and from work with children (who need accurate positive mirroring if they are to develop into lively adults). On the other hand, to fail to see that structure never exists *in* consciousness or that such a substantive self can never be achieved as an aim of therapy is to invite the continuation of human misery, including that portion of it which Sartre describes as the "conflict of consciousnesses." Only a reflective consciousness released from the struggle to create such a substantive self can respect either its own freedom or that of others.

The Implications for Psychotherapy

The implications for psychotherapy of Sartre's conception of the self as agent, object, and aim are both subtle and profound. As a therapist, one can work effectively to a certain point using the insights of the post-Freudian relational theorists, especially as these concern the impact of others on the development of a self. One can discover with Sullivan, Winnicott, and Kohut, for example, the origin of psychological disturbances in lack of adequate mirroring or reflection in childhood. Following the advice of Kohut, one can begin to work with clients to supply the missing needs for accurate reflection and other forms of human responsiveness—though one will probably not want to follow Kohut's idea that this involves actually building psychological structure.

One can then use the insights of Winnicott to consider questions of authenticity—the ways in which clients have substituted images which they believe will get the respect and approval of others for the truth of their spontaneous needs and desires. Again with Winnicott, one can explore the failure to develop an authentic self as this relates to a too intrusive or too neglectful parent who failed to allow a quiet sense of "going on being." Or one can experiment with Winnicott's idea that therapy is a situation involving "two people playing together"—that is, dissolving the serious world in favor of recognizing new possibilities.

One can even, following the ideas of Sullivan, approach one's client not as a fixed self but as a fluid self-system—though in doing so, one may wish to avoid Sullivan's physicalist metaphor of energy transformations. With all three theorists, one can respect the interpersonal nature of human reality, including the relationship between client and therapist. One can understand the extent to which other people have had and continue to have an impact on a client's developing sense of self. Yet despite all these useful insights, what will be found missing in post-Freudian relational theory is a clear and therapeutically useful conception of the self.

I believe that Sartre's description of the self as agent, object, and aim can clarify as well as take us beyond the insights of post-Freudian relational theory. Without some such understanding of the self, the aim of firming up the self as object (which is then confused with the self as agent) may become the goal of therapy. And though it is certainly true that the most important thing one can do at certain points in therapy is to provide accurate reflection, the attempt to provide missing structure may promote the very rigidity and misery which therapy ought to alleviate. Only a therapy which values the spontaneity of prereflective consciousness can emphasize self-acceptance in the sense of encouraging the client to reflectively validate his or her freedom. In this respect, even the attempt to hold on to joy, in terms of becoming a "happy person," is pathological. In fact, any other position than the reflective recognition and acceptance of oneself as responsible freedom will wrench away, constrict, and deny this very spontaneity. A therapy which does not understand this ontological truth, despite many very useful insights, is inclined to become a therapy in bad faith.

We can summarize the impact which a Sartrean view of the self might have on psychotherapy as follows:

1. If prereflective consciousness, or the self as agent, is translucid rather than opaque, then all therapeutic attempts to build structure *in* consciousness must be abandoned. In their place, the existentialist therapist would understand that a client's original difficulty lay in a faulty relationship between reflective consciousness and spontaneous consciousness, between the self as agent and the self as object, predicated on faulty mirroring or lack of adequate mirroring by the original others. The therapist would understand that the process of therapy is in part a matter of learning a new way of self-

reflection, partially through meta-reflection on one's reflective process. The "transmutation" that occurs is not, as Kohut believes, a matter of psychic incorporation of the therapist, but rather a matter of acquiring a new (reflective) way of being with one's (prereflective) self. To view or interpret this as the acquisition of structure may impede this process.

2. If the self as object—the ego—is no longer confused with the self of prereflective consciousness, then the therapist will be able to attend to the existential anxiety that accompanies profound change. This will lead the existentialist therapist to a new understanding of some forms of resistance as resistance not to unacceptable unconscious ideas but to the implications of change itself—that is, as resistance to the idea that one does not have a fixed nature. I believe it is extremely important for the therapist to recognize and deal with this "ontological" resistance. The question, "Who will I *be* if I change in [this or that significant way]?" is one which clients frequently ask, either implicitly or explicitly, as they consider the possibility of a fundamental shift in their way of being in the world. In a sense, the aim of existentialist therapy is just the opposite of contemporary psychoanalysis: Ultimately, it is not the establishment of a firm self or ego, but rather a "transcendence of the ego" (in the Sartrean as well as the Freudian sense of the term), which is the goal of existentialist therapy. The idea of becoming a substantive self or ego must be given up because such a self only reveals itself as an object of accessory reflection rather than as a subject.

3. In recognizing that the aim of consciousness is to create a self as value, the existentialist therapist would be able to understand in a different way defensive maneuvers, resistance, interpersonal conflict, and repetition of the past. In the attempt to create a substantive self, a client may avoid recognizing the implications of spontaneous behavior; resist therapeutic attempts to point out the impossibility of creating a substantive self; use others to attempt to create such a self; and repeat the past in order to ward off the appearance of the radically new experience which threatens his or her idea of being a substantive self. The existentialist therapist, in investigating all of this, would look not for unconscious ideas and affects, but for reflective distortions of spontaneous experience. Such distortions would not be regarded as deriving from a motive of pursuing pleasure and avoiding pain; rather, they would be viewed as deriving from attempts to preserve a self as meaning to which a client has great allegiance. Such a view does not require interpreting psychological distress as disguised pursuit of pleasure, since the pursuit of a self as meaning rather than the pursuit of pleasure as such is conceived to be the ultimate human "passion."

4. The existentialist therapist would be attuned to meanings in the client-therapist interaction beyond those usually conceived by traditional psychoanalysis. These would transcend the traditional understanding that therapy will be a forum for replaying old relationships, or the more recent understanding that accurate mirroring plays a crucial role in psychoanalysis, to allow an understanding of how clients (and therapists) may attempt to use the therapeutic process inauthentically in an attempt to create substantive freedom. For example, a client may (and probably will) want to use even the mirroring process to aid in the creation of a substantive self. This "tell me who I really am" process must be averted by pointing out that the client is capable of reflecting on his or her spontaneous experience and that the therapist is capable of misconceiving this. The question is, "Do you really want to give me that much power [to decide who you are]?"

Similarly, the discovery of other feelings and aims than those reflectively conveyed by parents may lead to an attempt to reify these new feelings and aims. I think, for example, of a client who repeatedly returned to therapy with the announcement, phrased in various ways, that last week he had finally discovered "who I really am." The therapist must in such cases resist the temptation to play God and assign a nature to the client—no matter how much the client seeks and desires this. Also, extreme caution must be used with respect to the tendency of therapy to develop a one-sided relationship at the expense of genuine reciprocity. The client must not emerge with the feeling that he or she is even more an object—the object of analysis—than when therapy began. Rather, the existentialist therapist should understand that it is the self as agent who must be encouraged and reflectively accepted in the course of therapy.

5. Finally and most importantly, the existentialist therapist would view the aim of therapy to be a radical conversion to a philosophy of freedom which would allow a reflective validation of the self of prereflective consciousness. Although accurate reflection, empathic resonance, and interpretation of the repetitions of past experience in present experience are all a part of existential psychoanalysis, as they are a part of Freudian psychoanalysis, they are not its final goal. That goal, as I have said, is recognition of one's prereflective self as responsible freedom. But this goal also affects the process and the interpretations made along the way. For example, one attempts to pursue the past, insofar as this is possible, in the mode of pure reflection rather than accessory reflection. This is very important, since in approaching the past it is quite easy to regard past events as determined from the outside rather than as chosen. Because prereflective consciousness is *con-*

sciousness of some external object, one remembers the past events and circumstances rather than oneself as an organizing *consciousness of* those events and circumstances. At the same time, one supplies a substantial "I" which was never there in the first place and attributes to it the property of being affected or caused by those events and circumstances, as rock rolling downhill is determined by physical forces. The problem with this view is that it solidifies consciousness and encourages bad faith. Too great a reliance on accessory reflection may indeed be the source of complaints that certain analyses encourage increasing knowledge *about* oneself while failing to provoke significant change.

The recognition that I *was* free, on the other hand, leads to the understanding that I *am* free. By emphasizing the therapeutic recovery of oneself as a past free agent, however, I do not mean to imply that the existentialist therapist should encourage clients to blame themselves for past events. In fact, self-blame frequently goes with a failure to recognize past agency rather than its opposite, since clients seem rather irrationally to assume that the blame lies in who they *were/are*—that the origin of their psychological difficulties is some kind of substantial flaw which exists in the self and environment at once. The radical conversion, on the other hand, offers the opportunity for a real assumption of responsibility in one's life—as opposed to either neurotic guilt or denial of agency. If I can really empathize with my past self at the choosing moment, then I can understand and appreciate my past self as a value-making process much better than if I take the more distant viewpoint of accessory reflection.

I can also, through meta-reflection, begin to purge the voices of the original others which I have incorporated into my reflective way of being—since pure reflection will provide a different vantage point on prereflective consciousness. For example, mother said anger was "bad," and I have been thinking of myself as "bad" when I am tempted to be angry. But pure reflection reveals to me not "badness" but anger. Recognizing this, I can begin to see what my past anger was about on a nonreflective level. I may similarly begin to name and reflectively understand past feelings and actions which were never named or reflectively understood. For example, I may give a name to the loneliness I felt as a child and thereby come to understand it and its motivating relevance to my present way of living.

Similarly, the attempt at pure reflection of immediately past events must be encouraged in therapy, as, for example, when one is investigating the client-therapist relationship in its contemporary dimensions. Therapeutic change involves more than anything catching oneself in the act of self/

world-making and changing the direction of the world one is attempting to make. For instance, one may catch oneself in the process of trying to impress the therapist with one's accomplishments as a way of avoiding a sense of inner emptiness and lack—which one can then explore. The fundamental direction of that change is movement toward the paradoxical realization that, though one must engage in the task of creating a self as value, one must never strive to *be* the self one has created—or to convince others to *be* the selves they have created or one would like them to create. Ultimately, the aim of psychotherapy is not building personality structure, but dissolving the illusion that consciousness or the psyche has structure and substance. The self as agent is free to create value.

As we come to the end of this discussion of how the basic project of creating a self affects existentialist therapy, one point needs to be reiterated. Although an existentialist approach along the lines of Sartre's philosophy outlines the process of self/world-making in terms of ontological insights, it in no respect dictates the particular character which an individual's world-making project will take. The existentialist therapist, as I have said, must never attempt to fix the meaning of symbols, in dreams or elsewhere, beforehand. Symbolic and other meanings emerge within the context of particular lives.Thus although the ontological outline is the same for all of us in that we are all pursuing the self as value, the particulars of how that pursuit takes place (and it can actually be discerned only in particulars) vary greatly from person to person. And while we can say that the goal of existentialist therapy is a radical conversion to a philosophy of freedom which involves giving up the belief that one can ever actually have a fixed self, the particular dimensions which such a conversion will take on in individual lives will also vary greatly. Furthermore, since lesser and greater modifications in an individual's project are always possible and may in fact be constantly occurring, the existentialist therapist must never approach clients as fixed psychological structures or static psyches. Both the methodology and the aim of existentialist therapy involve respect for and continual attunement to self and others as situated freedom.

5 · Sartre's Later Philosophy and the Sociomaterial World: A New Dimension for Existential Psychoanalysis

The Sartrean Dialectic and Existentialist Therapy

Sartre's earlier philosophy has thus far served us well in revealing the need for some major revisions in psychoanalytic metatheory which can help to account for, among other things, the new relational needs and disorders of the self discovered by many post-Freudian psychoanalytic theorists. According to the perspective developed in the preceding four chapters, this shift in psychoanalytic weltanschauung has significant implications for the practice of psychotherapy, especially with respect to providing an understanding of the future-directed dimension of a client's fundamental project and to apprehending and facilitating the moment of choice upon which significant change is based. Also, Sartrean revision of Freudian metatheory suggests that relations with others can be analyzed in terms of their significance to the fundamental project in ways which cannot be reduced to the simple desire to achieve pleasure or avoid pain.

Yet even though Sartre's earlier philosophy provides some crucial insights into the significance of the Other to one's definition of self, the earlier Sartre does not move beyond dyadic relations to develop a theory of groups and other social ensembles. Aside from a brief mention of the third party who objectifies the couple as an "us object" and the "we" of the common project, the "concrete relations with others" Sartre describes in *Being and Nothingness* are dyadic relations. Also, the specifically social implications of an individual's developing his or her fundamental project through the choice of various ways of *being*, *doing*, and *having* in a world held in common with others is simply not addressed to any significant extent.

The situation is very different in *Search for a Method* and the *Critique of Dialectical Reason*, where Sartre has taken on the task of describing and accounting for individual, group, and serial relations in a material world which is always *sociomaterial*. Although this shift does not, as some critics have argued, signify an abandonment of his earlier ontology, it is definitely an enrichment of his earlier position, which rests on the introduction of concepts not present in *Being and Nothingness*. Sartre's ambition in the *Critique of Dialectical Reason* is nothing less than to provide "Prolegomena to any future anthropology" in the European sense of the social sciences in general (CDR, p. 66). Or, as the subtitle of the critique indicates, the book's aim is to provide a "theory of practical ensembles." By practical ensembles, Sartre means human series and groups as they are connected to the sociomaterial world on the basis of survival-based need. Sartre also declares his intent in the *Critique* to solve "the fundamental problem of anthropology . . . the relations of practical organisms [human beings] to inorganic matter" (CDR, p. 72).

Although Sartre in *Being and Nothingness* had established an *ontological* basis for the relationship between human beings and the world, he had not yet discovered the *practical* relationship between them. Ontologically, this relationship does not change in Sartre's later philosophy: The free future-directed project based on negating consciousness still lies at the heart of all human enterprises. Indeed, the later Sartre still maintains that "the human dimension (that is, the existential project)" is "the foundation of anthropological Knowledge" (SM, p. 181). But this project is in the first instance a need-based project of organismic survival. It is *practical* first and *ethical* later.

This fundamental relationship between human beings and the sociomaterial world is also, Sartre now insists, a "dialectical" relationship. The word "dialectic" in its contemporary usage refers to the interpenetration of opposites. According to this view, which is derived from Hegel and Marx,[1] change is the distinguishing feature of reality. The "law of the negation of the negation," by means of which each state or phase of development is a synthesis which resolves the contradictions contained in the preceding synthesis at the same time that it generates its own contradictions, obtains in the movement of history. Yet although Sartre gains a basic understanding of the workings of the dialectic from his predecessors, he is neither a Hegelian nor a deterministic Marxist. Unlike Hegel and like Marx, Sartre grounds his understanding of the dialectic in the sociomaterial world. And like Hegel and unlike Marx, he locates the dialectic in its initial moment in the life of the individual.

Yet unlike either Hegel or Marx, Sartre refuses to subsume the individual in suprapersonal forces; he resorts neither to a Hegelian conception of the "World Historical Spirit" nor to the economic determinism of Marx to explain the movement of individual lives or of human history. Sartre considers both Hegelian "absolute knowledge" and Marxist "naturalistic" knowledge of the ends of history to be impossibilities. The reason, of course, is that human beings are fundamentally free. Also, according to Sartre, it is impossible for the philosopher or social scientist to take a position outside the movement of history from which to judge and categorize human affairs. Hence Sartre argues that by attempting to eliminate consciousness through objectivism, dogmatic Marxism has no recourse but to delegate the dialectic to a position outside of human history. As such, the dialectic becomes the "truth of Being as it appears to a universal consciousness" and thereby falls back into "complete dogmatic idealism" (CDR, p. 28).

Sartre describes his own position as one of "dialectical nominalism."[2] What he means is that he rejects the claims of both Hegelianism and Marxism to a dialectic which transcends individual praxis as its foundation and sustenance. The original negation of the negation, according to Sartre, is the needing individual negating the (projected) possibility of his or her extinction through work in the world. Thus Sartre believes that when we look at the real world, we do not find ideas or forces of production and exchange moving people; rather, we find people, through their impact on the world, creating social forces which subsequently make demands on their own and others' freedom—demands which can only be sustained by individual freedom. For Sartre, the dialectic "is not some powerful unitary force revealing itself behind history, like the will of God" (CDR, p. 37). Dialectical nominalism, unlike Hegelian idealism or Marxist economism, realizes that "there is no such thing as man" or history as distinguished from individual human beings (CDR, p. 36). It therefore insists on individual and group responsibility: If we are to have a more human future, we as human beings must create it.

Sartre also contends that the social scientist should place himself or herself within the human world that he or she is studying. The social scientist, according to Sartre, is not simply an observer who objectively notes the dialectical character of the object under study. Dialectical reason is an epistemology as well as a description of human reality. And knowledge in the social sciences, according to this view, is the dialectical knowing of a dialectical object which can only be known dialectically. Some of what Sartre means by this we have explored in previous chapters—especially in the discussion of the progressive-regressive method and of the fact that empathic comprehension supplemented by intellection is required for understanding in the human sciences. In the next three chapters, I compare the dialectical approach of existentialist therapy with the analytical approach of Lacanian structuralist psychoanalysis.

Here it should be noted that Sartre insists that in the human sciences, it is not a disadvantage for the social scientist to be a part of the system he or she studies. Although the Heisenberg principle of indeterminacy is making the objective observer obsolete even in the physical sciences, this idea that the experimenter is part of the experimental system is even more crucial to the human sciences. As Sartre puts it, "the only theory of knowledge which can be valid today is one which is founded on that truth of microphysics: the experimenter is part of the experimental system. This is the only position which allows us to get rid of all idealist illusions, the only one which shows the real man in the midst of the real world" (SM, p. 32).

Although today more social scientists are aware of the effects of the experimenter on the experimental system than was the case when Sartre first published these sentiments in 1960, objectivism in the social sciences is still far from dead. The problem with objectivist social science is that it falls into the error of expecting an active truth to reveal itself to a consciousness which has made itself passive. And this, Sartre maintains, is impossible, since "the scientist's passivity in relation to the system will reveal to him a passivity of the system in relation to him." It is for this reason, Sartre tells us, that "the dialectic as the living logic or action is invisible to contemplative reason" (CDR, p. 38).

Sartre, on the other hand, argues that "no one can *discover* the dialectic while keeping to the point of view of analytical Reason; which means, among other things, that no one can discover the dialectic while remaining *external* to the object under consideration" (CDR, p. 38). It is only as a meaning-engendering being that I as a social scientist have any chance of understanding the meanings engendered by others. For example, it is only from my own experience as part of a human series (a concept to be explained in some detail later on) or as a group member that I have any chance of understanding what serial alterity or being grouped means to others. Hence Sartre believes that the social scientist must enter into a dialogue with the object of study, a dialogue in which the investigator risks being personally touched and affected by the investigation. The social sciences, according to this view, require active involvement rather than passive analysis. The position of the godlike objective observer is impossible, and all attempts to mimic this position lead to distortions rather than to clarity in the human sciences.

Obviously, such a viewpoint is diametrically opposed to most traditional social science theory or even to traditional Marxism. Yet Sartre believes that traditional social scientists are deceiving themselves. Natural science provides a false model for the social sciences for the simple reason that human beings are not rocks or planets and human groups are not beehives. Predictability cannot be achieved in the human world because the free project, though not unsituated, is unpredictable. Genuine novelty, in which change cannot be reduced to identity, is a fundamental characteristic of the human world.

Actually, as Sartre points out, the attempt on the part of traditional social scientists to describe human affairs as if they were natural events involves a giant conjuring act:

> The procedure of *discovering* dialectical rationality in *praxis*, and then projecting it, as an unconditional law, on to the inorganic world, and then *returning* to the study of societies and claiming that this opaquely irrational law of nature conditions them, seems to us to be a complete aberration. A human relation, which can be recognised only because we are ourselves human, is encountered, hypostasised, stripped of every human characteristic and, finally, this irrational fabrication is substituted for the genuine relation which was encountered in the first place. Thus in the name of monism the practical rationality of man making history is replaced by the ancient notion of blind Necessity, the clear by the obscure, Truth by Science Fiction. (CDR, p. 33)

Not that Sartre would deny that certain moments of the dialectic are amenable to analytical classification or even that they can be expressed in mathematical formulas (CDR, pp. 177 and 561). But this is so because human beings encounter a thing world in which they must to some extent attempt to make themselves things in order to survive. A simple example is the human arm which I use as an extension to a crow bar in order to form a lever. A more complex example is the group which attempts to imitate a machine that acts effectively in the world. The group can therefore, from a certain perspective, be analyzed according to "a universal combinatory of functions" and thereby become the "object of an ordinal mathematics" (CDR, p. 561).

The problem with viewing the whole human scene in terms of the elements of it which can be understood analytically or even mathematically, however, is that this perspective ignores the fact that "the dialectic itself is beyond any mathematics" (CDR, p. 177n). In other words, the human motives which give significance to my making my arm into a part of a lever or supporting a group which attempts to work with machinelike precision lie beyond the grasp of mathematical analysis. Such an analysis is simply incapable of comprehending the "teleological structure" of human action, a structure which is always defined by its future-directed goal rather than by the inert structures which serve it in meeting that goal (CDR, p. 74).

Thus when analytical social scientists attempt to discover the "*hidden reality* of men and societies" in inhuman processes or static structures, they have reversed the truth of human affairs (CDR, 709). Processes and structures certainly exist, but they have been created and continue to be sustained by individual and group praxis.[3] To ignore this truth is to remove from them their intelligibility and to engage in perceptual and conceptual violence. Or as Sartre puts the matter, "Any philosophy which subordinates the human to what is Other than man . . . has hatred of man as its basis and its consequence" (CDR, p. 181). And this is true whether the "philosophy" in question is Marxist dogmatism, existentialist (Heideggerian) "idealism," or scientific positivism (CDR, p. 181).

Existentialist therapy, according to this view, is a dialogue in which the therapist as well as the client risks changing. Even more than other social science disciplines, psychotherapy is a living exchange rather than an antiseptic procedure. Traditional Freudian psychoanalysis has, of course, always recognized that it is the relationship which heals in the sense that the distortions of the transference are worked through within it. But the involvement of the analyst, that is, his or her deviation from a position of "technical neutrality" or (worse yet) being caught up in a "countertransference" which is often defined as *any* feeling toward the analysand, has been regarded as an error.

Existentialist therapy would also expect the therapist to avoid imposing his or her own issues on the client and to refuse to enter into the client's life as a participant in the usual sense (points I take up again in Chapter 8). But it would not therefore view absolute neutrality as an ideal position from which to conduct therapy. Hence Sartre, in the man with the tape recorder incident mentioned in Chapter 1, views as potentially pathological a situation in which the analyst is always an observer—the subject of the Look—while the analysand is always the object under observation. The client must realize that the therapist is a human being like himself or herself, or, to put this another way, the client must learn positive reciprocity within the context of therapy.

The ideas of *Search for a Method* and the *Critique of Dialectical Reason*, then, are relevant both for social science theory in general and for existential psychoanalysis in particular. Indeed, Sartre himself uses these ideas, together with many of his earlier concepts, in his biography of Flaubert. As for the relevance of psychoanalysis to social science endeavors in general, Sartre is even more adamant now about its value than he had been earlier. Attempting to create a marriage between Marxism and psychoanalysis under the auspices of existentialism, Sartre declares that psychoanalysis is "the one privileged mediation which permits [Marxism] to pass from general and abstract determinations to particular traits of a single individual" (SM, p. 61). This is important because, according to Sartre, the ultimate goal of social science research is to elucidate that "concrete universal": the unique historical individual. Unlike those lazy Marxists who overgeneralize because "they have forgotten their own childhoods" (SM, p. 62), Sartre would not engage in the "terrorist practice of 'liquidating the particularity'" (SM, p. 28) which reduces real people to economic abstractions—and which has at times corresponded to the physical killing of particular people. Existentialism instead "believes that it can integrate [with Marxism] the psychoanalytic method which discovers the point of insertion of man and his class—that is, the particular family, as a mediation between the universal class and the individual" (SM, p. 62). In doing so, Sartre believes that existentialism can correct the contemporary Marxist error of "reduc[ing] change to identity" (SM, p. 29).

Thus Sartre would ignore neither individual freedom nor the sociomaterial dimension of a person's life. Sartre defines existential psychoanalysis as "a method which is primarily concerned with establishing the way in which the child lives his family relations inside a given society" (SM, p. 61). After all, without understanding a person's childhood, we have no hope of understanding the path of his or her socialization or of his or her "personalization," that is, of what the environment brings and what the person adds. This is so because it is childhood which "sets up unsurpassable prejudices, it is childhood which, in the violence of training and the frenzy of the tamed beast, makes us experience the fact of our belonging to our environment *as a unique event*" (SM, p. 60). It is this unique event which the Sartrean dialectic attempts to discover. Whether a Marxist viewpoint is required to accomplish this is, however, a matter open to question. Indeed, Sartre himself later questioned whether the *Critique* was in fact a Marxist work.[4] It is certainly a work which allows us to add a sociomaterial dimension to the individualist approach of *Being and Nothingness*.

The Sartrean "dialectic" contains three "moments" (CDR, pp. 318–19), all of which have significance for (revised) existential psychoanalysis. The first moment, the moment of "objectification," is the moment in which individual need-oriented praxis inscribes itself in the sociomaterial world as a means to negating the possibility that it might fail to survive as an organism. An issue for clinical metatheory which arises from discussion of this moment concerns the substitution of survival-oriented "need" in Sartre's later philosophy for value-oriented "desire" in his earlier philosophy as a description of the basic relationship between the individual and the world. The questions we must ask are these: Are the two positions in any way reconcilable, and, if so, what impact does the new position have on Sartrean developmental theory? I believe that they are, and that the impact on Sartrean developmental theory is to deepen it in the direction of providing a link between organismically oriented needs and value-oriented desires.

The second moment of the Sartrean dialectic is the moment of "objectivity." This is the moment in which inorganic matter, infused with human meaning, "demands" of human beings a compliance to a pre-established future. It is the moment of the "practico-inert," or matter infused with human meaning and purpose. This idea that we never encounter anything but humanized matter is probably the most revolutionary concept of the *Critique* in that it is the basis for Sartre's whole social theory. Its significance for existentialist therapy is that it can help to account for the way in which an individual is inserted into a particular class or society at the same time that it explains how *things* too often come to dominate *people*—especially in the area of "work." It can help to clarify an individual's relations with previous generation(s) at the same time that it can define the serial impotence which lies behind a client's "other-directedness" and the "negative reciprocity" which may come to dominate a client's relationships in a situation dominated by scarcity. From this perspective, two aims of existentialist therapy would be to aid an individual, insofar as this is possible, in transforming other-directedness into self-directedness and negative reciprocity into authentic relatedness.

The third moment is the moment of "unification," or group praxis. Sartre's concept of group praxis as a negation of serial impotence introduces the new concept of the "ternary relation." And this idea of tertiary relations enables us to move beyond the binary relations of *Being and Nothingness*, which have proved so fruitful in elucidating the mother-child dyads of earliest infancy and childhood, to consider the power of the family as a *group* over its individual members. It also allows us to understand the kinds of groups that families may form and the significance of other groups, including the therapy group, to an individual's reconsideration of family norms. The third moment of the Sartrean dialectic, in fact, clearly moves existential psychoanalysis in the direction of social, and not simply individual, psychology.

Obviously, a single chapter of a book cannot hope to do justice to the complicated social philosophy of a dense volume such as the *Critique of Dialectical Reason*. I have therefore relegated certain issues, such as Sartre's Marxism, to the background. The sociopolitical implications of Sartre's later philosophy have, in any case, been adequately and admirably dealt with elsewhere.[5] In this chapter I want instead to consider the ways in which Sartre's later philosophy provides a social dimension for existential psychoanalysis which, though building on the ontology of *Being and Nothingness*, was not present in Sartre's earlier work.

Praxis, Need/Desire, and Sartrean Developmental Theory

The first moment of the Sartrean dialectic, the moment of *objectification*, is a moment which is ignored by positivist and Marxist social scientists alike. This is the moment of individual praxis which is all important to Sartre. It is the moment in which the negating individual inscribes his or her meanings in matter in the interest, first of organismic survival and later for other reasons as well. It is the moment of the "constituent dialectic," since everything is created and sustained by individual "totalizing" praxis—that is, by the individual comprehending and acting on the sociomaterial field. It is the moment with which the ontology of *Being and Nothingness* is concerned, though in his earlier philosophy Sartre demonstrates less of an appreciation of the sociomaterial world in which the individual objectifies himself or herself than he does in his later philosophy. In the *Critique*, such objectifying, goal-directed activity is referred to as "praxis" to emphasize the active nature of the for-itself as it lives its project in the sociomaterial world. Its opposite is "hexis,"[6] or simple re-creation of the status quo at the expense of genuine transcendence.

I make more of this idea of hexis than Sartre does (though I think the way in which praxis is derailed by the sociomaterial world is a major theme in all of Sartre's later work) for the simple reason that I believe that the transformation of hexis into praxis can be regarded as a major goal of (revised) existentialist therapy. Indeed, without authentic praxis, the moment of objectification is deprived of meaning—or it has only one (degraded) meaning: a restoration of the organism which rests on the submission of an enslaved freedom to the exigencies of the sociomaterial world. Such subservience is possible because restoration of the organism through the fulfillment of organismic needs is itself the first goal of praxis. And, of course, a certain amount of hexis is necessary in any life; it is, among other things, the security of the given.

By this time, the reader has probably already noted that Sartre, in his discussion of objectification in the *Critique*, substitutes the term "need" for "desire" as a description of the basic relationship between human beings and the world. Some have taken this substitution, along with Sartre's description of human reality as praxis rather than as consciousness or Being-for-itself, to indicate an abandonment of his earlier ontology. Although it is certainly true that the new terminology indicates a new emphasis on social awareness and action in the sociomaterial world, the idea that Sartre the Marxist has abandoned his earlier philosophy of freedom proves not to be the case. On the other hand, the shift in emphasis and the introduction of new ideas in Sartre's later philosophy do have significant consequences for the theory and practice of existentialist therapy.

Particularly significant for Sartrean developmental theory is his introduction, in the *Critique*, of a set of new terms to describe the *relationship* of the human individual to the sociomaterial world. These include "need," "praxis" and "hexis," and "totalization." Let us begin with "praxis," a term which is as old as Aristotle and which Sartre borrows from Marx.[7] Praxis, as we have said, is human goal-directed activity. More precisely, Sartre defines praxis as "an organizing project which transcends material conditions towards an end and inscribes itself, through labour, in inorganic matter as a rearrangement of the practical field and a reunification of means in the light of the end" (CDR, p. 734). Actually, despite this new sociomaterial orientation, praxis has much in common with nihilating consciousness as described in *Being and Nothingness*. Praxis, like the nihilating movement of Being-for-itself, is predicated on a relationship with the world as a perceived lack of future fullness. Like the for-itself, praxis is self-explanatory and transparent to itself, though Sartre adds that this intelligibility is "not necessarily expressible in words" (CDR, p. 93). Sartre still insists, in a sentence which might have come straight out of *Being and Nothingness*, that "consciousness, as apodictic certainty (of) itself and as consciousness of such and such an object" is the starting point for dialectical reason (CDR, p. 51). Praxis is human freedom, though not in the idealist sense of freedom without limitation. Even in Sartre's earlier philosophy, as we have seen, he had always conceived of freedom as situated freedom.

The difference is that in Sartre's later formulation the situation inevitably involves work on the sociomaterial world, which is designed, at the most basic level, to produce organismic survival; at the same time, praxis is inextricably interlinked with its sociomaterial milieu. Sartre therefore insists that "in an individual life, each *praxis* uses *the whole* of culture and becomes both synchronic (in the ensemble of the present) and diachronic (in its human depth)" (CDR, p. 55). The later Sartre is concerned with dissociating himself from some of his more radical earlier statements about one's being totally free in any situation. Although this is ontologically true, one must distinguish between an ontological freedom that allows one to freely live out the sentence which a society has passed on one and the kind of real freedom which a more genuinely human society might provide for everyone.

Nonetheless, Sartre still insists in the *Critique* that dialectical reason, in attempting to elucidate human praxis, must not reduce change to identity. Because praxis is not reducible to the material objects and social relations which it internalizes, it is capable of producing novelty. As Sartre notes, if we do not "distinguish the project, as transcendence, from circumstances, as conditions, we are left with nothing but inert objects, and History vanishes" (CDR, p. 97). It is for this reason that Sartre insists that "if there is any such thing as dialectical reason, it must be defined as the absolute intelligibility of the irreducibly new, in so far as it is irreducibly new" (CDR, p. 58).

Transcendence remains the key to Sartre's later philosophy as well as to his ethico-political position. In the *Critique*, however, Sartre wishes to locate transcending praxis at a much more basic level than that allocated to consciousness in *Being and Nothingness*. He therefore no longer terms the fundamental relationship between consciousness and its objects "desire"; instead, he designates this relationship as one of "need." Lest the reader think that the later Sartre has embraced some kind of instinctualism, however, we must hasten to add that need according to Sartre's conception is a human future-directed relationship with the world rather than an instinctual force. It is, like desire, a nihilating movement involving awareness of a present lack of a future fullness which is discovered in the world. Far from a "*vis a tergo* pushing the human laborer," need is "the lived perception of a goal aimed at, and this goal is, in the first instance, simply restoration of the organism" (CDR, p. 90). It is this "first instance" which distinguishes need in the *Critique* from desire in *Being and Nothingness*. The original negation of the negation quite simply is involved with survival itself.

Sartre describes praxis in the service of need satisfaction as proceeding by means of an activity which he terms "totalization." The totalization is an extremely important concept in the *Critique*, replacing the totality of traditional analytical social science theory both as the object of study and as the means by which the social scientist approaches this object. A totalization differs from a totality in that a totalization is a living, moving relation between the individual, or the group as sustained by individual praxis, and the world, whereas a totality is a static, inert whole. Sartre, however, claims that stasis is not a real characteristic of the human world. Praxis is always totalizing, detotalizing, retotalizing. A totality is a "fictionalized inert whole"; within dialectical reason, it functions as "a regulative principle of the totalization" rather than as a real entity. Like Being-in-itself-for-itself, which it resembles in some respects, it is that toward which human activity is heading rather than the point of arrival. For this reason, totalities as imaginary wholes come into the world through and are sustained by totalizing praxis (CDR, pp. 45–47). Even where a person has succumbed to the status quo, leading a life which is more hexis than praxis, there is still a moving retotalization which sustains that stasis or impasse. If one were really a static totality, one would not be able to feel bored or stuck.

If the totalization sounds like the world-making function of nihilating consciousness in *Being and Nothingness*, then this is so because the two concepts are, in fact, similar. The difference lies in the emphasis on the practical aspects of the totalization in Sartre's later work. From this perspective, need is lived as a "totalizing relation between the material being, man, and the material ensemble of which he is part" (CDR, p. 80). As such, a totalization is a "developing unification" of a practical field which is understanding and action at once; Sartre also uses the term for the field thus totalized, much as we use the word "work" in English to designate both the act of working and its products. Although totalizing praxis, like nihilating consciousness, is future directed grasping the present as the lack of a future fullness, that lack is in the first instance simply the projected lack of organismic survival unless one works on the world. At the most basic level, the totalization is the revelation of "the material environment, to infinity, as the total field of possibilities of satisfaction" (CDR, p. 80).

The problem for existentialist therapy with this description of the first moment of the Sartrean dialectic in terms of praxis, need, and totalization is that it fails to provide the link which will allow us to understand the connection between need as it is concerned with the restoration of the organism and desire as it is concerned with the creation of a self. In other words, the link between Sartre's earlier and later philosophy is missing. Yet surely Sartre has not abandoned his earlier ideas on desire, a conclusion which is amply illustrated by the Flaubert biography. Actually, this missing link between need and desire, though not present in *Search for a Method* and the *Critique of Dialectical Reason*, does show up in Sartre's unpublished writings from the 1960s, after he had completed the *Critique* and as he was working with the Flaubert material. In one of these manuscripts,[8] Sartre spells out the link we are looking for: Desire, he tells us, is socialized need, need which has through interpersonal relations been transformed from mere organismic longings into the desire for a certain kind of self.

Actually, as Sartre himself makes clear in the unpublished manuscript, need *never* appears in the already socialized human world in its pure form—except perhaps at birth. Otherwise, need is already socialized. And socialized need, as Sartre points out, is desire. It does not involve mere *reproduction of the organism* but *production of a self* at a more advanced level of the dialectic. It is the self as value which is the object of desire rather than the simple continued existence of the organism. And Sartre maintains that whereas pure need is "practical" in the sense of being survival oriented, desire is "ethical" in the sense of being value making. But just as the organic individual founds and limits the socialization of the serial individual of collectives and the common individual of groups while never appearing in a pure unsocialized state, so need, though nowhere to be found in its pure form, founds desire. Even in the *Critique*, Sartre is careful to point out that need is always socialized. For example, he states that "the labourer's work, his manner of *producing himself*, conditions not only the satisfaction of his need, but also the need itself" (CDR, p. 95). Yet as Robert Stone and Elizabeth Bowman note, this founding of the Sartrean dialectic on organismic need as the bedrock of desire is important because it "makes complete interiorization of impotence impossible" (1986, p. 208). There is a point in oppression at which the slave must revolt.

One can, however, go a long way toward distorting and denying needs before this revolt will occur. Throughout the *Critique*, Sartre points out that it is possible to turn praxis into hexis, changing transcendence into mere reproduction of the past/support of the status quo. In a sense, this re-creation of the past is an activity of free praxis, but it is an activity which undermines that freedom because people find themselves caught in the "passive activity" of obeying the exigencies inscribed in matter and the sociomaterial order. And while this turning of praxis into hexis is an inescapable aspect of being human, since it arises with the creation of the practico-inert, which is an inescapable outcome of the objectification process itself, Sartre objects to its overabundance in a world dominated by scarcity.

In such a world, needs are often denied or distorted through this transformation, even though the creation of the practico-inert is in the first instance intended to be need satisfying. Sartre cites the example of certain semiemployed day laborers in the south of Italy who, chronically malnourished, live their hunger as hexis. Since they expect only one meal a day or one every other day, they degrade their vitality accordingly to live in a state of semi-starvation (CDR, p. 95). Only the denial of that one meal, we might surmise, would be likely to arouse revolt against a situation which is otherwise deemed normal. Similarly, Sartre notes in the unpublished manuscript and in his biography of Flaubert, ordinary children from middle-class households may learn to deny or distort their needs—turning praxis into hexis.

Before we can fully appreciate this insight, however, we must first understand how need, through relations with others in the sociomaterial world, is transformed into desire. This idea is especially significant for existential psychoanalysis, as it will allow us to add some new insights to a Sartrean conception of developmental theory. In his unpublished manuscript, Sartre discusses how organismic disturbances which in their pure form are referred to as needs get transformed through interpersonal encounters into desires. From the beginning of life, the responses of others to an infant's organismic needs unveil that infant's *being* to him or her. To the infant's appeal, the adult caretaker responds by giving or withholding satisfaction. Gradually, through this interaction, appeal to the Other is transformed into demand or right over the Other. The infant comes to expect its cries to bring satisfaction in the form of mother's ministrations.

Sartre also explains that needs become intermixed—and symbolic of each other—in the context of the family. Alimentation, for instance, becomes sexual and sexual need becomes a way of eating. Artificial desires abstract themselves from cultivated needs. For instance, smoking may refer to eating, nursing, or sexuality. By the time a person reaches adulthood, no need appears in its pure form. All have been transformed into desires. Take eating, for instance. Neither the gourmet nor the ascetic experiences hunger as simple need. The gourmet subsumes simple hunger in an elaborate social ritual with an end which is not mere organismic survival but rather a particular kind of satisfaction which has aesthetic as well as nutritional goals. Nor can the ascetic with simple bread and bowl escape living hunger as desire since the ascetic's choice is ethical (value making) rather than merely nutritional. As for sexuality, it is, as we saw in Chapter 3, always much more complex than simple satisfaction of an organismic urge. Sexual desire involves a transformation of such organismic disturbances through language and fantasy into a demand to *be* (this or that kind of person) through (this or that kind of) sexual possession of (this or that) object.

The responses of the first caregivers are extremely important to the way in which an individual comes to live his or her needs/desires in the world. If the mother or primary caregiver responds with joy, acceptance, and understanding, then need, as Sartre tells us in the Flaubert biography, will be transformed into a desire that is felt as the perpetual possibility for action validating (or "valorizing," to use Sartre's own term) oneself and one's needs/desires in the world (FI, I:133–34). But if, as Sartre points out in the unpublished manuscript, the primary caregiver responds with irritation, disdain, or hostility, then need will tend to posit itself as illegitimate or culpable. The infant's need will have been socialized as a kind of primal *being guilty*—and this being guilty will come to be felt as an essential aspect of my being since each time organismic need is reborn (as it is perpetually reborn), my being guilty will be reborn. Not only my present, but my future (as need which has to be fulfilled) is implicated in this reproduction of guilt. For example, I am guilty for being hungry, sick, or "needy" in general—and I am ashamed of my needs/desires. Such guilt is a response to my *being there*, my very existence as a needing organism, which is reflected back to me as undesirable in this way or that by the original others. In psychotherapy, we constantly encounter such ontological guilt.

Sartre's example in the unpublished manuscript is anorexia.[9] The anorexic, Sartre hypothesizes, displays the desire for a guilt-free need that must be relieved of culpability by the Other's demand and supplication to eat. What the anorexic wants, Sartre tells us, is to experience a need that is *wanted* by the Other—as the anorexic's original need was apparently unwanted by the original others. The problem is that only a universal supplication could erase the original guilt—and this is impossible. Thus the meaning of anorexia lies in the movement of desire as a rejection-of-need-in-order-to-be-supplicated. Similarly, forbidden desire may look for a satisfaction that simultaneously punishes it and thereby purifies it—as happens in masochism and various other forms of self-destruction. Failure also is an example of need transformed into desire, in this case the desire to prove, by the impossibility of living, that there is an inverse to this impossibility—fulfillment in a more human world.

Obviously, though Sartre's examples are mostly negative, the transformation of need into desire can involve positive as well as negative development. Therapists, however, mostly encounter situations in which development has been painful, and Sartre's descriptions are extremely helpful here. Nor is Sartre, in his unpublished manuscript, unaware of the difficulties involved in a person's attempting to change the fundamental attitude formed in earliest infancy. This is so partially because the very eyes with which one will see new experiences have been clouded by this earliest experience, which must be retotalized each time one encounters something new. The past is surpassable, but only as taken into the detotalization and retotalization as a significant aspect of what is now practico-inert. As my original being there, this first experience of need as shaped by others into desire is very difficult to surpass in the sense of overcoming my guilt.

This is true because in objectifying myself I reproduce myself and this reproduction in the first instance means culpability (if I have experienced a negative response from the original others; otherwise, it means myself as gift, as possibility). My culpability gains the intimate force of need itself. The violence of my hunger, for instance, is the violence of my guilt. What I demand of the satisfaction of my desire is therefore a return to innocence—a restoration of an innocence I in a sense never had, since in discovering my need I discovered myself guilty before the original others. What I want is recognition of myself as innocent in the world of the Other; but this recognition is impossible—first, because even though the Other might change, it would be for other reasons than to validate me, and, second, because I presently structure reality in such a way that I probably could not see the change. Thus Sartre says that a long work on the part of the Other is required to free me of my guilt. Presumably, this is part of the work of psychotherapy. Its aim is not unsocialized need, but rather need/desire freed of the original condemnation.

Sartre's own approach to the Flaubert biography includes a description of the transformation of need into desire (or its failure) along the lines set forth in the unpublished manuscript. In *The Family Idiot*, Sartre attempts to show how an unvalorized child, Gustave Flaubert, through his interactions with the original others in his life, came to live his need more as hexis than as praxis and thereby to adopt the mode of "passive activity" as an integral part of his fundamental project. According to Sartre, Flaubert, as an "underloved" child, experienced as an infant the dutiful but cold ministrations of his mother. Madame Flaubert, Sartre hypothesizes, provided only the best physical care for her son, often anticipating in an overly protective fashion his needs before they even had a chance to manifest themselves. But in doing so, she treated her son as an object rather than as a subject, depriving him of the opportunity to develop an active sense of himself as affecting the world. At an "age when hunger cannot be distinguished from sexual desire" and when "feeding and hygiene condition the first aggressive mode of behavior," Sartre believes that Flaubert was deprived of a sense that he could aggressively satisfy his own needs/desires (FI, 1:48). Sartre describes the resulting condition as a kind of "anorexia" in which Flaubert fails to develop an active desire.

Flaubert's early passivity was not remedied by his encounter with a father who acted the paterfamilias and expected obedience. Even the part of Flaubert's interaction with his father which might have been expected to support him as an agent—his father's insistence on an active furtherance of the Flaubert family glory—escaped Gustave. He simply could not imagine what it meant to act in any real sense; instead, he playacted, dutifully producing the gestures expected of him by others. He also disappointed his father by his failure to learn to read as easily as his older brother, a failure Sartre attributes to the fact that reading requires an active participation of which the young Flaubert was little capable. As an escape from the adult world where he was Other to himself, Gustave sank into passive ecstasies in which a pantheistic union with nature had the real meaning of obliterating self and world together—a state in which, as Sartre says, "the soul *wants* nothing, *feels* nothing, *desires* nothing" (FI, 1:32). Later on, as an adult, Flaubert would complain of a "secret wound," which Sartre identifies as the "passive constitution" which resulted from his earliest interpersonal relations and of an ennui which never left him.

Before going on, I should explain what Sartre means by ascribing to Flaubert a "constitution," since it seems to imply a nature which would appear antithetical to the ontology of *Being and Nothingness*. Sartre, in *The Family Idiot*, divides an individual's life into three segments. The first of these is a person's "prehistory." This is the objective structure of the family into which the child has been born, including such things as class, social milieu, the character of the parents, and birth order. It will later be internalized by the child in this way or that. The second segment is the "protohistory," which refers to the earliest events in a child's life, including the "passional structure" which is the outcome of the earliest mother-infant interactions. The events of the protohistory lead to the development of what Sartre refers to as the child's "constitution." And if this sounds deterministic, it should be remembered that in developing a constitution, the infant still internalizes the external. It is just that Sartre recognizes the limitations of real choice (as distinguished from ontological freedom) which this involves.

Without a protohistory which includes the ability to affect the mother with one's needs, a child (as Sartre posits was the case with Flaubert) could hardly be expected to develop an "active" constitution. The constitution the child does develop will be included in the spiral of his or her development as a *this* which has to be transcended. Probably, we might add, the basic orientation toward life which is established in the protohistory is not likely to be overcome except through the deepest of therapeutic work. It will, however, be included in the next turn of the spiral of the child's life—his or her history proper, or "personalization." Personalization marks the advent of genuine praxis in the sense that the child begins to make something of what he or she has been made of—to act on the prehistory and protohistory which have been handed to him or her. But it is the constitution which will provide the original point around which the "spiral" of one's life will pass "again and again . . . but at different levels of integration and complexity" (SM, p. 106).

Flaubert, then, developed a passive constitution in response to indifferent handling by his mother. Hence he would later find himself complaining in a letter to his mistress of feeling like "a mushroom swollen with boredom" (FI, 1:142). He would envy less-talented souls who were able simply to feel and to act, and he would develop a sexuality which revolved around a fantasy of passive ravishment and which found its fulfillment in sporadic adventures with prostitutes and a long-distance relationship with the volatile Louise Colet rather than in real mutuality or commitment. As a mature writer, Flaubert would show a preoccupation with gestures, ceremonies, and objects rather than with reciprocal relations and with actions. Though he transformed his early project through an (imaginary) relationship with art which Sartre also deemed inauthentic, Flaubert was never able to overcome the passivity and isolation which derived from his original relations with others. He was never able to turn hexis into praxis or to learn the lessons of an active desire and real mutuality.

Actually, people similar to Sartre's Flaubert are not uncommon in therapy. I think especially of a client whom I shall call "John," whose life might be described as the epitome of hexis. John's mother, apparently an extremely self-centered, narcissistic woman, had consistently responded to him in ways that seemed designed to block the development of an active desire. In effect, she never heard anything which he asked of her. Instead, she substituted her own suppositions about who he was and what he needed or wanted for any communications he might have given her on the subject. John describes himself as being a very passive, "good" child as far back as memory goes. A particularly poignant memory involved a Christmas at home at about age eight. John had dutifully, but not very hopefully, made out a Christmas list. As custom had it, he and his brother were allowed to select one gift for opening on Christmas Eve. John selected a small package, which he imagined to be a toy car he had requested. When he opened this gift, his dismay at discovering "corn spears" (spears for holding corn on the cob) instead of the desired vehicle was greeted by the uproarious laughter of his mother. Not only could she not hear, but her not hearing appeared malicious. "From that time on," John told me sadly, "I decided never to put anything on my list which I really wanted—or probably even to *want* anything."

John's difficulties were very similar to those that Sartre describes for Flaubert. Although John did not become a writer (he was interested in writing), it was evident that he used reading as an escape from the real world. Asked about his hiding himself away in a world of books at a very young age, he replied, "Oh, yes, I *read* in order not to *be*." In his relationships with women, he was even more avoidant than Flaubert. After dissolving a marriage which was largely sexless by his wife's desire, he attempted to establish relations with other women. What he discovered was an extreme reluctance to even feel sexual desire in a woman's presence. On a rare occasion when he established a short sexual relationship with a woman, he described himself as lacking any feeling in his penis after penetration. "I was only aware of *her* and not of *myself* at all." His lack of desire showed up in other areas of his life as well. For example, he reported having to force himself to eat regular meals despite having no idea what he might *want* to eat. Also, even though he was a successful consultant in a technical field, he reported having no earthly notion about what he might want to *do* with all the money he made.

A seemingly casual remark which John made one day in therapy provided an opening into his dilemma. He commented that when people telephoned him, they frequently waited a moment after he answered "because they think I'm an answering machine." "Even you," he went on to say, "mistook me for an answering machine when you called the other day." I realized that what he said was true. And it occurred to me that the quality in his voice that caused him to be mistaken for an answering machine was a quality I often noticed there—the quality of not expecting anything from the other person. His childhood had foreclosed the possibility of learning to appeal to others for an answer or to expect/demand that his needs be met. At this point, John began to remember rather vividly what a "desert" (his word) his childhood had been. He had learned so well how to transform praxis into hexis that the whole world now appeared to be a similar desert in which he embraced the anti-value of "never desiring anything." As praxis began to be reawakened, he began to experience the pain, the humiliation, the anxiety, and the extreme loneliness he had previously avoided by deadening himself and curtailing his desires as completely as possible. Unlike Sartre's Flaubert, he was no longer bored.

Obviously, then, Sartre's account of the interconnection between organismic needs and relational needs or desires has implications for Sartrean developmental theory as well as for clinical practice. It should also be clear by now that Sartre has not abandoned his earlier interpersonal orientation for a new instinctualism. What he has done, however, is to give to organismic needs a significance that was missing in his earlier work. At the same time, it should be recognized that these needs gain significance and meaning only in a world which is from the beginning an interpersonal world. Hence it is only when organismic needs are met and shaped in a hospitable human environment that one's desire is shaped into a viable and real relationship with the world of objects and other people. Of course, as we saw in an earlier chapter, demand must be relinquished as a right over others if one is to develop relations in good faith. But unless the infant first experiences agency in being able to bring about the fulfillment of needs by the original caregiver, that infant will learn to live need as hexis rather than as praxis.

The young child in such a situation will learn to experience his or her being in the world of others as a being passive. Such a child will be more object than subject, and what will develop is something akin to the false self described by Winnicott. The problem, however, is that there is no true self to be uncovered; the release of spontaneity will require extensive work for a person to experience in a new way those needs which are perpetually reborn to be perpetually denied. The fact that they are perpetually reborn, however, allows the existentialist therapist to claim that a radical reorientation of oneself as a needing/desiring praxis is possible. The client in therapy must find a way within the therapeutic relationship to transform hexis into praxis—thereby discovering a viable future that the person has never before experienced. In this respect, on the individual if not on the group level, existentialist therapy might be conceived of as a revolutionary praxis.

*The Practico-Inert: Serial Alterity and Negative
Reciprocity as Issues for Existentialist Therapy*

The second moment of the Sartrean dialectic, the moment of "objectivity,"
is the moment in which worked matter, the practico-inert, returns with
claims on human freedom. The practico-inert is able to do this because
those claims have previously been written in matter by human beings. And
although Sartre, as a philosopher of freedom, tends to emphasize the negative characteristics of the practico-inert in a world dominated by scarcity,
the practico-inert has its positive side as well. It is both obstacle and opportunity. It is that through which I come to know myself as a part of my sociocultural heritage, that through which knowledge and opportunity are
passed (and in being passed are transformed) from generation to generation.

The practico-inert is also the thousands of exigencies written in matter
which enable me to live my life in an efficient manner without continually
"reinventing the wheel." It is not only the language which I speak and the
books which I read but also the streetlight at the corner which I obey and
the shop where I wait at the counter to buy my groceries.[10] It is that around
which my insertion into a particular class or milieu takes place. It is even the
natural disasters I experience, such as the volcano which destroyed Herculaneum or the recent earthquake in Armenia—since these occur in a humanized world where they are given a human significance (CDR, p. 180).[11] We
cannot escape the practico-inert. It is, Sartre contends, the very "motive
force of history" in that it is the practico-inert which provides the basis for
action in a common world (serial praxis) and which, through the creation of
serial impotence, motivates action in common (group praxis).

The practico-inert, however, is also the "anti-dialectic." As such, it replaces the conflict of consciousness in Sartre's earlier philosophy as the
Sartrean "hell." Indeed, one might say that in both *Being and Nothingness*
and the *Critique* hell is objectification—since it is the Other's objectification
of me that creates my misery in the former work while it is my objectification of myself (together with the objectifications of others) that creates the
practico-inert hell of the latter. What Sartre calls this "shifting hell of the
field of practical passivity" (CDR, p. 219) is a "place of violence, darkness,
and witchcraft" (CDR, p. 318) precisely because of its power to steal my
actions from me and to limit my freedom. It is because of this power of the
practico-inert to eat away at my own and others' freedom that Sartre, who
had noted in *Being and Nothingness* that I am constantly "sculpturing my fig-

ure in the world" (BN, pp. 463–64), now proclaims that all of us "spend our lives engraving our maleficent image on things" (CDR, p. 227).

The practico-inert, then, is that which eats away at my freedom by requiring that I obey its exigencies, thereby bending myself to those rigid and predetermined paths of action that are the "passive activity" of hexis rather than genuine transcendence. A machine in a factory, for instance, "demands" of the workers who service it that it be kept in working order, requiring them to submit to a "prefabricated future" in which the exigencies written in the machine take precedence over individualized action in which work is self-actualization (CDR, p. 188). Or a "brace and a bit and a monkey wrench" present a generalized future for anyone who uses them; they demand a similar usage of me and my neighbor (CDR, p. 186).[12] Even the language I speak suggests certain paths for my experience, paths which have been inscribed in the organized sounds and markings on paper which I have inherited from previous generations. Hence Sartre suggests that the "*scandalous absurdity*" associated with the exigencies written in tools is that they set up a "conflict between interchangeability and existence (as unique lived *praxis*)" (CDR, p. 260n).

Some people, of course, suffer more than others from the "hellish" side of the practico-inert. The factory worker, for example, would be more demeaned by the machine which he or she merely services to ends other than his or her own than would be a person who uses carpentry tools to build his or her own house. Similarly, the person who merely parrots the ideas and opinions of others without using them to help formulate that person's own unique experience would be living language more as hexis than as praxis.

At the same time, the meanings inscribed in tools—and all practico-inert objects are tools in the sense that they provide means to the satisfaction of needs/desires—are not as fixed as we might imagine. Indeed, as tools are made to "serve some other purpose" than was originally intended (actually, the moment a tool is created, it may already have begun to serve such a purpose), they lend themselves to the creation of new systems (CDR, p. 183). Consider, for example, the invention of gunpowder with its original meaning of greater power for destroying the enemy. What this invention helped to bring about was the collapse of the feudal system, since the knight on horseback thereby lost his privileged position in battle as protector of the realm. Similarly, we are only just beginning to suspect the possibilities for computer technology to transform the face of the socio-industrial world today.

Of course, tools cannot accomplish such changes on their own; a praxis (individual, serial, or group) must bend them to new ends. The point is that the tool is not a mere inert object. Sartre notes that the primitive tribesman also recognizes this when he calls the tool "sacred." He means that it contains "both a maleficent power [the power of solidified praxis as an indication of future behavior] and a threat [the threat of being used against oneself for purposes other than one's own]"—which is the contradiction long recognized as characteristic of the sacred (CDR, p. 183n).

Sartre, of course, understands that one *must* carve one's being in the practico-inert. An individual's life, from this perspective, is always some combination of hexis and praxis, freedom and necessity, exigency and value. Indeed, Sartre insists that dialectical rationality itself "must be seen as the permanent and dialectical unity of freedom and necessity" (CDR, p. 35). By necessity he does not mean an external or mechanistic fatality. Rather, necessity "arises in experience only when we are robbed of our action by worked matter, *not* in so far as it is pure materiality but in so far as it is materialized *praxis*" (CDR, p. 224). Necessity, though it erodes my freedom, emerges from it—it is *my* work alienated from me in a world which makes something different of it than I intended (CDR, pp. 226-27).

Just as freedom and necessity imply each other, so also are value and exigency "two different structures within a single process":

> The imperative character of exigency is due to the fact that materiality is animated by the *praxis* of the other and to the fact that this *praxis* is revealed to me as both human and alien: it signifies me and awaits me, but it is not *mine*: it is myself as nothing. Value, on the other hand, is a double movement: both the revealing of *my praxis* in its free development in so far as it posits itself as other within immanence, and the revealing of a future signification as an inertia which refers back to my freedom. (CDR, p. 248n)

There is no way to avoid objectifying myself in the world and having my praxis returned to me in an alien form. Furthermore, today's values become tomorrow's exigencies as they develop into a "system of values" adopted by a particular society.

The difference between value and exigency, praxis and hexis, therefore lies in the fact that value and praxis refer to the power of freedom to create novelty (even amid previously seemingly static structures) while exigency and hexis refer to the acceptance of the future as closed—as that "which cannot be transcended" (CDR, p. 247n). Obviously, all human projects are a partnership between the two. A completely open future would not be human.

Praxis must learn to define itself in the practico-inert world in such a way as not to be completely absorbed by it.

The question, then, is not whether hexis exists in my life—since it obviously does—but the extent to which it dominates my life. This is at least in part related to the extent to which I have fallen victim to "serial impotence" in a situation of scarcity. Sartre's concept of the series is undoubtedly one of the most significant and original contributions of the *Critique* to social theory. The human series, according to Sartre, is composed of individuals forming a social ensemble in which each reacts to a particular aspect of the practico-inert field, the "collective object," in an identical manner. As a social concept, the series lies between the individual and the group and provides an understanding of the link between the two in that it is serial impotence which motivates the formation of groups. Not all series, however, become groups. Sartre's most famous example—people queueing up to a bus—is unlikely to become a group unless something unforeseen happens, such as a group forming around a child who has been hit by the bus.

Since the bus queue illustrates all the aspects of the series which I wish to consider here, let us examine it more closely. The people in the bus queue are, like people in series in general, solitary, separate, interchangeable, and identical in their relationship to the collective object, the bus. The first individual in the line enters the bus first, not the individual who most deserves or needs to enter the bus (to use only two criteria for differentiation). The individuals in the bus queue, like individuals in series in general, are aware of each other: I wonder, for instance, if I will be able to get a seat on the bus. But the bus, like collective objects in general, does not provide a means to uniting me with these other people in any significant sense; rather, it becomes an index of separation cutting me off both from other people and from an authentic sense of self. We each stand in solitude as we wait for the bus and (usually) sit or stand in solitude once we have entered. In the bus queue, everyone "is the same as the Other in so far as he is Other than himself" in the sense of engaging in a generalized rather than an individual praxis (CDR, p. 260).

The locus of feeling, thought, and action in a series is always "elsewhere" rather than "here." Seriality therefore has more to do with hexis than with praxis. Its distinguishing characteristic is impotence rather than transcendence. Sartre refers to the "passive activity" of serial behavior as "recurrence." Recurrence is my acting as I believe the Other will act because it appears to be in my interest to do so. An outstanding example is the so-called free market of capitalism, which is in effect governed by recurrence rather than by individualist action. Another example is price, which "imposes it-self on me, as a buyer, because it imposes itself on my neighbor; it imposes it-self on him because it imposes itself on his neighbor; and so on" (CDR, p. 288). And though I am aware that I help to establish it, I am also aware that I can do nothing about it. There are, as Sartre points out, serial thoughts and serial feelings as well as serial actions. Scandal, as the judg-ment which no one claims and which is referred to as an impersonal "they," is an example of serial thoughts (CDR, p. 277); many other forms of "public opinion," including racism and anti-Semitism, fit here as well (CDR, pp. 652–54 and 716–34). Stereotypical love relations are an example of serial feelings.

Obviously, there is no harm in serial praxis if we are simply talking about a bus queue or a grocery line. In such situations, the formation of a series is a matter of mere convenience. But what if the individual who waits in the bus queue is not doing so as a means to further a project which includes gen-uine self-creation and the establishment of positively reciprocal relations with others? What if that person is heading for work in a factory where he or she has sold his or her labor in a situation involving competitive recur-rence with other workers for a job in which each will become the machine's "thing"? And what if this person, on boarding the bus, simply opens up that other collective object, the daily newspaper, and imbibes the paper's edito-rial opinions as his or her own? What if that person, on returning home, sits passively in front of another collective object, the television screen, absorb-ing but not critiquing or evaluating what he or she sees and hears, and then retires to bed? Will that person's dreams be serial, or will the crushed desire for individual praxis emerge with an unaccustomed violence? Actually, though one doubts that anyone is ever so completely immersed in seriality as our hypothetical example here, all of us to some extent act, think, and feel as other than ourselves. Sartre refers to the person who is fairly thor-oughly immersed in serial alterity as "other-directed"—borrowing a term from American sociologist David Riesman (1950) and giving it a philosophi-cal foundation.

Other direction is, from the perspective of existential psychoanalysis, a pathological condition. Often it involves a "manipulated series." Some "sov-ereign" person or group (see the next section for precise definitions) uses its influence or authority to induce fundamental relations of alterity in the members of a series in order to profit in some way from this seriality. The other-directed person has lost himself or herself in seriality. Other direction is, in fact, a kind of "worked seriality" in which a person has directed "his free *praxis* onto himself so as to be *like the Others*" (CDR, p. 643). Sartre takes two examples from a visit to the United States in 1946. One is the training of American salesmen, who must learn to manipulate themselves in order to manipulate their customers. The other is a radio phenomenon—the "top ten" records—which is used by broadcasters and record producers to promote sales.

The top ten records phenomenon provides an especially helpful insight into other-direction as a sociocultural phenomenon. It may be particularly relevant in an age where television advertising is much more pervasive and convincing as a tool for manipulating seriality than the radio broadcasts of the 1940s. After all, are we not continually asked to buy not only the record collection of the Other but also the soap, hair spray, automobiles, clothes, gum, toothpaste, and other products of the Other? And are we not asked to do this with the particular aim, it seems, of becoming the ideally desirable person (made visually manifest by the TV advertising model)—that is, no one?

In any case, the phenomenon which Sartre describes is this: In response to the announcement and playing of the top ten best-selling records of the week on several radio stations, listeners go out and buy records, increasing sales during the following week by thirty to fifty percent. According to Sartre, these listeners are responding serially to the announcement that others consider these the best records, and it is as Other that they buy either the top record or several top records. The individual record buyer than "listens to the selected record through Others and through himself as Other" in an "isolated ceremony" that "consecrates him *as Other* even in his own feelings" (CDR, p. 649). The record broadcast is successful because it persuades the listener "to buy what the Other is buying" (CDR, p. 669n). When the listener turned buyer later talks with peers about the record, this person will have the feeling of sharing something with others. Despite their being others to themselves, all of these people are mistaking manipulated seriality for genuine reciprocity. These buyers are not sharing their individuality, but are instead giving testimony to the fact that they are "really just the instruments of well-organized collectives" (CDR, p. 649). The truth is that this record buying is an act of recurrence. Each record buyer has acted "the same as the others in order to become the same as them" (CDR, p. 650), and the discussion among them is a ritual confirmation that both have succeeded.

Sartre points out that such appeals to act or buy as the Other can only succeed if "the serial individual has been produced from childhood as other-directed" (CDR, p. 651). One task of existentialist therapy will therefore be to discover to what extent seriality and other-directedness permeate a client's fundamental project—and how childhood may have prepared this person to engage in a project that includes the desire to become other than oneself. In this connection, I think of a young woman, whom I shall call Sherry, with whom I once worked in therapy. Sherry, who was in her early thirties, entered therapy at the suggestion of a friend because she found it extremely difficult to say no to people. She consequently found herself working sixty-hour weeks and continuing in a relationship (only mildly satisfying to her) in which her boyfriend made most of the decisions about where to go, whom to see, and what to do. In the therapeutic relationship, she seemed to expect advice and try to play the "good client"—an issue with which we worked in some depth.

What struck me most about Sherry in her initial interview was a certain "generic quality" to her dress, speech, and manner. She was pleasant and polite enough, but there was something about her that made it difficult for me to think of her as a "real" person in the sense of being a developed individual. Although she did not appear to be manipulative in any deliberate way, her manner had an inauthentic air that was hard to get hold of. I gradually discovered that this resulted from an extreme other-directedness in her fundamental project—an other-directedness which showed up, among other things, in her speech mannerisms. Instead of saying "I think" or "I feel," Sherry would say "you think/feel/say." For example, she might say to me, "When you're not happy, you just don't have any idea of why it's like that." By asking her to substitute "I" for "you," I soon confirmed something I had already begun to suspect: Sherry simply had no idea what she herself wanted, needed, or thought. For instance, she once stopped in the middle of moving to help a friend write a résumé because "you're supposed to be there for your friends." Most of her opinions were the generalized opinions of the "they say" variety—and their origins were the practico-inert wisdom of the popular culture of the day. When Sherry first began to look at this phenomenon, she was really frightened. She wondered aloud if "I [not you] even have a self." In a sense, of course, she did not have much uniqueness—though the fact that she was able as a free consciousness to grasp this meant she could begin to change.

Sherry's background provides one glimpse into how other-directedness is, as Sartre says, produced from childhood. Sherry's mother, who had come from a poor farming community and joined the middle class through her marriage, was extremely conscious of conventions. She was also somewhat tyrannical: It seemed natural to her to dictate not only the rules of the house, but her children's thoughts and feelings as well. The father, who was concentrating on his business, did not interfere and apparently appreciated the "orderliness" of his household. Sherry, on entering therapy, simply could not imagine contradicting her mother since her mother became unreasonably irate at the least sign of anything that smacked of differences. This woman's children, it seemed, required keeping in order like the furniture. At the same time, what dictated the mother's opinions and wishes for her children was public opinion—the "they" of middle-class respectability. Sherry remembered joining a girl scout troop, rather than the dance class she had wanted to join in grade school, because her mother insisted that "lots of successful children have been scouts" and "all of my friends' kids are in scouts."

Sherry was also aware that her mother hardly differentiated among the children: They were the generic "kids" and must do what "kids" are supposed to do. And though Sherry's younger sister had rebelled against this to some degree, Sherry herself was the "good daughter" who tried to please her mother. Indeed, this good-daughter motive was so strong that at a certain critical moment near the beginning of therapy, Sherry unaccountably decided to move back to her hometown because "my family misses me." Once this crisis was over, it became apparent that she was extremely fearful of facing the angry feelings she had toward her mother over squelching her individuality.

In Sartrean terms, what had happened in this family was serialization based on the existence of a "sovereign" at the center of the family group (a situation I discuss further in the next section). I believe it was partially because I was aware of the concept of serial praxis and other-directedness at the time I worked with Sherry that I was able to help her move toward developing a more authentic sense of self. Sherry began to look at the emptiness at the heart of her project—at the placement of the Other where there might have been a self. Although this was painful and difficult, she also began to get excited at the prospect of choosing something (an activity, a dress, a friend) "simply because *I* like it." This was obviously a totally new idea to her. Gradually in the course of the year during which I worked with her, Sherry began experimenting in her personal life—moving out of a roommate situation which was made difficult by her growing unwillingness to be acquiescent and suggesting activities to her boyfriend or even doing things on her own. Unfortunately, this relationship did not survive the changes since she had apparently chosen a very narcissistic man. The breakup, however, troubled Sherry only briefly, as she began dating and doing things with new friends.

In becoming aware of her own body rhythms and needs/desires, Sherry had started to live her own life rather than the life of the Other. Even her manner of dressing became more individualized. She told her boss "no" to the amount of overtime he had been extracting from her. And she organized and set up a training group for a program at work which landed her a promotion. Her excitement at discovering that "the sky doesn't fall in when I listen to myself" (she, of course, did not become narcissistic in doing so) was refreshing. The last time I saw Sherry I could not help being struck by the change in demeanor which had taken place since her first visit: In place of the polite, overly flexible young woman who had first come to see me was a real person with energy and enthusiasm.

While my work with Sherry demonstrates one of Sartre's points about serial impotence, the fact that it can deprive a person of an authentic sense of self, it does not illustrate the other—the fact that seriality, throughout history, has occurred in a field of scarcity. We must remember, however, in talking about scarcity that Sartre's theory of scarcity is a social theory, since for Sartre there are no facts which are not social facts. Hence scarcity is experienced differently by different people. For example, the fabulously rich heir to a mine might experience scarcity as "dispersal, poverty of means, and the resistance of matter" constituting impediments that threaten to slow down production. "For the heir, scarcity is the possibility of not coming into his inheritance unless he reorganises his field of actions as soon as possible" rather than a threat to his physical existence as such (CDR, p. 739). His workers, on the other hand, might experience scarcity as the lack in this particular field of decent work and wages. At certain times in the economic cycles of capitalism, scarcity might even be experienced as a scarcity of consumers rather than of products. Or it might be scarcity of time.

Ultimately, scarcity refers to basic needs. And even though the structures of capitalistic society relate only indirectly to basic needs, need is nonetheless "always present *as tension*" even in situations where it does not appear directly (CDR, p. 218). Most of us, after all, are at least dimly aware of the fact that two-thirds of the world's population remains undernourished (CDR, p. 123), and most of us have at least a peripheral fear of falling into the superfluous group. Nonetheless, because scarcity for Sartre is "*a human fact*, rather than the malignity of a cruel nature" (CDR, p. 140n), it is possible to think of overcoming it in a more just world.

In this world, however, the addition of scarcity to seriality "transforms separation into antagonism" (CDR, p. 221). And it is this transformation rather than the simple existence of the Other (as Hegel thought) which is the "scandal" of our common existence. In such a situation, violence, as "interiorised scarcity," becomes the basic structure of human relations (CDR, p. 815). This is not, however, necessarily an open violence; it is more often a structured violence in which a society, by the way it structures human relations according to classes and other criteria, chooses "its dead and its underfed" (CDR, p. 147). Exploitation, Sartre remarks, takes place not *by* violence but *in* violence (CDR, p. 153). And in a field of scarcity, violence (implicit or explicit) permeates all human relationships.

Actually, what Sartre is saying here is very interesting in light of his description of the conflict of consciousnesses in *Being and Nothingness*. Although his ontology has not changed, his ideas concerning the origins of interpersonal misery have shifted. The Other as the source of my objectification (as I am of the Other's) has not been superseded, as the following summary from the *Critique* illustrates: "It is impossible *to exist amongst men* without their becoming objects both for me and for them through me, without my being an object for them, and without my subjectivity getting its objective reality through them as the interiorisation of my human objectivity" (CDR, p. 105). Nor, as we can see from the Flaubert biography, has the significance of the objectifying Look been superseded as a means to understanding the origins of a person's neurotic distress: Sartre still claims that it was the critical Look of Flaubert's father, added to his mother's dutiful indifference, that helped to place Gustave in the untenable position leading to his neurosis (and to his becoming a writer). Yet the hostile Look of the Other now takes place in a sociomaterial context of (actual or possible) scarcity. And it is this scarcity which is viewed as lying at the heart of violence in human relationships—and not the mere existence of the Other as a witness and critic.

Since Sartre is usually regarded as a philosopher of human conflicts, I would like to emphasize the importance of this shift in perspective for existential psychoanalysis. What Sartre now regards as "normal" in human relationships not malformed by scarcity is something akin to the attitude of empathic understanding that he had already prescribed for the existential psychoanalyst in *Being and Nothingness*. Reciprocity, rather than antagonism, is fundamental. The term "reciprocity," for Sartre, means simply "a free exchange between two men who *recognize each other* in their freedom" (CDR, p. 110). Such recognition can be either positive or negative: I can use the fact that the Other's project is comprehensible to me because I, too, am human either to aid him or her in realizing it or to foil the Other's plans. In "pure reciprocity," however, I regard the Other not as an antagonist but as "another self," that is, as a person whom I recognize as being fundamentally like myself in his or her basic humanness. In such a situation, "my partner's *praxis* is, as it were, at root *my praxis*, which has broken in two by accident, and whose two pieces, each of which is now a complete *praxis* on its own, both retain from their original unity a profound affinity and an immediate understanding" (CDR, p. 131).

When I violate this affinity and solidarity with the Other, as I must do either implicitly or explicitly in a situation of scarcity, I myself suffer as well. Sartre comments that in attempting to destroy my adversary, "I cannot help destroying the humanity of man in him, and realising his nonhumanity in myself. . . . [In attacking my enemy] what I attack is man as man, that is, as the free *praxis* of an organic being. It is man, and nothing else, that I hate in the enemy, that is, in myself as Other; and it is myself that I try to destroy in him so as to prevent him from destroying me in my own body" (CDR, p. 133).

Later on, Sartre gives as an example the nineteenth-century factory owner whose own lifestyle (stiff collars and top hats for himself; corsets for his wife and daughters; repression of sexual and other needs/desires for all) represents the "presence of the oppressed in the oppressor in person" (CDR, p. 771). The suppression of his own and his family's organismic spontaneity is somehow intended to justify the factory owner's oppression of his workers at the same time that it proves him to be a "superior being" who deserves the favored position in which he finds himself. Yet the bourgeois owner suffers as well, as his own organismic needs are placed under strict surveillance, even if they cannot be fully extinguished. One wonders if something similar is at work in child abuse, where it is abundantly clear in the case of parents who were themselves abused as children that the child represents the "presence of the oppressed [one's own child self] in the oppressor [one's self, one's parent] in person." Often the thing which originally infuriates the abusive parent is the child's simple organismic needs—which the parent's parent had presumably failed to tolerate and which the parent now regards with suspicion and loathing in himself or herself as well as in the child.

Why, then, if in doing so we damage ourselves as well, do we develop antagonistic relationships in a situation of scarcity? Sartre suggests that this antagonism initially develops out of a simple fear of being the "superfluous man" in a world where there is "not enough for everybody" (CDR, p. 128). That this fear exists at the edges of consciousnesses even in the most affluent bourgeois homes is attested to by those ubiquitous parental maxims: "Eat your [whatever loathsome dish the child is trying to avoid]—don't you know that the children in [whatever impoverished country is currently in the spotlight] are starving?" Or the parent may say, "Study hard—do you want to grow up to be a garbage collector?" In fact, I once had a client who admitted to getting his doctorate partially out of fear of becoming a garbage collector.

Sartre describes the negative reciprocity which results from the recognition of scarcity in the following way:

> In pure reciprocity, that which is Other *is also the same*, but in reciprocity as *modified by scarcity*, the same appears to us as antihuman in so far as *this same man* appears as radically Other—that is to say, as threatening us with death. Or, to put it another way, we have a rough understanding of his ends [for they are the same as ours], and of his means (we have the same ones) as well as of the dialectical structures of his acts; but we understand them as if they belonged to *another species*, our demonic double. Nothing—not even wild beasts or microbes—could be more terrifying for man than a species which is intelligent, carnivorous and cruel, and which can understand and outwit human intelligence, and whose aim is precisely the destruction of man. This, however, is our own species as perceived in others by each of its members in the context of scarcity. (CDR, pp. 131–32)

In such a situation, violence will be perceived as counterviolence (CDR, p. 133) in which the Other is always the "one who started it" (CDR, p. 149).

Scarcity therefore provokes the development of Manichaeism—a situation in which I and my group or subgroup are perceived as "good" and/or "human" while the others are perceived as "evil" and/or "subhuman." Manichaeism is obvious in the conflicts between nations and between well-defined groups and subgroups (races, classes, interest groups) within a society. Prejudice of various sorts is an outstanding example. But Sartre argues that such antagonism also implicitly invades relationships between friends and family members (CDR, pp. 152–53n). In the context of "diffused violence" created by scarcity, it is always possible to view even one's best friend as an "alien wild beast" whose intent is one's own destruction (CDR, p. 150). Friendly and not so friendly "competition" is often a veiled form of such antagonism.

Within families, it is possible that Sartre's idea of antagonism based on scarcity of parental supplies better explains sibling rivalry than Freud's explanation of instinctual sexually based jealousy. Those supplies obviously include not simply the means to fulfilling organismic needs but also the lack of love or validation of those needs, which might well be in part the result of shaping the child to live in a society where scarcity of resources requires a dulling of active praxis in favor of hexis. After all, who could expect a still "needy" parent to respond well to the needs of a child? In any case, I believe that negative reciprocity is a viable concept for understanding certain kinds of extremely negative and destructive interactions which develop between family members.

Obviously, such negative reciprocity may be exacerbated in cases of real economic deprivation or perhaps even homelessness—although it is also possible that in such situations people might learn to support each other. The example I will use involves the learning of negative reciprocity in an "ordinary" middle-class household since this is the population with which I usually work in private practice. My client, whom I shall call Polly, was a young divorced woman in her mid-thirties with a ten-year-old son and a live-in boyfriend. During the course of therapy, Polly broke up with her boyfriend and entered a more compatible relationship. It was in the context of this "good" relationship that she became suspicious of the continued presence of an old symptom which did not vanish because of her newfound confidence in her partner.

This troubling symptom was unfounded jealousy. Polly was jealous of anyone her lover spent time with—of his women friends most of all, but also of his family and his men friends. She also admitted that she found it difficult to be with him or with anyone else who was close to her in a group situation. Apparently she either felt jealous that her friend was giving others more attention or that others were giving her friend more attention. She also felt a compulsion to entertain or be the center of attention in groups. On her own, she kept up a hectic pace of achievement-oriented activities. All of this made her miserable, as her adult mind told her that her companion was reliable and her responses were unreasonable and that her hectic pace left her drained and uneasy. In fact, as it turned out, all this frantic activity ("too many pots boiling on the stove," as Polly described it) kept at bay certain deep feelings of inadequacy and sadness. Nonetheless, Polly could not restrain herself from "punishing" her lover with angry withdrawal for any time he spent with friends. And "slowing down" admittedly made her very anxious.

Part of Polly's problem with jealousy seemed to derive from a desire to have her lover provide her with constant positive mirroring. Polly simply felt that she did not really exist when she was not being mirrored. But as Polly worked on these issues in therapy, it became increasingly clear that there was another source to her difficulties as well: She had grown up in a family where negative reciprocity was the norm. Polly's father, a businessman to whom "success" was extremely important and who failed to conceal his opinion that the three children his wife had insisted on having were a financial burden and a bother, nonetheless paid attention to his children in one way. He arranged competitions among them—for attention, grades, or whatever. Even at the family dinner table, he set up a ritual in which the child with the best story received money as a reward. Polly usually won the prize, resulting in a feeling that it was "not OK" just to be herself—that she had to be interesting and entertaining. In fact, she complained bitterly of feeling that if she did not entertain or perform, "I would just be invisible and worthless." Apparently this was how her older sister, Mary Ann, felt, whereas her younger brother, John, gained attention by self-destructive rebellion. Polly, however, in addition to winning the competitions, was regarded by her mother as "my best child." It would appear at first that she had the best from both parents. In fact, her older sister now lived a life that was continually in crisis, and her younger brother was an alcoholic still living at home. The truth, however, is that Polly, the seemingly "normal one," did not escape unscathed.

The effects of negative reciprocity even on the "winner" became very clear in a break-through session with Polly during the second year of therapy. Polly came in vaguely annoyed with her sister, who had been "wasting my time" regaling her with the latest details of the sister's "latest crisis." Polly felt concerned, frustrated, and helpless to do anything about Mary Ann's constant "problems." She also felt vaguely guilty. After all, even her parents had called suggesting that Polly might be able to and in fact ought to find a way to help "poor Mary Ann."

I suggested a Gestalt dialogue with Mary Ann, which revealed some very interesting things not only about Polly's feelings concerning Mary Ann but also about her feelings regarding her mother's favoritism and her father's competition mongering. In the course of this role playing, Polly's anger and guilt toward Mary Ann turned into anger with her father for setting up competitions between them which Mary Ann always lost and which left Polly feeling guilty and sad for Mary Ann, whom she now realized felt like "another self." This made Polly more aware of her own terror over the possibility of being in Mary Ann's position since it was obvious that "*somebody* in the family had to lose." There was in this family, in other words, a scarcity of validation.

In this session, it also became clear that the competition mongering of Polly's father was reinforced by her mother's very obvious preference for Polly over Mary Ann. And, indeed, it was in the dialogue with her mother that an emotional "explosion" occurred for Polly. Polly became aware that she felt very distant toward her mother and tried to keep her at arm's length. In the dialogue, she physically held up her arms and hands to ward her mother off. At first, she thought this was out of sympathy for her sister in not receiving the same "love," and it was certainly true that Polly as a child had obviously felt deeply Mary Ann's wounds. But as it turned out, the "love" for which Mary Ann so envied Polly turned out to be not genuine love at all but a voracious narcissism on their mother's part. Polly's fear was of having the "life sucked out of me" by a vampire mother who wished to use Polly to fill up her own emptiness in a marriage where there was little emotional contact. The mother had even agreed with the father to send Mary Ann away to boarding school in high school, but had resisted sending "my Polly" because she needed her so badly. Mary Ann, of course, had felt this as a terrible rejection, while Polly had pitied Mary Ann at the same time that she felt the danger of engulfment by her mother grow stronger.

When Polly was finally able to get deeply angry with her mother in this dialogue (she had found it easier earlier in therapy to get angry with her father, but she had continued to insist up until this point that she felt only pity for her mother) and to demand her own release as a narcissistic extension of her mother, she felt much clearer about the relationship with her sister. At this point, Polly experienced a deep sadness about the seemingly impassable gulf which had been placed between the children in this family by their father's competitive games and their mother's narcissistic favoritism. I suggested that Polly talk with her sister *not* about her sister's problems, but about her own unhappiness in a family where jealousy and rivalry were a natural outcome of a situation of negative reciprocity in which *nobody* was able to receive genuine love and validation. She followed my suggestion and was surprised to find herself developing a closer relationship with her sister.

At the same time, she felt more involved in a deeply caring relationship with her lover, one in which she felt less jealous and more "peaceful"—a word which, she noted, she had never before applied to her own life. At this point, Polly expressed a desire to terminate therapy and I agreed. Although she knew that some of these issues would continue to come up, she felt that she now had "the tools to understand and deal with them." I think she meant that she had developed a meta-reflective process which served her well in dealing with the remnants of her old project.

Obviously, the two families described in this chapter were permeated by serial alterity and/or negative reciprocity. These issues, I am finding, come up again and again within the context of individual psychotherapy. I am also aware that such issues might prove even more poignant in working with families or individuals experiencing genuine economic deprivation. Two cases, of course, cannot hope to illustrate the whole spectrum of uses to which Sartre's concept of the practico-inert can be put in the context of psychotherapy. That usefulness is itself much larger than our discussion of other-directedness and negative reciprocity. It encompasses as well such things as the significance of an individual's insertion into a particular class and/or milieu, the nature of relations between generations, the quality of an individual's insertion into the world of work, and the way in which an individual relates to what Sartre in the Flaubert biography refers to as the "Objective Mind" of his or her era. While there is not enough time or space in a single section to mine the whole rich potential which the practico-inert holds for the theory and practice of psychotherapy, these ideas deserve at least a brief treatment.

Take, for instance, an individual's "class-being," which arises as a consequence of the serial relationship of an ensemble of people to particular aspects of the practico-inert. Although groups develop within classes, a class is not a group. Rather, it is "a shifting ensemble of groups and series" (CDR, p. 638)—a "totalised series of series" (CDR, p. 315). Belonging to the anti-dialectic (CDR, p. 806), class-being pervades every aspect of our lives and becomes part of the facticity upon which future freedom must play itself out.

In the following passage, Sartre describes how we are all continually conserving as we supersede our class-being as we learned to live it in our families of origin:

> What was once both a vague comprehension of our class, of our social conditioning by way of the family group, and a blind going beyond, an awkward effort to wrench ourselves away from all this, at last ends up inscribed in us in the form of *character*. At this level are found the learned gestures (bourgeois gestures, socialist gestures) and the contradictory roles which compose us and which tear us apart. . . . At this level also are the traces left by our first revolts, our desperate efforts to

go beyond a stifling reality, and the resulting deviations and distortions. To surpass all that is also to preserve it. We shall think *with* these original derivations, we shall act *with* these gestures which we have learned and which we want to reject. By projecting ourselves toward our possible so as to escape the contradictions of our existence, we unveil them, and they are revealed in our very acting although this action is richer than they are and gives us access to a social world in which new contradictions will involve us in new conduct. Thus we can say both that we continually surpass our class and that class reality is made manifest by means of this very surpassing. The realization of the possible necessarily results in the production of an object or an event in the social world; this realization is our *objectification*, and the original contradictions which are reflected there testify to our *alienation*. (SM, pp. 100–101)

One of the goals of existentialist therapy, from this perspective, will obviously be to understand the way in which a particular individual has been inserted into his or her class and/or social milieu—as Sartre has attempted to do in his explication of Flaubert's relationship with the French bourgeoisie of his day.

At the same time that Sartre insists that class-being must be taken into account in understanding an individual's project, however, he is also clear that the approach he is recommending must not resort to Marxist reductionism. For example, he faults contemporary Marxists for attempting to thoroughly reduce the French poet Paul Valéry to his class affiliations. Such approaches, according to Sartre, fail to yield an understanding of the individual in all of his or her rich particularity as a "concrete universal" who internalizes but is not reducible to the sociomaterial world from which he or she comes. "Valéry," as Sartre points out, "is a petit bourgeois intellectual, no doubt about it. But not every petit bourgeois intellectual is Valéry" (SM, p. 56).

Although the work of existential psychoanalysis has been enlarged to include socialization, it still involves elucidation of the individual project in terms of individual choices. In approaching this individual project, however, we must not forget that to deny one's class affiliations is to indulge in bad faith since one is thereby refusing to face an aspect of one's facticity—a form of inauthenticity of which Sartre accuses Flaubert and the writers of the Second Empire. And just as Sartre believes that contemporary Marxists are too often guilty of ignoring the concrete in favor of the universal, so we must also admit that contemporary psychotherapists are too often guilty of ignoring the universal in favor of the concrete or individual.

I believe that this sociomaterial "blind spot" on the part of psychotherapists can be particularly detrimental when they are working with people from a different class than their own or when they are working with people who have passed through the ever-permeable barriers between classes and whose projects bear the imprints of that surpassing. Sartre, in the Flaubert biography, makes much of the way in which Achille-Cléophas's movement from the peasantry to the minor bourgeoisie affected his family relations and particularly the self-perceptions of his sons. For one thing, those sons could never, in their own eyes or in the eyes of their father, be quite so wonderful as he because they could never aspire to the marvelous achievement of moving into a higher class.

Sartre's account reminds me of a client who, like Gustave Flaubert, had developed a sense of personal deficiency based in part on his feeling that he could never match the marvelous "rags to riches" trajectory of his father. His task was to find a self in a world that seemed to be completely dominated by his father's myth of rising. At the same time that the son's work in therapy revealed the grandiosity of the father's project, it also seemed to point to a social unsureness on the part of the father—an unsureness which appeared to be covered over by a blustering contempt for the "softness" of his middle-class wife and sons. Sherry's mother, in the case described above, also seems to demonstrate the difficulties which the movement from one class to another can impose on a family. Interestingly, in my own experience as a therapist, it is usually the children rather than the parents who come into therapy. Only a clinical depression of mammoth proportions, it seems to me, is likely to bring the "self-made man" to the therapist's office.

The connection between the generations, however, is a complex one and not a simple matter of cause and effect. As Sartre points out, the previous generation passes along the culture, the material means, and even the language which are the tools with which the new generation must work. But the new generation does not simply accept the objectifications provided to it. Regarding the materialized praxis which it has inherited from the previous generation as "an inert object which needs to be rearranged," the new generation goes on to transcend in one way or another the legacy of its fathers (CDR, p. 666). Even history, our collective past, is rewritten by each generation according to changes in the future-directed projects of its members; thus social memories (like individual memories) change over time (CDR, p. 56).

It must be emphasized, however, that the members of a new generation cannot simply make anything whatever of their inheritance; even revolutionary praxis must inscribe itself in a practico-inert world that is resistant because of prior inscriptions. One lives, for good or ill, within a particular culture and with certain sociomaterial constraints—which, to be overcome in a realistic fashion, must first be taken into account. Consequently, though the investigation of continuity and conflicts between generations must not remain on an abstract general level in existentialist therapy, neither can the existentially oriented therapist afford to ignore what the particular members of a generation have in common.

What makes a certain amount of generalization possible is the common relationship which the members of a particular class, society, or generation have to the practico-inert. It is because of the claims of the practico-inert, and not because of some mysterious suprapersonal unity or mechanistic determinism, that membership in a particular class or generation leads us to have certain common characteristics. In the Flaubert biography, Sartre refers to the cultural heritage of a generation as the "Objective Mind" of that generation. This idea of the Objective Mind, despite its Hegelian ring, does not represent a return to idealism. The Objective Mind, according to Sartre, is nothing other than the cultural practico-inert at a particular moment of history. Sartre himself is especially interested in investigating the literary works which influenced the generation of writers of the Second Empire, of whom Flaubert was one of the leading lights.

The Objective Mind of Flaubert's generation, Sartre tells us, was flawed because the writers of the Second Empire were presented with contradictions which were realistically insuperable—contradictions passed on to them by their literary "grandfathers," the eighteenth-century philosophes, and their literary "elder brothers," the romantic writers. The grandfathers enjoin those who follow them to create through their works a rational "universal" art which serves all mankind, but which really invokes a bourgeois definition of "man." By contrast, the European romantics, who have aristocratic rather than bourgeois leanings, enjoin their followers (who are unhappily bourgeois rather than aristocratic) to take a stance of beauty for its own sake and a hatred of the bourgeoisie.

The neurotic solution—and Sartre insists that the solution of the Second Empire writers must be neurotic because the Objective Mind of the period is filled with contradictions that admit of no "real" solutions—of the writers of

Flaubert's generation is to embrace the universal calling of the philosophes without their idea of service and to embrace the love of beauty of the romantics combined with a generalized misanthropy. "Art for art's sake" and the renunciation of the duty to communicate are the earmarks of these writers. Asked for an impossible solution, they embrace the imaginary as demoralization because all avenues for a real solution have been foreclosed. Flaubert, Sartre maintains, was eminent among these literary "Knights of Nothingness" partially because his personal history predisposed him to take the position required by the "Objective Neurosis" of the period.[13]

Obviously, then, in addition to exploring the individual dimensions of a client's fundamental project, the existentialist therapist who is aware of Sartre's later work must also be prepared to explore the cultural contradictions which an individual is living and how these affect that client's life. An obvious negative example is the Objective Mind of the generation in Germany which chose Adolf Hitler as its leader; perhaps the cultural practico-inert at this time was not simply neurotic, but psychotic in the grandiosity combined with rage which are its earmarks. In any case, there is no doubt that this situation is one which Germans—and the rest of the world—will have to try to reconcile themselves to (or escape from) for some years to come. An example which might be considered positive by many people is the Objective Mind of the generation of the 1960s and 1970s in the United States and Europe. During this time, new meanings concerning racial, colonial, and sexual equality were inscribed into the Euro-American tradition of freedom, equality, and individual opportunity as this had been handed down in numerous documents and proclamations by previous generations.

As a therapist who is now beginning to encounter a new generation of clients—those who are making something different of what the generation of the 1960s and 1970s (my own generation) has made—I am finding this idea of social continuity with a difference increasingly fascinating. Indeed, it has occurred to me that a study of the lives of members of my own generation in terms of the impact on them of the civil rights movement, the Vietnam War, the sexual revolution, the women's movement, and so on might be extremely interesting—particularly if it could be extended to include what is now being made (positively and negatively) of those experiences both by the people who lived them and by their children.

Such studies have, of course, occasionally been done. An example is the studies of the impact of their parents' concentration camp experiences on the "children of the holocaust." What has not been done to any great extent is to look at the impact of *everyone's* sociomaterial depths on the creation of a number of individual projects. A task of existentialist therapy, from this perspective, would be to take into account the common relationship to the practico-inert of members of a particular generation in elucidating a project which is nonetheless individual for all its connections with the sociomaterial world—a task Sartre himself undertook in his elaborate examination of Flaubert's connections, reactions, and contributions to the Objective Mind of his generation in the third volume of *The Family Idiot*.

One significant way in which an individual must connect with his or her sociocultural milieu is, of course, through work in the world. Since Freud's famous definition of the normal individual as one who is able "to love and to work," psychoanalysis has been interested in an individual's relationship with the world of work. But this interest has been largely a theoretical interest in work as neutralization or sublimation of libidinal energy and a clinical interest in work as manifesting aspects of the transference. Certainly, transference issues cannot be avoided, especially, for example, when one works with a client who repeatedly relates to employers as if they were parents and to co-workers as if they were siblings. On the other hand, transference is not the whole story, and even the relationship of present work difficulties to past experiences may require an understanding of principles which are not present in Freudian metatheory. As therapists, we are often reluctant or unable to examine the effects which a client's work conditions have on the quality of that person's life—or the way in which learning to live one's needs as hexis in childhood may have prepared the way to accepting boring, repetitive, and overly restrictive work conditions as "normal."

There is, of course, from a Sartrean perspective an interplay between the work conditions a society presents to its members and the way in which one is prepared to live those conditions in childhood. Understanding this relationship is not a simple matter of deciding which factor (work conditions or childhood experience) to place in the position of an independent variable. Rather, from the perspective of existential psychoanalysis, it will be necessary for the investigator to explore the past as ground for present distortions of the self in the workplace while he or she must at the same time refuse to reduce present difficulties to mere psychological phenomena. There is, after all, a real sociomaterial world with which the individual must interact in terms of work in order to survive and/or prosper.

Let us take, for example, Sartre's worst case scenario—the worker in a factory who is dominated by the hexis of a machine's demands. Obviously, this worker has not ceased to have human needs; on the other hand, the use of the machine to meet survival-based needs has to some extent relegated the production of a self at a more advanced level of the dialectic to the worker's less central leisure-time activities. His or her work involves not the creation of a new individualized future, but the re-creation of the (past) static future which is written into the machine. Not only this, the machine will invade even the recesses of the worker's most intimate thoughts and feelings.

Sartre cites as an example certain studies which show that women factory workers, as they work, engage in fantasies of sexual abandonment which may or may not have any correspondence to their actual love life. In doing so, Sartre maintains, they only find a way to better service the machine— since what is required by the machine is a kind of semi-automatism on the part of the worker, "an explosive mixture of unconsciousness and vigilance." In order to perform her job effectively, the worker must not really think in an active way; for example, worries about her children are likely to distract her from her work. Rather, she must induce in herself a state in which the mind is "absorbed but not used" (CDR, p. 233).

The solution to this dilemma is the sexual fantasies. By engaging in them, the woman worker attempts to modify the "desert of boredom" produced by the machine through an escape into interiority. But because in doing so she merely finds a way to better serve the machine, Sartre declares that "the deepest interiority [thus] becomes a means of realising oneself as total exteriority" (CDR, p. 234). Hence it is in a sense appropriate to say that "it was the machine in [the woman worker] which was dreaming of love" (CDR, p. 233). In another sense, of course, the compliance with the dictates of the machine is founded on free praxis—which in this case is merely subjectivity as "the verdict which compels us to carry out, freely and through ourselves, the sentence which a 'developing' society has pronounced on us" (CDR, p. 71). The tragedy of degraded and reified freedom is that it is still freedom.

Since it is our childhoods which have prepared us to accept this verdict, it is the task of existential psychoanalysis to find out how this is so. For example, in Sherry's case, it was her obedience to her mother's tyrannical other-directedness which prepared her to be exploited by her employer. Obviously, as therapists, we must be aware not only of the real conditions (the demand of the machine or other work situation for a certain kind of activity requiring a certain kind of attentiveness) and the childhood situations but also of the present life circumstances which dispose a person to accept a less than human work situation. As for the larger sociopolitical issues, although they are interconnected, they do not bear directly on our work with clients.

In all of these ways, Sartre's concept of the practico-inert enables us to enlarge the individualist perspective of existential psychoanalysis delineated in

Being and Nothingness to include a sociomaterial perspective. Instead of viewing a client's project only in terms of individual choices of ways of doing, being, and having in a largely dyadic universe, Sartre's later philosophy also mandates that existential psychoanalysis look at a person's work in a sociomaterial world containing certain exigencies from the past which affect and shape or misshape that project. It mandates a consideration of seriality and negative reciprocity as they affect a person's life project. And it mandates a look at the connection between generations that is achieved in and through the sociomaterial world.

Existential psychoanalysis, in other words, must consider the ways in which a person's project is concurrently "centuries old" and completely new. As Sartre puts the matter,

> I totalise myself on the basis of centuries of history and, in accordance with my culture, I totalise this experience. This means that my life is centuries old, since the schemata which permit me to understand and to totalise my practical undertakings (and the set of determinations which go with them) have *entered the present* (present in their effects and past in their completed history). In this sense, diachronic evolution is present (as past—and, as we shall see later, as future) in synchronic totalisation: their relations are bonds of interiority and to the extent that critical investigation is possible, the temporal depth of the totalising process becomes evident as soon as I reflexively interpret the operations of my individual life. (CDR, p. 54)

Human reality, in the *Critique* as in *Being and Nothingness*, is still a temporalizing project linking past, present, and future—but that past-present-future now has a social as well as an individual dimension.

Human reality is "synchronic," partaking of present sociomaterial relations, and "diachronic," living the past as present and as projected future while detotalizing and retotalizing it. The aim of existentialist therapy, in such a situation, is not to detach the individual from the sociomaterial world, since this is impossible. Rather, it is to investigate with a client the sociomaterial dimensions of his or her project with an end to increasing the domain of praxis, or real freedom, and to decreasing the domain of hexis, or resignation to the status quo, as an individual endeavors to make something new and more satisfying and meaningful of what he or she has been made of from a sociomaterial perspective. It is also, as we shall see in the next section, to aid that person in investigating the opportunities and pitfalls of group praxis as an antidote to serial impotence, negative reciprocity, and the impasses created by contradictory imperatives inscribed in the practico-inert.

The Regulatory Third Party, Fraternity-Terror, and the Family as Group Praxis

The third moment of the Sartrean dialectic, the moment of "unification," arises as a negation of the serial impotence instituted by the second. Groups attempt to nullify the "recurrence" or repetition in everyone of the same relation to a collective object by transforming individual praxis into common or collective praxis. For example, when the workers in a factory organize themselves into a union, they are no longer each subjected to the same impotence with respect to that collective object, the factory. Together they are able to demand better working conditions, shorter hours, and so on. Similarly, people organizing themselves into a group can better deal with an emergency like a natural disaster or a food shortage than can those same people relating serially to the same event. Where a single individual experiences impotence, the group has power.

All this, however, is ordinary and not particularly philosophically profound. Sartre's originality with respect to explaining this third moment of the dialectic arises from two new concepts which allow us to understand the efficacy and power of groups without resorting to some theory of groups either as hyperorganisms or as simple social contracts of the individual-to-group variety. These concepts are the "regulatory third party" and "fraternity-terror." They explain how group members come to share a common praxis at the same time that this common praxis ultimately rests on an individual praxis which is always and everywhere being transformed by the individual's inclusion in groups. Because the group is derived from and maintained by individual praxis, however, Sartre refers to group praxis as the "constituted dialectic" to distinguish it from the "constituent dialectic" of individual action. This idea of the group as the constituted dialectic will have, as we shall see, significant implications for our understanding of family issues in the context of existentialist therapy and for our understanding of the way in which the therapy group can be utilized to counteract destructive family norms.

The constituted dialectic rests on a new concept of the third party which is both similar and dissimilar to Sartre's concept of the third in *Being and*

Nothingness. Sartre in his earlier work describes human relations as primarily dyadic, consisting of the eternal subject-object alternation which provokes the "conflict of consciousnesses." The third person there is simply an addendum to the idea of objectification, with Sartre noting that two people can be objectified by a third as an "us object" (BN, pp. 415-23). In the *Critique*, however, he seems to reverse himself by declaring that "the *real* relation between men is necessarily ternary" (CDR, p. 109). The truth is that this is a contradiction in appearance only. Binary relations are still conceived to be the "necessary ground of any ternary relationship" (CDR, p. 109), its ontological foundation if you will, since it is still my experience of the Other's Look that reveals to me the existence of other consciousnesses. But in the "real" world—that is, in the inevitably social world—relations are never simply dyadic. This is so because it is the third party who "makes reciprocity visible to itself" (CDR, p. 116). In other words, it is the third party who provides the context and the perspective within which dyadic relations come to know themselves reflectively. Within the context of the group, as we shall see, everyone takes the position of this third party who makes the reciprocal relations of the group visible to itself.

Let us take a look, for example, at the inevitably ternary nature of human relations in that seemingly most intimate and exclusive of dyadic relationships: the relationship between two people who have just fallen in love. Sartre had already noted in *Being and Nothingness* that lovers will often attempt to avoid for a time the objectifying Look of third parties because they do not wish to be fixed from the outside as an us object. Yet the truth is that the lovers cannot escape the Look of the third, since this Look is the implied presence in absence which allows them to constitute themselves as a couple in the first place. Nor can this young couple, from the perspective of the *Critique*, simply "degroup" itself and start afresh as members of a self-sufficient duo—as many a young couple has learned to its chagrin. Each will carry his or her groupedness, especially membership in the family of origin, into the new relationship. What is true for the young couple is also true for the rest of us. The degrouped single individual, Robinson Crusoe, simply does not exist. One is always and everywhere grouped, even before birth since loyalty is expected in advance to the family and its groups. Of course, one may subsequently defect from old groups and/or join new ones. The point is that one does not first exist as a separate individual who later joins groups. One is fundamentally grouped from the beginning of life.

At the same time that one is a "common" or grouped individual from the beginning, however, it is also true that individual, organic praxis sustains groups. The secret of this apparent paradox lies in Sartre's idea that the group is formed and maintained by a ternary relationship among its members in which each acts to the others as a regulatory third party rather than by some kind of union of consciousnesses in a hyperorganismic whole. First cousin to the objectifying third who united the dyad as an us object in *Being and Nothingness*, the regulatory third is no longer an instrument of alienation but an instrument of unification. This is so because the regulatory third, standing together with others as *a part of* the group rather than observing others from a position *apart*, totalizes the others as a participant in a common action on a particular sociomaterial field—acting, obeying, and commanding for the group and demanding that others do likewise.

In such a situation, serial alterity has been overcome by common or group praxis. Whereas in the series, the locus of action is always "elsewhere," in the group it is always "here"; whereas in the series, I act as an "Other," in the group I and the Other act as a "myself." This allows for a "we" which transcends the "we" of the common project of *Being and Nothingness*—a "we" which rests on a transformation of individual praxis into common praxis and with it the transformation of the organic individual. As Sartre points out, the individual in a group undergoes a metamorphosis. The grouped individual is "constituted as different from what he was on his own." He or she experiences and internalizes the "adopted inertia, function, power, rights and duties, structure, violence and fraternity" of the group and actualizes these new reciprocal relations as "his new being, his sociality" (CDR, p. 510).

At the same time that the organic individual is fashioned into a common individual through such socialization, however, the fact that groups are founded on individual praxis rather than on some kind of mystical union of consciousnesses leaves them vulnerable to dissolution. Thus although group praxis, as an antidote to serial alterity, may sound like an ideal solution to recurrence, there is a worm in the apple. Unless the group has formed to handle a single emergency (such as meeting a natural disaster or rescuing a child from a well) after which it will naturally dissolve, individual praxis poses a threat to the group and with it to the security and effectiveness which the group affords its members. As Sartre puts the matter, one is never simply *in* a group as the contained is *in* a container. As a group member, my anguish consists precisely in the inextinguishability of individual praxis: "I am *inside* but I am still afraid that I may be outside" (CDR, p. 586). From my own viewpoint and from the viewpoint of the other members of the group, there is always the possibility that I might detotalize and retotalize the group in such a way as to undermine its very foundation. Therefore, if groups are to continue to exist, they must continually work on themselves as well as work on the world. The group is always a double negation—of serial impotence on the one hand and individualist action on the other.

The negation of individualist action takes a form which Sartre describes as "fraternity-terror." Fraternity refers to the offer of inclusion in activity for the common good, and terror to the threat of death or, what amounts to the same thing, ostracism from the group if one does not live according to its requirements or norms. In other words, the group demands that its members abjure certain forms of freedom as a necessary condition for the preservation of the group. It does so through the exaction of the "pledge," implicit or explicit, by means of which the organic individual promises to continue acting as a common individual at the expense of his or her future freedom.

Such a pledge may be given beforehand by an individual born into a particular group—as in the pledge of military service on the part of all males born into most tribes or nations. Sometimes the pledge is ritually renewed at puberty, as in the puberty rites common to most tribal cultures; Christian confirmation and Jewish bar and bat mitzvahs are also examples of such ritual renewals of the pledge. The pledge is necessary because the group, much as it might like to be a hyperorganism or a machine, is unable to accomplish this. This is why the traitor receives such severe treatment by most groups: He or she is a living reminder to the group that the freedom of each poses a constant (implicit) threat to the group's continued existence (CDR, p. 589n).

The degree of fraternity versus the degree of terror in a particular group, together with the degree of genuine community versus serial impotence, varies with the kind of group and with its contexts. Sartre delineates four different kinds of groups, classified according to increasing levels of organization: the group-in-fusion,[14] the pledged or statutory group, the organization, and the institution. Each of these groups has more structure and more differentiation of function than its predecessor. And since seriality increases as the group becomes more and more permeated with inertia, each is more invaded by serial impotence to the point where the institution, especially if it is also bureaucratized, is permeated with seriality. The problem is that structure, though it is an attempt at efficiency in dealing with the environment and control in dealing with the danger of individualist revolt, signifies ossification. Sartre's favorite kind of group, as the reader might guess, is the one with the least structure—the group-in-fusion which arises as a response to a particular situation. His least favorite is obviously the institution, which he believes signifies the "systematic self-domestication of man by man" (CDR, p. 606).

The group-in-fusion arises as a direct response to serial impotence. A group is likely to form on the face of a collective when a gathering of people suddenly begins to live serial impotence as something which might/must be overcome. Ultimately, this movement from series to group is motivated by need, with organismic survival providing a univocal link of interiority with nature which points to a limit beyond which needs cannot be shaped or denied. As I begin to read my own fate in the fate of the Other, including the impotence of both of us before the collective object or sovereign group, I come to see the Other not as an alien Other but as another self destined like myself for extinction unless we engage in a common action. Obvious examples include people facing the possibility of death from a common natural disaster, such as a fire or flood, or of starvation from a common lack of resources. Sartre's own example is the storming of the Bastille at the moment when the people of Paris came to read the presence of the king's troops as the likelihood of their own deaths (CDR, pp. 351–63). Of course, less urgent matters can also provoke group formation so long as people see their needs/desires and their neighbors' as being equivalent and inextricably linked in terms of the possibility of fulfillment.

The group-in-fusion, however, is not a prearranged covenant between people, but rather the development of a spontaneous common action based on a new totalization of the common field in which I and the Other act for and through each other, becoming a group of "myselves" as a replacement for the collection of "Others" which had locked us together in serial impotence. This involves the development of group praxis, as each person fashions himself or herself as a regulatory third party who totalizes the others as a group as they totalize him or her. In the group-in-fusion, with its lack of structure, anyone may perform any function—for example, the person nearest the stump becomes the "myself" who urges the others on to the Bastille. In the group-in-fusion, there is therefore the greatest amount of fraternity and the least amount of terror since the energy of the group is focused almost entirely on the task at hand. The problem is that once the emergency has passed, if the group is to continue to exist, it must work on itself as well as work on the world. It is here that the group-in-fusion evokes the pledge and with it the threat of death/ostracism which constitutes the bonds of fraternity-terror in a pledged group. Terror increases and fraternity decreases as groups become more structured, moving from pledged groups to organizations to institutions.

With the institution, the serial impotence which motivated group formation in the first place has been replaced by an institutional impotence. Seriality has re-entered the picture in the form of everyone's loyalty to a sovereign individual or group. Actually, sovereignty has evolved because the group has become a debased community, attempting to replace the energy of spontaneous common activity with the efficiency of a machine. The group, at the point where it becomes institutionalized, is endangered by individual praxis. Thus each person attempts to save the group by expelling "freedom from himself in order to realise the endangered unity of the declining group as a thing" (CDR, p. 606). The model for the institution is the "forged tool." Each person, in order to perpetuate the institution, must make himself or herself into a "stereotyped praxis" supporting a rigid future that is in reality a reproduction of the past (CDR, pp. 606-7). Obviously, in such a situation, the danger of serial dispersal will be great since creative energy will be severely limited. For this reason, as organizational ossification increases, terror dominates and fraternity lessens. The wielding of this terror, however, is no longer simply in the hands of each person as a regulatory third party. Rather, it is focused in the hands of the sovereign individual or group and its agents.

Sovereignty, according to Sartre, is only possible if a group has ossified to the point where genuine community is no longer possible. Such a debased community may then seek a false sense of oneness by substituting the organic unity of the sovereign individual for the missing real unification of genuine community. If this happens, then secondary alienation re-enters the group and reserialization occurs in a situation where the members of the group are no longer the same and every elsewhere is no longer here. In the sovereign, the group has produced an individual who is "other than all because he cannot become a regulated third party."

As an untranscendable third party, the sovereign comes to represent "violence without reciprocity" (CDR, p. 615). As a member of an institutionalized group with a sovereign leader, each individual finds himself or herself supporting group praxis not as the action of a developing unification of myselves but as "an actualisation of the Other's [the sovereign's] freedom" (CDR, p. 616). Only the sovereign is able to be himself or herself—and, of course, even the sovereign cannot really do this because of the constraints of the organization (CDR, p. 619). As for the group members, they subsume their freedom in the freedom of the sovereign. Hence "the sovereign is present in everyone as Other in the moment when he is obeyed" (CDR, p. 621). In fact, the sovereign is produced and maintained by terror; through the sovereign's agents, the group is held together by (implicit or explicit) violence, which is necessary to counteract a return to seriality. Genuine community, which sovereignty is supposed to safeguard, would actually be a threat to it and so disappears.

Thus the final step in the struggle against seriality is marked by a return to seriality in the form of the impotence of everyone before the king (or other sovereign individual or group), who now occupies the place vacated by the collective object. What this whole situation masks is the fact that genuine sovereignty—as distinguished from the quasisovereignty of the regulatory third party or the pseudosovereignty of the king or other ruling group— resides only in individual praxis or "man himself as action, as unifying labour, in so far as he has a purchase on the world and is able to change it" (CDR, p. 610). In a sense, the sovereign in the decaying group takes the position of the missing God in the search for Being-in-itself-for-itself; in fact, Sartre argues in the *Critique* that the institution of sovereignty is a false solution because "neither God nor the totalised group [as opposed to the totalizing group] actually exist" (CDR, p. 610). In other words, the resort to sovereignty is an evasion of freedom and responsibility, both individual and group.

As we come to the end of this discussion of groups, it would be well to remember that the real social landscape is not as schematic as I have presented it here. For one thing, groups do not necessarily develop in an orderly succession from group-in-fusion to institution with an eventual return to seriality as the outmoded institution is abandoned like a dead leviathan by a new generation which has simply lost interest. Instead, we find every order of emergence and decay and, as we have previously seen, many varieties of interactions between series and groups. As Sartre points out, there is no "formal law" that compels groups to pass through the logical succession from group-in-fusion to institution.[15] Also, the presence of existing groups may either provoke the emergence of new groups (as happened with the king's army and the people storming the Bastille) or inhibit their formation (as is the case with the manipulation of series by groups). Furthermore, there may be a combination of forms. For example, why might we not explain the presence of groups with charismatic leaders as combinations of two opposite forms, since they appear to have both the urgency and the vitality of the group-in-fusion and the subsumption of individual freedom in a sovereign of the institution?

Where a group does emerge, it is important, for social science in general and for existential psychoanalysis in particular, to investigate its character and its degree of fraternity versus terror as a way of determining whether or not this group provides a viable solution to the problem of serial impotence. As an ontological negation and a practical realization, the group can either empower or disempower an individual—depending on whether or not a person as a common individual (or ontological negation of organic praxis) is part of a group which is an energetic community promising the realization of a goal (practical realization) which has genuine meaning for all, or whether the group member is participating in a group which has ossified to the point of demanding little more than obedience to the status quo, or passive activity. In the latter case, as with the series, the problem is that one's project has become permeated with hexis rather than with praxis—that one views the demands of the institution as "the way things are" rather than as a means to transcendence. Although this debased community may still offer security, it is in some ways worse than no community at all—especially since it may inhibit the formation of new, genuinely vital groups.

I think we can now begin to see the significance of Sartre's theory of groups for existentialist therapy. If the existentialist therapist is to make full use of the new social concepts presented in the *Critique*, he or she must add to an understanding of those dyadic relations which have proved so useful in deciphering the mirroring needs of earliest infancy and childhood an understanding of the way in which ternary relations govern all social relations, including relations within the family. The family as series and as group must be explored, together with its bonds of fraternity-terror and its claims on the freedom of the individual.[16] The kind of group represented by a particular family—or the extent to which a family has been able to group itself at all as opposed to remaining serial—must be considered. The family of origin is, of course, crucial to this exploration. But membership in the present family and other important groups must be explored as well. If a family has broken apart at some point, the impact of this on the children's capacity for being grouped must be explored. Similarly, the strength of the family in effectively dealing with difficult circumstances, such as accidents, natural disasters, and death, must be considered. And the efficacy of the therapy group as a means to breaking the terror which keeps people bound to other dysfunctional groups must be explored.

An appreciation of Sartre's theory of groups and of series will therefore allow existentially oriented therapists to go beyond the individualist analysis which sometimes cripples our ability to help an individual. As with the exigencies of the practico-inert and the traps of serial behavior and thought, it is important to recognize the ways in which groups, especially institutionalized groups, may deform an individual by imposing a conformity to group norms which is a matter of hexis rather than of praxis. At the same time, vital groups offer the most efficient (and many times the only) means for overcoming hexis and serial impotence. Obviously, then, the existentialist therapist will want to examine a client's group affiliations—and the impact that being grouped or not being grouped in this way or that has on a client's fundamental project. In particular, the therapist will want to aid a client in moving away from serial impotence into a sense of community, if this is a problem, or else in escaping the demands of fraternity-terror imposed by a group (frequently the family group) which is providing security at too great an expense to individual happiness or genuine community.

Sartre himself was aware that the family provides fertile ground for illustrating his theory of groups. Having noted in the *Critique* that the paterfamilias of the traditional authoritarian family is an example of sovereignty, he takes up in *The Family Idiot* the exploration of a particular family, that of Gustave Flaubert, as an example of the effects of a semipatriarchal family on one of its members. Achille-Cléophas Flaubert, according to Sartre, was a mixture of bourgeois liberalism and traditionalism. The brilliant son of a peasant family in which his father and two brothers were veterinarians, Achille-Cléophas was sent to school in Paris where he won a scholarship to medical school. As the chief surgeon of Rouen, he had clearly climbed out of his humble beginnings. His marriage to Caroline Fleuriot gave him pretensions even to nobility, as Caroline was connected on her mother's side to the minor nobility. Like the father mentioned in the previous section who had left behind his humbler beginnings, Dr. Flaubert was something of a tyrant in his relations to his family. His wife, who was nine years younger than he, bent her will to his—admiring, adoring, and obeying him. His sons, whom he imagined would become doctors like himself, were valued primarily as assets to the Flaubert family glory. In this respect, as we have seen, Gustave was a disappointment; Achilles, on the other hand, succeeded in his appointed task of following in his father's footsteps as the favored successor.

In such a family, what is required of the children is a "strict surrender of the individual to the family group" (FI, 1:68). Hence because each of the sons "was bursting with pride at being a Flaubert, neither of them knew the dignity of being himself" (FI, 1:71). For Achilles, this lack of individualism is rewarded by being allowed to fill his father's shoes. For Gustave, who was the favorite of neither his father nor his mother, it adds to the earlier wound. Although family life in such a situation resembles more of the atomization of a "common solitude" (FI, 1:70) than the solidarity of a genuine community, Gustave suffered more than Achilles or Caroline. Intensely jealous of his older brother, he became generally envious and resentful. Later, when he wished to escape from the alternative profession of law which his father had chosen for him, Gustave could not risk direct confrontation. Instead, he allowed his body, through the passive activity of a psychosomatic illness which has usually been identified as epilepsy but which Sartre regards as hysteria,[17] to accomplish this task for him. Direct disobedience to a father whom he invested with the authority of a medieval lord if not with that of God Almighty was unthinkable. According to Sartre, at a time when the conjugal family with its greater freedom for wife and children and its greater appreciation for the individuality of its children was becoming common, the Flaubert family remained semipatriarchal and restrictive in a way that was fifty years behind the times. Such families are still more common today than most of us would like to admit.

In addition to the difficulties of the traditional patriarchal family, therapists today often meet with a variation on the paterfamilias which is even more destructive to the individuality and self-esteem of family members. Dr. Flaubert, for all his tyrannizing over his family, at least represented the stability of a person who offers his family a recognized place in society. The contemporary "family tyrant," who often brutalizes both wife and children in an overtly violent way, offers no such security or stability. Similarly, therapists often meet with families that either combine tyranny with extreme serial alterity or that have failed to form cohesive groups at all. Sometimes several divorces have compounded the difficulties of forming a new group out of the remnants of an old one. Research into the effects of such degrouping and regrouping, such as that of Judith Wallerstein (Wallerstein and Blakeslee, 1989), is just beginning to assess the damages.[18]

In any case, one cannot help thinking that the seemingly greater prevalence of what are referred to in therapeutic nosology as borderline and other severe personality disorders may have at least something to do with the greater degree of seriality in contemporary families. Indifference, as I noted in earlier chapters, may be even more pathogenic than overt criticism; I might add that lack of belonging to a coherent and reliable family may be more damaging than participation in a group which is less than optimally growth promoting. Perhaps bonds forged more in terror than in fraternity are preferable to no bonds at all.

In working with individuals, therapists must not, however, mistake what are actually phenomena relating to the bonds of fraternity-terror for individual aberrations or the effects of seriality. As Sartre points out, it is often true that "what people call *fanaticism, blindness*, etc., is really fraternity-terror as experienced in another group and in so far as we, *as individuals*, treat it as an emotional occurrence *in individuals*" (CDR, p. 518). Since some of the stubbornest fixations in therapy derive precisely from these structures of fraternity-terror in the family of origin, no amount of analysis of purely individual motives will dissolve them. Instead, they must be looked at as phenomena arising from the way in which an individual was originally grouped—and as the terror which arises at the thought of giving up a way of behaving/feeling/believing/thinking which appears to be critical for inclusion in the family group at all. And since, as we know, one's experience in one's family stands as a prototype for experience of the world in general, since one's family was once one's whole world, giving up such prejudices may appear to a client to be tantamount to giving up membership in the human race. Often the therapy group can help in overcoming this illusion.

As an example of the power of both the family bonds of fraternity-terror and the efficacy of group therapy as contrasted with individual treatment in helping to break the maleficent power of these bonds, I think of a client whom I shall call Jan. Jan, who was a member of a women's therapy group which met once a week for several years, was an attractive, divorced woman in her mid-forties with a college-aged son and daughter. Jan's family of origin played a greater role in her adult life than contemporary families sometimes do. Jan and four of her five siblings still lived in the area where she had grown up and all participated in managing the family business. The father, though deceased, was a pervasive presence in the family, both because he had been a powerful (often despotic) personality and because the business which he had created and which still supported the family seemed somehow to embody him. His "ghost" was constantly lurking around its corridors. When Jan first came into therapy, she maintained that she simply did not understand her own discontent and difficulties in sustaining a satisfying relationship with a man, considering the fact that she had come from such a "good, close-knit family." As it turned out, this myth of the perfect family—which was enforced by unusually strong bonds of fraternity-terror— became the focal point for her therapy. If Jan wished to be a part of her family, it appeared, she would simply have to support this idea of its "perfection."

The truth about Jan's family, as the reader might suspect, appeared to be very different from this initial image of perfection. Jan's mother, though a dutiful wife who stayed home to care for husband and children, was personally distant and inaccessible. She was a paragon of efficiency, not of warmth. Family outings, Jan remembered, were more a matter of marching along together "like little soldiers" than of real fun and pleasure. Indeed, Jan herself remembered getting sick to her stomach every Sunday when the family went for its mandatory outing in the country. As for Jan's father, he apparently had an irascible temper and a penchant for planning his children's lives. He was also quite critical, especially of Jan's older sister, Joan, with whom he frequently had loud arguments. "As for me," Jan was able to concede later in her therapy, "he never really saw me. He only saw his blueprint for who he thought I was or should be." On those occasions when her father's temper brought him close to violence with one family member or another, Jan remembered, her mother would pack the children into the car and drive around for an hour. When they returned home, the point was to pretend that nothing had happened. The "perfect family" was back in order.

Many of Jan's early therapy sessions centered around her feelings about her older sister. Joan, though a rebellious child, had evolved into a staunch defender of the family myth. When Jan began to question this myth, Joan was adamant about how *she* saw *her* family: There were simply no problems that Joan remembered; even the fights she had had with her father, which had so disturbed her younger sister, Joan now viewed as having had the beneficent effect of strengthening her character. Mostly, however, Joan remembered her childhood as happy and harmonious. As for her father, she viewed him as heroic and was happy to see herself as being like him. Joan, however, as Jan gradually revealed to the therapy group, had quite a few family problems herself. Like her parents, she had had five children, but these children were far from lacking in difficulties. Indeed, their problems ranged from anorexia to suicidal depression. Although Joan blamed her ex-husband and their divorce for her children's problems, it was Joan and not their father to whom all of her children were at one point refusing to speak. Joan nonetheless maintained that *she* was happy, that *she* had had a perfect upbringing, and that *her* family of origin was still a close, wonderful group—with the single exception of Jan, whom Joan viewed as full of unjustifiable complaints about the past. And, of course, Joan viewed her own second marriage as achieving the "perfection" she had missed on the first try.

Although Jan also did some individual therapy, it is to the women's therapy group that I attribute much of the credit for Jan's gaining the strength to eventually break with her family myth. Jan, as the group came to realize, not only came from a family which regarded itself as close and problem-free; she also tended to develop relationships with men and even friendships with people who similarly used idealization as a defense. Each time Jan encountered one of these "perfect" people, she gave herself a hard time for her own "imperfection" and "inability to be satisfied." Soon the perfection theme—and its source in Jan's family of origin—became quite familiar to the group. Rather like a Greek chorus, they began to express in unison their disbelief in the perfection of whatever friend or lover Jan was currently enhancing with the family myth. Sometimes this took the form of laughter, sometimes of expressions of concern—but Jan could no longer deny that the group saw through her family myth and its current embodiments. At the same time, the group also provided the experience of belonging to a different kind of group—one in which all kinds of feelings, and not just positive ones, could be honestly expressed.

As Jan began to work with this material and to contemplate dissociating herself from the family myth, she alternately experienced extreme distress and a growing sense of authenticity. Her terror at the thought of defection was great, as she imagined herself standing alone with no family or friends. And as she lamented her lack of feeling of belonging and her terror over being "completely alone," ostracism became a major theme in her therapy. She expressed a wish to bring her sisters, her mother, and a current lover into therapy. Indeed, she convinced a woman friend to join the group for a short time, and later she brought a lover for several couple's sessions. Apparently I and/or the group were supposed to convert these people so that Jan would not feel so alone in defecting from the family myth.

At the same time, Jan realized that her own relations with her children were quite different from the family relations in her family of origin and that she had a real closeness with them which her family criticized as "overindulgence." She could also see from her experience in the group that not all groups are so massively attached to denial of negative feelings/thoughts as a condition for membership as her family had been and continued to be. As Jan began to be more centered in herself, she found the strength to end her latest, highly unsatisfying love relationship over her lover's protests that the two of them were—or could easily be—the "perfect couple." As Jan faced the anguish, loneliness, and pervasive sense of unrealness she had experienced with her original "perfect family," her loyalty to this mode of existence began to crumble. In its place was the gradual development of a new sense of "space" and centeredness in herself—and with this a freedom from the terror of not belonging which she had never before experienced.

Therapy groups, of course, have many other functions than the choral one which I have described here—functions which have been adequately described by other group therapists.[19] For example, the therapy group is likely, especially in the beginning, to feel like a duplicate of the family group and the client is likely to inadvertently go about trying to confirm this impression. Group leaders make excellent proxy parents and group members excellent proxy siblings. In this way, the therapy group, like all other groups, can be made to serve the interests of preserving the norms of fraternity-terror established by the original family group.

For example, when Jan first joined the therapy group, she felt that she had to smile continually and show her good-spiritedness in order to gain the group's approval. She also felt a great uneasiness, like being "put on the spot by my Dad," whenever her turn to speak came; and she tried to recede into the background, a strategy which had worked in her family to keep her out of the battles she saw her sister get into with their father. Obviously, these "projections" of the family group onto the therapy group must be challenged and investigated. Jan's group, for instance, soon challenged her assumptions: They let her know that they responded to her when she was real, not when she was pretending to be cheerful. She reacted to this with disbelief and later with gratitude. But for Jan the group was more than a vehicle for working on transference; it was also an experience of a different way of being grouped—a way which allowed her to break the old bonds of fraternity-terror which had kept her trapped for so long in a painful and unfulfilling life project.

Furthermore, whereas the therapy group is useful for a person such as Jan, who is attempting to free herself from destructive family norms, it is perhaps even more significant for the client who has never been adequately grouped at all than for the client who has been unhappily grouped. For the person who grew up in a situation of serial alterity, the therapy group, if such a person can be included within it, can be critical to overcoming the loneliness and alienation which tend to pervade this person's life. I think, for instance, of a client whom I shall call "Craig." Unlike Jan's family, which fits the authoritarian group style where serialization is a by-product of centering on the father as sovereign, Craig's family was the closest in my experience to a disconnected series living under a single roof. He, his father, his mother, and his younger brother each, as he described them, "sat silent in our isolated little worlds." Outsiders or even extended family members rarely entered the tomblike atmosphere of this household. Eating together was rare and was done largely in silence; family activities were unheard of.

When Craig spoke in the therapy group (he was often silent), his lack of reaching out to other group members produced little response at first. He was as isolated as before. When he complained about this, group members pointed out that he seemed to be monologuing—that he seemed not to *want* a response. This was painful for Craig since he could see that other group members "feel more like they belong here than I do." Isolation, as he saw it, was his "fate." Then one night, when Craig was talking about the pain of his isolated life, he seemed to be actually sharing this pain rather than intellectualizing about it.

When I realized that the other group members were involved with his story, I called his attention to the fact that "everyone seems to be right here with you." For the first time, Craig started to cry as he replied, "My whole life has been so *lonely*, I just don't know what to *do* with this." I believe this experience with the group was less a "corrective emotional experience" than a challenge to the status quo—a glimpse of the possibility of turning hexis into praxis and with it an awakening to the pain of his previously deprived existence. Obviously, Craig had a long path to travel before he could allow himself the experience of belonging to an outside group, but he had at least begun to internalize the pledge which is implicit in the therapy group—the pledge to support the norm of honest sharing and emotional presence.

Sartre's theory of groups, then, provides both a new way of looking at personal history and a new way of utilizing the therapy group to counter the destructive elements in family history. It might also provide some new insights for doing family therapy as well. In addition to the family of origin and the contemporary family, the existentialist therapist will probably also want to investigate with a client his or her experiences with early and later peer groups, with contemporary groups at work and in the community, and with intergroup relations (family, work, or other). The therapist will want to see what kinds of expectations a person has about being grouped (or not being grouped)—and to use this both as a way of understanding contemporary life and as an inroad into earliest experience. Moreover, perhaps looking at the family group as a development within classes and within particular social milieus will provide further keys to understanding an individual's dilemma. Obviously, from this perspective, the ultimate aim of existentialist therapy would be to see the individual involved in a group that provides genuine community—a goal which Sartre believes is extremely difficult to attain in a situation of scarcity, but one at which we must nonetheless aim. And as therapists we must remember that even though we rarely see them in the course of our professional work, relatively happy families do exist.

Sartre envisions something much larger. Although he questions whether this will ever be completely possible, he would like to see the emergence in some future socialist society of "a true inter-subjective community in which the only real relations will be those between men" (CDR, p. 307n)—that is, of a community in which the practico-inert is made to serve human relations rather than the reverse and in which human beings will be able to risk a transparency with each other that has as its concomitant a greater self-knowledge and self-acceptance than is usual at the present time.

Sartre does not describe the specifics of this genuine future society since he believes they will have to be discovered in the process of creating it. Nevertheless, he does give some hints as to what it will be like. Obviously, it will avoid as much as possible the reification of people which exists in all existing technological societies. In doing so, it will place a value on the creation of what Sartre refers to as "immaterial matter" (CDR, p. 183)—the divesting of things of their power over people. It will be a society in which scarcity and class divisions will have been overcome and in which positive reciprocity predominates in human relations. It will be a society whose social structures are closer to the group-in-fusion than to the institution or the bureaucracy. And it will be a society which encourages not only freedom of thought, but "*revolutionary* freedom of thought" (BEM, p. 134). In short, it will be a society in which hexis is greatly reduced and authentic praxis greatly encouraged.

The possibility that such a community, though it may never actually exist as such, could be considered a kind of heuristic principle—a norm toward which groups (including families) and societies might consider themselves to be moving—is a topic I have considered further in an article (Cannon, 1985). But whether or not such a community ever comes to exist on a large scale, it is obvious that Sartre's later philosophy adds a new dimension to existential psychoanalysis—a dimension that allows us to understand the experience of being grouped as a phenomenon referring to the regulatory third party who did not yet exist in the largely dyadic relations described in *Being and Nothingness*. The appreciation of the phenomenon of fraternity-terror which results from this understanding is, I believe, also new to depth therapy in general. And though systems analysis has long been familiar in family work, a systems approach usually neglects the individual in favor of the group. It is in this respect analytical rather than dialectical. I believe that the Sartrean dialectic gives adequate weight to both the individual and the group. Because it is the individual who sustains groups (though deeply influenced in his or her being by the experience of being grouped), it is possible to degroup and to regroup in a more life-enhancing and authentic fashion.

Conclusion

We are now in a position to summarize the impact of Sartre's later philosophy on existential psychoanalysis and to consider how the present chapter prepares us to answer, in the next three chapters, the challenge of Lacanian structuralist psychoanalysis to Sartrean existential psychoanalysis. Sartre's later philosophy, as we have seen, does not discard the fundamental ontology and insights into human conflicts so richly provided in his earlier work. The task of existential psychoanalysis, in the later as well as the earlier philosophy, is still to discover and elucidate an individual's fundamental project of being. And the aim of the existentialist therapist remains that of aiding a client in the difficult task of encountering and accepting himself or herself as a responsible freedom with respect and caring for the free projects of others.

The difference between Sartre's earlier and later work is that the fundamental project in his later work has acquired a sociomaterial dimension which is foreign to *Being and Nothingness*. Although human freedom still lies at the heart of the Sartrean dialectic, it is a freedom which discovers itself in an inescapably social world within which the power of humanized matter, of groups, and of series is recognized in a new way. Existentialist therapy must no longer simply discover the individual depths to a client's project; it must also elucidate the sociomaterial depths of that same project. The beginning point of this investigation is no longer just the desiring individual; it is also the needing individual behind the desiring individual—an individual enmeshed in a world of humanized matter and alienated (in the secondary sense) from his or her authentic project but capable, because this person is free, of transforming hexis into praxis. It is the aim of existentialist therapy to aid a client in this endeavor.

In attempting this task, the existentialist therapist will differ from the analytical social scientist in that the therapist will not attempt to occupy an objective position apart from the client's difficulties. Instead, the existentialist therapist must use his or her own humanness to attempt an empathic comprehension of the client's difficulties, thereby gradually building the kind of authentic relationship which is often missing in the client's life. What this means is that in order to understand a client's experiences, the existentialist therapist must bring to bear his or her own awareness of having needs shaped into desires in earliest childhood, of being the "thing" of humanized matter, of experiencing serial impotence, and of being subjected to the fraternity-terror which binds group members together in constructive and destructive ways. Without this social dimension, a therapist may be tempted to interpret individualistically phenomena which are really signs of group praxis, serial reactions, or the class-being of a class which is different from the therapist's own. Furthermore, the impact of the family of origin as a group, as differentiated from the impact of one's earliest dyadic relations, can hardly be understood without these new concepts—or the possibilities of group therapy realized to their best advantage.

I also believe that Sartre's social theory provides an answer to the challenge not only of analytical social theory in general, but of structuralism in particular as a contemporary analytical approach. Particularly important here, of course, is the challenge of Jacques Lacan's structuralist approach to psychoanalysis to Sartrean existential psychoanalysis. As we shall see in the following chapters, the existentialist therapist, unlike the Lacanian analyst, has no need to "play dead" in order to cause the dead structures of the psyche to appear. Instead, the existentialist therapist attempts to answer with his or her own aliveness the aliveness or spontaneity which the client wishes/fears to allow himself or herself to experience. Lacanian analysis, unlike existentialist therapy, demonstrates in the extreme the error which Sartre attributes to analytical social science theory in general: In the words of an English poet, it "murders to dissect." From a Sartrean perspective, the progressive moment must be added to the regressive moment for full understanding to occur—and for a client to be able to assume his or her freedom within the bounds of his or her particular personal and sociomaterial constraints. Those constraints certainly include, as Lacan thinks, the constraints of language itself—though Sartre, as we shall see, would view language as a practico-inert field rather than as unconscious structure.

6 · A Challenge to Existential Psychoanalysis: Ego, Mirror, and Aggressivity in Sartre and Lacan

Introduction

In Chapters 1–4, we saw how Freud's failure to develop beyond the paradigms of nineteenth-century materialist science contributed to the failure of contemporary psychoanalytic theorists to get beyond the illusion of substance as they attempt to describe the development of the ego or self. Although many of these theorists show unusual insight into earliest relational needs, especially needs for mirroring as these affect personal development, most of them nonetheless fail to transcend the reification of the psyche that is implicit in Freud's structural hypothesis. In Jacques Lacan, we encounter a psychoanalytic theorist who counters this egological orientation with ideas which, at first glance, sound quite Sartrean.

Lacan, like Sartre, claims that the ego is not a subject but an object of experience—and that current psychoanalytic attempts to buttress or build the ego are misplaced. Indeed, Lacan has nothing but contempt for most post-Freudian psychoanalytic theorists from the ego psychologists to the culturists to the British object relations theorists. Like Sartre, he objects to any attempt on the part of the analyst to colonize the analysand by substituting his or her own reified ego for that of the analysand. And like Sartre, he believes that the only legitimate position the analyst may take toward the analysand is a position of "ignorance." However much the analysand may attribute to the analyst the position of the "subject supposed to know," the analyst must never be taken in by this.

On the other hand, though Lacan, like Sartre, emphasizes the "interpersonal" nature of the analytic experience—the fact that discourse is always addressed to an Other—Lacan's view of the analyst as "Other" differs significantly from Sartre's in that for Lacan the Other whom the analysand addresses is really the linguistic unconscious (the "Other [A]") for which the analyst as the "other" (lower cased) stands as a substitute. And though Lacan, like Sartre, refuses to regard adjustment to the cultural norm as the aim of psychoanalysis, the "full speech" at which Lacanian analysis aims is not at all the same thing as Sartrean authenticity; rather, it is the realization and acceptance of the analysand as the plaything of the linguistic unconscious.

Similarly, though Lacan places great emphasis on the "mirror stage" in which a young child discovers himself or herself in the other person, the Lacanian mirror is quite different from the Sartrean in that it refers not to the discovery of the other person as a subjectivity through my experience of myself as an object but rather to the alienation of myself (ego) in the other. Thus when Sartre and Lacan discuss ego development and each quotes approvingly Rimbaud's statement that "I is another" (Sartre, TE, p. 97; Lacan, 1966, p. 23, and 1978, p. 7), the similarities between the two statements are more apparent than real. Sartre means that reflective and prereflective consciousness can never merge; Lacan means that I literally take the other person for myself and that this situation of fundamental alienation can never be overcome.

To confuse matters further, Lacan's version of the linguistic unconscious is in some ways similar to Sartre's concept of the linguistic practico-inert—the difference being that Lacan, as a structuralist, believes that language "speaks" the person, whereas Sartre ultimately holds the contrary position. Furthermore, Lacan's concept of desire, which is linked with his linguistic theory, is similar to Sartre's ontological concept of desire in that it is defined as a *manque à être*—a lack of being or (as Lacan prefers) a "want-to-be" rather than a Freudian "wish" (*Wunsch*).[1] Lacanian desire is also, like Sartrean desire, a socialization of need. On the other hand, desire in the symbolic order (as opposed to the primitive desire of the mirror stage) is for Lacan a movement from signifier to signifier rather than a value-making process, as it is for Sartre. From a Sartrean perspective, as we shall see, Lacan as an analytical social scientist sometimes does a good job of analyzing the moment of the antidialectic, but he is incapable of adequately grasping the dialectic of intentional praxis which lies behind it.

All of this tells us that a comparison of Sartre with Lacan is not going to be a simple matter. Lacan, who I believe proposes the only other major challenge besides Sartre's existential psychoanalysis to orthodox Freudian metatheory, makes matters even more difficult by claiming to be an orthodox Freudian providing an approach to Freud which is a "return" to the master's teachings rather than the revisionist fare of the post-Freudian psychoanalytic theorists. To support this claim, Lacan argues that the post-Freudian theorists are mistaken in emphasizing the early mother-child relationship at the expense of the Oedipus complex, that they are incorrect in discarding the death instinct, that they are simply wrongheaded in emphasizing ego development over the influence of the unconscious, and that their attempts at a humanistic perspective are a deviation from Freud's own attempts to create a "scientific" metapsychology. Lacan, in fact, goes so far as to argue that Freud himself would have taken a psycholinguistic position similar to Lacan's if the necessary training in structural linguistics had been available to him. Indeed, Lacan contends that Freud intuited the discoveries that later became formalized by structural linguistics and that *The Interpretation of Dreams* paves the way for later linguistic analysis "by the sheer weight of its truth" (1966, p. 162).

Obviously, this argument is not acceptable to orthodox Freudians. Nonetheless, Lacan has influenced, in one way or another, a whole generation of French psychoanalysts, and his controversies with the International Psychoanalytic Association (IPA) have left a deep scar in the French psychoanalytic community.[2] There is one way in which Lacan is right in thinking that his approach is closer to orthodox Freudianism than the approaches of contemporary psychoanalytic theorists. Lacan, like Freud but unlike the more humanistic post-Freudians, is a reductionist who is searching for a "scientific" explanation for psychic phenomena that is experience-distant rather than experience-near. He finds this not in discredited biological or physical theories but in structural linguistics. In this respect, and despite Lacan's being influenced to some extent by Sartre's own philosophical predecessors (Hegel, Husserl, and Heidegger) and probably also by Sartre himself, Lacan is definitely non-Sartrean. Indeed, in this respect the post-Freudian theorists discussed in earlier chapters are closer to Sartre than is Lacan. While their scientific positivism is being eroded, Lacan's new synchronic version of determinism remains hardy and secure.

Yet despite this major difference, Sartre does not simply reject the ideas of the structuralists in general or of Lacan in particular. Instead he attempts to confront and incorporate structuralism into existentialism with an accompanying "sea change" comparable to that undergone by Marxism and psychoanalysis. This is particularly evident in the second book of the *Critique of Dialectical Reason*, where Sartre explicitly critiques the ideas of his old friend and contributor to *Les Temps Modernes*, Claude Lévi-Strauss. But it is also evident in the whole of the *Critique*, which seems at least in part intended to counter the analytico-synchronic perspective of structuralism with the synthetico-diachronic approach of Sartrean dialectical reason.[3]

Sartre, as I noted in the preceding chapter, views analytical social science approaches (including structuralist analysis) as having something to contribute to the dialectical process. But he maintains that analysis without synthesis deforms and distorts the human individuals and groups which it attempts to understand. At the same time, however, Sartre respected structuralist technique enough to contemplate using it in the unfinished fourth volume of his biography of Flaubert to analyze *Madame Bovary*. That he never got around to completing this analysis perhaps testifies in part to his inherent distaste for structuralism (see Barnes, 1981, pp. 374ff). In any case, Sartre never conceived of structuralism as a replacement for an existentialist approach to biography; at most, it might provide an interesting supplement to it.

As for Lacan, there is little doubt that his view of the development of the ego was to some extent influenced by both Hegel and Sartre. Though Lacan's first presentation of his concept of the mirror stage (*stade du miroir*) antedates both *The Transcendence of the Ego* and *Being and Nothingness*, nothing remains of the paper he delivered at a meeting of the International Psychological Association in Marienbad in 1936. The first *published* version, which dates from a paper delivered to the International Congress of Psychoanalysis in Zurich in 1949, specifically refers to Sartre's "philosophy of being and nothingness" (though Lacan does not mention Sartre by name) as providing something of value in naming the "existential negativity" which lies at the heart of primary aggressivity; at the same time, Lacan goes on to say that "existential psychoanalysis" is essentially erroneous in maintaining the "self-sufficiency of consciousness" (1966, p. 6). Since it is obvious that Lacan knew Sartre's work at this time, it seems probable that his own view of the mirror stage was influenced by Sartre's account of the Look. Later, Lacan would recommend Sartre's account of the conflict of consciousness as essential reading for future psychoanalysts. Yet despite this praise, Lacan himself, in the passage just quoted, points to a major divergence between his own thinking and that of Sartre. Sartre, like Hegel, begins with consciousness as a cornerstone of his theory; Lacan does not. The result is an antihumanism of which Lacan is proud but which Sartre rejects. In doing so Sartre rejects as well the major premises of Lacanian analysis. Hence Sartre's appropriation of Hegel, as we shall see in the next section, is very different from Lacan's.

Indeed, Sartre would contend that Lacan, in dispensing with the conscious subject as the starting point for his theory, gets rid not only of the ego as controller of the psyche but also of the possibility for authentic action and genuine relationship. The Lacanian mirror, unlike the Sartrean, is not the other person as a conscious subject who sees me as an object, but my own reflected image in a literal mirror which, augmented by the greater motoric wholeness which I see reflected in my human counterpart, gives me the illusion of a bodily integrity which I do not in fact possess. Such "mirroring" leads me not to form an image of myself as an object, but to substitute the other's image in the place of a self. Hence while Sartre's ego is a construct of reflective consciousness, albeit a construct which is highly influenced by the reflected appraisals of others, Lacan's ego is an adoption of otherness (my own illusory mirror image plus the image of my human counterpart) in the place of a self.

The Lacanian ego, unlike the Sartrean, therefore does not admit of transformation by meta-reflection on the distorting reflected appraisals. Aggressivity, according to this view, arises not out of my attempt to use the Other who mirrors me to create a self, as in Sartre, but out of the fact that I am condemned to mimic the desire of the other along with his or her physical characteristics; it therefore cannot be obviated by the recognition of my own and the Other's freedom, since there is no freedom in Lacan to recognize. The natural consequence of Lacan's position, as I shall attempt to show, is that reality itself vanishes along with the conscious subject; as for the Lacanian antidote to this loss of self and world in the "imaginary order," although subsequent submersion of the subject in the "symbolic order" of language might be said to allow the construction of a kind of reality, it forever divides one from direct experiencing. Obviously, Sartre would not agree with this characterization of human reality.

Hegelian Themes in Sartre and Lacan

In order to better understand the differences between Sartre's and Lacan's conceptualizations of the ego and the mirror, we need first to look at what each writer has made of Hegel's account of the master-slave relationship. Although both Sartre and Lacan originally encountered Hegel in a common source, Alexandre Kojéve's "left-Hegelian" lectures at the Ecole des Hautes Etudes between 1933 and 1939,[4] and although both object in the final analysis to Hegelian idealism, there is a great divergence between Sartre's and Lacan's appropriations of Hegel—a divergence based on Sartre's acceptance and Lacan's rejection of Hegel's idea that consciousness is the starting point for these investigations. This difference has led Lacan to diverge from Hegel in the direction of a kind of physicalization of the conflict Hegel describes, while it has led Sartre to diverge in the direction of greater emphasis on and more subtle understanding of the workings of individual consciousnesses and of intersubjective relations.

Let us begin with Hegel's own views. According to Hegel, it is through the recognition of the Other (person) that I first become conscious of myself in the mode that is described as self-consciousness. Before this initial recognition, consciousness of external objects exists but consciousness of self does not. In this situation, as Hegel puts it, there is "self-certainty" (subjective reality) but no "truth" (objective reality). I experience, but I do not know myself objectively as an experiencing self. For this, I need recognition from the Other. Yet according to Hegel, my first awareness of the Other is not as a fully developed other person but as a "sublated" Other. In other words, the Other is not a real person in his or her own right but is rather "another self." This other self, however, is a danger to me in that he or she threatens my self-sufficiency and therefore becomes a source of conflict. Hence at the same time that I desire the Other's recognition, I desire the Other's death because I do not wish to depend on the Other's acknowledgment of me. This initiates a kind of primary aggressivity in which I attempt to prove my mettle as a subject through a fight to the death based on pure prestige. The problem with this is that my own death renders me a mere object rather than a self-consciousness, whereas the death of the Other leaves me without the objective recognition I need to achieve the truth of self-consciousness.

My next move will be to assume one of two positions: Either I will decide that my life is of supreme value and refuse to risk death, thereby assuming the position of the slave, or I will continue to risk death but will enslave the Other rather than kill him (Hegel, of course, uses the masculine pronoun), thereby assuming the position of the master. The master's solution is to make himself the essential consciousness while relegating the slave to the position of the inessential consciousness. As a subsidiary consciousness, the slave loses importance as a unique interiority and becomes important only insofar as he is a consciousness of the master. As for the master, he has proven his worthiness as a freedom (to himself and the slave) through his willingness to go beyond mere existence and risk his life in a battle to the death—a refusal of contingency that the slave was not willing to make.

This solution, however, also proves to be unstable, since an inessential consciousness cannot very well give an essential consciousness the recognition it requires.[5] And, indeed, the master-slave conflict is only the beginning of a dialectical movement whose end, reached through various meanderings of the World Historical Spirit, is Absolute Knowledge. At the point of Absolute Knowledge, temporality, as the moving aspect of a dialectic that always points beyond itself, has no meaning since self-identity has been achieved in the form of equivalence to world-identity.

Obviously, neither Sartre nor Lacan will follow Hegel here. Both maintain that human reality remains what Hegel refers to as an "unhappy consciousness"—a consciousness hopelessly divided against itself. And Lacan would even deny that this division is wholly conscious. Nor would either Sartre or Lacan agree with Hegel's view of history as a dialectical development of which the various moments connote spiritual progress. Rather, they would follow an interpretation of Hegel which regards his account of the development of consciousness as psychologically rather than historically descriptive. At this point, however, differences appear in Sartre's and Lacan's appropriations of Hegel.

Sartre, of course, has provided his own critique of Hegel's view of intersubjectivity in part three of *Being and Nothingness* (pp. 235–44). Although Sartre accepts Hegel's ideas that consciousness is the starting point for the investigation and that the battle for recognition is fundamental, he criticizes what he believes to be Hegel's erroneous identification of self-consciousness with self-knowledge. Although Sartre believes that Hegel's account of the Other is superior to Husserl's in that for Hegel "the negation which constitutes the Other is direct, internal and reciprocal," whereas Husserl's account is merely external (BN, p. 238), he nonetheless believes that Hegel, too, fails to solve the problem of solipsism. According to Sartre, Hegel's attempt to arrive at the "I am I" of self-consciousness and self-identity is misplaced since there can never be an equivalence between the first and the second "I" in this proposition. Hence the whole attempt to escape the contingency of life, to cease to be mere objects in nature (which is the meaning of the life and death struggle in Hegel), is mistaken.

What is at issue, according to Sartre, is not my own or the Other's existence as body-object but *otherness* itself. And otherness cannot be overcome either by the risk of life or by taking otherness into myself. The ego, as we have seen in previous chapters, is not on the side of the for-itself but on the side of the in-itself. There is no coincidence between my consciousness for myself (basic intentionality), my consciousness of myself (reflective consciousness), and my knowledge of the Other's consciousness of me. Thus Sartre argues that Hegel, by viewing the Other as an object through whom I apprehend my own objectness, removes the possibility of apprehending the Other's consciousness of me since I could apprehend this only in an Other who is a subject and not an Object. It is for this reason that Sartre believes that the Other as mirror in Hegel "is clouded and no longer reflects anything" (BN, p. 242).

What will be required for the Other's power as a mirror to be restored is an apodictic certainty of the Other as another consciousness similar to the certainty I have of my experiencing self. As we saw in earlier chapters, Sartre finds this apodictic certainty in the experience of the Look. Although the Look does not overcome the ontological separation which Hegel attempted to supersede in the direction of the Whole, it does release me from the solipsism implied in a perception of the Other only as an Other object. It also provides a new interpretation of the master-slave conflict. The fight to death and the desire to enslave or to be enslaved still refer to the attempt to achieve a sense of self, but this is no longer an empty, abstract identity: for-itself equals for-itself. Rather, the Other who apprehends me is a particular Other who does not constitute me in my being (as in Hegel) but who interests himself or herself concretely and "ontically" in the empirical circumstances of my life. It is this Other who pierces me to the heart of my being by making me aware of myself as a transcendence transcended.

As for the master-slave conflict, it becomes part of the sadomasochistic circle discussed in Chapter 3. In this context, the attempt to enslave or to be enslaved in the sense of giving primacy to one's own or the Other's consciousness no longer involves an attempt to recover myself as I am through the Other but an attempt to recover myself as an object for another consciousness. Thus, although Sartre follows Hegel in insisting on the importance of the desire for recognition, this recognition serves not the achievement of a real self-identity but the illusory quest for substantive freedom. And, as we have seen, transformation of aggressivity in Sartre does not rest on a Hegelian higher synthesis involving Reason and Spirit and leading eventually to Absolute Knowledge; rather, it rests on a concrete acceptance of the otherness of the Other, on a respect for the Other's freedom as such. Later, Sartre would insist that positive reciprocity, except in a world dominated by scarcity (which, of course, is our world), is the norm of human relations—remarking that violence derives not from the mere existence of the Other, as Hegel supposed, but from interiorized scarcity (CDR, p. 815).

Lacan's appropriation of Hegel is quite different from Sartre's. Instead of beginning with consciousness and the battle for recognition from the Other as a subject, Lacan begins with the body and the attempt to appropriate the other person as an image of motoric wholeness. Thus we might say that whereas Sartre takes a step away from Hegel toward giving more credit to the recognition of the other person as a subject, Lacan physicalizes Hegel by making the body and its image the focal point of his inquiries into the early stages of human development. Although Lacan claims that his own account of the mirror stage supports "the fundamental Hegelian theme—man's desire is the desire of the other" (Lacan, 1975, p. 146)—his conceptualization of primitive desire is, in fact, neither Hegelian nor Sartrean. Lacan means literally that the young child, mistaking himself or herself for the other person, learns to substitute the other's desire for objects in the world for the child's own desire; human conflicts result from the inevitable collision of desires which follows from this proposition.

In order to understand how Lacan is using Hegel, we must therefore first provide an account of his theory of early development, which includes both the mirror stage and a state he refers to as "transitivism." Before doing so, however, we should note that Lacan is less exact than other developmental theorists in pinpointing the exact ages and sequence of the "stages" of early development. At times, for example, he seems to say that transitivism follows the mirror stage, whereas at other times they appear to be concomitant. What does seem clear is that transitivism comes to an end at about two and a half years of age with the advent of the Oedipus complex. The exact timing is not so important since, as one critic notes, Lacan's mirror stage should be regarded more as a "structuring situation" than as an actual stage which can be exactly placed chronologically (Green in Smith and Kerrigan, 1983, p. 166); I believe the same is true of transitivism. As Lacan puts this matter, his account of "anteriority is not chronological but logical" (1975, p. 170).

Part of the reason for this refusal to precisely pinpoint pre-Oedipal reality appears to be Lacan's insistence that life before the advent of language, before the individual's insertion into the symbolic order at the time of the resolution of the Oedipus complex, can only be reconstructed symbolically—through the very language which transforms it. Hence, even though the mirror stage and transitivism provide the underpinnings of the symbolic order, they can never be approached directly, without the intervention of that order, in the course of analysis.

Despite these reservations about a literal reading of Lacanian developmental theory, Lacan does give some fairly clear indications about the chronology of the mirror stage. It begins at about six months of age and lasts until the acquisition of language at about eighteen months. Before this, in the stage that Lacan designates "autoeroticism" the infant had been aware of objects only in terms of the pleasure or unpleasure they bring. Obviously this is not Freudian autoeroticism, or primary narcissism, since Lacan (1966, p. 181) agrees with the majority of post-Freudian theorists that the human infant has a rudimentary intersubjectivity which is present almost from the beginning of life.

The mirror stage begins when the six-month-old baby becomes fascinated with his or her mirror image, greeting it with a "flutter of jubilant activity" in which the baby leans forward to hold the image in his or her gaze. The baby at this time is also fascinated with his or her motorically developed counterparts—older children or mother—with whom he or she comes to identify. Lacan believes that this fascination with mirror images and images of others derives from the "motor incapacity and nursling dependence" of the infant, which signal the *specific prematurity of birth in man*" as compared with other animals—the "foetalization" of the human infant (1966, pp. 2 and 4).

Lacan also thinks that the behavior of the infant before the mirror might indicate a special case of the need for an imago of one's species, seen in pigeons and locusts as well as human beings, to provoke maturation. Such "mimicry" may be more complex in human beings (the young chimpanzee, for instance, soon loses interest when it discovers that there is no other chimp behind the mirror), but it indicates a connection between animal reality and human reality in the imaginary order. The mirror image, according to Lacan, anticipates a sense of motoric wholeness and integration which the infant does not yet possess. The consequence is that the primordial "I" is based on what Lacan refers to as the "Ideal-I," or the ideal ego, as opposed to the ego ideal, which belongs to the symbolic rather than the imaginary order. Thus, though most commentators believe that Freud uses the terms "ideal ego" (*Idealich*) and "ego ideal" (*Ichideal*) interchangeably and as precursors to his concept of the superego, Lacan points out that Freud does in fact use all three terms to make a distinction which is important to Lacan. The ideal ego, unlike the ego ideal, is based on a "fictional" identification with an image of wholeness that is intended to negate the human being's "organic insufficiency in his natural reality" (Lacan, 1966, pp. 2 and 4).

The ego itself will always bear signs of this fictional, imagistic origin. This is the first alienation, and it refers to an absolutely crucial gap which structures human reality as temporal—as referring from present insufficiency to future wholeness:

This development is experienced as a temporal dialectic that decisively projects the formation of the individual into history. The *mirror stage* is a drama whose internal thrust is precipitated from insufficiency to anticipation—and which manufactures for the subject, caught up in the lure of spatial identification, the succession of phantasies that extends from a fragmented body-image to a form of its totality that I shall call orthopaedic—and lastly to the assumption of the armour of an alienating identity, which will mark with its rigid structure the subject's entire mental development. (Lacan, 1966, p. 4)

The result is that at the same time that the ego develops as an imaginary wholeness, the fragmented body (*corps morcelé*) becomes a staple of dreams, of children's play, and of certain psychotic episodes; it is also, Lacan notes, an inspiration for the horrific visions of an artist such as Hieronymus Bosch. We are apparently never sure of our wholeness since it originally developed as a mirage. Similarly, the ego is symbolized in dreams by a fortress or stadium, standing for our need to defend ourselves against fragmentation.

As for the aggressivity that Hegel believes lies at the heart of human relations, Lacan, following Charlotte Bühler, finds its origins in the situation he calls "transitivism." Transitivism refers to the tendency of the young child, before the middle of the third year, to confuse his or her actions with those of counterparts. The child will say, "John hit me," when the child hit John, or "I fell down," when Francis was the one who fell down; indeed, the child will cry when something has actually happened to the other child. Lacan tells us that it is in transitivism, at the point of conjunction between the specular *me* and the social *I*, that the "paranoiac alienation of the ego" takes place. This happens because of the very confusion of self with other and self with mirror image which lies at the heart of ego formation. This confusion, which is not to be mistaken for introjection (Lacan regards introjection as a symbolic rather than an imaginary function), is the source of a "paranoiac" projection which is absolutely fundamental not because I am dumping my desires on the other (the usual conception of projection) but because the ego is at its source formed out of the desire of the other (Lacan, 1966, pp. 1–7).

The basic aggressivity which is introduced in transitivism derives from the fact that in identifying with the other's body, I come to identify also with his or her desire. I want what the other wants. In one of his seminars, Lacan gives the analogy of a little machine which gains its direction from the imprinting of another little machine. Since each little machine is thereafter intent on the point where the other is going, the inevitable result is a collision—a collision that is obviously Lacan's version of the Freudian notion of sibling rivalry (Lacan, 1978, pp. 51 and 54). The intensity of such rivalry, whether with siblings or playmates, derives from the fact that pre-Oedipal, or presymbolic, desire "is seen solely in the other": "At first, before language, desire exists solely in the single plane of the imaginary relation of the specular stage, projected, alienated in the other. The tension it provokes is then deprived of an outcome. That is to say that it has no other outcome—*Hegel teaches us this*—than the destruction of the other" (Lacan, 1975, p. 170; italics mine).

Thus the subject's desire is confirmed only in an absolute rivalry with the other, in a projection outside which implies the "impossibility of all human coexistence" (Lacan, 1975, p. 171). Indeed, Lacan believes that without the mediation of recognition, which is a function of the entrance into the symbolic order, "every human function would simply exhaust itself in the unspecified wish for the destruction of the other as such" (1975, p. 171). Transitivism is therefore a "drama of primordial jealousy" (Lacan, 1966, p. 5) that points to the Hegelian theme of desire for the death of the other.

Lacan gives as an example of this primary aggressivity a little girl scarcely old enough to walk who hits her playmate from next door (around whom she has constructed her first identifications) over the head with a good-sized stone. Triumphantly and without the slightest trace of guilt, she announces her deed: "*Me break Francis head.*" In doing so, Lacan tells us, she "displays the most fundamental structure of the human being on the imaginary plane—to destroy the person who is the site of alienation" (1975, p. 172). The aggressivity which characterizes transitivism does not, of course, disappear from adult human relations. It appears in such phenomena as competitiveness, war, and the linking of aggression with "strength" in Western thought (Lacan, 1966, p. 25). Transitivism also survives, Lacan tells us, in the familiar phenomenon of the double as it appears in literary productions and in dreams.

Lacan also links the early confusion of self with other to pre-Oedipal sexuality. In identifying with the desire of his or her mother, Lacan tells us, the pre-Oedipal child comes to identify with the all-fulfilling object of the mother's desire—the phallus which the mother lacks. This is neither the real penis nor the symbolic phallus which is (as we shall see in the next chapter) the primal "signifier"; rather, it is the "imaginary" phallus. At first believing that the mother *has* this imaginary phallus, the child a little later, upon comprehending her lack and her desire, wishes to impersonate it—a situation which is Lacan's refashioning of Freud's idea that the child, in the mother's unconscious, stands for the penis of which she has been deprived. It is also Lacan's rendition of the Hegelian desire for recognition. In the next stage of development, this identification is overcome by the appearance of the father (who stands between the child and the mother) and by the entry of the child into the symbolic-linguistic order which this precipitates. At this time, Lacan believes, the imaginary phallus is superseded by the symbolic phallus—the "Desire-of-the-mother" by the "Name-of-the-father."

Obviously, though Lacan repeatedly cites Hegel's insights into the origins of human aggressivity and the nature of desire as being similar to his own, Lacan's is a strange Hegelianism. This is so because, as I have said, it is a Hegelianism that denies the primacy of consciousness. Hence Lacan does not really conceive of transitivism as the battle for pure prestige envisioned by Hegel (though Lacan sometimes implies this correlation), but rather as a battle over objects which each child, mimicking the desire of his or her counterpart, grasps as his or her own. Indeed, the heart of transitivism can be seen in Lacan's parable of the little machines which imprint each other rather than in a Hegelian struggle for objective awareness of self. Even Lacan's version of the desire for recognition from the primordial object involves not recognition as a person, but recognition as the imaginary phallus—as that which the mother lacks rather than as that which I am.

In other words, for Lacan the meaning of transitivism and the identification with the imaginary phallus is not the attempt to incorporate otherness into the self as a means to objective truth (Hegel) or substantive freedom (Sartre). It is the adoption of otherness in the place of a self. I do not discover myself either as a subject or as an object in the (Hegelian) Other; rather, I lose myself (insofar as one can be conceived to have a self in a philosophy that denies the primacy of consciousness) in the (Lacanian) other.

As for the transcendence of aggressivity (which I consider in more detail in the next chapter), Lacan's view is again pseudo-Hegelian rather than genuinely Hegelian. It is certainly not Sartrean. Lacan seems to follow Hegel in developing an idea of "pacification" through universalization—through a movement into the world of "law and command" that is associated with language and culture (see Hegel, 1807, pp. 294–363). Lacan notes, in a passage similar to certain passages in Hegel linking language with law and authority,[6] that "the dialectic of the ego and the other is transcended, is placed on a higher plane, in relation to the other, solely through the function of language, in so far as it is more or less identical, and at all events fundamentally linked with what we should call rule, or better still, the law" (1975, pp. 156–57).

Yet because there is no original consciousness in Lacan, the "I" is not a point from which Absolute Knowledge in the Hegelian sense can develop; it is instead a "subject" constantly subverted by the unconscious linguistic order which creates it. And though the laws of the linguistic unconscious (which, as we shall see, are the "laws" of metaphor and metonymy) indicate a kind of rationality, this rationality is the product of neither the individual consciousness (Sartre) nor of the World Historical Spirit realizing itself in existence (Hegel). As Lacan is fond of saying, "There is no Other of the Other." There is nothing behind the static linguistic order which subverts human beings to its structures.

Ego, Mirror, and Intersubjectivity in Sartre and Lacan

Lacan, then, is not a Hegelian idealist. Neither, however, is he a Sartrean existentialist. Lacan's qualified praise for Sartre's phenomenological accounts of the Look and the conflict of consciousnesses does not imply an acceptance of Sartre's ontology. The truth is that where Sartre rejects Hegelian idealism in the direction of an untranscendable individual consciousness which alone is responsible for creating value and which in the course of doing so posits a self as an object (ego) which is always divided from the transcendent consciousness which posits it, Lacan rejects Hegelian idealism in favor of a physicalist view of human conflicts transcended by a static linguistic structure out of which the "I" as the successor of the specular ego emerges. Yet despite this fundamental difference, it is not surprising (considering the fact that Hegel provides a common source and that Lacan had read Sartre) to find that Lacan's account of the ego and mirroring is not completely at odds with Sartre's. This is, however, a similarity with overshadowing differences.

We have seen, for example, that Lacan follows Sartre in describing human reality as a temporalization which attempts to move from present insufficiency to future wholeness. Indeed, Lacan goes so far as to suggest that analysis works "from the future to the past" because even though the analyst may think that he or she is "looking for the patient's past in a dustbin," it is actually "a function of the fact that the patient has a future that you can move in the regressive sense" (1975, p. 157). And even though Sartre would certainly agree with this statement, he would nonetheless disagree with Lacan's attempt to link future-directedness to animal ethology (or, as we shall see later, with the movement of language) and with Lacan's view that the lack inherent in desire refers initially to a desire for motoric development and an image of physical integrity rather than to a desire for substantive freedom.

Still, Sartre would agree with Lacan's conceptualization of the ego as an object which is more often an object of misunderstanding (*méconnaissance*) than of understanding. Indeed, Lacan echoes Sartre when he compares the human subject to a paralytic who has been hypnotized by his or her image in a mirror (the ego); Sartre had similarly described the ego as a "false representation of itself" with which consciousness has "hypnotized itself" (Lacan, 1978, p. 50; TE, p. 101). The difference, of course, is that Sartre's subject is paralyzed by the image of a substantive self which the ego represents, whereas Lacan's paralytic is hypnotized by the substitution for a self of its own mirror image or the image of its counterpart. Nonetheless, both theorists would agree that the ego represents a kind of rigidity which it is the task of psychoanalysis to call into question.

For this reason, both would also agree that contemporary psychoanalytic theorists are mistaken in their attempts to build ego structure in the psyche rather than to confront the illusory nature of the ego. Lacan, in fact, repeatedly faults the ego psychologists and British object relations theorists on this score, insisting that such attempts at structure building in the psyche are examples of an unacceptable objectification and manipulation of the analysand on the part of the analyst. And he further implies that the ideal analyst would be egoless (Lacan, 1978, p. 246), though he agrees with Sartre on the practical necessity for an individual to develop an ego. Sartre has similarly suggested on occasion that the annihilation of the ego might be a desirable goal. On the other hand, Sartre's position is different from Lacan's in that the ego as an object for reflective consciousness (though contaminated with the voices of others) is quite different from the ego as a fundamental alienation in which the desire of the other takes the place of a self. For this reason, it is possible from a Sartrean perspective to conceive of a transformation of the ego that is not possible from a Lacanian perspective.

As for the Look and the conflict of consciousnesses, Lacan recommends Sartre's *Being and Nothingness* as "essential reading for an analyst" because it so brilliantly captures "the entire phenomenology of shame, of modesty, of prestige, of the specific fear engendered by the gaze" (1975, p. 215). Yet on closer inspection, one discovers that Lacan believes that Sartre is mistaken about the origins of the Look or the "gaze" (as Lacan scholars usually translate *le regard*) in one's human counterpart. In support of this idea that the gaze, though linked to my human counterpart, really points elsewhere, Lacan cites Sartre's own admission that as soon as I turn to look at the Look, it disappears; instead, all I see is eyes. Also, Lacan notes, Sartre himself admits that I apprehend the Look in places other than real persons: I experience the Look in the window behind which I suspect a person lurks, in the sound of rustling leaves, or in the footsteps in a corridor at the end of which I am acting the voyeur (Lacan, 1975, pp. 215 and 220, 1973, pp. 85–85). Sartre, of course, would reply that these experiences gain their significance from the Other's Look, which is already a part of my intersubjective repertoire. As for the fact that the Look disappears when I turn to look at the Other's eyes, this happens because in so turning I assume the position of a subject confronting an Other as object.

Lacan, on the other hand, presents us with suppositions about the origins of the gaze which underscore his profound differences with Sartre—differences which in the end lead Lacan to adopt a position that (despite Lacan's repeated insistence on the significance of intersubjectivity) reintroduces the problem of solipsism. Lacan believes that the gaze does not really originate in my human counterpart (the Lacanian—lower case—"other"), but rather in the linguistic unconscious—the great Other (*le grand Autre*), to be written hereafter as the "Other(A)" to distinguish it from the other person, the Sartrean "Other" and the Lacanian "other." Although the mirror stage and transitivism remain backdrops for understanding the significance of the gaze, its real significance lies in the interaction of the "I" with the linguistic unconscious.

Yet the situation, as is often the case with Lacan, is not quite this simple. This is so because Lacan believes that the linguistic unconscious itself refers to one's original relations with others. Indeed, the linguistic unconscious, according to Lacan, comes into existence with the repression of the mirror stage and the primal attachment to the mother at the time of the entry of the symbolic father into the child's life—leading to a lifelong linking of the desire for recognition with other people. As Lacan scholar Ellie Ragland-Sullivan notes,

> Mirror-stage infants act in such a way as to attract the attention of the Real other [mother], whose *parole* [speech] they "introject" and subsequently desire *qua* Other(A). This drama is reenacted throughout life via substitutive others whose recognition is sought. . . . When the mir-

ror stage ends, the mother is repressed as a record of primordial, corporal, identificatory meaning. (1986, p. 76)

The mother reappears, then, as the subjective experience of the gaze of some imaginary other pointing to the unconscious origins of the conscious subject. The conflict is no longer a conflict of consciousnesses but a conflict between the ego and the Other(A) via the path of others. In this way, Lacan adds a third term to Sartre's subject-object conflict, transforming (or deforming, depending on one's position) it entirely.

Thus according to Lacan, although human conflicts may appear on the horizon of the experience of the gaze, their actual origin is not my desire to co-opt the Other as a mirror for me as an object (as in Sartre) but my desire to mimic the other and thereby gain a self. And though Lacan views as irrefutable Sartre's idea that love is at bottom the desire to be loved (1975, p. 216), he nonetheless rejects Sartre's fundamental ontology. At the same time, this rejection means that Lacan's and Sartre's views of the "fundamentally narcissistic structure of love" (or, we might add, the fundamentally narcissistic structure of inauthentic love, according to Sartre's later formulations) are on closer inspection quite different. When Lacan says that narcissistic love "is essentially an attempt to capture the other in oneself, in oneself as an object" (1975, p. 276), he is practically quoting Sartre on the masochistic position. What he means, however, is that one loves in the other person "one's own ego [which, we remember, is modeled on the mirror reflection and the counterpart and hence is in no way an actual reflection of self as subject or object] made real on the imaginary level" (Lacan, 1975, p. 142). In other words, Lacan conceives of both the self and the other as objects, not subjects. According to this conceptualization, there is no subject-object alternation and no possibility for transformation through coming to respect one's own and the Other's freedom.

Such transformation as there is results from the entry of the lover into the symbolic order. The "active gift of love," as distinguished from narcissistic love, involves the bestowal of a symbolic promise in words such as these: "You are my husband, you are my wife" (Lacan, 1975, pp. 216-17). Yet though Lacan insists that love in the symbolic order moves beyond "imaginary captation" (a neologism indicating, one presumes, capture, captivation, bestowal of headship) toward the "being of the loved object, toward his particularity" (1975), p. 142), one cannot help wondering how the bestowal of roles leads to an appreciation of particularity. In any case, Lacan believes that despite this symbolic overlay, love at the most profound level involves a disturbance in the symbolic order made possible by the origins of affectivity in the imaginary order. When you are in love, Lacan maintains, you are "mad" because love involves a "veritable subduction of the symbolic, a sort of annihilation, of perturbation of the function of the ego ideal"—which, as we remember, is distinguished from the imaginary ideal ego by its participation in the symbolic order. Love "opens the door . . . to perfection"—and perfection, of course, is the longing for an imaginary wholeness (Lacan, 1975, p. 142). Hence, the captation which we wish our beloved to experience with respect to us, this desire which we have to become "for the other that in which his freedom is alienated" (the Sartrean "object limit of our freedom"), is not motivated by a desire for substantive freedom (Lacan, 1975, p. 217). Rather, it is motivated by a love of self which is not self-love at all but a love for the image of wholeness by means of which the Other originally captured what might have been a self.

Actually, if Lacan is correct in his conception of the origins of the gaze and of human conflicts, then the problem of solipsism remains unanswered and the intersubjectivity on which Lacan repeatedly insists is meaningless. A question asked by one of Lacan's students in a seminar on the gaze points to this difficulty. Lacan has just remarked that it is the dialectic of desire as related to the Other(A) which explains why the gaze disorganizes the field of perception when a student remarks, "But I don't understand how others will reappear in your discourse." Lacan's seemingly flippant reply is, "Look, the main thing is that I don't come a cropper!" (1973, p. 89). The problem, I think, is that others as other subjects or consciousnesses do not appear anywhere in Lacan's work. But perhaps this is only natural in a psychological metatheory which views the ego, as Ragland-Sullivan notes, as "an organized object, which functions as a subject"—an object which is always verifying and recomposing itself "in relation to objects 'out there' [who also think they are subjects]" (1986, p. 96, brackets in original). In other words, in place of Sartre's subject-object alternation, Lacan substitutes a relationship of objects in which each is constantly chasing its own mirage in the other.

The Sartrean Ego: Possibilities for Transformation

The implications of a Lacanian perspective on the ego and intersubjectivity for psychotherapy are not, I believe, optimistic in the same way that a Sartrean perspective may ultimately be said to lead to a kind of tough optimism. Clearly, Lacan's view of human relations in no way allows a position of authenticity or genuine intimacy since consciousness (one's own and the other's) is rejected as a starting point and since mimicry of and rivalry with the other is seen to be fundamental. As for the Lacanian ego, since it is purely and simply a mirage, it cannot admit of purification. Even if the Lacanian analyst succeeds in undermining the ego by making the analysand aware of its specular origins, there is no spontaneity of consciousness that can thereby be released. In Sartre, on the other hand, one can conceive of a kind of purification of the ego effected by the same radical conversion to a philosophy of freedom which allows for authentic relations with others. Although the early Sartre primarily emphasizes the negative aspects of the ego, there is, as Hazel Barnes notes, a positive side to the Sartrean ego.[7] There are also, as Sartre himself recognizes in the Flaubert biography, positive as well as negative possibilities for ego development—possibilities which are not present in a Lacanian perspective on the ego.

The question Barnes addresses is this: What would an authentic relationship with one's own ego be like? In other words, what kind of transformation would the purifying reflection effect on this relationship? If the ego does not simply disappear, which seems unlikely, it would have to be different from the ego of the person in bad faith. Obviously, the answer must be implicit in Sartre's description of bad faith with its implications about the nature of good faith. Just as authentic love involves giving up the idea of using the other person to create substantive freedom, so an authentic relationship with one's own ego must involve giving up the ego as a means to an inauthentic substantialization of the self. We know Sartre's own description of the ego as it is usually lived by the person in bad faith: This person reverses the order of the ego's formation, assuming an underlying substantive ego which generates psychic states and qualities which in turn determine one's behavior. The ego is thereby assumed to be a *cause*, or source, rather than an *effect*, or product. The person relating to his or her ego in this way is guilty of the form of bad faith which denies freedom in favor of facticity. As Barnes points out, however, this cannot mean that a person living in good faith has no ego. There is, after all, a second form of bad faith, the denial of facticity, and surely the person aspiring to an "egoless" state would be guilty of this form of inauthenticity.

Barnes suggests that an authentic relationship with one's own ego would involve recognizing that the ego is an object—that its "I" is the narrator (consciousness, of course, is the author) of a story which one tells oneself about oneself and which one must continually modify and revise as one modifies and changes one's relationship with the past in the direction of the future. At the same time, one would take responsibility for the ego one has created/is creating as the principal of one's personal narrative. Obviously, the kind of story one tells oneself about oneself has a real effect—similar, as Barnes notes, to the real effects produced by the "social imaginary" of literary works which Sartre discusses in the Flaubert biography. Telling myself a story in which the ego is substantive support for a set of qualities and states will have a very different effect than telling myself a story in which the ego is the objective unity of qualities and states which I realize I have set up as reflections of free conscious choices. In the second situation, I may still speak of "love" and "hate," for instance, but I will understand that it is free consciousness rather than a substantialized ego which supports these states. I may at any moment change, and as I change I must change the narrative unity which is my ego.

This is very different, however, from becoming egoless or failing to develop an ego. If I fail to develop an ego, as Barnes notes, the result might be at best a person who is a mere weather vane, moving impulsively in the wind with each external stimulus but certainly not living responsibly or meaningfully. At worst, the result might be psychosis, and Barnes gives as an example R. D. Laing's discussion of the case of Julie, whom Laing describes as a "chaotic nonentity" (Laing, 1959a, pp. 178–205). Julie, it seems, is an example in the extreme of the kind of borrowed identity which Lacan describes as normative for ego development. She is literally a precipitate of all past object identifications, speaking now in the voice of one family member and now in the voice of another—with an occasional fleeting sense of being a unified person. From a Sartrean perspective, Julie's "ego"—or rather her lack of ego development—might be viewed as an aberration based on her failure to develop a coherent "story line" which would allow her a sense of self. Julie's associative word salad, which from a Lacanian perspective might indicate a failure of inclusion in the symbolic order, in fact testifies to this dilemma. She says that she is a "tolled bell," which Laing interprets to mean "told belle." She also calls herself "Mrs. Taylor," meaning that she is "tailor-made," a "tailored maid," or "made, fed, clothed, and tailored" but denied genuine autonomy (1959a, pp. 187 and 191). On entering the hospital, Julie told the in-take psychiatrist that she was not a real person but that she was trying to become a person (Laing, 1959, p. 178).

Laing, on questioning Julie's mother, discovered that Julie had been a perfectly obedient child, even asking her mother to tell her everything she must do, until the age of fourteen when her mother began to encourage her to be more autonomous, to date, and to go to parties. At this point, Julie accused her mother of not having wanted her, of refusing to let her be a person, of keeping her from breathing, and of smothering her. We can see from Laing's interviews with the mother why Julie might have felt this way. According to Julie's mother, Julie, unlike her older sister, had been a "good" baby—that is, undemanding and never "a trouble" (Laing, 1959a, pp. 182–83). She never cried for her feeds, was weaned without difficulty, was toilet trained at fifteen months, and generally did as she was told. Laing comments that whether the mother's memory is accurate or not, what is significant is that she praises in her child exactly those things that might connote an "inner deadness" (Laing, 1959a, p. 183).

Julie's mother, however, does not understand her daughter's difficulties. After all, Julie was her favorite child, the one for whom she "did everything"—meaning, apparently, that Julie's mother tried to live Julie's life for her. In doing so, she stifled all impulses toward autonomy. An incident which Julie's mother recounted concerning her daughter at about the time of weaning gives some insight into how this may have happened. At this time, Julie had tried to play a "throwing-away" game with her mother similar to the *fort-da* game described by Freud with respect to his grandson. The difference from the usual version of this infantile game was that Julie's mother inverted the roles, which she had played in the usual way with Julie's sister. "I made sure that *she* [Julie] was not going to play that game with me," she tells Laing. "*I* threw things away and she brought them to *me*"—as soon as she could crawl (Laing, 1959a, p. 185). Julie's mother also believed that the separation anxiety which Julie showed until the age of three by "going crazy" if her mother was out of her sight signaled how much her daughter loved her (Laing, 1959a, p. 186).

Julie, as Laing describes her, apparently never developed autonomy, a will of her own, a sense of being the source of her own actions. Instead, she was, according to her mother, a child who always did as she was told. When she was "told" to be more autonomous as a young teenager, this proved to be a contradiction she could not sustain. The possibility for praxis had been too severely limited too early. Hence the overt trouble began when Julie's mother, no longer satisfied with the nonentity she had created, began "to order this shadow to act as though it were a person" (Laing, 1959a, p. 193)—a task of which Julie was incapable. When, at age seventeen, Julie became psychotic, she accused her mother of having murdered a child wearing Julie's clothes.

In a sense, of course, Julie was right. Her autonomous self, which was linked to her chance to develop a coherent ego, had been murdered. According to this view, the fragments of personalities who occupied her body—whom Laing came to recognize as the "bad mother," the "good sister," and the "compliant child"—were not remnants of earliest ego identifications in the Lacanian sense, but rather signs of a radical failure *to be* in the existentialist sense of creating a self out there in the world. Tragically, Laing occasionally encountered the embryonic stirrings of a person who seemed to be Julie herself—but this was always ruthlessly squashed by the internalized voices of others.

Another manifestation of difficulties in ego development is the position of the neurotic, who does not (like Julie) fail to develop a coherent ego but whose ego is a false representation of the self based on the views of others. Sartre himself presents us with an extreme example of neurotic ego development in the Flaubert biography[8]—an example which has implications for a Sartrean perspective on "normal" ego development as well. Sartre maintains that Flaubert's basically passive "constitution," deriving, as we have seen, from the failure of his mother in her dutiful handling of him as an object to evoke his active participation as a subject, leads to the formation of an ego which "scarcely belongs to him" in any real sense (FI, 1:165).

Flaubert's ego, Sartre tells us, is a matter of "belief" rather than of "truth," since truth emerges out of the engagement of a praxis in its project through the mediation of (humanized) things of which Flaubert is incapable. Since Flaubert is incapable of the activity that is required for verification, he simply accepts as truth what is "affirmed by others and etched into [him] by them" (FI, 1:164). And since his relationship with his own ego as a psychic object is similar to his relationship to external objects and to language (which, as we shall see, he regards as the possession of the grown-ups with only an incidental and external relationship to himself), Flaubert has no means for verifying the opinions of others on the basis of which he has formed his ego. He may try to playact the feelings and sentiments attributed to him, but he has no means of verifying them in his being. He therefore "limits himself to supporting passively the synthesis effected by the Other" (FI, 1:156). The result is that he never develops an authentic ego.

Sartre understands that the reader of *The Transcendence of the Ego* is likely to object at this point by noting that "the ego in everyone is a determination of the psyche and that it is entirely conditioned by others, full of alien determinations which we can grasp only in their abstract significance but cannot *see* because they only appear *to others*" (FI, 1:167n). This is so, of course, because the qualities that describe me are names provided by the

Other. It is from the viewpoint of the Other that I am "spiritual or vulgar, intelligent or dull, open or closed." But even though this is true, it is also true that my ego "is, in form at least, the pure correlative of . . . reflective ipseity" (FI, 1:167n). That is, the ego is my turning on myself to reflect on what I am—however much this reflection may also be influenced or contaminated by the views of others or however much I may be said to discover and take an interest in the act of reflecting *because of* the presence of the Other.

Thus in reality there are always two parts to the Sartrean ego—the "reflective ipseity" which is its basic structure, and the judgments of others (especially the original others) which figure in its construction. When I become aware of these judgments, as Sartre points out, I leave the reflective terrain and attempt to consider them through the Other's eyes; I then try to relate the Other's observations to my own acts or gestures. In "normal" development, I either accept or reject the Other's determinations; in either case, I use them "to reshape the object-unity of my reflective experience, the ego." The ego thereby becomes not only a reflection but a promise: I take a vow to *be* this kind of person, to realize these qualities in myself. And this activity allows my ego as a psychic object to become "a sector of knowledge and truth"—which also means, of course, that it can be a "sector of nonknowledge, error, and bad faith" (FI, 1:168n). At any rate, it is not merely a sector of "belief" which has no real relationship to my experiencing self, as is the case with the false ego of Flaubert.

The neurotic ego of Flaubert, and even the psychotically fragmented ego of Julie, on the other hand, appear very close to the Lacanian norm. Sartre tells us that since Flaubert is passive, since he has not developed an active relationship with external objects, other people, language, or his own ego, his ego "is not only a psychic object but an *external and other object* introduced into the subjectivity from without." We might, Sartre goes on to say, even describe Flaubert's self as "allogenous"—as born solely of otherness (FI, 1:168n). Lacan, of course, proposes that the *normal* ego is allogenous in the sense of being a mere mimicry of the other. This is so because for Lacan there is no "reflective ipseity" at the base of ego formation; the Lacanian ego is purely and simply other in its entirety.

From a Lacanian perspective, then, Flaubert and even Laing's Julie with her bits and pieces of others which serve the place of an ego merely demonstrate more dramatically than most of us the essential otherness of the ego. How Lacan would go about working therapeutically with their situations, I am not sure—except to say that he would probably view Julie's psychosis as a failure to enter the symbolic order. In any case, it is certainly clear that Lacan's characterization of the ego as "other" to the core makes impossible a therapeutic transformation such as the one I have described as possible from a Sartrean perspective. But perhaps this is not surprising in a metatheorist who rejects the primacy of consciousness, as Lacan does.

Image, Reality, and "Normality" in Sartre and Lacan

Actually, I think the heart of this dilemma concerning the Lacanian ego can be found in Lacan's insistence that the ego belongs fundamentally to the "imaginary" order and therefore is inaccessible to the test of "truth" in the Sartrean sense. Lacan's imaginary order, I have noted, refers to the specular origins of the ego. It is to be distinguished from the symbolic order of language and culture, which is superimposed upon it, and from the order of the "real"—to which Lacan gives an odd definition which is significant for our discussion. Lacan frequently refers to the real as the "impossible" (1973, p. 167). It is, he says, "the accident, the noise, the small element of reality, which is evidence that we are not dreaming" (1973, p. 60).

At other times, Lacan defines the real as "plenitude," observing that there is "no absence in the real" (1978, p. 313). Here and also when he insists that the world in which we live is always a "humanized, symbolised world, the work of transcendence introduced by the symbolic into primitive reality" (1975, p. 87), Lacan sounds quite Sartrean. But then we find that Lacan identifies the real with traumas and with hallucinations (1975, p. 66); indeed, Lacan insists that the real is "that which is unassimilable," not in the Sartrean sense of a "transphenomenality of being" but absolutely unassimilable (1973, p. 49). Furthermore, Lacan does not conceive of a consciousness that infuses the world with symbols as a manifestation of its own transcendence (as Sartre does); rather, he believes that symbols produce the person—that the person is the plaything of the symbolic order.

In a situation like this, the ego obviously is not going to admit of transformation through a Sartrean return to the "truth" (reality) of one's own experience since the problem is not inauthenticity in the Sartrean sense but the nature of the human condition as fundamentally illusory. Sartre, of course, though he would agree with the idea that we never encounter pure Being-in-itself without the addition of human significance and meaning, would not agree with Lacan's closing off of human experience from world experience. Indeed, he would characterize such a closing off as a neurotic choice of the imaginary in the Sartrean sense—a choice with which Sartre credits

Flaubert. Furthermore, Sartre would object to Lacan's definition of the imaginary order as originating in the "image" I form of myself in the mirror and the "image" of the Other's greater maturational wholeness with which I identify since this is to place the image as a content within consciousness.

On the other hand, Lacan's assertion that I "imagine" myself to be the mirror image or the other who I am not would fall within Sartre's definition of the imaginary as a nihilation of both the real self and the real world. After all, I can enter an unreal world "only by unrealizing myself in it" (PI, p. 188). There is, of course, no reason why one might not create this unreal self out of a fantasy involving the mirror. Sartre, in the Flaubert biography, conceives of a scene in which Flaubert, viewing himself in the mirror in an erotic state, fantasizes that he sees there not a real man but an imaginary woman. However, Sartre would not define the "normal" ego as resting on a substitution of the imaginary for the real, as Lacan does. He would instead see it as some kind of healthy interaction between imaginative consciousness and reality-oriented consciousness. But before we can understand these differences fully, we must take a look at Sartre's theory of the imagination.

In *The Psychology of Imagination*, Sartre defines an image as "an act which envisions an absent or non-existent object as a body, by means of a physical or mental content which is present only as an 'analogical representative' of the object envisioned" (p. 26). The *analagon*, or analogue, is, briefly speaking, some material on which I hang the unreal image produced by the act of imagining. The analogue can be a photograph or portrait, brush or pen strokes on a piece of paper, a piece of carved marble, sounds, the human body in the act of producing an impersonation of a real or imagined person, the flame, cloud, or rock formations which serve as analogues for faces or other objects, or the emotions, movements, and words on which mental images are hung. It can even be the mirror image in which Sartre suggests that Flaubert, in his masturbatory fantasies, imagines that the hands of a man caress the imaginary body of a woman. In all of these cases, we animate a certain material (the analogue) "in order to turn it into a *representation* of an absent or of a non-existent object" (PI, p. 72). One wonders if Sartre would consider the rapid eye movements (REMs) discovered by recent sleep researchers to be analogues for the dreams that seem to accompany so-called REM sleep.

The important thing is that Sartre views the act of imagining as radically different from the act of perceiving in that the latter is a mode of consciousness directed toward what *is* (the real), whereas the latter is a mode of consciousness directed toward what *is not* (the imaginary). Imagining involves a double negation—first of the real perceptual world from which I withdraw and then of the image which does not belong to it. We might surmise from *The Psychology of Imagination* and other writings that a healthy relationship with the imaginary for Sartre is one in which the individual stays anchored in the real while retaining the capacity to go beyond the real which is characteristic of the imagination. And, indeed, it is this idea of a balance between the imaginary and the real and the attendant idea that one can deviate in one direction or another, overemphasizing either the imaginary or the real, which solves an apparent paradox in *The Psychology of Imagination*.

Although throughout most of *The Psychology of Imagination*, Sartre insists on the magical, impoverished character of the imagination as opposed to perception, toward the end of the book he surprises the reader by noting that without this capacity to imagine—to create the unreal—human beings would be totally engulfed in the real. Indeed, Sartre identifies this capacity to imagine with the very nihilating power of consciousness itself, stating that "every concrete and real situation of consciousness in the world is big with imagination in as much as it always presents itself as a withdrawing from the real" (PI, p. 270); hence it "is because he is transcendentally free that man can imagine" (PI, p. 271). A consciousness which does not imagine would be a consciousness "completely engulfed in the existant and without the possibility of grasping anything but the existant" (PI, pp. 271–72). And though this is impossible, Sartre asserts that it is the person who avoids imagining, the person who "is crushed in the world, run through by the real, who is closest to the thing" (PI, p. 272). This would be, of course, the person who engages in the form of bad faith which relies on an overemphasis on facticity—the person who attempts to be absorbed by the "serious world." Such a person misses even the significance of the real since the "imaginary . . . represents at each moment the implicit meaning of the real" (PI, p. 272).

On the other hand, Sartre certainly does not endorse a preference for the imaginary over the real. To engage in such a preference, one presumes, would be to embrace the second form of bad faith: overemphasis on transcendence. The most extreme example of this is the psychotic, who attempts to negate the real world entirely—presumably because of the intolerable pain it has caused. Of course, the psychotic is no doubt doing this because the so-called real or serious world is too weighty—because it offers no real paths to self-realization. In this sense, such a flight could be considered an overemphasis on facticity as well, since one believes that one cannot alter the intolerable constraints of the real. It is for this reason that Sartre tells us that the schizophrenic allows himself or herself to become "imprisoned" in the imaginary, thereby experiencing it as a trap for his or her freedom.

The hallucinatory act itself, Sartre continues, is "a pure event that appears suddenly to the patient while his perception disappears" (PI, p. 216). This interpretation of hallucinations (with which Sartre was personally familiar from a medical experiment with mescaline given him by his friend Daniel Lagache when he was a psychiatric intern[9]) correlates with the information given me in two interviews with my friend Joanne Greenberg in which I questioned her about the hallucinatory experiences which are fictionalized in *I Never Promised You a Rose Garden* (1964):

> *Cannon:* What do you mean by *seeing* a hallucination? Do you see one in the same way that you see me?
>
> *Greenberg:* It isn't really *seeing* in that sense. It's more *being aware*. You see but you don't see—rats out of the corner of the eye. When you're in that state, the world isn't real—it's X-ed out. The hallucination is a metaphor for some inexpressible anguish. It says, "I am adrift. I am bereft. I am somebody for whom gravity and the laws of the universe do not apply."[10]

In this same interview, Greenberg confirms Sartre's impression that the psychotic person in some way recognizes the difference between hallucinations and perceptions and that the very meaning of the hallucinations is an escape from the perceptual world.

Greenberg also agrees with Sartre that the "poverty of the hallucinatory material" derives from the fact that one has cut off the "real" world and hence cannot enrich oneself with it. Perhaps this is so, Sartre says, because "the unreal always receives and never gives" (PI, p. 198). Because I can only find there what I have put there, the pure imaginary lacks "the depth and richness" of the real (PI, p. 199). Or, as Sartre says in another place,

> It is . . . a mistake to look upon the world of the schizophrenic as a torrent of images possessing a richness and a glitter, which compensates for the monotony of the real: it is a poor and meticulous world, in which the same scenes keep on recurring to the last detail, accompanied by the same ceremonial where everything is regulated in advance, foreseen; where, above all, nothing can escape, resist or surprise. In

brief, if the schizophrenic imagines so many amorous scenes it is not only because his real love has been disappointed, but, above all, because he is no longer capable of loving. (PI, p. 212)

Greenberg agrees:

> Creativity and psychosis are about as far apart as two experiences can be. Creative things learn and grow. In psychosis, there's no meaning, no future, the world is senseless. The whole thing is stuck. What I resent about all this talk about the creativity of mental illness is that it fails to recognize that mental illness is stuck. The hallucination is "dead end productions." How can meaninglessness be creative? Mental illness is boring in a way that's inconceivable. If there's no learning, all there is is reacting. It's boring because there's no place to go.[11]

Greenberg, like Sartre, believes that there must be interaction between imagination and the world for creative living to occur. When a person feels that any viable traffic with a real future has been cut off, such "normative" interaction cannot occur.

Of course, I do not have to hallucinate to become trapped in the imaginary in an unhealthy way. Actually, though this is not unhealthy, I am "imprisoned" there every night in my dreams. The dream, according to Sartre, "is a consciousness that is incapable of leaving the imaginative attitude" (PI, p. 238). It is a consciousness "completely deprived of the faculty of perceiving, [a consciousness] isolated from the real world, imprisoned in the imaginary" (PI, p. 239). The dreamer, who cannot engage in reflection so long as he or she is dreaming, continues to lay hold of image after image. There is no conjecture in dreams: Instead of saying to myself in a dream that I could have had a revolver in my hand, I suddenly find a revolver in my hand. Since these images are merely a matter of belief, not of knowledge, one has only to think a thought imagistically for the dream to change.

Dreaming therefore involves a "spellbound spontaneity" that has the "nuance of fatality" because events in a dream occur as if a consciousness cannot help but imagine them (PI, p. 245). The dreamer's "'enchanted' consciousness" (PI, p. 254), Sartre notes, "can help us to conceive what a consciousness would be which would have lost its 'being-in-the-world' and which would be by the same token, deprived of the category of the real" (PI, p. 255). One cannot help wondering if such a consciousness is not akin to the Lacanian subject, who has little if any traffic with the real either in the imaginary mode or in the symbolic mode. In any case, while Sartre certainly does not view the dream as emanating from the unconscious, he does not deny that one might inquire into the "symbolic function of images" (PI, p. 232)—a task which would be undertaken differently in existential psychoanalysis than in Freudian psychoanalysis (and one that ought to be undertaken in future inquiries).

In addition to entering into the imaginary each night in our dreams, all of us probably also use the imaginary as an escape from the real at times. For instance, Sartre points to the everyday example of the individual who, separated from a loved one, is somewhat disappointed upon reunion with the person to find that the real loved one does not match his or her image—an image which can be made to conform more easily to one's desires than the real person (PI, p. 208). Or perhaps, like Annie in Sartre's *Nausea*, we wish to imagine our loved ones as remaining the same so that we can measure our own changes by them (N, pp. 182–206). Or again, we may be like the person who has prepared himself or herself for an action by imagining it, only to be confronted by the divergences between the real situation and the imagined one. If this person goes ahead and performs the action, obstinately ignoring the change from imaginary to real which has occurred, his or her actions will appear "stiff and abrupt," as though that person is refusing to recognize that he or she is dealing with a real interlocutor by repeating the lines from the imaginary dialogue (PI, p. 210).

Furthermore, I think that what is usually referred to as "transference" involves a kind of superimposition of the imaginary (drawn, albeit, from real past experience) on the real. And, indeed, this may be why it is so easy to project parental criticisms onto strangers who have not yet had a chance to become real. Interestingly, this phenomenon of substituting an imaginary person for the real person and/or an imaginary self for a real self also frequently occurs in a person's most intimate love relationships. Sometimes in doing therapy with couples, I have noted that the partner actually closely resembles the problematic parent—and the act of imagination involves fantasizing that one is still a small child in one's partner's power. At other times, the partner seems to me to have in reality very few of the imagined characteristics. The latter situation is almost always accompanied by an odd phenomenon: The person doing the fantasizing avoids really looking at the partner when he or she is describing the "imaginary" relationship. Sometimes merely looking and listening will begin to dispel the illusions—although the need to substitute an imaginary ogre (or prince/princess) for the real partner will also need to be explored.

Actually, Sartre notes, the act of imagining involves two selves: the derealized real self and the imaginary self that takes its place (PI, p. 210). Understanding this can be an important matter for therapeutic investigation—as it proved to be, for example, in the case of a mild-mannered client who engaged in murderous fantasies. This client, who had also experienced hallucinations some years previously, found that part of his task in therapy was to humanize this anger and make it "real"—a crossing of the bar which changed its character. I have noted, in fact, that people are often afraid of their fantasies, as this client was, for the simple reason that they grasp the possibility that the unreal emotions and images of imaginative states refer to what is missing in the real. What they fail to understand is that "realizing" that missing element changes it in a fundamental way. Sometimes, of course, people do dimly recognize this, as was the case with a client who clung tenaciously to her fantasies out of a deep conviction that the real world could never measure up. Certainly it was not so easily manipulable as the fantasy world in which she had lived for so many years. Like Sartre's Flaubert, this client had made a fundamental choice of the imaginary over the real—a choice which proved very recalcitrant to therapeutic intervention and which was based, like Flaubert's, on earliest experience filled with such a lack of valorization of her own real needs/desires that it hardly seemed worth the effort to try to discover them.

Sartre's biography of Flaubert further clarifies the meaning of such a choice together with the differences between a Sartrean and a Lacanian perspective on the significance of the imaginary for (normal or pathological) ego development. According to Sartre, the roots of Flaubert's choice of the imaginary over the real lie in those childhood experiences which made him capable of "belief" but not of "knowledge" or verification. Sartre therefore links that failure to develop a sense of praxis—the substitution of hexis for praxis—with the development of an imaginary identity or ego. Because Flaubert is incapable of engaging with the world, with the real, he becomes subject to the traps of the imaginary.

Instead of becoming a real child, Flaubert becomes an imaginary child, playacting the roles expected of him by adults rather than developing an authentic sense of self. Later in his childhood, he would develop a penchant for acting, even writing plays so that he could act in them, and he would dream of becoming a great actor. He would also join his schoolmates in creating a collective character, the Garçon, who mocked ordinary human reality and the bourgeois values of parents by embodying the grossest of appetites. In connection with another figment of Flaubert's imagination, the

Giant who looks down on humanity with scorn, the Garçon is part of a growing spirit of misanthropy in Flaubert. This misanthropy would find its final embodiment in an art which, according to Sartre, attempts to demoralize—"to devalorize the real by realizing the imaginary" (quoted by Barnes, 1981, p. 188).

Flaubert's misanthropy, Sartre argues, is to some extent born of an envy of those who, unlike himself, have learned to desire spontaneously. Like Lacan's mirror stage child, Flaubert wants to desire and to possess that which satisfies the others who possess it. He envies them their satisfied desire. Sartre, however, does not view as a matter of "normal" development Flaubert's inability to feel a spontaneous desire which is his own. Instead, he notes that Flaubert's failure indicates a fundamental "anorexia" in his approach to life. Hence the lack of praxis in Flaubert's fundamental project happens not because of some inevitable identification with the Other in place of the self, but because Flaubert, as an unvalorized infant, has come to find himself incapable of the engagement with the real which allows for authentic living. Lacan would view this as the norm since for Lacan, reality itself is "the impossible." In any case, he certainly would not regard as abnormal or neurotic Flaubert's development of what Sartre regards as a false ego based on the designations of others which are left unchecked by referring them to one's own authentic experience.

Sartre, of course, would not agree with Lacan that the self is fundamentally derealized from the beginning of life, except in the case of pathologies of the imagination such as that which he ascribes to Flaubert. If the ego is to be regarded as basically and unalterably imaginary in the Lacanian sense and if there is behind the ego no transcendent consciousness which can grapple with the real, self and world are together caught up in an imaginary morass. From a Lacanian perspective, there is purely and simply no way of orienting oneself in the real—though there is (as we shall see in the next chapter) a way of orienting oneself in the symbolic. Nonetheless, it seems to me that this blurring in Lacanian metatheory of the imaginary and the real (in the sense that my entrance into the imaginary is based on an imaginary identification with a real other) at the most basic level of personality formation leads to a therapeutic perspective in which there is no way to counter alienation and the sense of living a false life. In such a situation, not even one's desires are one's own (as they are even in Freud), since in appropriating the other in place of a self my desire is to desire what the other desires. And while neither I nor Sartre would deny that in mental disturbances such confusions do occur, one can hardly recommend them as being the norm.

Conclusion

We can now see that Lacan's discussion of the development of the ego, though it bears a superficial resemblance to Sartre's idea that the ego is a subject rather than an object, is in the end anti-Sartrean. While Lacan does indeed follow Sartre in maintaining that the ego is an object rather than a subject, he does not posit a subject which creates this object and is responsible for it. Instead, he proposes, at the heart of human development, a substitution of the other for the self as agent that makes of human reality an alienation which (in the imaginary order at least) is without remedy. In terms of this adoption of an image of the other where there should be a self, human reality is at its core based on imaginary identifications and has no traffic with the real. Nor is there any possibility for transforming the illusory nature of the Lacanian ego, since it is not, like the Sartrean ego, based on a reflective ipseity which might allow meta-reflection on one's own reflective process and hence, at least to some extent, a purging of the distorting views of others.

Aggressivity, according to Lacan, results from this adoption of otherness (I want what the other wants) and not from a Sartrean desire to use the Other to create a substantive self. There is therefore no possibility for overcoming this primary aggressivity with a Sartrean transformation based on a radical conversion to a philosophy of freedom and a consequent learning to respect my own and the Other's freedom. Indeed, there is no freedom in Lacan. And since for Lacan both the other person and I are objects (egos) rather than subjects, it would appear that intersubjectivity is meaningless. Lacan maintains that it is not—and that the taming of primary aggressivity is achieved through the adoption of a common world predicated on the child's entrance into the symbolic order. In the next chapter, we shall see whether this solution works or whether it, like Lacan's account of the ego, ultimately throws us back into a position of solipsistic isolation and self-alienation.

7 · Sartre and Lacan on the Nature of Language: Existentialist versus Structuralist Metatheory

The Structuralist Challenge to Existentialism

The question I address in this chapter is whether or not the entrance into the symbolic order saves Lacanian metatheory from the imaginary morass in which we left it at the end of the last chapter by allowing the Oedipal stage child to enter the human community. The answer is somewhat complex because Lacan's belief that language makes the person cannot be simply dismissed as absurd. In a certain sense, Lacan is correct, and Sartre acknowledges this when he observes a connection between Lacan's idea that the "unconscious is structured like a language" and his own conception of the practico-inert. "In my view," Sartre says, "Lacan has clarified the meaning of 'unconscious' as discourse which separates through language, or if you prefer, as counterfinality of the spoken word in which verbal groupings are structured through the act of speaking into a practico-inert grouping." Like all aspects of the practico-inert, language contains exigencies that eat away at my freedom and produce counterfinalities in the sociomaterial world over which I have no control. Sartre goes on to say, "These verbal groupings express or constitute intentions which determine me without being mine" (Sartre in Contat and Rybalka, 1974, 1:482). In this sense, language makes the person.

On the other hand, it is not true that Sartre has been converted to Lacanian structuralism. Even if Lacan's statements about unconscious linguistic structure may be reinterpreted in the light of Sartre's idea of the practico-inert (and I am sure that Lacan would not accept this reconceptualization), it would remain true that Lacan fails to take into account the power of speech as praxis. And it is speech as praxis which saves the individual from being the mere plaything of linguistic structure. Furthermore, from a Sartrean perspective, language as structure is really not unconscious at all. Rather, its power comes from the exigencies written in matter—a matter which is in this case the squiggles on paper or the sounds out of which words are made. And like all practico-inert objects, language can be detotalized and retotalized by the practical activity of the human beings who create and sustain it. For this reason, a "healthy" approach to language for Sartre is not, as it is for Lacan, constituted by the realization that one is the plaything of unconscious structure; rather, it is the ability to speak in the sense of using language as praxis (as opposed to a submission to language as hexis) to fashion one's own enterprises and to fulfill one's own (material and interpersonal) needs/desires.

This difference between Sartre and Lacan becomes even clearer if we place it within the larger context of Sartre's dialogue with structuralism, which finds its most thorough expression in his critique of Lévi-Strauss in the second book of the *Critique of Dialectical Reason* (1960a, pp. 479–504). Although Sartre begins by praising Lévi-Strauss's accurate and enlightening discovery of complex structures in primitive or tribal societies, he hastens to add that Lévi-Strauss's analytical account of social structures must be supplemented with a dialectical perspective.

Hence Sartre criticizes Lévi-Strauss's formula for the structures of exogamy governing the marriage possibilities between two groups. In *The Elementary Structures of Kinship*, Lévi-Strauss argues that in a primitive society where cross-cousin marriages are allowed and parallel-cousin marriages prohibited, marriage itself is regarded as an exchange of women similar to the linguistic circulation of words. Sartre disputes neither the existence of these structures nor the possibility of representing them through mathematical formulas. But he does deny that this is the end point of the investigation. After all, it is organizing praxis which sets up the kinship structures in the first place and it does so with an aim or purpose, which Sartre suggests is "to combat, *as far as possible*, scarcity [of women for marriage] and its consequences to the social 'ensemble'" (CDR, p. 483). The real source of the seeming inertia represented by such social structures is the pledge by which each group agrees to abrogate its future freedom (in this case, marriage to any woman whatever) in exchange for an organized set of inextricably interconnected rights and duties which allow both stability and satisfaction (in most instances).

Sartre maintains that structure itself is the objectified form of function as lived praxis. As such, it is "active passivity"—a kind of hexis produced and sustained by the group as a condition of future praxis. Its difference from the actual passivity of the physical structure of material objects is that the group, under the pressure of new circumstances, can entirely dissolve its structures. Sartre therefore argues that praxis cannot be reduced to the structures which it produces since "it is more and it is different; it is the free concrete realization of a particular task" (CDR, p. 489). The group, Sartre goes on to explain, "acquires inertia in order to struggle against inertia; it absorbs the passivity which enables matter to sustain the passive syntheses which it needs in order to *survive*; it is *precisely* not, in itself, a passive synthesis, and its passivity sustains the active synthesis which is *praxis*" (CDR, pp. 489–90). Hence it is only by "*silently ignoring* the practical totalisation as the support and reason for the inertia" (CDR, p. 492) that Lévi-Strauss and others can view structures as objective realities and inert totalities. In doing so, they kill the intelligibility of the structures under consideration.

Lévi-Strauss answers Sartre in the final chapter of *The Savage Mind* (1962) by attacking as prescientific Sartre's conception of the dialectic as totalizing praxis. Like "wild" or "untamed thought" (*le pensée sauvage*), the Sartrean dialectic, according to Lévi-Strauss, is able up to a certain point to grasp its objects. For example, it is quite capable of "doing what every anthropologist tries to do in the case of a different culture: to put himself in the place of the men living there, to understand the principle and pattern of their intentions, and to perceive a period or a culture as a significant set" (Lévi-Strauss, 1962, p. 250). But Lévi-Strauss believes that this approach cannot accomplish the fundamental scientific task of placing the data on a different plane—that of an abstract structural analysis which avoids the pitfalls of contextual analysis and with them androcentric and ethnocentric prejudices leading to incorrect conceptualization. For example, Lévi-Strauss claims that Sartre's insistence on the *historical* nature of the dialectic reduces to subhumanity those repetitive tribal societies which do not possess a history in our sense. Sartre's "gratuitous contrasts" between primitive and civilized societies, Lévi-Strauss goes on to say, merely reflect his earlier postulate of a "fundamental opposition . . . between myself and others" (1962, p. 241).

As for Sartre's concepts of the practico-inert and the totalization, Lévi-Strauss dismisses both. The practico-inert, he maintains, is a prescientific concept which "quite simply revives the language of animism" (1962, p. 249). And the totalization has been taken for granted since Malinowski—and Malinowski's defects have demonstrated its shortcomings as a fundamental method. Hence Lévi-Strauss believes that "this supposed totalizing continuity of the self" is really "an illusion sustained by the demands of social life" and not a social science concept at all (1962, p. 256). And while Lévi-Strauss admits that dialectical reason is useful in putting "the human sciences in possession of a reality which it alone can furnish them [that of concrete understanding]," he nonetheless believes that "the properly scientific work consists in decomposing and then recomposing on a different plane" (1962, p. 250). Sartre's problem, Lévi-Strauss concludes, is methodological: "He who begins by steeping himself in the allegedly self-evident truths of introspection never emerges from them" (1962, p. 249). Sartre, according to Lévi-Strauss, remains trapped in the Cartesian cogito—which he does not escape by his attempt to "sociologize" it (1962, p. 249).

Aside from the fact that to my knowledge no one other than Lévi-Strauss has ever accused Sartre of racial or ethnic chauvinism, it should be obvious what Sartre's reply to Lévi-Strauss would be. From what position outside the social system, Sartre would ask, would the social scientist presume to judge the social system? Also, does this "idealist" outside position not in effect do away with an understanding of the very social events one is trying to conceptualize? While Lévi-Strauss believes that the Sartrean dialectic is "only a point of departure, not one of arrival" in social science methodology (1962, p. 250), Sartre contends that the structuralist analytic must be subsumed within the Sartrean dialectic. Sartre himself did not directly reply to Lévi-Strauss's response to him, presumably because Sartre believed that he had already said what needed to be said.

Sartre's criticism of Lévi-Strauss for his failure to see intential praxis behind static structures is a criticism that might be levied against structuralism and poststructuralism in general. Translating Ferdinand de Saussure's structural linguistic emphasis on language over speech into a general emphasis on structure over event (that is, on the abstract possibilities of a system over concrete lived happenings), structuralists in general have preferred a synchronic study of cultures, psyches, or texts which looks at their static interrelationships to a diachronic consideration of their movement through history. The overgeneralization to which this perspective leads is again perhaps nowhere better illustrated than in Lévi-Strauss's own attempt to apply the linguistic concepts of "phonemes" and "binary oppositions" to a study of cultures and myths. The basic point of such an application for Lévi-Strauss is not, of course, the discovery of a transcending consciousness which creates these structures (as it would be for Sartre) but rather the discovery of universal structures of the mind which govern all human endeavors.

What Lévi-Strauss attempts to do is to construct a grammar of myths by analyzing single myths, relating these to other myths within the same culture, and relating these myths and their transformations to similar myths and their transformations in other cultures. As Jonathan Culler points out, "Lévi-Strauss would argue that his procedure is analogous to the study of a linguistic system: in both cases one compares syntagmatic sequences in order to construct paradigmatic classes and examine those classes so as to determine the pertinent oppositions between members of each paradigm" (1975, p. 44). Yet, as even a sympathetic critic such as Culler admits, there is a problem with Lévi-Strauss's linguistic analogy in that structural linguistics teaches that two items can be taken as members of a paradigm class only when they replace one another in a given context; but in attempting to construct a semiology of myths across cultures, Lévi-Strauss extends his paradigm classes to the point where they become extremely far-fetched (Culler, 1975, pp. 44–51). If there is a universal language of myths, Lévi-Strauss may be its only proficient speaker.

Similarly, Lévi-Strauss's attempt to describe kinship systems as stemming from universal mental structures that make the circulation of women equivalent to the circulation of words in a language has been criticized for its failure to recognize that kinship structures involve more than this (for example, the organization of groups; the transmission of rights, property, attitudes, and expectations; and the circulation of goods) and that the circulation of women is not linguistic in the sense of being a coded communication (Dan Sperber in Sturrock, 1979, pp. 23–24).

I believe that Lacan similarly errs in attempting to reduce everything to unconscious linguistic structure without adding human intentionality and meaning. The problem is that in reducing the conscious subject to a mere "effect of the signifier" (Lacan, 1973, p. 207), Lacan removes from the human subject the possibility of meaningful transformation. Lacanian structuralism, as a new positivism, has moved from a determinism based on historical causation (which includes Freudian determinism) to a determinism based on (unconscious) structural causation. Both forms of determinism are manifestations of an analytical reductionism in social science theory against which Sartre aimed the arguments of *Search for a Method* and the *Critique of Dialectical Reason*. And although analysis has a place in the Sartrean approach, Sartre believes that only dialectical reason can allow an understanding of the humanness of human individuals and groups.

Hence though Lacan and Sartre come close to agreeing on certain issues, their metatheories are in reality worlds apart. From a Sartrean perspective, Lacan does have valid things to say about the power of language/culture as (practico-inert) structure, but he does so at the expense of totally denying the creative power of praxis. And it is this denial of praxis that finally makes of structuralism in general, despite the leftist political leanings of most of its proponents, a new philosophical conservatism in that structuralist analysis can explain stasis but not change. In this respect, it shares the limitations of Freudian psychoanalysis in failing to explain how change can take place in the context of psychotherapy or elsewhere.

Language and Desire: A Lacanian Revision
of Freudian Metatheory

The developmental stage which follows the mirror stage and transitivism, according to Lacan, is the Oedipal stage with its accompanying insertion into language and culture. Lacan believes that the child at this stage of development moves from the mother to the father, from the specular ego or "me" (*moi*) to the linguistic "I" (*je*), and from the imaginary to the symbolic order. The ego and the mother do not, of course, disappear, but the whole pre-Oedipal stage is repressed into the unconscious. In fact, it is at this point that both the unconscious and consciousness as it is commonly conceived come into existence. Sexual differentiation and gender identity also begin here. In fact, Lacan says that it is with the insertion into the symbolic-linguistic order that "desire becomes human" (1966, p. 103, 1975, pp. 155 and 173). Since Lacan has already speculated that animals are capable of specular identification, we must conclude that he means this literally. Language—the fact that one becomes a "speaking animal"—literally makes the little human animal human.

Because of the introduction of language, desire, in the symbolic order, takes on a different character than desire in the imaginary order. Already prefigured in the imaginary order as a gap between the baby's disorganized body and his or her ideal ego, the gap now reappears as an unfillable lack of being (*manque à être*)[1] which is characterized by a movement from word to word and object to object. Lacan, as we shall see, identifies this movement with metonymy, modeling his view of unconscious linguistic structure on the work of Ferdinand de Saussure and Roman Jacobson in structural linguistics—though Lacan's use of their insights is heavily influenced by the anthropological appropriations of their work by Lévi-Strauss.

At first glance, it would appear that Lacan, in attempting to unite the Freudian Oedipus complex with structural linguistics, has produced a misalliance that does not admit of reconciliation. Actually, the combination may in fact be forced at times. But what Lacan does with the Oedipus complex is on the one hand to ally the father in the Oedipal triad with the symbolic-linguistic order and on the other to ally the prohibition against incest with the structures supporting the exogamous kinship systems described by Lévi-Strauss. According to Lacan, what is important for the child's entry into language is not the presence of the real father or the imaginary father but the symbolic father. And the symbolic father is so necessary to Lacan's system that he declares that even without a biological knowledge of father-hood, the father would have to be invented—as one might say, for example, that the mother was impregnated by a water spirit. The symbolic father is equivalent to what Lacan designates as the "law of the Name-of-the-father" with its religious-legalistic connotations. The Name-of-the father in French (*nom-du-père*) also suggests the "no" of the father (*non du père*), which is pronounced similarly. Lacan believes that the symbolic father is, in effect, the dead father of *Totem and Taboo*. In this respect, the Name-of-the-father is simultaneously equivalent to the introduction of guilt and to the entrance into the symbolic order of culture and language (the heritage of fathers now dead).

Of course, someone or something must symbolically pronounce the "no" of the father if the child is to enter into language and culture. A failure or "foreclosure" in the area of the prohibition against the desire for union with the mother will leave the child psychotic. This prohibition and the subsequent entry into language are Lacan's version of Freudian "primal repression,"[2] which is necessary for the child to develop normally. If repression of the primal relationship occurs normally, it will leave the child forever searching for substitutes for the original object. The "object a" (sometimes designated the *objet petit a[utre]*, the "small object other," but usually left untranslated in accordance with Lacan's request, which was based on a wish to stress the relevance of the *objet a* as a kind of algebraic symbol) can be anything from people to words to ideas; it is anything that momentarily appears to fill the gap created by the "no" of the father.

As such, the *objet a* is a continual movement away from at the same time that it is a continual attempt to recapture the *jouissance* which has been lost through primal repression. Lacanian *jouissance*—a word usually left untranslated but generally meaning "enjoyment," "sexual pleasure," and even "ecstasy"—is not to be confused with the Freudian pleasure principle with its insistence that pleasure derives from reduction of charge. Nor is Lacanian primal repression exactly the same as Freudian primal repression. According to Lacan, primal repression sets up a continual movement of desire from object to object which is conceived to be the source both of linguistic development and of transference in its more general sense—which Lacan redefines as this very movement from object to object. It is for this reason that Lacan claims that transference, contrary to traditional psychoanalytic opinion, is not the opening to the unconscious but its closing. It is the *objet a* that provides the stopper (Lacan, 1973, pp. 129–34).

The entry into language of the Oedipal stage child is facilitated by the discovery of the phallus as primary signifier and by the experience of (symbolic) castration. Lacan's version of the castration complex is one in which the child's recognition of the third (separating) term, the father (both symbolic and real), dashes forever his or her hopes of being the phallus for the mother—that is, of being the sole object of her desire. The castration complex therefore does not involve a real fear of organ loss, as Freud thought, but an emotional loss contingent upon the forswearing of primal union with the mother. Symbolic castration is experienced by both boys and girls. The successful resolution of the Oedipus complex leads to sexual differentiation, whereas an unsuccessful resolution leads to various "abnormal" solutions to the problem of sexuality or, in extreme cases, to a psychosis precipitated by failure of the symbolic father to intervene successfully in the mother-child dyad. The price of not being castrated is apparently being mad.

It should be emphasized that sexual differentiation for Lacan is a cultural-linguistic matter rather than a biological one, as it was at least in part for Freud.[3] Yet these cultural-linguistic distinctions are based on an aligning of oneself on the plus or minus side of what Lacan refers to as the "primal signifier"—the phallus. Although the phallus is not the biological organ, just as the Name-of-the-father is not the biological father, it does in some respects refer to the penis just as the symbolic father is often confused with the real father. For example, Lacan notes that the penis, as "the most tangible element in the Real of sexual copulation," easily offers itself as a "primary symbol" (1966, p. 287). Nonetheless, Lacan goes on to say, the phallus "can only play its role when veiled," as in the Greek mysteries, for it is only thus that it serves as a "sign of the latency with which any signifiable is struck" (1966, p. 288). The image of the mother as possessing the phallus—the Freudian "phallic mother"—derives from the child's experience of her as the first person to transmit the symbolic order and to indicate the place of the phallus in it. In this sense, she "contains" the phallus. The sexual identity of both boys and girls is first established in relation to the mother's attitude toward the phallus and toward the child's relationship to it. Awareness of the father's attitude, if he is present, comes later.

In "normal" heterosexuality, the movement is from attempting to *be* the phallus for the mother to *having* or *not having* the phallus, which is at this point associated with the penis. The boy, identifying with the father, takes up the former position while the girl takes up the latter. This will have serious consequences for relations between the sexes, which will be asymmetrical rather than complementary. Because the phallus is identified with the symbolic order (Lacan says in no uncertain terms that it is a "fact" that "the symbolic order, in its initial operation, is androcentric" [1978, p. 261]), women will come to serve as objects of a cultural-linguistic-matrimonial exchange among men in the manner described by Lévi-Strauss. Because they are thus submerged in and transcended by the symbolic order, they will inevitably find their relationship to it problematic (Lacan, 1978, p. 262), and they will consequently wish to use men as means to status in the social discourse.

Men, on the other hand, will want to use women as a means to wholeness—to imaginary unity—and will regard "the woman" (who, as Lacan observes, does not really exist as a category [1985, pp. 137–48]) as access to their own unconscious being or truth. They will also regard her as an impersonation of the phallus, which, since she does not *have* it, she can be imagined to *be* (Lacan, 1966, p. 322). Depending on his relationship with his own unconscious, a man will either degrade a woman in an attempt to avoid his own sense of castration or he will exalt her, sometimes endowing her with a power equivalent to God as identified with the gaze of the Other(A) (Lacan, 1985, pp. 137–48, 153, and 160). As Ragland-Sullivan observes, a man makes love to complete himself, whereas a woman makes love to gain access to the status conferred by the phallic signifier (1986, p. 293).

Yet despite this account of gender differentiation, there is for Lacan no "genital drive" leading to a purely "genital love" which is the goal of psychosexual development, as many post-Freudian theorists have contended (Lacan, 1966, pp. 245 and 287, 1975, p. 139). This is so because men and women are not products of biology but effects of the symbolization process. Gender and gender roles are not determined by one's sexual organs but by the position one takes with respect to the phallus as the instigator of castration or loss of the primal mother. In the case of the "normal" woman and the homosexual male, the position taken is that of first experiencing and later denying loss of incompleteness. As for the fetishist or the transvestite, the former refuses to give up the idea of the phallic mother, substituting the fetish for her missing phallus (as Freud suggests), whereas the latter impersonates her. For the neurotic, especially the hysteric, sexual identity is much more problematic than for the so-called normal person because of the neurotic's continual pull to the imaginary order, whereas for the psychotic, sexual identity has never gelled because the psychotic has never experienced (or has rejected) symbolic castration. The psychotic, having refused a relation to the primal signifier, is consequently set adrift in an ocean of detached signifiers.

Lacan regards the phallus as the first pure signifier because it sets up the first set of "binary oppositions" which the child, at the stage of entry into language, learns. One must locate oneself with respect to the phallus in order to enter the social order, taking up a position of plus (*toute*, usually male) or minus (*pas-toute*, usually female) with respect to it. To do so means to enter a social order that has been established before one's birth and within which one is expected to take on certain predetermined gender roles. Because the phallic signifier is the first pure signifier of difference (the mirror stage, or course, refers to identity or sameness), it becomes the reference point for the child's developing capacity to use signifiers. Having instituted a cut or gap between the infant and the mother, thereby relegating the mirror stage experience to the primordial unconscious, the phallic signifier has instituted that lack of being (*manque à être*) by means of which desire (now become human) will play itself out in an endless movement along the signifying chain.

Lacan therefore reinterprets Freud's account of his young grandson's play with the bobbin-reel (the *fort-da* example described in Chapter 2) as an instance of the connection between separation and symbolization at the juncture where the child enters the symbolic-linguistic order. Rather than demonstrating the child's attempt to "master" his mother's departure through play, this incident, according to Lacan, shows the beginning of the child's insertion into language. Lacan says that the phonemes "ooh" (*fort*, go away) and *da* (here) create a binary opposition and a "presence in absence" which mark that entry. Although these are not actually phonemes in the strict linguistic sense, since they appear to have reference, one sees Lacan's meaning. From this point on, the child will find himself or herself increasingly lost *in* at the same time that he or she is created as a subject *by* the linguistic order.

Lacan also believes that Freud is correct in linking this throwaway game with the repetition compulsion and the death instinct, since repetition with variation is the meaning of metonymic displacement itself and since "the symbol manifests itself first of all as the murder of the thing, and this death constitutes in the subject the externalization of his desire" (Lacan, 1966, p. 104). As death opens its jaws in the gap created by the primal signifier, a kind of Heideggerian "Being-toward-death" (Lacan frequently mentions Heidegger in this connection) assumes an important place in Lacanian analysis. We might also say that the child, deprived of the hope of union with the mother, uses words as "transitional objects" (Winnicott's "transitional object" is one of the few concepts introduced by post-Freudian theorists of which Lacan approves [Lacan, 1966, pp. 250 and 312]). Forever after, words will provide a dual path toward and away from the primal *jouissance*, which is forever foresworn and at the entrance to which the phallic signifier stands like the angel guarding the gates of Eden. Yet primal repression, at the same time that it implies renunciation and loss, is the beginning of cultural individuation.

Lacan believes that it is with the insertion of the individual into the symbolic-linguistic order that both the conscious subject (*je*, I) and the unconscious subject (Other[A]) come into existence. The subject, as defined by Lacan, is simply "the one who speaks." Not to be confused with Sartrean consciousness, the Lacanian conscious subject (*je*) is far from being an intentional praxis. Created by and existing only through language, the Lacanian subject is in many ways identical to the linguistic shifter. According to Lacan's oft-repeated definition, "The signifier is that which represents a subject for another signifier" (1966, p. 316, 1973, pp. 207 and 236). The conscious subject is therefore no more the "real self" than the specular ego is. Its origins also lie outside, in the Other, though this time the Other referred to is not the specular ideal but the grand Other (Other[A]) of one's sociolinguistic heritage. This is the Other who speaks in unexpected places—in dreams, jokes, slips of the tongue, and symptoms.

It is the Other(A) whose discourse the linguistic unconscious, as opposed to the specular m(Other) unconscious, is. As Lacan says over and over again, "The unconscious is the discourse of the Other" (1975, p. 85, 1978, p. 89, and elsewhere). Or again, as Lacan is fond of repeating, "The unconscious is structured like a language" (1966, p. 234, 1973, pp. 20 and 149, and elsewhere)—and, indeed, comes into existence with language. Antedating a child's birth, the Other of the cultural-linguistic order "speaks" the child rather than the child it. "*Ça parle*" (it speaks) rather than "*je parle*" (I speak) is the truth of being human according to Lacan (1966, pp. 125 and 284). The real subject, as opposed to the specular ego or the conscious subject of discourse, is therefore the unconscious Other(A) whose domain is the "other scene" described by Freud in *The Interpretation of Dreams*. The conscious subject is a "decentered subject" which is constituted as a defense mechanism against the truth of the unconscious. Truth itself comes to exist only with the linguistic order, and the return to the Other(A) is its test (1966, p. 306, 1975, pp. 228 and 259).

Before these ideas about the decentered subject and the subject of the unconscious can be understood, however, a brief review of Lacan's appropriation of structural linguistics is necessary. According to Lacan, it is this relationship to structural linguistics, and not Freud's physicalist and biologistic metaphors, that will place psychoanalysis on a firm scientific footing. Indeed, Lacan argues that Freud had an implicit understanding of linguistic laws that he was unable to formulate precisely because the theory on which these laws are based had not yet been articulated (1966, p. 162, and elsewhere). Hence Lacan, in effect, proposes to edit Freud from the vantage point of Saussure and Jacobson.

From Saussure, Lacan takes the twin concepts of the signifier and the signified. He follows Saussure (1916) in emphasizing that language works both phonetically and semantically through a recognition of differences—though Saussure does not, of course, define primary differentiation as sexual differentiation along the phallic signifier. Saussure divides the "sign" into two components: the signifier (*signifiant*), or image-acoustical component, and the signified (*signifié*), or conceptual component. Neither the signifier nor the signified is directly related to the world around us, to things themselves, since the signifier is not a thing but a notion of a thing. The linguistic sign is also arbitrary, both because there is no natural link between the signifier and the thing it signifies (not the signified) and because the signified can be divided up in different ways—for example, as colors are in different languages. Thus for Saussure, language is form and not substance, and he is more interested in language (*la langue*) than in speech (*la parole*) because he believes that the study of language as the theoretical structure which must be obeyed if we are to communicate allows us to grasp the principles on which language functions in practice (speech). This idea is the source of Lacan's discussion of the "law of the signifier" and of his understanding that this law must impose itself on the child if he or she is to become human.

Lacan, however, radicalizes Saussure. Taking as a starting point Saussure's idea of an arbitrary relationship between the sign and the thing, Lacan proclaims, in a discussion which is actually rather Sartrean and phenomenological, that things themselves are unknowable. It is for this reason that he defines the domain of the real, as distinguished from the imaginary and the symbolic, as the "impossible." What is neither Sartrean nor Saussurean in Lacan, however, is his inclination to divorce language from reference in any sense. Following Lévi-Strauss, Lacan inverts the Saussurean relationship between the signifier and the signified, giving primacy to the signifier:

$$\frac{\text{Signifier}}{\text{signified}}$$

for Saussure's

$$\frac{\text{signified}}{\text{signifier}}.$$

Lacan also places a double bar between the signifier and the signified, intending thereby to indicate a cut or break between the two. The signifier is now viewed as occupying the structuring position, and the signifier and the signified are no longer conceived to be inextricably interconnected (recto and verso of a single entity, the sign, as Saussure thought) or even as existing at the same level. The metaphor of the piece of paper is replaced in Lacan by an image of the signifying chain as "rings in a necklace that is a ring in another necklace made of rings" (1966, p. 153). Another of Lacan's metaphors is the Borrhomean knot: In the world of the signifier, there is no clear demarcation between inside and outside, conscious and unconscious; instead, there is an imperceptible gliding of one into the other without a differentiation between them.

Lacan's double bar points to the character of Otherness which signification maintains because it refers to the whole unconscious linguistic system. In order to understand how Lacan views the signifier as constantly "sliding" or "gliding" beneath the signified and therefore as leading to distortion (Freud's *Entstellung*), however, we must first understand Lacan's appropriations of Jacobson. It is from Jacobson (Jacobson and Halle, 1956) that Lacan borrows the idea of phonemes and binary oppositions which Lacan, following Lévi-Strauss's appropriation of these concepts for other than strictly linguistic uses, applies in his own account of the *fort-da* story discussed above. It was also Jacobson who renamed Saussure's laws of combination (syntagmatic relations) and substitution (paradigmatic relations) by the rhetorical devices of metonymy and metaphor; Jacobson then related these rhetorical devices to Freud's account of primary process "thinking," asserting their "primary significance and consequence to all human endeavors"—to the operation of dreams, magic rites, and charms, as well as to the structure of everyday discourse (Jacobson, 1962, p. 113). Where Jacobson identifies metaphor with identification and symbolization and metonymy with condensation and displacement, however, Lacan identifies metaphor with Freudian condensation (*Verdichtung*) and metonymy with Freudian displacement (*Verschietung*).

According to Lacan, metaphor is to be defined as "the structure of the superimposition of the signifiers" (1966, p. 160). As Ragland-Sullivan notes, it is therefore to be regarded as "first a function and only second an iconic mode of meaning" (1986, p. 255). Metaphor is the function by which one signifier can be substituted for another, rather than simply a figure of speech with a reference outside. In the course of this substitution, there is a "crossing of the bar" between the signifier and the signified where the first signifier is relegated to the place of the signified. Lacan gives as an example the line, "His sheaf was neither miserly nor spiteful," from a poem by Victor Hugo in which the hero, Booz, is replaced by his "sheaf" in the metaphor. Where the item under the bar (the signified) is unconscious, this can lead to the formation of symptoms which are unintelligible to the conscious subject. And, indeed, Lacan tells us that a symptom is "a metaphor in which flesh or function is taken as the signifying element" (1966, p. 166). The overdetermination of dreams is likewise a consequence of metaphoric substitution through dream images acting as signifiers for unconscious signifieds. Since Lacan conceives the initial metaphoric substitution to occur at the point where the subject enters language and renounces the idea of dyadic union with the mother, substituting the presence-in-absence of the word for the libidinal object, this account of the unconscious use of metaphors is hardly surprising.

As for metonymy, it also has its origins in primal separation. But metonymy is not so much the substitution of one object for another as the movement from object to object—what Lacan frequently refers to as "this intersubjective game of hunt-the-slipper in which desire makes itself recognized for a moment" (1966, pp. 104–5, and elsewhere). Once the original gap has been created, the subject is ever hungry for the *objet a* which will fill it. Desire become human is itself metonymic. Thus metonymy is both a forward movement and an attempt to return to the primordial object via displacements, an attempt to regain the paradisiacal experience. Unfortunately, desire is a perpetual lack, a want-to-be (*manque à être*) which can never be fulfilled and which therefore moves endlessly from object to object. Linguistically, metonymy involves a word-to-word connection instead of the word-for-word substitution of metaphor (Lacan, 1966, p. 164). In this sense, it is the very movement of language itself.

Obviously, Lacan means something more than the part for whole substitution which is the usual definition of metonymy. Metonymy, Lacan contends, operates according to a "veering off of signification [which is] used by the unconscious to foil censorship" (1966, p. 160). In dreams and fetishes, metonymy manifests itself as the displacement of one object by another—for example, of the "glance at the [mother's] nose" that has replaced the original "shine on the nose" required by one of Freud's fetishistic patients for sexual arousal. Transference and love relationships also operate according to the laws of metonymy, though they also refer back to the imaginary order; as metonymic displacements, they involve repetition with variation.

Aside from one's suspicion that Lacan, like Lévi-Strauss, is using linguistic structure to explain too much, there are other serious objections to Lacan's theory of the insertion of the individual into language which we must make from a Sartrean perspective. For one thing, Lacan's account appears to make the individual a mere epiphenomenon of the cultural-linguistic order, however carefully he explains that linguistic structure carves this same individual out of the bedrock experience of an imaginary order which is itself fundamentally alienated. One might, indeed, paraphrase Lévi-Strauss's statement that he does "not intend to show how men think in myths but how myths think in men, unbeknownst to them" (1964, p. 12) by saying that Lacan intends to show "not how men think in langauge but how linguistic structure thinks in men, unbeknownst to them."

Behind all of this, of course, lies the structuralist emphasis on structure over event. But the synchronic determinism which results from this emphasis opens Lacan's theory to the objections we have made to deterministic psychoanalysis in general—that it denies the philosophical premises which might sustain a theory of change in psychotherapy. One might, of course, take Lacan's definition of the goal of psychoanalysis as a movement from "empty speech" to "full speech" as a sign that transformation is possible. Yet on closer inspection, it appears that full speech has nothing to do with the genuine communication which might be promoted in existentialist therapy. It is instead openness to the "meaning" which "insists" in the linguistic unconscious. If that unconscious is (as I maintain in the next section) in reality simply the Other's praxis as it is inscribed in the linguistic practico-inert, then this can only lead to maintenance of the status quo.

As I noted, this is one of the difficulties with structuralism in general. While most of its practitioners were affiliated with the political left, the analysis of structure to the exclusion of consciousness in their work does not allow for the possibility of change—social or individual. This is particularly evident in Lacan's account of the development of gender differentiation. Consequently, the question asked by feminist apologists as well as feminist critics concerns whether or not Lacan's account of the phallic signifier implies support for the patriarchy. Even if we disregard some of Lacan's more disagreeable remarks, such as his idea that the female genitals have a character of emptiness which causes them to be less desirable than male genitals (see Ragland-Sullivan, 1986, p. 286), there is ample evidence that his theory, unlike Sartre's, does not allow for going beyond the status quo in gender relations.

The feminist apologists for Lacan (Mitchell, 1974; Mitchell and Rose in introduction to Lacan, 1985; Ragland-Sullivan, 1986) have claimed that he is not a "phallocrat"—pointing out that his view of gender is that it is "constructed" rather than biologically determined. Yet appearances to the contrary, Lacan's position is not equivalent to that expressed in the opening lines of Book II of Simone de Beauvoir's *The Second Sex*: "One is not born, but rather becomes, a woman" (1949, p. 249). Both writers agree that the crucial matter is not biology. But what Beauvoir means by this is that one's childhood, one's immersion into society and culture, together with the ascriptions of the original others, point out the paths through which one becomes a woman. What Lacan means is that the differentiation accruing around the phallic signifier leads to the assumption of gender roles. And while it is possible that this might change, it seems unlikely. After all, without "castration," culture and language themselves would not, according to Lacan, stick in such a way as to fashion a linguistic subject out of the little human animal.

Indeed, certain feminists, taking Lacan at his word, have demanded that women renounce the symbolic order, which is not theirs, and return to a oneness with the pre-Oedipal mother (see Marks and de Courtivron, 1981; Moi, 1987). The literary results of this effort promise to be idiosyncratic in the extreme. The feminist writers who take seriously Lacan's idea that the symbolic order is necessarily androcentric are not simply attempting to use the "language of the oppressor" to undermine the oppressor, as Sartre claims the African poets in *Black Orpheus* are doing. Rather, they are attempting to use language to undermine language, with no hope of redeeming language (as a practico-inert field) from its sexist bias.

Here is Xavière Gauthier on the subject of women's language and writing:

But perhaps if we had left these pages blank, we would have had a better understanding of what feminine writing is all about. In fact, what surprises us is the fact that men and women seem to speak approximately the same language; in other words, women find "their" place within the linear, grammatical, linguistic system that orders the symbolic, the superego, the law. It is a system based entirely upon one fundamental signifier: the phallus. And we can marvel (like Thérèse Plantier in *C'est moi Diego* [I am Diego]) at the fact that women are alienated enough to speak "the language of Man." "*If there is a madman, then it's definitely Woman.* Believing themselves to be emancipated, women had access to universities where they were fed by force a language in which everything, verbs and subjects, was masculine. And so, having lost their minds, women believed they could be men, equal to their masters in adopting their grammar and syntax. Completely divorced from themselves without knowing it, women were transformed into this Crazy Sex which was nicknamed the 'Second Sex.'" (In Marks and de Courtivron, 1981, p. 162)

Fortunately, the women writers in Marks and de Courtivron's selection do not leave its pages blank—and, indeed, most of the contemporary French feminists represented there continue to register their protests in the usual syntax of the "masters."

Still it seems worth noting that while Sartre's ontology has inspired perhaps the most significant book in all of feminism in Beauvoir's *The Second Sex*, Lacan's metatheory has inspired a revolt that seems to be almost nihilistic in its essential import. After all, if the primal signifier is the phallus and if culture is androcentric in essence, then where is a woman to go except outside it? Yet, as Ragland-Sullivan notes, there is no outside to go to. The return to the pre-Oedipal mother cannot be a return to an essential femininity since masculinity and femininity are themselves created by the phallic signifier (Ragland-Sullivan, 1986, pp. 267–308). One would therefore presume that women are doomed to occupy the place of the second sex—exalted and denigrated but never recognized as equals.

Of course, one could say that as a man—for instance, a man in Lacanian analysis—gets more in touch with the voice of the Other in himself and with his own castration, he will no longer need to identify these with women and with femininity. But there remains the difficulty that culture is, by virtue of its association with the Name-of-the-father, androcentric. As Ragland-Sullivan, who is perhaps the best of the Lacanian apologists, notes, changing this androcentric orientation would from a Lacanian perspective amount to changing nothing less than the whole unconscious symbolic order, the Other(A) (1986, p. 306). But Lacan himself, as Ragland-Sullivan also notes, was "generally pessimistic about the possibilities of altering the Symbolic order" (1986, p. 303). And rightly so, since there is no transcendent subject who might effect such change.

From a Sartrean perspective, of course, the power of language and culture as practico-inert are also recognized, along with the fact that change is not an easy matter. It is possible, however, since one is struggling not with an unconscious Other from whence one is created as a subject, but with the Other as (prior) praxis inscribed in the practico-inert. And though the Sartrean subject does not exist outside of language, any more than consciousness anywhere exists separately from its objects, the fact of human transcendence makes it possible to struggle with a cultural order that makes one as one makes it. Like Lacan, Sartre would not deny the fact that women have been associated with otherness in most cultural situations; that is, of course, the central thesis of Beauvoir's book. But he would deny Lacan's premise that this sociocultural determination is inherent in an unconscious symbolic-linguistic order which itself creates the speaking subject. Beauvoir's book shows what has gone wrong; Sartre's idea that the symbolic-linguistic order can be changed through revolutionary praxis suggests what might need to happen for women to achieve equal status with men. This is not an easy matter since even from a Sartrean perspective the presence of the mother as first witness is going to affect subsequent relations between men and women.[4] To this extent, Lacan is correct in thinking that change will be difficult—but it is certainly not impossible from a Sartrean perspective.

This brings us back to the issue of change in general, especially therapeutic change, which is also difficult though possible from a Sartrean perspective because there is a transcendent consciousness at the heart of the therapeutic enterprise. Opacity lies in the *inertia* of the practico-inert, not in the human *praxis* which organizes and sustains it or infuses it with new meanings. From a Lacanian perspective, on the other hand, it is difficult to see how change might occur in psychotherapy. Of course, Lacan claims that the slightest alteration in an individual's structuration in the symbolic order changes everything, so we might imagine that Lacanian analysis must address itself to finding the key to such changes. This, I believe, is in fact the case (though Lacan's writings offer few case examples), and it is a point to which we shall return in the next chapter. Still, as with deterministically oriented psychotherapy in general, there is the question of how the Lacanian analyst, if the analyst is not himself or herself a transcendent consciousness, can aid the analysand in effecting such changes. How is one to change a cultural-linguistic order of which one is the plaything rather than the originator? I believe that Sartre's concept of language as practico-inert and speech as praxis, while it takes into account the difficulties inherent in changing the exigencies inscribed in the sociomaterial world, will allow the solution that Lacanian analysis does not.

A Sartrean Reply: Language as Practico-Inert

A serious Sartrean challenge to Lacan must attempt to account for those phenomena which Lacan explains by applying the insights of structural linguistics to psychoanalysis. I contend that Sartre's account of the insertion of the individual into language provides the starting point for such a critique. Of course, Sartre's philosophy, unlike Lacanian analysis, is neither a philosophy nor a psychology of language, as Sartre himself makes clear—though he concedes that a philosophy of language could be extrapolated from his work (Sartre in Schilpp, 1981, p. 17). Therefore, what we expect from Sartre is not a precisely developed linguistic system, but an idea of how language fits into his overall philosophy and how the individual's insertion into language fits into existential psychoanalysis. In the *Critique*, Sartre states unequivocally that language is practico-inert. The act of speaking, however, is not. And speech as praxis has priority over language as practico-inert.

This does not mean, of course, that some of what Lacan says about the effects of language as structure will not appear true from a Sartrean perspective; indeed, Sartre understands that language involves an inscription of otherness in the heart of my being. Such otherness is "unconscious" in the sense that it is usually unexamined. It is not, however, unconscious in the sense of being a realm beyond consciousness. And like all aspects of the practico-inert, it may be lived either more as praxis or more as hexis. It is to the exigencies written in language as practico-inert structure that Sartre refers in the statement quoted in the introduction to this chapter where he sees an affinity between Lacan's dictum that the "unconscious is structured like a language" and his own view of the counterfinalities of the written and spoken word.

On the other hand, it is equally true that Lacanian analysis, from a Sartrean perspective, must appear mistaken in its attempt to attune the analysand to the "discourse of the Other" without at the same time attempting to restore speech as intentional praxis. This leaves structuralist psychoanalysis open to the criticism which Sartre makes of the structuralist anthropology of Lévi-Strauss in the *Critique*. While structuralism accurately describes a certain moment of human affairs—that of the practico-inert or the antidialectic—it is analytical rather than dialectical in placing static structures rather than totalizing praxis at the heart of social science research. In this respect, structuralism is seriously one-sided in its approach to understanding human individuals and groups. From the perspective of existentialist therapy, the point would be to examine the insertion of the individual into language (as Sartre does with Flaubert) with an end to increasing the domain of real freedom, or praxis, and to decreasing the domain of hexis, or acceptance of oneself as "spoken" by one's own language and culture rather than as "speaking" in the sense of intentional (self-) creation.

Language, as antidialectic, betrays the characteristics of all practico-inert objects: It is matter (in this case, "disturbances of the air" [CDR, p. 98] or squiggles on a piece of paper) infused with human meanings and requiring human praxis to sustain those meanings. And though I use language as a medium through which to objectify myself, this medium is, like other aspects of the practico-inert, treacherous in that I must work with a matter which is already alive with the meanings of past others and which may be twisted by future others to their own ends—as, for example, when my statements, written or oral, are turned against me or used toward ends which are not my own. Sartre therefore notes that "whenever I form a sentence its meaning escapes from me, is stolen from me; meanings are changed *for everyone* by each speaker and each day; the meanings of the very words in my mouth are changed by others" (CDR, p. 98). Like the practico-inert in general, language also bestows a sense of exigency derived from the inscriptions of the others who have engraved it with their meanings through the ages. Speaking is not a private but a public act which "does not consist in inserting a vocable into a brain through an ear, but in using sounds to direct the interlocutor's attention to this vocable as public exterior property" (CDR, pp. 98–99).

As a practico-inert repository of past praxes, language is both a way of preserving cultural continuity and an invitation to hexis. Sartre agrees with Lacan that the insertion into language is equivalent to insertion into the sociocultural order—that otherness comes to be inscribed into my project through language. He states that the "Other in me makes my language," but he hastens to add that language is also "my way of being in the Other" (FI,

1:12). Otherness, for Sartre, is not all there is to speech, and he laments the fact that speaking may at times become almost pure hexis, pure otherness. A striking example of language as "idea-hexis" is the racist/colonialist language that supports the status quo in a situation of oppression. Racist slogans, Sartre points out, are not really "thought" at all—that is, they are not capable of verification or falsification. Rather, they are mindless repetitions of serial ideas which belong to everyone and no one. Behind such slogans, as with all idea-hexis, is the "secret hope that thought is a stone" (CDR, p. 300n). Indeed, the racist slogan appears to have the "materiality of a fact [precisely] because no one thinks it" (CDR, p. 301n). Certainly, all mindless repetition similarly conveys a sense of "thought" as hexis, though this does not mean that one may not use a conventional phrase in the service of a linguistic act which is primarily praxis (see Sartre's discussion in FI, 1:601).

Language is also, like the practico-inert in general, capable of codification and possibly even of quantification. In other words, it is accessible to analysis. Although a living language is never a closed system, it appears, like other practico-inert objects, to be an inert totality defined by the structural relations of its parts. Thus Sartre would agree with Lacan and the structural linguists that the study of language involves a study of the relations between mutually conditioned elements in a system and not between self-contained elements. On the other hand, language is really a totalization. Sartre points out that "the sentence is an actual totalisation where every word defines itself in relation to the others, to the context and to the entire language, as an integral part of the whole." Language, he goes on to say, "contains every word and every word is to be understood in terms of language as a whole; it contains the whole of language and reaffirms it" (CDR, p. 99). He repeats this idea in the Flaubert biography, noting that "no one doubts that the whole of language is needed . . . for the sentence to define its own being and its meaning, which is nothing but *differentiation*" (FI, 1:27). Obviously, Lacan would agree.

Furthermore, Sartre is as aware as Lacan of all the associations, possibilities for substitution, connotations, and sound relations by which sentences imply more than they say and sometimes suffer a deviation of meaning. Sartre even defines a form of bad faith with respect to language which involves a denial of the capacity of language and other people to derail one's project as speaker or writer. Sartre tells us that the practitioners of *L'Arts Absolu*, including Flaubert and Mallarmé, attempted to exclude all chance from their literary productions. Flaubert, for instance, struggled desperately

to find precisely the right word which would produce only a specifically intended response.

This position is comparable to the second form of bad faith discussed in
earlier chapters: the denial of facticity. It is unrealistic because chance necessarily plays a role in every aspect of life, including speech and literary production. The person of action, unlike the aesthete, realizes that his or her
project will be stolen by others because he or she is aware of its relationship
with "the whole of materiality through the mediation of men and the whole
of man through the mediation of materiality" (IF, 3:189; quoted by Barnes,
1981, p. 276). When one contrasts this position with that of writers such as
Flaubert and Mallarmé, who, as "Knights of Nothingness," attempt to take
a position outside of humanity and outside the sociolinguistic order, one realizes that it is an impossible aim. These writers cannot make themselves
"*other than man*" (IF, 3:145; quoted by Collins, 1980, p. 156)—they cannot occupy the Hegelian position of Absolute Knowledge or make themselves
gods. The refuge of the imaginary will not save them from the contingent
world. The book will remain "a human enterprise that partially escapes its
author and thus reflects his facticity as well as his freedom" (IF, 3:191; quoted
in Collins, 1980, p. 158).[5]

If it is possible to live one's linguistic facticity in bad faith, however, it is
also possible to live one's linguistic freedom in bad faith. And, indeed, this is
the deeper form of bad faith exhibited by Flaubert as portrayed by Sartre. It
is also, I believes, a form of inauthenticity which is endemic to structuralism
in general and to Lacan's account of the insertion of the individual into language in particular. The difference is that Flaubert's inauthenticity is a matter of lived experience, whereas Lacan's is a matter of psycholinguistic theory. In any case, according to Sartre, speech/writing is—or ought to
be—praxis. He notes that "language as the practical relation of one man to
another is *praxis* and *praxis* is always language (whether truthful or deceptive) because it cannot take place without signifying itself" (CDR, p. 99).
The verb "signify" is important here. Sartre does not use "signification" in a
purely linguistic sense, as Lacan and the structuralists do. Rather, he uses
the term to indicate the intentional act of meaning creation. For Sartre, this
involves not just speaking and writing but all meaning-oriented activity—
that is, all human praxes. "Speaking," Sartre maintains, "is nothing more
than adapting and enriching a behavior which is already verbal, that is, already expressive in itself" (FI, 1:28).

Similarly, in *Being and Nothingness*, Sartre maintains that language arises
with my discovery of the necessity to express myself in a world where there

are others. He notes that while "psychological and historical problems exist with regard to the existence, the learning and the use of a *particular* language, there is no special problem concerning what is called the discovery or invention of language." That discovery, he goes on to say, is exactly equivalent to my discovery of my Being-for-others:

> Language is not a phenomenon added on to being-for-others. It *is* originally being-for-others; that is, it is the fact that a subjectivity experiences itself as an object for the Other. In a universe of pure objects language could under no circumstances have been "invented" since it presupposes an original relation to another subject. In the intersubjectivity of the for-others, it is not necessary to invent language because it is already given in the recognition of the Other. I *am* language. . . . Language is therefore not distinct from the recognition of the Other's existence." (BN, pp. 372–73)

Thus for Sartre, there is no moment of entry into the symbolic-linguistic order in the Lacanian sense (though Sartre would not deny that the child learns at a certain point in time to speak and that this makes a difference). Rather, speech is an enrichment of behavior which is always already signifying.

The signifying act in Sartre therefore opens onto the world of reciprocal relations with others, either directly or through the mediation of other practico-inert objects. Thus "truth" in Sartre is not merely linguistic; verification, as we have seen, involves checking out the indications that the Other's words give me about the world which we share in common and which is, admittedly, partially created by language. Without this possibility of verification, words would be a matter of mere belief, leading to the creation of a false ego and the development of a lifestyle which is primarily other-directed. Not that all of us do not start out, as children, with some mixture of belief and truth—but most of us (unlike Sartre's Flaubert) move in the direction of verifying the statements of others in important areas.

Signification for Sartre does not imply a self-referential closed system, as in Lacan. For Sartre, what the signifier signifies—the signified—points outward toward the phenomenal world; although one can never get to Being-in-itself as it is, one is not hopelessly trapped in a linguistic universe without reference. The signifier points both to the humanized object and to the other person, to reciprocity, since it is the purpose of words to "carry the projects of the Other into me and . . . my own projects into the Other"

(CDR, p. 98). Where this does not occur, where words are appreciated for their opacity rather than for their transcendent capacity, "aestheticism" takes the place of genuine praxis. It would seem that structuralist psychoanalysis, by defining the real as the "impossible" and by insisting that language is a closed structure where one glides from word to word without external reference, recommends the perspective of the aesthete—which is just the perspective that Sartre sees as the key to Flaubert's neurosis.

Flaubert's position as an aesthete, according to Sartre, derives ultimately from a childhood in which he found himself "badly anchored in the universe of discourse" (FI, 1:15–16). And while some readers, aware of Flaubert's status as one of the world's great novelists, might wish to be as "badly anchored" as he, Sartre in his biography does make a good case for a stylistic analysis even of Flaubert's greatest works as exemplifying this linguistic "failure." Obviously, this failure has its origins in those experiences of early childhood in which Flaubert's relations with his mother failed to provide him with a sense that he could actively seek to fulfill rather than merely passively suffer the satisfaction or denial of his needs. Because he experienced only the dutiful ministrations of a cold mother, Sartre maintains that Flaubert never came to know "that first communication, the reciprocity of tenderness" (FI, 2:17) on which all later (verbal and other) communication will rest. For this reason, Sartre maintains that language for Flaubert comes to be a gesture rather than an act—representation or playacting rather than presentation.

According to Sartre, we are all capable of having the world derealized when we are unable to respond to its demands through effective action. He gives as an example an experience of Gide's one night in a Venetian lagoon where he was threatened by gondoliers who were deliberating over whether to take his wallet or perhaps his life. Sartre himself had a similar experience during the Second World War, when he was caught between German and French guns and faced being shot by either side depending on whether he advanced or retreated. In both situations, there was no real action that either man might have taken to save himself, and in both situations there was a feeling of unreality, pretense, role-playing about the scene. Sartre proposes that this is what Flaubert's entire life is like (FI, 2:15–17).

Sartre contends that the young Flaubert's passive constitution prevents him from even conceiving of speech as action or as reciprocity. For speech to be real praxis, according to Sartre, it must refer to one's earliest experience as praxis: One must be active from the beginning. This is exactly the converse of Flaubert's earliest experience as presented by Sartre. Hence it is that words wound him, his whole body quivering with the shafts of arrows as if he were a "little Saint Sebastian." Words wound Flaubert because they do not apply to *his* experience in the same way that they apply to the experience of those "loved sons" who are "princes" in their exercise of the "sovereignty that these denominations legitimatize." Words, Sartre tells us, are value laden. They refer to "the autonomy of spontaneity, to the synthetic unity of experience, to all the structures of praxis"—and in doing so, they refer to a "creative and sovereign spontaneity that the child [Gustave] has never encountered in himself" (FI, 1:148–49). Words, those practico-inert objects, have been endowed with the past praxes of others—so that they may be invoked in the interest of future praxis. But praxis has never been awakened in Flaubert; from earliest infancy, his experience has been hexis.

Hence it is that the child Gustave comes to regard words as opaque; they are a material gift, like a music box given to him by the adults but bearing no reference to his own experience (FI, 1:14). For this reason, Gustave is unable to conceive of speech as reciprocity. For him "dialogue is not the actualization of reciprocity through the Word, it is an alternation of monologues" (FI, 2:18). And though it is true that Flaubert has to maintain his passivity, just as he has to learn language, he does so (as he himself complains) without that sense of freedom which is the earmark of praxis. Although Flaubert is forced to learn the language of praxis, its meanings are never measured by "subjective certainty" based on active experience (FI, 1:342). Gustave misses the "transcendental indication" in words which is an invitation to "*escape from the self toward*" the world (FI, 1:152) for the simple reason that he has never genuinely learned to act.

Instead, Flaubert develops a form of action which Sartre refers to as "passive activity" and he learns the "feudal" relationship of adoration, but he never learns the reciprocity which leads to actual engagement with another as another transcendence—to reciprocal love, antagonism, or mutual aid. He never learns to subject belief to verification. Hence it is that Sartre explains a family story about Gustave at age six in which the future writer is told by a servant to "go into the kitchen . . . and see if I'm there." The dutiful child trots into the kitchen to ask, much to the amusement of the other servants. Sartre comments that if "Gustave, aged six, confuses sign and meaning to the extent that the material presence of the sign is the evidence that guarantees the truth of the meaning, he must have had a poor initial relationship with the Other" (FI, 1:14). Like Lacan's mirror stage infant, then, Gustave learns not a distinction but a "confusion of self and Other": "He is himself as an Other and for an Other" (FI, 1:145). A little later, Gustave will have difficulty learning to read for the same reason: Reading requires an active synthesis of the material, which he finds exceedingly difficult.

Sartre reminds us that Flaubert all his life expressed an affinity for animals, children (who are often treated as small animals), and severely mentally disabled persons. Flaubert's sympathy was for those creatures on the horizon but not quite included in the cultural-linguistic order. One of the characters of his juvenilia, Djalioh, is a half-man half-orangutan who feels deeply but communicates badly. Flaubert clearly identifies with him. Flaubert, unlike those loved children who regard themselves as princes, has been received with indifference. He is therefore, Sartre tells us, "wild grass"—he does not fit into the cultural-linguistic order where action and reciprocity are expected. "No mouth," Sartre says rather poetically, "gave Gustave, that weed, the language of useless plants, the only language that would be his own." Later on, he would try to invent it. For the time being, "he never feels what he expresses and never expresses what he feels" (FI, 1:149). For Flaubert, only the stupors and half-mystical experiences into which he had sunk since he was a child are "real."

As for communication, because Flaubert never feels that words represent his own experience, he exaggerates and playacts, but he does not communicate. He is excluded from the dialogical exchanges which are the mark of true communication between people because

> he is unaware that every word is a right over the Other; that every sentence, even a purely informative one is imposed as a question, a solicitation, a command, an acceptance, a refusal, etc., in the interminable conversation men have pursued over the centuries; that every question is answered, even by silence; that any two persons, different as they may be, when placed in each other's presence, carry on a dialogue, though fully intending to keep quiet, because even in the most complete immobility they are necessarily seeing and visible, totally signifying and totally signified. For the child Gustave—and later for the man—dialogue is not the actualization of reciprocity through the Word, it is an alternation of monologues. (FI, 2:17–18)

Even these monologues, however, are external. These "*alien phrases* that designate him from the outside and implant themselves in his head" do not really belong to him—do not really designate *his* feelings and *his* experience and he does not communicate this (FI, 2:18).

As for inclusion in a common project, Flaubert is also incapable of this because he is incapable of the common action on the world which it requires. Knowledge is based on immediate evidence, and Flaubert, since he has not learned to act, is capable only of belief. For this reason, he "can under no circumstances consider himself a solid link in a chain of collective operations" (FI, 1:154). Collective knowledge is first "rigorously impersonal and then it is us and then me." It is through evidence that "I appeal from rigorous impersonality to the historical community, and from others to myself; I recover myself by losing myself." But such common activity is an ethical enterprise—"an act that establishes the person but can only be accomplished on the foundation of a previously recognized *value*" (FI, 1:154). Since Flaubert has failed to develop the sense of reciprocity and world orientedness which would enable him to act as a solid link in such collective operations, we might say that the cultural-linguistic-historical order is "foreclosed" to him—he can represent it, but he can never become an active participant in it.

What is thereby foreclosed to Flaubert is not the Lacanian Name-of-the-father, but the ability to make speech a verbal act. And though his father's demand for obedience later adds to Flaubert's passivity, it is not originally the absence of the phallic signifier but the absence of reciprocity with the first Other (his mother) which has laid the stage for this foreclosure. Although others name him, Flaubert does not know how to name himself or his experience—and it is this absence of intentionality in speech, an absence which Lacanian psycholinguistic theory does not recognize, which has crippled him. Forever after, he will be interested in ceremonies of naming, as when he has Emma and Leon go through their ceremony of invoking nature in the course of the ripening of their love in *Madame Bovary* (FI, 1:17); or he will be interested in indications that others, like himself, are spoken objects rather than speaking subjects—as when he collects commonplaces in his *Dictionnaire des idées reçues*.

Indeed, Flaubert's *Dictionnaire* perhaps illustrates more clearly than anything else his attitude toward language. What interests Flaubert is not language as living praxis but "human significations in the process of petrification" (FI, 1:605). The " 'moving sidewalk' of banalities" which he enjoyed capturing in his dictionary illustrates this process. Flaubert (like Lacan) apparently "does not believe that *people speak*" but rather that "*people are spoken*" (FI, 1:602). Or again, Sartre maintains that language for Flaubert "is nothing but stupidity, since verbal materiality left to itself is organized semi-externally and produces a kind of *thought-matter*" (FI, 1:603). Sartre gives as an example the following entry under "railroads": "Talk about them ecstatically, saying: 'I, sir, who am speaking to you now—I was this morning at X; I left by train from X, where I had taken care of my business, and in X hours I was back here'" (FI, 1:600). Sartre comments that while it is true that all travelers were at the time making such remarks about railroads (as they would later make them about airplanes), Flaubert catches only the "stupidity" of the commonplace while missing the expression of naive and spontaneous emotion common to everyone experiencing the "marvel" of railway travel for the first time. Flaubert is unaware of the praxis indicated by the truisms.

Hence, whether ironic or serious, Flaubert will remain, as Sartre says, a "choirboy of language," ceremoniously serving an alien mystery but never making it his own (FI, 1:153). For Sartre, this substitution of otherness in the place of self through language does not lead to an openness to unconscious Being, as in Lacan, but to a use of language which is in the final analysis incantatory and magical rather than a work on the world. Linguistic truth, for Sartre, is world oriented rather than unconscious oriented, as in Lacan. Hence Sartre notes that in normal development the signifier is not divorced from the "real existence of the signified." On the other hand, in pathological development, "the development of language is arrested" and verbal processes "seem meaningless." "We have encountered such imprisoned thought," Sartre goes on to say, "in magical formulas, in riddles, and in the *carmina sacra*; we find it each night in our dreams" (FI, 1:14). As a way of life, it is, as we saw in the last chapter, a sign of a (pathological) choice of the imaginary over the real.

Thus we might say that a healthy insertion into language is for Sartre exactly the opposite of the one Lacan envisioned. Flaubert, Sartre tells us, is in a certain sense not wrong. The problem is that for Flaubert, as for Lacan, sensitivity to language as "thought matter" (practico-inert) eclipses recognition of speech as praxis. It is certainly true, Sartre admits, that "every pronounced speech contains within it the counterfinality that consumes it" (a point with which not only Lacan but also Derrida would agree) and that a word is a "a ready-made idea since it is defined outside us by its differences from other words in the verbal spectrum." But it is equally true that in another way "we are all intelligent," even when we express ourselves in commonplaces, in that "commonplaces are words in the sense that, by using them we move toward a thought that is always fresh" (FI, 1:603). In addition, praxis as genuine creativity is always striving to find new ways to express (and create through expressing) novel experience. According to Sartre, "invention characterizes speech." Under favorable conditions, we will invent—

"if not, we will have badly named experiences and live them badly" (FI, 1:29). Speech, after all, is behavior, and discourse and lived experience are changed by each other.

It is the creative aspect of language, in which "intelligence is a dialectical relationship between verbal intention [which is world-oriented] and words," that Flaubert—and Lacan—neglect. And it is this neglect that leaves Flaubert in a constant "state of *estrangement* in the face of words [which] represent the outside transferred to the inside, the interior grasped as exterior" without the intervention of free praxis (FI, 1:603). In this respect, Flaubert is something like Lacan's "decentered subject" who realizes that he is decentered—that is, the analysand who has come to terms with the otherness from which he or she emanates. Yet it is precisely because Flaubert's desire is the "desire of the Other" (Lacan means the linguistic unconscious, but we have seen how this is predicated on a repression of the desire of/for the m[Other] on the part of the mirror stage child) that he is estranged from himself; and it is precisely because he is unable to communicate his own desire in words—indeed, because he has not been allowed to develop into an actively desiring subject—that Flaubert mimics others.

Lacan, I would contend, by neglecting intentionality and denigrating consciousness, takes a position close to the one that Sartre ascribes to Flaubert. And by placing the source of otherness not outside in the practico-inert but inside in unconscious linguistic structure, he considers "normal" the kind of alienation which Sartre describes as symptomatic of "an internal disorder of language" (FI, 1:148). Lacanian alienation is unsurpassable not in the sense that Sartrean primary alienation is unsurpassable because I cannot refuse to objectify myself in a practico-inert world that is already filled with the objectifications of others; rather, it is unsurpassable because it is this Otherness which creates me as a speaking subject. From a Sartrean perspective, Lacan has got it backward: The "symbol" does not "beget intelligent beings," as Lacan (1975, p. 142) thinks; rather, intelligent beings beget and sustain symbols, albeit in a world already filled with symbols and in which there is no return to a prior state of nature which pre-exists and retains its purity outside of the cultural-linguistic order (FI, 1:28).

Of course, if by unconscious structure Lacan means only that one is *not usually conscious* of linguistic structure and that cultural and familial meanings are often imposed on us without our critical awareness, then he would simply be talking about the practico-inert and Sartre's agreement (in the statement quoted at the beginning of this chapter) with his idea that the "unconscious is structured like a language" would represent a real convergence of thinking. There are certainly times when Lacan talks as if this might be the case, as when he discusses the way in which an individual is inserted into his or her "prehistory"—that is, this person's place in the family system or particular class and/or culture. Lacan also says that the unconscious is "that which is inside the subject, but which can be realized only outside, that is to say, in that locus of the Other in which alone it may assume its status" (1973, p. 147). As such, the unconscious is transindividual. Or again, Lacan contends that the unconscious "is neither primordial nor instinctual; what it knows about the elementary is no more than the elements of the signifier" (1966, p. 170).

Yet if all this sounds as if Lacan is simply talking about the cultural-linguistic order itself, an order which for Sartre is practico-inert, then we must remember that the unconscious for Lacan is also that which speaks the subject from the "other scene" where dreams, slips of the tongue, and jokes develop. It is the locus from which symptoms which are undecipherable to the conscious subject emanate. It is that which "speaks me" without my being aware of it. It is the reason why transcendence and any ideas I may have of myself as a unified subject are illusions. It is the guarantor of "truth" and of "Good Faith," the very "kernel of our being" (Lacan, 1966, pp. 172–73 and 234) from which we each derive as a "decentered subject." It is also the reason why Lacan rejects the existential-phenomenological view of intentionality. As Ragland-Sullivan points out, when Lacan speaks of consciousness, he does not mean consciousness of *something*: "Instead, consciousness has become a mode of perception which negotiates Desire via substitutions" (1986, p. 91). It is in the dimension of the Other, the unconscious, that "the recognition of desire is bound up with the desire for recognition" (Lacan, 1966, p. 172). Hence it is there, in the repressed primal relationship with the mother and in the linguistic laws which have been placed there in the wake of the encounter with the primal signifier, that the various substitutions with which I fill my life make sense.

There is, of course, a sense in which Sartre would agree that language "speaks" the subject. It is not from the realm of the unconscious, however, that this speaking occurs. Because language is practico-inert, it is imbued with past praxes. Thus like the practico-inert in general, it contains exigencies. For example, it is presently difficult—though it is becoming possible—to speak many languages in the world without having oneself imbued with the implicit sexism of the generic "he."[6] It is also true that having once applied a word to an experience, the whole history of associations to that word carry us along. For instance, Sartre discusses the way in which the application of the word "love" to tender feelings endows that tenderness "with a past, a present, a future, an objective essence constituted by the historical evolution of mores, of folk wisdom, with a positive value and often an antivalue that bear witness to the contradictions of the current ideology or opposing ideologies" (FI, 1:28).

The way in which a quality such as love or hate becomes associated with the ego is, of course, familiar from Sartre's early work. What is different here is the recognition of the power of the word in inducing the tender emotions, the desire, as a means to preserving the "being" of love as a practico-inert linguistic reality linking one to the history and culture in which the word is spoken. I believe that it is the power of the practico-inert which produces the strange phenomenon of the relationship that is changed (sometimes for the worse) by marriage; the meanings inscribed in the word "marriage" by others, including, of course, the couple's families of origin, come to invade and change the simple feelings the couple previously had for each other and in some sense to direct the relationship.

Sartre does not say that it is absolutely wrong to submit to the exigencies discovered in the linguistic practico-inert. After all, they are paths as well as roadblocks, and, indeed, it is the teleological implications of words which Sartre believes disturb and estrange Flaubert. Certainly, Sartre would agree that where the project of loving (despite its cultural-linguistic associations and imperatives) involves a commitment including real feelings and mutuality, it can benefit both parties. But where the word does not apply to the felt reality of the individual, where it simply induces playacting, as Sartre believes was the case with Flaubert, it becomes an obstruction. In this case, the subject is literally spoken by words which alienate him or her from any authentic sense of self. On the other hand, words can also liberate by implying a path for praxis and by naming something that previously had remained hazy because it was unnamed. Sartre notes that "nothing exists that does not require a name, that cannot be given one and cannot even be negatively named by the bankruptcy of language." At the same time, "*nomination* from its very origin is *an art*" and "invention characterizes speech" (FI, 1:29).

It is true, then, that experience is often prescribed by language, but it is equally true that through invention, through creativity, one finds new paths for expressing experience through language—which in turn affect future experience (one's own and others'). In one sense, language can be perceived as a totality, with an interrelationship among its parts. But as we have seen, the sustenance of a totality always involves totalization—and the history of languages shows that they are developing totalizations. As for individual expression, it is always a totalization, although the relative linguistic health or illness of the individual can be related to the extent to which the individual either uses language creatively or allows his or her experience to be passively dictated by language (or perhaps fails to find ways of expressing that experience in words at all)—in other words, to the relative degree of praxis or hexis, authenticity or other directedness, in an individual's linguistic project. Sometimes, as in cases of social oppression, what is required is to disrupt the usual workings of language—to divert and twist the meanings of the very words of the oppressor in order to make them vehicles of revolutionary praxis, as Sartre, in his preface to *Black Orpheus* (1948), credited the black African poets who wrote in French with doing.[7]

In individual psychotherapy, too, part of the task is revolutionary linguistic praxis in the sense that the client must invent a new (to him or her) way of talking about significant past (also present) experiences which were badly named, misnamed, or not named at all. This power of naming in psychotherapy cannot be overemphasized. It is the path through which release of spontaneity is largely achieved. Obviously, from a Sartrean perspective, this path leads from a past in which language was used to distort or twist or deny experience through a present moment of revolutionary praxis (the "psychological instant") in which expression becomes more real as one heads off into a future which appears different partially because it can be more truly and realistically named. The release of speech as intersubjective praxis through the substitution of dialogue for monologue or genuine communication for playacting would also be a goal of existentialist therapy. What the path of transformation might be from a Lacanian perspective, or whether transformation is possible at all in Lacanian analysis, is the subject of the next chapter.

Conclusion

As we come to the end of this discussion, I think it will be apparent that Lacan has not escaped from the solipsistic quandary in which we left him at the end of the last chapter. The "real" still lacks adequate representation in his system. For this reason, although Lacan may be right in saying that we encounter nothing *outside* the symbolic-linguistic system (pure Being-in-itself), he is from a Sartrean perspective mistaken in advocating a view of language in which "signification" refers only to the relationship among linguistic components and not to human world-making activity (the workings of praxis on the practico-inert). Hence though Sartre would agree with Lacan that language creates the subject in the sense of providing paths for praxis and limitations in the form of hexis and linguistic counterfinalities, he would not agree that this is the whole story. What is significant for Sartre (and for existentialist therapy) is what the person has made of what he or she is made of linguistically and otherwise—and what that person might make of this through a reorienting linguistic praxis.

I suppose the crux of the matter is that for Sartre there is an intentional praxis which creates and sustains the linguistic practico-inert which it takes into its project, whereas for Lacan there is not. Hence from a Sartrean perspective it is possible to achieve a meta-reflective position on one's fundamental attitude toward and insertion into language and to change directions. For Lacan, as we shall see in the next chapter, the most that is possible is an understanding and acceptance of the fact that one is the plaything of the linguistic unconscious—that one is (in the Sartrean sense) a signified rather than a signifier, an object pretending to be a subject. Lacanian analysis, from this perspective, is conservative and supportive of the status quo— even to the point of insisting that the entrance into language is predicated on a gender differentiation that is supportive of patriarchy (though it has other possibilities as well). Certainly, as a new synchronic determinism, Lacanian metatheory offers no better explanation for the transformative possibilities of depth therapy than does traditional Freudian (diachronic) determinism.

Language, for Lacan, ultimately refers neither to intentional praxis nor to intersubjective relations, but rather to the relationship of the conscious subject to the unconscious Other(A)—the subject beyond the subject which is no subject at all in that it is an "acephalic," nonintentional subject. For Sartre, on the other hand, language is fundamentally intersubjective (since it arises with my Being-for-others) and world-open. Consequently, there is the possibility both for the action of authentic speech and for the meta-use of language to reflectively purge the distortions handed down by the original others. And this is possible, as we have seen, because the ego and language are not for Sartre (as they are for Lacan) unalterably other in the sense of deriving solely from the specular image overlaid by the Other(A). Hence, though Sartre would not deny that language is other in the sense of containing exigencies placed there by others which affect me at the most profound levels of my being, he would deny that this in itself makes it impossible for me to exercise the creative power of speech. One's life in the world of language, like one's life in the practico-inert world in general, is an inescapable mixture of praxis and hexis, freedom and necessity. The question is rather which predominates. Certainly, one of the aims of existentialist therapy, as contrasted with Lacanian analysis, would be to release or restore the creative power of language where it has been undermined by a client's earliest intersubjective experience.

8 · Clinical Implications:
Sartrean Revolutionary Praxis versus Lacanian *Amor Fati*

Introduction

From the discussion in the preceding two chapters, it would appear that the critical question for Lacanian analysis is whether and how change is possible from this metatheoretical perspective. Obviously, change is possible from a Sartrean perspective, although this becomes more complex in the later philosophy with the introduction of the practico-inert. We have seen in earlier chapters what the goals of change are from a Sartrean perspective. Now we must ask what the goals of change are in Lacanian analysis. In other words, what are the marks of a successful Lacanian analysis? These are not easy questions to answer, especially since Lacan himself gives so few clinical examples.[1] Still, Lacan has said that the sole purpose of his teaching is to train analysts, and Stuart Schneiderman, in his introduction to the only book in English with extensive examples of Lacanian case studies, *Returning to Freud: Clinical Psychoanalysis in the School of Lacan*, insists that "any approach to Lacan that does not see his theory in its relationship to analytic practice is doomed to an irreducible obscurity and confusion" (1980, p. 9). Lacan apparently did not mean his theory to be a plaything for literary critics and other intellectuals. He meant it to have an impact on clinical practice. The problem, however, as I see it, is that Lacan, by making the linguistic unconscious the source and director of "subjecthood," leaves us with an extremely unclear idea of who is to change and how this change is to occur.

It may be, as Lacan says, that "the slightest alteration in the relations between man and the signifier . . . changes the whole course of history by modifying the lines which anchor his being" (1966, p. 174). The question is: Who is to effect the change, individually and/or historically? It may also be, as Douglas Collins notes, that psychoanalysis "becomes for Sartre what it was for Hesnard and Lacan: the discovery of the invading Other within an unhappy host" (1980, p. 109). The problem is that in Lacan it is hard to see who the host is, other than the "animal" who learns to speak (that is, the subject's biological underpinnings), since the little human animal is suffused with otherness from the mirror stage identifications onward and since it is the Other(A) who creates the conscious subject. It therefore becomes difficult to see how a kind of absolute self-alienation can be modified, much less overcome, from a Lacanian perspective.

Actually, I do not think these problems are finally theoretically or even practically surmountable, though I do think that the Lacanian analysts make some interesting and even valid discoveries along the way. Nonetheless, I believe that Sartre's theory of praxis and the practico-inert, with its implications for a possible movement from hexis to praxis, provides a better clinical path for dealing with the otherness which is ensconced in the heart of our being than Lacan's theory of the Other(A). And I contend that Sartre's idea of the therapist as another person is fundamentally at odds with Lacan's idea of the therapist as stand-in for the Other(A), the linguistic unconscious, and that the aims of Sartrean existential psychoanalysis are fundamentally different from the aims of Lacanian structuralist psychoanalysis. Described briefly, the aim of Lacanian analysis might be said to be a kind of Nietzschean *amor fati* or love/acceptance of the fate of being the plaything of the linguistic unconscious predicated in part on a recognition of the specular origins of the ego. The contrary aim of Sartrean existential psychoanalysis could be described (as I have said in earlier chapters) as transformation to a more authentic mode of living—"revolutionary praxis" on the individual level.

Lacanian Analysis: Transformation or Amor Fati?

Throughout Lacan's work, despite the paucity of case histories, we find scattered indications about what Lacanian analysis does, or, sometimes more clearly, what it does not do. First of all, Lacanian analysis is not egologically oriented; rather, it is oriented toward an opening up to the Other(A). Lacanian analysis is not "ego analysis" but "discourse analysis"—both the conscious discourse of the subject and especially the unconscious discourse of the Other(A) which is the source of conscious discourse (Lacan, 1975, pp. 62–70). Its aim is "full speech" as opposed to "empty speech" (a point I shall take up below). Lacan's position is therefore the opposite of most post-Freudian psychoanalytic theorists. With the single exception of Melanie Klein, whose work Lacan once offered to translate (Macey, 1988, pp. 220-21), we have seen that these theorists are more interested in the development of the ego from earliest infancy, a task suggested by Freud, than they are in the workings of the unconscious. They prefer the structural to the economic hypothesis of Freud.

Lacan, of course, is not a follower of Klein. Although, like Klein, he would emphasize the unconscious, it is an unconscious of linguistic laws rather than an unconscious of primitive instinctual forces. Still, Lacan obviously prefers Klein, whose cases he cites from time to time, to the ego psychologists and the British object relations theorists.[2] With the exception of Winnicott's transitional object, Lacan universally rejects the major ideas of the majority of post-Freudian theorists. He especially regards the attempt by ego psychologists and object relations theorists to reconstruct the development of the ego and to restructure the ego in analysis as undermining the power of the Freudian achievement. For Lacan, such approaches are a domestication of Freud in the interest of a false ideal of genital bliss to be achieved in so-called normal development or (a word that Lacan, along with Sartre, does not relish) "adjustment." As for the concentration of these theorists on the mother-child duo in early infancy and childhood, Lacan insists on a "return to Freud" in the sense of placing theoretical and clinical emphasis on the "third term" of the Oedipal conflict—though, as we have seen, this is an Oedipal conflict which has been radically reinterpreted by Lacan.

Lacanian analysis would therefore concentrate not on analyzing or structuring/restructuring the ego but on bringing the analysand to an understanding of the illusory nature of the ego in the interest of a fuller attunement to the subject beyond the subject who is introduced through the phallic signifier and the experience of castration—the Other(A). As Lacan insists again and again, the aim of psychoanalysis is not, as many contemporary psychoanalysts seem to believe, to strengthen the analysand's ego, to substitute the strong ego of the analyst for the weak ego of the analysand, or to in any other way manipulate the analysand with the precepts or example of the analyst. Lacan complains that such an analysis leads the analysand to a "reinforced alienation" (1966, p. 274). In attempting to strengthen the ego, contemporary analysts fail to recognize that the ego is an illusion, a mirage, a center of misunderstanding (*méconnaissance*) (Lacan, 1975, p. 53). Indeed, the ego, far from being a force for reality organization and cooperation with the treatment, "represents the center of all the resistances to the treatment of symptoms" (Lacan, 1966, p. 23). This is so, of course, because the ego is organized around the specular images which give the individual a sense of imaginary coherence and order based on identification. In other words, ego analysis takes place on the plane of the imaginary, whereas Lacan believes that effective psychoanalysis is played out "on the frontier between the symbolic and the imaginary" (1978, pp. 254–55).

This perspective leads Lacanian analysts to a different treatment in analysis of such issues as transference, resistance, repetition, and repression. Lacan links repetition with the desire to maintain the static illusion of the unified ego through the use of signifiers and regression with the structural traces of previous periods as they are preserved in the signifiers rather than with an actual movement backward to a prior "stage" of development. He regards the contemporary analyst's attempt to overcome the analysand's resistance through analysis of the defenses as "inquisitorial"—a position he believes is based on an idea of the analysand's "ill will" (1975, p. 30). Indeed, he sometimes insists that the only real resistance in analysis is the resistance of the analyst (1978, p. 324), which presumably results from the analyst's resistance to the truths of the Other(A) and attachment to the illusory ego. In any case, Lacan believes that if the analyst lets go of his or her need to structure and direct the patient (Lacan insists that the analyst must direct the treatment but not the patient [1966, p. 227]) and listens to the discourse of the Other(A) as it appears in the discourse of the patient, then there will be no need to analyze and struggle with the analysand over the analysand's resistances and defenses.

As for the transference, the analyst needs to recognize that the actual focus of the transference, the place where the patient situates the analyst, is the Other(A). It is the analyst as the "subject supposed to know" (*le sujet-supposé-savoir*), but who does not really know, who takes the place of the unconscious Other at the beginning of analysis (Lacan, 1973, p. 269). In the course of the analysis, the analysand uses this misconception to get to know his or her unconscious. This does not happen, according to Lacan, by the analyst's calling the analysand's attention to disparities between what the analysand thinks the analyst is doing (or being) and what is actually the case. To proceed in this way is to totally mistake the nature of transference, which acts simultaneously in the three registers of the imaginary, the symbolic, and the real and is not therefore a real case (however unconsciously motivated) of mistaken identity (Lacan, 1975, pp. 112–13). As a replay of the past in the register of the imaginary, the transference provides not an opening to the unconscious but a closing of the unconscious. Desire, for the moment, has been tossed an *objet a* which assuages its hunger and prevents the backward movement along the chain of the signifiers which leads to an understanding of the original composition of the subject.

What, then, is the analyst to do? We have seen that the Lacanian analyst does not analyze the ego and its defenses; rather, he or she waits for the opening of the unconscious and apparently reinforces this by responding. In the following passage, Lacan has just condemned the practice of conducting the analysis of the transference on the basis of an alliance with the healthy part of the analysand's ego and "appealing to his common sense by pointing out to him the illusory character of certain of his actions in his relation to the analyst" (Lacan, 1973, pp. 130-31). He goes on to say:

> This is a thesis that subverts what it [analytic practice] is all about, namely the bringing to awareness of this split in the subject, realized here, in fact, in presence. To appeal to some healthy part of the subject thought to be there in the real, capable of judging with the analyst what is happening in the transference, is to misunderstand that it is precisely this part [represented by the transference] that closes the door, or the window, or the shutters, or whatever—and that the beauty with whom one wishes to speak is there, behind, only too willing to open the shutters again. That is why it is at this moment that interpretation becomes decisive, for it is to the beauty one must speak. (Lacan, 1973, p. 131)

While this passage may be an example of what some critics have referred to as Lacan's "occultation" of the unconscious (see Antoine Vergote in Smith and Kerrigan, 1983, p. 217), what it makes clear is that Lacanian analysis is not an analysis of defenses and resistances or even an analysis of the transference in the usual sense; it is instead an attempt to speak directly to the unconscious Other(A).

Lacan's (famous or notorious) experiments with "short sessions" were apparently one practical attempt to surprise the "beauty" and get her to "speak." Against the objections of the International Psychoanalytic Association (IPA) to this deviation from standard practice, Lacan argued that leaving the analysand unsure about the length of the session speeds up the process of analysis by lessening a routine which has long been recognized to foster avoidance and allowing the analyst to punctuate the session wherever the punctuation might naturally fall—rather like a metric beat or a Zen master surprising his students (Lacan, 1966, pp. 44 and 100-101). Furthermore,

Lacan argued, since the unconscious is timeless, standard sessions make little sense. The IPA did not agree. Lacan's short sessions were only the most blatant example of the heterodoxy which finally got him expelled from the organization as a training analyst in 1963.[3]

The short sessions, however, were discarded after a time and, at any rate, were not central to the practice of Lacanian analysis. In what other ways, then, does the Lacanian analyst attempt to induce this opening of the unconscious? First, he or she does this by keeping silent. Lacan insists that the analyst must not instruct, overinterpret, or otherwise get in the way of the opening of the unconscious through the thread of the signifiers in the practice of free association. This silence of the analyst is not, however, a nonresponse since the speaking of the analysand implies a response, even if that response is silence. The analysand, for his or her part, attempts through the transference to get the analyst to enact the part of the *objet a*, to enter the imaginary loop of the ego to alter ego relations which constitute the analysand's everyday interactions (Lacan, 1978, p. 324). The analyst must reject all of the analysand's "demands," that is, the analysand's concrete indications of what the analyst must do in order to satisfy the analysand (at bottom, this is a demand for love or recognition) in the interest of provoking an opening up of the analysand's *desire*.

This desire, which Lacan defines as the splitting that results from the subtraction of need (for organismic satisfaction) from demand (for recognition or love) (1966, p. 287), occurs in what Lacan refers to as the "defiles of the signifier" (1966, p. 264 and elsewhere). Desire, Lacan says in another place, "begins to take place in the margin in which demand becomes separated from need: this margin being that which is opened up by demand, the appeal of which can be unconditional only in regard to the Other, under the form of the possible defect, which need may introduce into it, of having no universal satisfaction (what is called 'anxiety')" (1966, p. 311).

Most analysts, in Lacan's view, reduce desires to demands (1966, p. 262) and thereby fail to get at the symbolic regression which leads to cure. Through demand, the analysand's "whole past opens up right down to earliest infancy," and the analyst, by "supporting" that demand through failing to satisfy it, allows "the signifiers in which [the subject's] frustration is bound up to reappear"—to, as it were, recross the bar of repression and gain access to conscious cognition (Lacan, 1966, pp. 254–55). What is important in the recovery of the past, however, is not that the analysand *relive* his or her history but that the analysand *reconstruct* it and by doing so *restructure* the signifying chain by which he or she has been constructed (Lacan, 1975, p. 13).

Lacan suggests that the analyst must take the position of the dummy (*le mort*) in a game of bridge in order to introduce the fourth player—the Other(A), who is the partner of the analysand and "whose hand the analyst, by his tactics, will try to expose" (1966, p. 229). The Lacanian analyst, in fact, plays dead. He "cadaverizes" his position—"either by his silence when he is the Other with a capital O, or by annulling his own resistance when he is the Other with a small o" (Lacan, 1966, p. 140). Only by playing dead, according to Lacan, does the analyst become the one to whom the discourse of the Other(A), by whom death enters the human scene in the sense that the word is the death of the thing, is addressed. Thus Lacanian analysis works by means of the analyst's refusing the position of the *objet a* in favor of the position of the Other(A).

Lacan therefore notes that the

> analyst partakes of the radical nature of the Other, in so far as he is what is most inaccessible. From this point on, and beginning at this point in time, what leaves the imaginary of the ego of the subject is in accordance not with this other to which he is accustomed, and who is just his partner, the person who is made so as to enter his game, but precisely with this radical Other which is hidden from him. What is called transference happens precisely between A [the Other(A)] and m [*moi* or ego], in so far as the a [*objet a*], represented by the analyst, is lacking. (1978, p. 324)

Hence it is that Lacan insists (though he knows it is impossible) that the ideal analyst, far from displaying his or her "strong ego" for the emulation of the analysand, would be "egoless" (1978, p. 246).

Only by diminishing his or her own ego involvement will the analyst be able to act as the "harmonic vibration" which allows the passage of the "fundamental speech" of the Other(A) to the conscious subject (Lacan, 1978, p 325). Thus Lacan, far from endorsing the image of the analyst as an empathic or living mirror offered by theorists such as Heinz Kohut,[4] views the proper function of the analyst to be that of the "empty mirror" through which the analysand's discourse with the Other whom he or she is truly addressing on the other side of the "wall of language" may pass (Lacan, 1978, p. 244). The resolution of the transference therefore hangs not on the dispersal of illusions but on the analysand's progressively discovering the

"Other he is truly addressing, without knowing it, and of him [*sic*] progressively assuming the relations of transference at the place where he is, and where he didn't know he was" (Lacan, 1978, p. 246).

Lacan is being characteristically enigmatic here, but his students know by now how to interpret the enigma. It is in terms of a frequent reference to Freud's famous dictum, "*Wo Es war, soll Ich werden*," which Lacan goes on to mention. Translated as, "Where id was, there ego shall be," in the Standard English Edition (Freud, 1923, p. 80), this has usually been interpreted to mean that psychoanalysis seeks to increase the dominion of the reality principle over the pleasure principle, to bring id impulses under the control and understanding of the ego.

Lacan absolutely rejects this rendition, noting categorically that Freud did not mean that "the ego must dislodge the id" (Lacan, 1973, p. 44). Instead, Lacan views this statement as an imperative commanding the return to the Other(A). He retranslates Freud's statement, citing Freud's deletion of the definite articles (*das Es* and *das Ich*) as a reason for discounting the idea that Freud was referring to the psychic structures ego and id (Lacan, 1966, p. 128). According to Lacan, Freud meant to say, "There where it [the linguistic unconscious] was, it is my duty that I should come to being" (Lacan, 1966, p. 129). Ragland-Sullivan interprets this to mean, "Only in the movement of seeing oneself emerge from the unconscious can knowledge become truth" (1986, p. 12). Furthermore, Lacan playfully identifies *Es* with *S*, which is now considered to be not the conscious subject but the real subject, the Other(A), who speaks in the conscious subject's unconscious. "At the end of [psycho]analysis," Lacan says, "it is him [S] who must be called on to speak, and to enter into relation with the real others. Where the S was, there the *Ich* should be" (1978, p. 246). One should return to one's unconscious origins and use them (one wonders how) as a basis for intersubjectivity.

These ideas point to the meaning of that "full" or "veridical" or "true speech" at which Lacanian analysis aims. Ideally, this would be a speech which occurs without the disrupting intervention of ego identifications—though Lacan admits that even after a Lacanian analysis, the ego does not "volatilize" and the analysand "doesn't go to heaven, disembodied and pure symbol" (1978, p. 325). Rather, the ego is little by little linked with a subject who has come to identify with the Other(A). Full speech, according to Lacan, differs from "empty speech" in that it "realizes the truth of the subject." In empty speech, on the contrary, the subject "loses himself in the machinations of the system of language"—a statement which might sound Sartrean except for Lacan's explanation that this loss entails an entanglement in "the labyrinth of referential systems made available to him by the state of cultural affairs to which he is a more or less interested party" (1975, p. 50). I take this to mean that movement inward toward the unconscious is preferable to movement outward toward the social order.

Again Lacan may appear Sartrean when he says that the goal of analysis can only be "the advent of a true speech and the realization by the subject of his history in his relation to a future" (1966, p. 88). What Lacan means by assuming my history, however, appears to be more similar to Nietzschean *amor fati* than to Sartrean responsibility—in other words, it seems to imply an acceptance of what *is* as inevitable rather than a movement toward genuine transcendence. The analysand's "truth," according to Lacan, is "the signification taken on in his particular destiny by those givens which are peculiar to him and which one can call his lot" (1978, pp. 325–26). Thus although I may call on my counterpart to recognize me through his or her speech, the real recognition I require is the understanding of my destiny which I will find in the Other(A).

In order to understand myself as a product of the "discourse of the Other," I must understand what this discourse is. It is neither an abstract discourse nor the discourse of my counterpart or even my slave, Lacan says. It is instead "the discourse of the circuit in which I am integrated" and where I am "one of its links." It is the "discourse of my father" in that I am doomed to repeat his mistakes, "not simply because I am his son, but because one can't stop the chain of the discourse, and it is precisely my duty to transmit it in its aberrant form to someone else" (Lacan, 1978, p. 89).

Obviously, this is a kind of synchronic determinism in which a human being is caught in a symbolic circuit. Lacan reiterates this idea in an oft-quoted statement from the lecture known as the "Rome Discourse" wherein he first laid out his system as a psycholinguistics: "I identify myself in language, but only by losing myself in it like an object. What is realized in my history is not the past definite of what was, since it is no more, or even the present perfect of what has been in what I am, but the future anterior of what I shall have been for what I am in the process of becoming" (1966, p. 86). Lacan does not mean that down there in the future I am projecting an in-itself-for-itself. He means that at the moment the subject enters the stage of history "the die has already been cast." "Don't you feel that there's something derisory and funny," he asks his students in a seminar, "about the fact that the die has already been cast?" (1978, p. 220). According to Lacan, the aim of analysis is to lead the analysand back to "his signifying dependence" (1973, p. 77). After all, as Lacan puts it, "somewhere in the Other, it knows." And *it* knows "precisely because it is upheld by the signifiers through which the subject is constituted" (Lacan, 1985, p. 158).

I think we can now decipher the meaning of Lacan's enigmatic statement that the lofty goal of the psychoanalyst is nothing less than to act as a "mediator between the [Heideggerian] man of care and the [Hegelian] subject of absolute knowledge" (1966, p. 105). The "man of care" (according to Heidegger, the structure of consciousness is *sorge* [care or concern]), aside from representing the cares or troubles which the analysand brings the analyst, is the conscious subject with all his or her (albeit illusory) involvements, whereas the "subject of absolute knowledge" is the Other(A). Lacan, however, is no metaphysician. He declares categorically that "there is no Other of the Other" (1966, p. 311): There is no point outside the linguistic system from which to judge it. The subject of absolute knowledge, in an ironic reversal of Hegelian idealism, becomes the Lacanian acephalic subject (Lacan, 1978, p. 167, and elsewhere). This subject without a head, this subject which is no subject at all, is the "truth" to which the Lacanian analyst would have his or her analysands return.

The analysand's return is therefore to a symbolic order which Lacan links with the death instinct and which "is simultaneously non-being and insisting to be"—a symbolic order "in travail, in the process of coming, insisting on being realised" in the history of the analytic subject (Lacan, 1978, p. 326). In such an order, the Lacanian analysand must discover that before his or her birth the analysand had been constituted "in the chorus line" of concrete discourse as a message which "is entirely located in the succession of messages" (Lacan, 1978, p. 283). The Lacanian analysand, then, is a decentered subject who recognizes his or her decenteredness—a person who recognizes that he or she is caught up in the "gears" of language and therefore "isn't master in his own house" (Lacan, 1978, p. 307). It is at the point where the analysand recognizes his or her dependence on the signifiers, one presumes, that the Lacanian analyst graces the "true speech" of the analysand with a reply (Lacan, 1966, p. 95).

The problem with Lacan's system is that it is a system which closes in on itself, continuously swallowing its own tail. For the transparency of a consciousness opening out onto the world, Lacan substitutes "the opacity of the signifier that determines the I" (1966, p. 307). No genuine praxis is possible in a system where the conscious subject is merely an "effect" of the unconscious signifiers (Lacan, 1973, pp. 126 and 207) and where the signifier is the determinant of a signified which glides ceaselessly beneath it (Lacan, 1966, p. 299). As Antoine Vergote notes,

Actually, [for Lacan] the subject of discourse is fundamentally the subject of "modern game theory." . . . The subject is but the locus of the combinative production of autonomized signifiers. The clinician might even wonder if this is not the nonsubject of schizophrenia, the one who is the stake of the word but who is no longer playing the game of language. (In Smith and Kerrigan, 1983, p. 202)

Certainly, Lacan means to distinguish between the language of the psychotic, which, having never been anchored in the phallic signifier, lacks "anchoring points" (Lacan, 1966, p. 303) which can give it sense, and the language of the normal person or the neurotic. The question, however, is whether intelligible discourse can be accounted for in a system which denies both intentionality in the phenomenological sense and reference. If the "reality of the subject" is unconscious (Lacan, 1978, p. 58) and if this unconscious subject lacks a head with which to think in the usual sense, then madness would seem to be the norm of human reality. Lacan says that belief in the ego, since it is a mirage, is a kind of madness (1978, p. 247). But is not Lacan's insistence on the primacy of language over all else also a kind of madness? Lacan says that psychoanalysis induces in the subject a "controlled paranoia" (1966, p. 15); one wonders if Lacanian analysis might not, if it succeeds in its avowed aims, produce an actual schizophrenia.

This point about the linkage between Lacanian analysis and psychosis is reinforced by an unlikely source: Lacanian Jacques-Alain Miller's explication of Lacan's interview with a psychotic patient published in Stuart Schneiderman's book as "A Lacanian Psychosis" (Lacan in Schneiderman, 1980, pp. 19–41). Miller argues that this psychotic man (who had, in any case, read Lacan's *Ecrits*) demonstrates Lacan's theory of the linguistic unconscious. The patient was subject to the delusion of "imposed speech," in which he could not recognize himself as the speaker. He responded with what he called "reflexive statements," which he did recognize as coming from himself. Miller contends that the patient "witnessed in this way [through the imposed statements] the emergence of the discourse of the Other, but directly, without this soothing misapprehension of the reversal that makes us believe that we speak, when in fact we are spoken." Lacan, responding to this, asks, "How do we not sense . . . that the words we depend upon are imposed on us, that speech is an overlay, a parasite, the form of cancer with which human beings are afflicted?" (Miller in Schneiderman, 1980, p. 49). The question which this Lacanian psychosis brings up "is no longer 'What is a madman?' but 'How can one not be mad?' " (Miller in Schneiderman, 1980, p. 48). One wants to know why indeed, from a Lacanian perspective, we are not all mad—since this attentiveness to the truth of the unconscious is exactly the point of Lacanian analysis.

The truth of the human subject, according to Lacan, lies in the inhuman interrelation among the signifiers, in linguistic structure—leading to an insistence on the primacy of the "letter" over the "spirit" in discourse:

> Of course, as it is said, the letter killeth while the spirit giveth life. We can't help but agree, having had to pay homage elsewhere to a noble victim of the error of seeking the spirit in the letter; but we should also like to know how the spirit could live without the letter. Even so, the pretensions of the spirit would remain unassailable if the letter had not shown us that it produces all the effects of truth in man without involving the spirit at all. (Lacan, 1966, p. 158)

Lacan therefore inverts the Cartesian dictum in this way: "I think where I am not [in the Other(A)], therefore I am where I do not think [in my everyday discourse]." Hence it is that "the ring of meaning flees from our grasp along the verbal thread" (Lacan, 1966, p. 166)—and this is true of the so-called normal person, who does not recognize it, as well as of the psychotic. Perhaps the little bit of ego, itself an illusion, which remains at the conclusion of a Lacanian analysis saves one from psychosis.

In any case, it would appear that Lacanian analysis rescues the analysand from one alienation, the specular identifications of the ego, to immerse him or her in another, the otherness of the linguistic order itself. Lacan says,

> If *it* speaks in the Other, whether or not the subject hears it with his ear, it is because it is there that the subject, by means of a logic anterior to any awakening of the signified, finds its signifying place. The discovery of what it articulates in that place, that is to say, in the unconscious, enables us to grasp at the price of what splitting (*Spaltung*) it has been constituted. (1966, p. 285)

The split subject, the subject beyond a subject, the acephalic subject, the "fading" subject, the subject who is not a subject in the usual sense—these are the concerns of Lacanian analysis. One is tempted to say that what is revealed here is the madness of a metatheoretical system which denies intentionality and reference. The result, one might conclude, is a therapeutic practice which offers no escape from the linguistic order which creates the conscious human subject, but which the conscious human subject does not create. In the next section, I will consider how a therapeutic practice informed by Sartrean premises, without simply rejecting all of the insights of Lacanian analysis, can offer a way out of this dilemma by resituating intentional praxis at the heart of the therapeutic endeavor.

A Sartrean Critique of Lacanian Analysis

The aim of depth therapy from a Sartrean perspective would be just the opposite of the aim of Lacanian analysis. It would be to increase the domain of real freedom in which Lacan simply does not believe, to transform hexis into praxis. Existentialist therapy would involve a movement not inward toward the symbolic unconscious, but outward toward an intersubjective and practico-inert world which can be grappled with and changed. From a Sartrean perspective, the only time an individual is the mere plaything of the signifiers is when, like Flaubert, this person has been badly inserted into language—by which Sartre means that he or she has accepted language as hexis rather than as praxis, as that which determines me without my using it to determine myself in return. Yet this is exactly the aim of Lacanian analysis—to bring the analysand to an appreciation of his or her "signifying dependence." Sartre would not, of course, claim that we are absolutely free with respect to our use of language; his position is not that of Humpty Dumpty in Lewis Carroll's *Alice in Wonderland*.[5] To believe that one can absolutely control the meaning and the impact of one's words is, as we have seen, just as much a matter of bad faith as to believe that one is absolutely a product of the symbolic order. Yet Sartre would aim at greater linguistic freedom, based (as we have learned from the Flaubert biography) on the recognition that words, far from being magical invocation, have reference and relevance to the "real" world of which the linguistic order itself, as a practico-inert field, is a part.

Thus unlike Lacanian analysis, a therapeutic practice based on Sartrean principles would not aim to take a client from recognition of the illusory nature of the ego to recognition of the "truth" of the linguistic unconscious. Rather, to the extent that the world of symbols imposes itself on me without my learning to use it to name and shape my experience, existentialist therapy would recognize that the world of symbols itself can become a support for an imaginary rather than a real existence (as Sartre claims happened with Flaubert). Although otherness will always invade a person in the form of the exigencies of the practico-inert, including those of the linguistic order, there is still for Sartre a translucid consciousness which supports—and may therefore cease to support—this otherness. Where such a view of praxis as free future-directed activity is missing, reality becomes a dream—or, at most, a disturbing "noise" in the street soon to be forgotten. Far from perceiving a disparity between phenomenal reality and the linguistic order, Sartre believes that the latter must come to be a means for grappling with—and possibly changing—the former.

Nor does Sartre see the ego as arising from a different area of experience than the linguistic order, since the ego requires for its reflective support certain linguistic determinations first learned from the Other. Yet even though the ego will remain on the side of the practico-inert (rather than simply "on the side of the in-itself," as in Sartre's earlier philosophy) if for no other reason than that it is sustained by these designations, the Sartrean ego is, as we have seen, amenable to purification where the Lacanian ego is not. This is so, of course, because for Sartre there is a prereflective consciousness to do the purifying; for Lacan, on the other hand, the otherness of the ego is absolute since it is composed entirely of identifications, whereas the "conscious" subject is composed entirely of significations. These differences in perspective will necessarily lead to significant differences in therapeutic approaches both to the ego and to insertion of the individual into the order of language.

To begin with, it should come as no surprise that the therapist with a Sartrean orientation will use as his or her main tool exactly that empathic comprehension and mirroring which Lacan proscribes.[6] Indeed, Sartre prescribes comprehension, which he defines as the understanding of individual or group praxis in terms of the purposes of its agents, as the primary method of inquiry for the social sciences in general. Later, apropos of the Flaubert biography, he explains that the "necessary attitude for comprehending a person is empathy" (quoted by Barnes, 1981, p. 9). Empathic comprehension, as we noted in an earlier chapter, is supplemented by intellection where this is necessary to grasp that which goes beyond individual praxis in the life of an individual or a group. But while Sartre admits that it is always possible to learn something about people from the perspective of analytical reason, structuralist or traditional, he believes that an exclusively analytical approach leaves out the one thing which makes human affairs comprehensible: free future-directed praxis.

Thus although one may certainly reduce any human action to its component elements, even creating an "ordinal mathematics" out of the "ossified structures of groups" (CDR, p. 561), one will not thereby understand the thing which makes us human—the ability to create, admittedly out of a sociomaterial world which already is, the "irreducibly new" (CDR, p. 58). Sartre therefore points out that while there is "no human action [including, of course, the act of speech] which cannot be decomposed, dismembered, transformed, and infinitely varied by an 'electronic brain,'" it would nonetheless "be impossible to construct or use an 'electronic brain' except within the perspective of a dialectical *praxis* of which the operations under consideration were merely a moment" (CDR, p. 562). It is this all important moment of praxis, of which contemporary artificial intelligence people as well as structuralist psychoanalysts might well take note, which analytical social science in general ignores.

Sartre maintains that the structuralist effort to analyze passive structures at the expense of praxis is a mistake. Although one may, as Lévi-Strauss claims he would like to do, invent a "genuinely logico-mathematical analysis" of social data (Lévi-Strauss, 1964, p. 31), this is not enough. And while Lévi-Strauss himself admits that his own use of mathematical symbols is purely illustrative and not meant to prove anything, Lacan is not quite so humble in his use of what he refers to as "mathemes" in his various (pseudo)mathematical graphs and charts and in his attempts to create "algorithms" of human experience. Lacan does not mean these as part of the truth of human existence; he believes that they illustrate this truth insofar as they graph the unconscious structures which create human subjects. Hence though Lacan repeatedly refers to psychoanalysis as "dialectical," his view of the dialectic is of an external combinatory of signifiers. And though Lacan claims that the therapeutic relationship is necessarily intersubjective, it is an intersubjectivity in which one of the partners plays dead.

Obviously, the existentialist therapist will not play dead. He or she will instead use his or her own humanness to understand the humanness of clients. This does not mean that the therapist will accede to the "demands" of the client; Lacan is right in thinking that Freudian "technical neutrality" guards against the analyst's becoming involved in the web of the analysand's neurosis. On the other hand, if the primary demand of any human being is a demand for recognition, as Lacan says, then the existentialist therapist does in a sense accede to this demand. There are, however, many machinations and strategies standing in the way of the client's asking for genuine recognition, strategies which were adopted in the wake of an original interpersonal failure. The existentialist therapist does not bow to these. Nor does the therapist with a Sartrean orientation try to accept the role which the parents originally abdicated—the role of valorization which ought to have given the infant a sense of absolute value. Since existentialist therapists are not Kohutian self psychologists, they will not try to fill in a client's missing "ego structure" in this way.

The key to working with failed mirroring is not to assume the parental role (Lacan is right about this), but rather to work with the client so that he or she can see what is missing and thus awaken from the sleep of hexis which this lack has induced. In this way, the therapist offers a mature version of positive reciprocity, which does involve recognition, instead of the infantile version of total acceptance. After all, the therapist is not a parent and can never take the place of a parent. Also, the goal of existentialist therapy is twofold: to awaken in the client the desire for recognition which was squelched in the first place and to promote the mutuality which transcends this position by encouraging the client to abdicate the hope of being the "object limit" of anyone's freedom. In this respect, existentialist therapy, like Lacanian analysis, is not oriented toward psychogenesis and real regression—though it would not avoid creating opportunities within the therapeutic context in which affective states which were previously proscribed could be experienced. Such affective unblocking would aim at facilitating an opening to a new present/future reality—though the means for facilitating this would, of course, differ depending on the complaint and the person.

Whatever approach it takes, however, existentialist therapy differs from Lacanian analysis. The latter is oriented toward acceptance and assumption of one's history as it is written in the laws of the signifiers, whereas the former would aim not at *amor fati* but at revolutionary praxis. The existentialist therapist does not have to play dead for the simple reason that he or she is not standing in for a symbolic order whose ultimate meaning is the murder of the thing in the advent of the word. Certainly, negation or lack of being is primary in Sartre's description of Being-for-itself, but Sartrean negation derives from a consciousness seeking to fill its lack in a future fullness rather than from a subject enmeshed in and created by the symbolic order.

Although Sartre might conceivably agree that *pro-jecting*, negating consciousness has invented language as a means to making absence present, he would never agree that language creates the lack. Rather, he would insist that negating consciousness is fundamentally and unalterably signifying (in the Sartrean sense of creating meaning) whether the material which it inscribes with significations be words, other material objects, or (at the level of fundamental need) the simple biological organism re-created down there in the future. And although the linguistic practico-inert may turn back on an individual to suggest or prescribe paths for praxis, this is not because the linguistic order has created the human subject, as Lacan thinks, but because the prior praxes inscribed there produce exigencies in the form of rigidified teleology.

As materialized praxis, words have reference. The paths they suggest (by both describing and prescribing) are paths in the world, not links in a self-enclosed system. Hence where words do not point to experience, where they are opaquely appreciated in themselves, as Sartre claims was the case with Flaubert, something is definitely wrong. The point of existentialist therapy, in working with a person such as Flaubert, would not be to induce in him or her a recognition of "signifying dependence" but to awaken linguistic praxis. Existentialist therapy would not aim at communication with the elusive Other(A), though it certainly would involve an examination of the practico-inert structures which have created exigencies in one's life. Rather, it would aim at promoting as authentic a communication as is possible with one's fellows. In a sense, the existentialist therapist, like the Lacanian analyst, answers the client at the point where "true speech" emerges. But Sartrean true speech differs from Lacanian true speech in that for Sartre such speech is addressed by a free praxis to another free praxis whose freedom is accepted and respected; it is an opening to the other person rather than to the Other(A). Of course, Lacan also insists that true speech is intersubjective, but what he seems to mean by this is that it is addressed from one self-conscious link in the signifying chain to another rather than from free praxis to free praxis.

At the same time that there are fundamental disagreements, however, existentialist therapy would not deny the validity of all of Lacan's discoveries. Like other analytically oriented social science approaches, Lacanian analysis has a piece of the truth—though this piece, for full comprehension, must be recast in terms of the Sartrean dialectic. For instance, the Lacanian analysts in Schneiderman's collection do good work with examining what they call the patient's "prehistory"—the patient's position as a link in a particular cultural-familial system. Sartre, in the Flaubert biography, similarly considers an investigation of an individual's prehistory to be important to understanding both that individual's "protohistory" (the earliest mother-child interaction, which shapes the person's affective "constitution") and "history" (the person's historicization of himself or herself, the fundamental project).

Yet Sartre, unlike Lacan, does not attribute everything to the person's place in a particular transgenerational cultural-linguistic chain. Instead, he is interested in what an individual makes of what he or she is made of—the moment of praxis which Lacan in effect denies in favor of an account which makes everything of the practico-inert heritage. For Sartre, on the other hand, an individual is both constituted and constituting—and the important thing is to increase the domain of real freedom, to reconstitute oneself in such a way that the domain of hexis decreases.

Similarly, Sartre would not deny the importance of the effects of the father or of the cultural-linguistic order on individual development, nor would he disagree with the importance this is given in the cases reported in Schneiderman's collection. Although Lacan has accused Sartre of failing to find a "third term" which transforms the subject-object dyad (Lacan, 1975, p. 224), this is a valid criticism only for Sartre's earlier philosophy. In the *Critique*, as we have seen, the third term in the form of the regulatory third party is made the basis of social organization. As for the importance of the father, Sartre had as early as the biography of Baudelaire (1946a) recognized the connection between the failure of the father to intervene successfully in the mother-child dyad and the development of narcissism. In Baudelaire's case, Sartre maintains, it was the late and traumatic intervention of his mother's second husband, the authoritarian General Aupick, in the "incestuous couple" of mother and son which fixed Baudelaire's fate as a narcissist. As Douglas Collins notes, the influence of Angelo Hesnard's *L'individu et le sexe: Psychologie du narcissisme* is apparent in Sartre's study of Baudelaire's narcissism (Collins, 1980, pp. 60–79). According to Collins, "Before Jacques Lacan and Melanie Klein, Hesnard showed that the father, as the third party in the oedipal situation, is not only the hated and feared rival, but also the agent whose presence brings to a close the unlimited relationship between mother and child. If the separation of the child from the mother is particularly traumatic, the child becomes narcissistic" (1980, p. 66). This, of course, is exactly the trauma which Sartre presents Baudelaire as having suffered.

Actually, Baudelaire's childhood, as depicted by Sartre, is in some ways similar to Sartre's own. At the time of the death of his natural father when he was six, the young Baudelaire is depicted as feeling himself justified in his existence through the adoring eyes of his mother, as was Sartre himself. But his enjoyment of being part of this "incestuous couple" ended too abruptly when Baudelaire's mother married General Aupick a year later and afterward sent her son away to boarding school (Sartre also appears to have been affected by his mother's remarriage to Joseph Mancy, though this happened much later, when Sartre was twelve). Baudelaire, according to Sartre, would spend his life resenting this event and attempting to recover a sense of self as object through an overly developed reflective consciousness: "He was at once inside and outside, object and witness for himself; he introduced other people's eyes into himself so that he could look at himself as though he were another person" (B, pp. 85–86). One wonders if a similar decision to capture oneself as object through reflection is not at work in all narcissism—a decision which is extended to others who come within the narcissistic circle since their task is obviously to adoringly reflect the narcissist if they are not to be scornfully rejected by him or her. Certainly, behind narcissism lies a "wound" to self-esteem similar to the one Sartre says Baudelaire suffered.

Yet despite this almost Lacanian interpretation of Baudelaire's narcissism, it should also be noted that Sartre, unlike Lacan, has no love either for fathers or for the rules or laws of conventional society which they seem to represent. In his autobiography, Sartre announces his agreement with "the verdict of an eminent psychoanalyst: I have no Superego" (W, p. 19)—a development he attributes to the fortunate (for Sartre) circumstance that deprived him of a father before he was a year old. Perhaps if Sartre had undergone the analysis he proposed to Pontalis at the time he was working on his autobiography, he would have discovered that his grandfather had served as more of a father figure than Sartre himself realized. We cannot, however, for this reason discount Sartre's lifelong aversion to the prefabricated destinies he saw fathers as laying on their sons. As for himself, Sartre says, "Amidst Aeneas and his fellows who carry Anchises on their backs, I move from shore to shore, alone and hating those invisible begetters who bestraddle their sons all their life long. I left behind me a young man who did not have time to be my father and who could now be my son" (W, p. 19). Rather than the son of a dead man, whom he in any case did not remember, Sartre was given to understand that he was "a child of miracle." Sartre attributes his own "incredible levity" and sense of freedom to the impressions these early experiences left on him (W, p. 21).

The situation in the Flaubert household, as presented by Sartre in *The Family Idiot*, is just the opposite to Sartre's own. Sartre depicts Gustave's older brother, Achilles, as following the path of accepting such a prefabricated future, while Gustave, dispossessed from the beginning, finds a way out—albeit one which involved the "passive activity" of inventing on the psychosomatic level a nervous illness (hysterico-epilepsy) which prevented him from following the law career his imperious father had chosen for him. Part of Flaubert's dilemma, however, derives from his inability to use his father to find viable paths for himself in the world. It is his early maternal deprivation, rather than a too prolonged symbiosis or a failure of his father to assume the proper authority, which makes this impossible. According to Sartre, Flaubert, like many children whose first bonds with their mothers proved unsatisfying, looked to his father for a second mothering rather than for fathering. When his father also rejected him, it was more like a traumatic "second weaning" than the loss of a model for world making (FI, 2:24). Thus *The Family Idiot* is an indication of the possible uses of fatherhood as well as a comment on the abuses of patriarchy as represented by Achille-Cléophas Flaubert. Obviously, not all fathers are as authoritarian as those whom Sartre imagines as laying, or attempting to lay, prefabricated lives on their sons. We may therefore read Sartre's usual stance against fatherhood as a personal predeliction which is not a necessary consequence of his philosophical position.

What is fundamental in Sartre's later philosophy, however, is a matter which is also of great significance for existentialist therapy: his idea that human relations, linked in a world of humanized matter, are always ternary. The first third party may well be the father (or his representative) who intrudes into the mother-child dyad. But the importance of the ternary relationship in Sartre's philosophy is ultimately that it makes group relations, including relations within the family as a group, possible. The family, then, as a little unit organizing itself in the larger practico-inert field, becomes the transmitter of one's sociocultural heritage. One's mode of insertion into the family will therefore have great bearing on one's way of inserting oneself into later groups or into one's society as a whole. For Sartre, it is not just the father but the family group as a shifting complex of dyadic and ternary relations which shapes the mode of an individual's insertion into the practico-inert world of language and culture.

Where the traditional patriarchal family resembles the institutionalized or authoritarian group, the father (or mother) will, of course, assume more importance as each of the family members becomes serialized in relation to the patriarch or matriarch. But to believe, as Lacan does, that the third term is only a matter of the intrusion of paternal authority (in whatever form) is, from a Sartrean perspective, to fail to take ternary relations far enough. According to Sartre, aggressivity marks the authority-ridden family not because of a failure of the paternal metaphor which prevents specular identifications from being detoxified by the symbolic order, but because seriality in some form has invaded the family structure and positive reciprocity has failed to become the predominant mode in family dynamics.

The existentialist therapist would therefore work not on introducing a client with problems in the area of reciprocity to the law of the Name-of-the-father, but on looking at how a particular combination of earliest dyadic relations with failure in the family group itself (including the client's developing choices as a member of that group) has led to the development of these particular difficulties. This, of course, is the kind of analysis Sartre conducted on the Flaubert family. It is, I would submit, more complex than Lacanian analysis in that it considers not only the father, mother, and child but also the whole complex of family relations and relational failures.

Lacan and the Lacanian analysts are, however, again correct from a Sartrean perspective in seeing desire as linked to the symbolic-linguistic order. As we saw in Chapter 5, Sartre, like Lacan, believes that need is transformed into desire as the child becomes acculturated. Sartre would also agree that desire, unlike need, is that which on principle cannot be fulfilled. But this is so for Sartre because desire aims at the impossible goal of Being-in-itself-for-itself and not because it passes along an unending chain of elusive signifiers with their origins in the linguistic unconscious. According to Sartre, the lack has been instituted by negating consciousness, not by the linguistic order. Therefore, from a Sartrean perspective, it is possible to transform need/desire lived as hexis into need/desire lived as praxis at the same time that it is possible to transform negative reciprocity into positive reciprocity in interpersonal relations. And this transformation of conflictual relations is possible not because of a linguistic "pacification" of specular identifications, as Lacan believes, but because it is possible to arrive at a position where one respects and claims as a fundamental value one's own and the Other's freedom. Obviously, a therapeutic practice based on Sartre's assumptions about desire will be radically different from a therapeutic practice based on Lacan's assumptions. The future, for Sartre, is open, whereas for Lacan, it is in a certain sense closed.

Finally, Sartre would have to agree that Lacanian analysis has some beneficial contributions to make to psychotherapy in its refusal to substantialize the ego. Yet although Sartre agrees with Lacan in viewing the ego as object rather than as subject and though he often sees the ego as a source of misunderstanding, the existentialist therapist would not take the Lacanian view of the ego as total mirage. The ego, as I noted in Chapter 6, is redeemable from a Sartrean perspective. Yet it is precisely to the extent that an individual's ego is other-directed (which to some extent, of course, the ego always is) that it is a false ego. Thus existentialist therapy would not aim at a Lacanian reduction of the ego in favor of an assumption of one's place in the symbolic order, but at a purging of the ego of as much of its alienating otherness as possible.

A Sartrean perspective does not, of course, suggest that the ego can cease to be "on the side of the in-itself" or that it will lose its affiliations with the practico-inert. One cannot step outside one's concrete situation, one's language, one's culture, and one's moment in history. It does mean, however, that one can begin to reflect on one's assumption of an identity (including cultural identifications) to the extent that it is based on the unchecked designations of others. If one is as passive as Flaubert, this may mean finding a way to verbalize one's experience of oneself as passivity and from there to begin the painful project of turning hexis into praxis. From a Lacanian perspective, it is difficult to see how one could do anything with the ego other than to discover and acknowledge its fundamental existence as illusion. But since for Lacan there is no translucid consciousness involved in the construction of the ego, it is difficult to see how any movement toward authenticity is possible. The most one could expect from such an analysis is an exposure to the rules of the game in which one is a pawn of the unconscious signifiers. But even then, to whom would they be exposed?

In summary, a therapeutic practice based on the metapsychological principles of Sartre would emphasize the link between praxis and the practico-inert, between individual freedom and sociocultural necessity, while giving primacy to praxis. It is to be contrasted with Lacanian analysis in that Lacan seems to have eyes only for what Sartre refers to as the linguistic practico-inert and thereby to advocate a therapeutic system which, taken to its logical conclusion, would promote hexis rather than praxis, stasis rather than change. If we take Sartre at his word, we have to recognize that a disembodied freedom without a practico-inert world in which to exercise itself is an impossibility; however much Sartre stands on the side of freedom over necessity, praxis needs the practico-inert. Thus while the existentialist therapist would encourage a movement from hexis to praxis, this would always be with the understanding that the practico-inert is the ground of praxis. Whereas for Lacan the symbolic order subsumes praxis, for the therapist with a Sartrean orientation desirable change is a movement from "being spoken" to "speaking," from passivity to authentic action. Thus while it is certainly true to say that in a world where praxis always occurs in conjunction with the practico-inert one is in some sense an effect as well as a cause, it is simultaneously true that for existentialist therapy the goal is to increase the domain of the individual as cause.

For the existentialist therapist, then, subjecthood is not to be found in the linkage of the signifiers. Rather, it is to be found in one's objectifying actions in a practico-inert world, including the linguistic order, in which one is always making something new of what the exigencies inscribed in the practico-inert have made of one. Existentialist therapy must also be sensitive to the ways in which an individual's desire has been cut off, muted, or deviated by other people directly or indirectly through the exigencies of the practico-inert, sometimes to the extent that a person moves toward the imaginary rather than toward the real. Such a person must be encouraged to find a way to reinsert himself or herself not only into the symbolic order but also into the real (practico-inert) world. From a Lacanian perspective, engagement is not what I am looking for; rather, I am looking to assume the opacity of the signifiers which constitute me. The difference in these positions, I believe, makes a great deal of difference to the way one conducts therapy—either from the position of otherness itself (by impersonating the Other[A], by playing dead, and by assuming that one's task is to bring one's patient to an appreciation of his or her "signifying dependence") or from the position of sameness which is comprehending praxis. Obviously, I prefer the latter to the former of these two positions.

Conclusion

As we come to the end of these three chapters answering the challenge of Lacanian structuralist psychoanalysis to Sartrean existential psychoanalysis, I think it might be well to summarize our findings. Although Lacanian analysis at first seems promising as an alternative to the egological emphasis of most post-Freudian psychoanalytic theory, it does not fulfill this promise. I believe this is so because Lacan, like the structuralists in general, throws the baby out with the bath water. Intending to discredit the transcendental ego, the structuralists deny the notion of transcendent consciousness altogether. Lévi-Strauss even accepts Paul Ricoeur's description of his own version of structuralism as "Kantism without a transcendental subject" (Lévi-Strauss, 1964, p. II). In fact, Lévi-Strauss goes so far as to assert that the aim of structuralism is "not to constitute but to dissolve man" and in doing so to provide for "the reintegration of culture in nature and finally of life within the whole of its physico-chemical conditions" (Lévi-Strauss, 1962, p. 247). Certainly, Lacan would see this aim as a return of the speaking subject to the linguistic unconscious which constitutes that subject.

To take the viewpoint which apparently is Lacan's—that human reality has its origins in a situation of mistaken identity (the specular ego) and that the order of the signifiers is ascendant over the signifying human subject—is from a Sartrean perspective to take a position beyond the world which eliminates the possibility for genuine praxis. The Lacanian ego does not admit of transformation in the same way that the Sartrean ego does; and the truth of the Other(A) is a dead rather than a living truth. The true speech at which Lacanian analysis aims is a speech which is not true speech in the Sartrean sense at all since, as Lacan says, it is a "speech which is in the subject without being the speech of the subject" (1978, p. 171).

Although Sartre would consider language to be practico-inert and although he is aware of its exigencies, he would maintain that if speech is not praxis, it serves no authentic purpose and opens up no genuine intersubjective possibilities. The opacity which Lacan attributes to the signifiers is for Sartre an opacity combined with praxis which points not to a controlling unconscious realm which lends an opacity to the human subject it defines, but rather to a common practico-inert field which all of us must work and work as creatively as possible. For Sartre, the person who is attracted to the opacity of language itself rather than to the transcendent possibilities of speech is a person who is fleeing—or who has somehow failed to get a taste of—his or her freedom.

At times, Lacan's account of the return to the "truth" of the signifying chain which has been lost in the Other(A) sounds simultaneously like a great mystery and a great boredom, resembling the automatic writing of the surrealists whom Lacan admires (see Macey, 1988, pp. 44-74) and who suppose themselves to be putting Freud's great discovery of the unconscious to work in their automatic writings. I think this may be so partially because Lacanian analysis is ultimately on the side of stasis rather than of movement—of death rather than of life. Lacan himself says that life is "a detour, a dogged detour, in itself transitory and precarious and deprived of any significance" (1978, p. 232). Life, he goes on to say, "doesn't want to be healed. . . . All that life is concerned with is seeking as much repose as possible while awaiting death" (1978, p. 233).

One might, of course, agree that a life enmeshed in the opacity of signifiers without reference is indeed a living death. I do not, in any case, see a basis for Lacanian analyst Moustapha Safouan's idea that the Lacanian journey through the corridors of death leads to a courtyard where the analysand experiences "death's death" (in Schneiderman, 1980, p. 166). Rather, it seems to me that any metatheory which is to be life-oriented must provide a sense of intentionality and freedom that allows an opening toward the phenomenal world in which engagement, individual and group, is possible. A psychotherapy based on Sartrean metatheoretical principles, as I have argued throughout this book, offers such a possibility for authentic transformation based on a transformation of self and world together—since for Sartre the two are indivisible.

9 · Conclusion:
Toward a Sartrean Clinical Practice

Sartrean Metatheory and the Practice of Psychotherapy

Throughout this book, we have noted a compatibility-incompatibility between Sartrean existential psychoanalysis and traditional Freudian and post-Freudian psychoanalysis. Obviously, Sartre has learned much from Freud just as subsequent existentialist theory has much to learn from the post-Freudian psychoanalytic theorists. Sartre's own appraisal of the significance of psychoanalysis increased rather than decreased with time to the point where, in *Search for a Method*, Sartre asserts that psychoanalysis is the "one privileged mediation" (p. 61) which would allow a Marxist-oriented social theory to achieve an appropriately concrete understanding of particular individuals and particular historical events. His three-volume (unfinished) biography of Flaubert is both a final synthesis of all his philosophical ideas and a tribute to his persistent attempts to revise and refine existential psychoanalysis. Yet at the same time that the later Sartre remains convinced of the value of a psychoanalytic approach which takes into account the insertion of the individual in childhood into that person's class and culture, he also revises both Freudian psychoanalysis and Marxism from an existentialist perspective. The resulting metatheory is neither traditionally Marxist nor traditionally Freudian in its refusal to accept either historical or psychological determinism.

The later Sartre continues to place the existential project and free individual action, or "praxis," at the heart of group and other social relations. He continues to reject Freudian drive theory in favor of an intentionality which is meaning oriented, to favor a view of consciousness as translucid and free over the Freudian idea of the psyche as substance and structure, and to see

314

self-deception in terms of bad faith and reflective misconception or failure of conception rather than in terms of unconscious motives. While admitting in the Flaubert biography to the enormous impact of the early mother-child relationship on the very way in which a child comes to grasp self/world as praxis or hexis, activity or stasis, Sartre nonetheless views an individual's "personalization" as a constantly developing project which includes this original "constitution" even as it surpasses it. A life, according to such a view, involves not static repetition or fixed character structure but a spiral which "passes again and again by the same points but at different levels of integration and complexity" (SM, p. 106).

Although need rather than desire now provides the bedrock connection between the individual and the sociomaterial world, need (like desire) is defined as a future-directed project, the project of renewal of the organism, and is seen as being slowly shaped by one's experiences into desire. The later Sartre, unlike the earlier Sartre, also recognizes the enormous power of groups and of the practico-inert, particularly of the family group and of language and culture, to shape an individual's project; but he insists at the same time that free individual praxis creates and sustains groups and other cultural forms. Presumably, radical change through conversion to a philosophy of freedom is still possible.

Thus while the later Sartre attempts to account for the insertion of the individual into language and culture, he nonetheless rejects the new synchronic determinism represented by structuralism. And although Sartre believes that structuralism has some contributions to make in analyzing cultural and linguistic structures, he maintains that structuralism, like analytical social science in general, fails to account for novelty. Sartre would therefore refuse to view Lacanian analysis as providing a solution to the problems in post-Freudian psychoanalytic theory surrounding the idea of a substantialized ego—an idea to which Lacan and Sartre both object. In disposing of transcendent consciousness along with the transcendental ego, Lacanian analysis appears to leave no room for either individual freedom or significant therapeutic change.

Indeed, in some respects mainstream post-Freudian psychoanalytic theory has more to offer than Lacanian analysis to the psychotherapist with an existentialist orientation. Although from a Sartrean perspective the traditional post-Freudians are incorrect in substantializing the ego and the self, they have nonetheless provided more in the way of understanding the interpersonal needs of childhood and the needs for an authentic sense of self than the Lacanians. It is the understanding of these nondrive-related needs on the part of the theorists discussed in this book which have caused me to propose that the new wine of post-Freudian psychoanalytic insights bursts the old bottles of traditional psychoanalytic metatheory. These bottles are not mended, however, by Lacanian structuralist psychoanalysis. What is needed is a metatheoretical perspective which accounts both for the new relational needs and for cultural "necessity" without denying the primacy of the free individual. I argue that Sartrean metatheory provides such a perspective.

In the third chapter of this book, I noted that the needs for adequate mirroring, emotional resonance, and interpersonal relatedness from earliest infancy discovered by the post-Freudian drive theorists in reality point to an overthrow of the Freudian pleasure principle in favor of a Sartrean concept of the significance of the Other as subject (rather than as need-gratifying object) to a child's developing sense of self. The objective is not instinctual gratification but human valorization. A Sartrean approach to human development would therefore look for a series of existential crises leading ideally to the development of a mature capacity for reciprocal love in which I am able to respect my own and the Other's freedom rather than for the laying down of a firm ego structure. Failure to develop this capacity would be regarded as leading to sadomasochistic and other relations in bad faith in which one attempts to *use* others to create a self. Sources of such failed reciprocity, as well as those failures in self-esteem which are omnipresent in therapy, would be investigated from the perspective of attempting to understand how the looks, touches, and words of the original others led to the development of present difficulties.

As for the Sartrean ego, it must be viewed as an object of consciousness rather than as a psychic structure in consciousness. Thus the goal of therapy is not to strengthen the ego in the Freudian sense, but rather to promote accurate self-reflection together with a confrontation with the ontological truth that one can never become a substantive entity—though one may certainly value and take responsibility for the ego (in the Sartrean sense) or self one has created and is continually in the process of creating/re-creating.

Similarly, although existentialist therapy has something to learn from the ideas about the self proposed by the post-Freudian relational theorists discussed in Chapter 4, the self from a Sartrean perspective can never be viewed as substantive. And although these theorists understand very well the interpersonal origins of most psychological distress, they create confusion by discussing the self as if it were simultaneously a substantive entity and an active center of personality organization and choice. We have seen that much of this confusion can be cleared up if we follow a Sartrean distinction between the self as agent, the self as object or ego, and the self as aim or value. Indeed, faulty relations between reflective and prereflective consciousness, in which the self as agent fails to accurately reflect or understand the self as object as this relates to the self as value, are responsible for much human misery. Nor does existentialist therapy aim at the discovery of a "true self" hidden somewhere beneath the disguise of a "false self," as psychoanalytic theorists following Winnicott would insist. Rather, it aims at a radical conversion to a philosophy of situated freedom which will undermine the various structures of bad faith or lying to oneself about one's freedom or one's facticity which have kept one trapped in interpersonal and intrapersonal inauthenticity.

"Pure reflection" is the reflective mode in which such change is able to take place, since it is only in something approaching pure reflection that I am able to let go of that false substantializing by which accessory reflection turns choices into qualities or states of being and thereby to grasp my fundamental project as an existential choice. Pure reflection, therefore, can precipitate one of those psychological instants in which a new choice of a way of being in the world may be made. Since such instants are feared as much as they are hoped for, it is the task of the existentialist therapist to be aware of their appearance and of that form of resistance which cannot be understood as resistance to this or that disclaimed feeling or idea but as *resistance to change as such*. The repetition compulsion, according to such a view, may be reconceived as a desire for the security of the known over the fearful confrontation with a self who never *is* but is instead always in the process of *becoming*. If the therapist understands that such resistance is a matter of existential anguish rather than a manifestation of the death instinct, then the therapist will be better able to aid the client in confronting that anguish and letting go of the past.

Lacanian structuralist psychoanalysis, although it notes the problem, does not provide a comparable solution to the substantialization of the ego or the self on the part of mainstream post-Freudian theorists. This is so because Lacan replaces a view of the psyche as substance and psychological structure (ego, superego, id) with a view of the psyche as imaginary imprinting underlying linguistic structure. Although Sartre's association with the structuralists may in part have provoked him to attempt to develop in his later philosophy a social theory which goes beyond the individual psychology and dyadic relations described in his earlier work, he accepts structuralism as representing only a part of the truth of human affairs. By taking the moment of the linguistic practico-inert as the whole truth and by making the conscious subject a plaything of the unconscious symbolic-linguistic order, Lacan appears to invert the actual state of affairs and to leave Lacanian psychoanalysis without a viable approach to change.

The later Sartre rejects all analytical social science approaches in favor of a dialectical approach which gives priority to event over structure and reintroduces the existential project as the basis for the dialectical relationship between human beings and the material world. Existential psychoanalysis can, of course, learn something from Lacanian analysis in recognizing the power of language in shaping an individual's project—though an existentialist perspective will insist that the power of language comes from the exigencies inscribed in a practico-inert field rather than from unconscious "laws." Like Lacanian analysts, existentialist therapists will want to look at a client's prehistory as well as at his or her history. They will want to question how a client was inserted into his or her family group and through this into the larger history and culture. Existentialist therapists will, however, want to move beyond structuralism to question from a Sartrean perspective the ways in which serial and group relations, including other-direction and the structures of fraternity-terror, inhibit a client from changing in a positive direction. And in addition to recognizing the power of the practico-inert and of groups in shaping an individual's fundamental project, they will want to look at what a client has made of what he or she is made of—at the novelty which each individual and each generation introduces, whether positive or negative. And they will want to encourage the conversion of hexis into praxis.

In working with clients from these perspectives, existentialist therapists will, of course, regard their own role in the therapeutic enterprise differently from either Lacanian analysts or traditional Freudian analysts. Throughout this book, the emphasis has been on a view of the client-therapist relationship which is nontraditional in regarding the therapist as a participant in a therapeutic process which aims not at objectivity in the usual sense but at empathic comprehension. This does not mean, of course, that therapy is an enterprise like any other, that the therapist does not have a sense of the direction of the therapy, or even that those phenomena which Freud refers to under the heading of "transference" do not occur. They certainly do. But the existentialist therapist sees both the transference and his or her own role in handling it differently than the traditional Freudian analyst does. I have noted, for instance, that transference is an aspect of a person's future-directed project rather than mere repetition of the past. Sartre believes that it emanates not from a repetition compulsion associated with the death instinct but from a fundamental choice of self in a particular interpersonal world which may have imaginary as well as real components. Furthermore, an existentialist perspective on the client-therapist relationship would not reduce the whole relationship to the workings of transference and countertransference. Rather, a part of the goal of therapy would be a movement toward positive reciprocity within a developing real relationship.

Perhaps these differences can be further clarified by taking another look at the incident of the man with the tape recorder mentioned in Chapter I. Pontalis, who is certainly an eminent psychoanalyst, regards Sartre's insistence on publishing the transcript of this incident in *Les Temps Modernes* as proof positive that Sartre does not understand the role of transference in the psychoanalytic process (Pontalis in BEM, p. 220).[1] And there is no doubt that Sartre, who did not know the clinical process firsthand, did not fully understand these issues. Yet the man with the tape recorder's appearance in his analyst's office with a device which might help him turn the tables on his analyst, reversing the subject-object roles in the therapeutic dyad, perhaps points to a "transference" issue of which Freud himself, lacking a Sartrean perspective on the subject-object conflict, was undoubtedly unaware.

I am referring, of course, to the fact that children experience an imbalance in the Look: The Look of the parents at the child is more powerful than the child's Look at the parents for the simple reason that the parents, as the first powerful others, have more impact on the child's developing sense of self. Thus most of us resonate to some extent with the idea of a powerful Look which cannot be looked at—the Look of God, if you will. It is also probably true that to some extent clients always project this all-powerful Look onto their therapists. Indeed, we have seen that a part of the therapeutic process involves the therapist's acting as a counter to the parents as original mirrors—thereby facilitating the client's taking a meta-reflective position on his or her own reflective process as it is contaminated by the voices of the original others. But I believe it is equally important for the therapist, by the end of therapy, to have decisively refused this position of power. In other words, I think it is important, insofar as this is possible, for the Looks of the therapist and the client to be equalized. Otherwise, though the client may have learned much in the therapeutic context, he or she has not learned the positive reciprocity between equals which is one of the aims of existentialist therapy.

It is obvious from the dialogue which the man with the tape recorder records with his analyst that reciprocity is exactly what this man's analyst does not wish to allow. Rather, he wishes to designate without being designated—to look without being looked at. In a parody of Aristotle's idea of God as the "unmoved Mover," we might designate the therapist who takes such a position as the "unlooked-at Looker." It is this illusion of om-nipotence which the intrusion of the tape recorder apparently breaks, finally reducing the terrified analyst to emitting a series of cries for help which cul-minate in "a final dismal sound like a dying animal—followed by a long si-lence" (BEM, p. 218). There is no doubt that the analysand's act is an act of aggression—or is it, as Sartre maintains, an act of counteraggression? In any case, it not only breaks the analyst's "neutrality," it also exposes his posture as the all-knowing observer for the ruse that it is.

Sartre comments that he finds this incident fascinating because it spot-lights "the irruption of the *subject* into the consulting room, or rather the overthrow of the univocal relationship linking the subject to the object"— that is, the analyst to the analysand. The analysand's rebellion is provoked by the analytic situation itself—a situation in which the analyst, as "the in-visible and silent witness to the discourse of the patient . . . transforms his speech, even as it is uttered, into an object." Sartre continues,

> Why? For the simple reason that there could never be any reciprocity between these two figures, the one lying on the couch, his back to an-other sitting down, invisible and intangible. . . . [The analysand] is dis-appointed, it is true; he takes it out on his doctor and some will say that he thus merely demonstrates an incomplete transference, gone awry. But how are we to answer him when he tells us that a 'patient's' cure has to begin with a face-to-face encounter in which each person takes his chances and assumes his responsibilities? . . . The interpretation should be proposed to *him* in the course of a long common adventure, in *interiority*, and not 'come' to him anonymously, like stone tablets. This particular subject hopes to gain some comprehension of himself as a damaged, derailed subject. For lack of any inter-subjective collabora-tion, he 'acts it out'—as analysts say—which means he turns praxis, and the situation, upside-down. In the 'Psychoanalytical Dialogue,' the roles are reversed, and the analyst becomes the object. For the second time, a rendezvous of man with man is missed. This episode, which some people will find funny, represents a tragedy of impossible reciproc-ity. (BEM, pp. 200–202)

Existentialist therapy aims not to repeat this tragedy. Sartre, however, is not simply objecting to the technique of having the analysand lie on the couch.

Indeed, in a footnote, he states that "depth psychology . . . presupposes a general loosening of self-abandon on the part of the patient, and thus makes the couch mandatory." Rather, Sartre is objecting to a situation in which "no progress will be made unless both approaches [reciprocal humanness and the loosening of ordinary reality, which is achieved by some technique such as lying on the couch and free associating] are grasped together" (BEM, p. 205).

A therapist working from a Sartrean orientation, then, will approach the people he or she works with in therapy not from a position of godlike objective observation or even from a position of immovable and antiseptic neutrality—though we have seen that there are times when neutrality is an appropriate counter to a client's attempts to suck the therapist into the client's interpersonal project. There are also times, and some modern psychoanalytic theorists are recognizing this (see, for example, Masterson and Klein, 1989), when other attitudes are more appropriate—for example, empathic mirroring, confrontation, collegial working on a common project, or even sharing of self.[2] Obviously, sensitivity to the client and the situation ought to determine the therapist's response.

On the other hand, existentialist therapy is neither a matter of manipulation nor of nonparticipation. In fact, the existentialist therapist, unlike certain modern Freudians who attempt to model an unchanging healthy ego for the analysand, risks change along with the client in the therapeutic process. This risk is inherent in an approach which prescribes empathic comprehension supplemented by intellection, together with active engagement with the object of study, as the appropriate means to knowledge in the human sciences in general. The necessity for such risk is even more evident in the practice of psychotherapy than in other social science approaches since psychotherapy is by definition both a common project and a combination of knowledge and praxis. If in my work as a therapist my own humanness is the only means I have to understanding/affecting the humanness of my client, then it is obvious that in order to achieve that understanding/efficacy, I have to risk myself. One cannot engage deeply with a client in the (mutual) project of therapy without being in turn deeply affected by that project.

Furthermore, as I have noted, the existentialist therapist does not take the position of the one who knows what is in the client's unconscious. Although as a therapist I may suspect that the client is hiding things from himself or herself through various strategies of bad faith, I will understand that the truth has not been reached until the client recognizes it. In other words, I will accept Sartre's dictum that the "final intuition of the subject is decisive" in existentialist therapy (BN, p. 574). Nor will I, as an existentialist therapist, attempt to reach the "truths" of the linguistic unconscious by playing dead or impersonating the Other(A), as the Lacanian analyst does. From a Sartrean perspective the Other(A) is simply the antidialectic of the linguistic practico-inert and not the Lacanian unconscious subject beyond the conscious subject. Rather than the object of unconscious forces or structures, the client in existentialist therapy is regarded as a conscious subject who plays an active role in the therapeutic process—the role of allowing that pure reflection from which deep change springs. And it is the client's discoveries in the mode of pure reflection, and not the speculations of the therapist (however probable), which provide the truths of existentialist therapy.

The existentialist therapist, unlike either the Lacanian or the traditional Freudian analyst, will also not forget that good therapy is both regressive and progressive—that it attempts to establish the conditions under which a given fundamental project came into being (including the individual's insertion into language and other practico-inert structures) together with the ways in which the individual has come to transcend those givens in a particular direction. Instead of reducing human lives to static structures or unconscious forces, the existentialist therapist will attempt to catch the future-directedness of a client's past or present project—where a client was/is going as well as where he or she came from. While it is certainly true that good psychoanalysts (like good therapists of any persuasion) have their portion of humanness and empathic comprehension, the emphasis in traditional psychoanalysis on investigating the past as ground to the neglect of the future as meaning has sometimes led to those therapeutic impasses in which a client seems to learn more and more *about* the past conditions of his or her difficulties without experiencing significant change. Traditional psychoanalysis neglects the psychological instant and the fear of change as such which are so important to existentialist therapy.

Finally, the existentialist therapist will not hide behind a generalized nosology in order to distance himself or herself from clients, nor will he or she neglect the sociomaterial as well as the individual strains in a client's fundamental project. There is, of course, some usefulness in nosological categories such as neurotic, psychotic, borderline, narcissistic, and schizoid if one understands that they are descriptions of general strategies for solving the problem of Being rather than actual illnesses. But these categories should not be used to exempt the therapist from attempting to fully understand a client's project in all of its rich particularity—including the particularities of the structures of bad faith which the person may have adopted. After all,

there are many concrete means—many ways of doing, being, and having—
which I may employ to flee my freedom and/or to flee my facticity. Indeed,
the existentialist therapist must even avoid falling into ontological overgeneralization. As Sartre points out over and over again, the ontological
structures manifest themselves not *behind* concrete lived experience but *in*
lived experience. Hence concreteness and particularity take on a significance in existentialist therapy which they do not have in other systems.

There is, however, one area where the existentialist therapist should be attentive not to particularity but to its lack. This is where a client has adopted
strategies of other direction in response to serial impotence, simple submission or hexis rather than genuine praxis in response to the exigencies of the
practico-inert, or conformity to group norms in response to the pressures of
fraternity-terror. Of course, there is a sense in which all of us are "concrete
universals" rather than concrete individuals. But where the general tends to
efface the particular so that one's own life is lived as the life of the Other,
this situation needs to be recognized and worked with. To the extent that an
individual has become "overgeneralized" or "overuniversalized," it is the
task of existentialist therapy to work toward the awakening of authentic individual and/or group praxis as an antidote to serial impotence, other direction and overconformity. Although Sartre's social theory adds a new dimension to existentialist therapy, it does not change its fundamental aim—to aid
a person in matching the ontological freedom which is the condition of our
being human with a greater practical freedom to live, to love, and to engage
in an authentic process of self-creation which is fluid rather than static. The
later philosophy adds the caveat that this self-making process must occur in
a sociomaterial world whose exigencies and counterfinalities we attempt to
recognize without allowing them to crush us.

In approaching a client's past/present experiences of being grouped or of
submitting to the exigencies of the practico-inert, the existentialist therapist
will need to use his or her own experiences in the sociomaterial world as a
basis for understanding—just as one hopes that the therapist will be able to
use his or her own experiences of turning hexis into praxis and of developing positive reciprocity in pointing to the direction of healing. Yet it is only
to the extent that the therapist is aware of the sociomaterial depths of his or
her own project, the insertion into his or her own class or social group in
the family of origin, that the therapist will be able to aid the client in exploring this dimension of the client's fundamental project. If the therapist does
not understand that his or her own life (like the life of the client) is "centuries old" at the same time that it is completely new, then the therapist will

perhaps explore well the individual dimensions of a client's difficulties without taking into consideration the sociomaterial dimensions. Or, worse yet, the therapist may mistake a group or serial phenomenon for an individual symptom without catching a glimpse of the interconnection between the two.

Obviously, the ideal existentialist therapist will be able to use the insights of both the early and the later philosophy of Sartre to aid a client in clarifying both the individual and the sociomaterial dimensions of that client's project. It is a large task. And though most of us will probably fall short of this ideal, it does remind us of the immense complexity of the issues involved in the practice of psychotherapy.

While I have throughout this book attempted to suggest ways in which the metatheoretical premises of Sartre can be applied to clinical practice, I think it might be helpful, now that we have come to the end of this process of laying out those premises, to give a more detailed clinical example. The case history in the next section does not demonstrate all of the insights I have discussed here and in preceding chapters, but it does demonstrate many of them, including the ways in which needs may be shaped as hexis rather than as praxis; the power of fraternity-terror in enforcing family norms; the significance to clinical insights of a Sartrean view of the ego as object versus the Freudian view of the ego as a center of reality orientation; the impact of failed mirroring in early childhood on later difficulties; the importance of considering ontological issues in "diagnosing" a client's "problem"; and the effect on the therapist of participating in the joint project of therapy.

I would also like to note that this book is intended as a beginning, a prologue to Sartrean studies in existentialist therapy, rather than as any final word on the subject. I am aware, as I said in the first chapter, that others have used Sartre together with other existentialist philosophers to develop a more generalized existentialist approach to psychotherapy. Although I find those approaches very interesting and useful, my own approach has been to try to explore the significance of a systematic application of Sartre's ontology and social philosophy to the issues of depth psychotherapy. In comparing and contrasting Sartre's metatheory with traditional and not so traditional psychoanalytic approaches, I have not, of course, had time to follow many interesting avenues of inquiry, both theoretical and practical. Therefore, in the final section of this chapter, I suggest some directions for future inquiry—though I am sure there are many others. My own hope, as I said in the introduction, is that this book will provoke further inquiries into the usefulness of Sartre's ideas for clinical theory and practice.

A Sartrean Case History: Martha the "Marvelous Mirror"

The case I will discuss here is the story of "Martha," a young woman in her early thirties who at the time she began therapy with me was working as a psychotherapist at a local college and experiencing an acute personal crisis. Before beginning to tell Martha's story, I should probably say why I chose it. Although Martha's story might not be the most dramatic example of Sartrean themes among the people I have worked with, I think it does provide a significant illustration of those themes which is in no way unusual among my clients in general. I thought that a fairly typical example might be more useful than one which was more striking but less "usual." At the same time, of course, Martha was very much an individual with issues and concrete choices which were particular to her and her alone. I hope that the reader will find the story of our unraveling the various turns in her original project as engrossing as she and I found it to be in the joint work of psychotherapy.

The reader has probably already noted, however, that Martha's case is unusual in at least one respect: Martha was herself a psychotherapist. Because this was so, I think it may be easier for me to talk about the impact her therapy had on her therapist, especially as it touched on issues surrounding our common profession. Certainly, I am deeply affected when I work with other clients as well, but it seemed somehow less difficult to identify this in my work with Martha. Also, Martha's issues as a therapist augment the points I wish to make about how it is impossible for the therapist as a person *not* to be involved (for good or ill) in the therapeutic process—and how the choice of the profession of psychotherapy always relates to the therapist's own fundamental project. Finally, I have chosen Martha's story because she very graciously permitted me to tell it in some detail—though I have changed certain distinguishing features in order to protect her identity.

As Martha worked with me (once, twice, and occasionally three times a week) over a three-year period, her work seemed to fall into three more or less distinct stages. The initial stage, which lasted around seven to eight months, involved an exploration of the crisis which had brought her into therapy and its relationship to the ontological structure of her fundamental project. Although we explored some of Martha's personal history during the first stage, this work deepened considerably during the second stage, which lasted approximately a year and a half. During this time, Martha was increasingly challenged to confront and to understand her fundamental project both in its regressive and progressive dimensions—and to question how she came to be who she thought she was and to see whether she wished to continue to live her life as she was living it.

As her work deepened during this second stage, Martha found herself increasingly confronting issues which probably had their origin in a past she no longer remembered or had never personally lived—issues which undoubtedly originated during infancy and earliest childhood (which Sartre refers to as a person's "protohistory") and even in the family situation into which she was born (which Sartre designates as one's "prehistory"). In working with such material, one is dealing with highly elusive feelings, impressions, and convictions which have never been reflectively examined, partially because they go so far back and partially because they seem to be so much a part of the fabric of what oneself/one's world *is* that one has never thought to challenge them. The final seven or eight months of therapy dealt primarily with the existential crisis which developed as Martha faced the ramifications of her work and confronted the possibility of making profound and far-reaching changes in her fundamental project of being.

I should probably add that in dividing Martha's therapy into "stages," I do not mean to imply that the same themes did not appear again and again throughout the course of therapy or that there was not considerable overlap between them. Rather, I think that something like the gradual deepening of insight leading to an existential crisis of greater or lesser intensity which inaugurates a radical reorientation of a client's fundamental project such as I describe here often happens in existentially oriented psychotherapy. This is one of the ways in which I find Martha's therapy "typical" of many clients with whom I have worked. I am not at all sure that this is as typical of the experience of depth therapists working from more traditional models. Although I do not deny that Martha's difficulties might be explicable from other points of view or even that my work with her was influenced by the insights of classical and contemporary psychoanalysis, I contend that attention to the ontological/existential issues made a great deal of difference to the resolution of her difficulties in the context of our work together.

Stage One. The first stage of therapy dealt primarily with investigating the ontological structure of Martha's fundamental project and some of its historical underpinnings as these related to the severe personal crisis with which she entered therapy. This crisis, as often happens, revolved around the breakup of a love relationship. Martha's lover of three years had just left her—as it turned out, for a relationship with a man. The fact that "Mark" was bisexual was not so much the issue, however, since Martha had known this from the beginning. Nor was the problem exactly that he had left her for someone else, though this was deeply painful to her. The relationship, it seems, had been on a downward spiral for almost a year anyway. What was shocking to Martha was the effect the dissolution of this relationship had on her.

As Martha described it, she felt completely disoriented by Mark's leaving, as though he had taken with him her sense of who she was. "Nothing seems real," she told me. "I can't get my feet on the ground. I just feel like running and there's no place to run to." She experienced extreme panic over being alone, a panic which sometimes impelled her to call (or call on) friends in the middle of the night. She felt that she was very "forgetful" and "disconnected"—as though she were going through the motions of living without really being present. Sometimes she could not remember what she had done or said in a recent interaction. At the same time, Martha carried on in her head endless dialogues in which she attempted to "justify my existence" to her former lover. In fact, only at these times did she lose the anxiety which otherwise characterized her mental and emotional state when she was alone. It was replaced by pain and depression over the impossible task of "convincing a phantom of my value as a person."

We began our work together with the focus of Martha's own attention—the lost love relationship. Indeed, for several months, Martha did nothing but talk obsessively about Mark. Her pain was so palpable and the sense I had of her fragility so strong that most of the time I simply lent a sympathetic ear, reflecting back what I heard about her difficulties. During this period, I had an image of myself as a life raft at which Martha was clutching in the midst of a stormy ocean. Her hopes of restabilization seemed to rest on my constancy. After about two months, when I felt that Martha was a little stronger, I began to confront her about the meaning of her obsessive ruminations about her former lover, suggesting that there must be something which these "dialogues" were giving her that she held so tenaciously to them.

This led to the first crisis in therapy. Martha withdrew, saying she was unsure whether I could understand her. She also began to lecture me about therapeutic method—claiming she deserved from me the same "unconditional positive regard" she offered to her own clients as a Rogerian nondirectional therapist. This was the initiation of what Martha herself would later designate the "marvelous mirror" theme—the idea that Martha ought somehow to be able to find the ideal mirroring she attempted to offer to others, friends and lovers as well as clients. As it turned out, one of the most difficult—and significant—tasks which Martha would face in therapy would be accepting the fact that I was not and could not be the perfect mirror which she longed to find in a therapist.

For the time being, I replied that it was hard to watch Martha continue to wound herself in this way without saying something. Her rage at me over this confrontation grew more vocal before it began to subside, as she appeared to make a new choice to look more deeply at the meaning of these dialogues in the larger context of her life and at the significance of her desire to find the perfect mirror. In most of her relationships, it seems, Martha had played the listener, the facilitator, the "mirror." In this position, she had rarely felt that her feelings and concerns took center stage or were even of much interest. During a two-year marriage during graduate school, for example, she had "nurtured" her husband through his Ph.D. and then split up with him when he moved to another city to begin a successful career. But although this was painful, it was nothing like the pain she was experiencing now over the breakup with Mark. She began to ask herself why this was so.

Martha's relationship with Mark, as she told it, had not been totally different from her other relationships in the beginning. Indeed, at first she had listened to him, drawn him out, even discussed with him in detail the ambiguities of his sex life—all in the interest of establishing an "openness" which she valued in relationships. As time went on, however, Mark had suggested that this openness was not exactly reciprocal and had indicated that he wished to know more about Martha as well. At first tentatively and then more and more obsessively, she began to tell him. The problem was that at the same time that Mark seemed to want to know her better on a "friendship" level, he distanced her physically. "Sex itself was OK," as Martha put it, "but he didn't want to hold me or cuddle with me." This caused Martha great pain—to the point where, as she said, "My skin burned with longing for his touch." During this time, if she reached out to him and saw him pull back, as she frequently did, she responded by weeping profusely, sometimes for hours. And she started to keep mammoth journals which she insisted on reading to him. Sometimes she went into rages if he seemed disinterested or critical. I reminded her of her recent rage with me over my lack of perfect mirroring, and she agreed that this felt somewhat similar—although she insisted that the experience with Mark had been much more intense.

The problem Martha experienced with her memories of this relationship, which had deteriorated considerably when they decided to live together during the third year, was that she "hated the person I became with him." She was now deeply chagrined by some of her behavior—for example, when she had put her fist through a window or when she had knocked dishes off a table in her rage over Mark's indifference to her. Finally, as the last year of their relationship dragged on, Martha had become severely depressed as Mark pulled away more and more. Although she still maintained in the back of her mind the hope that things would improve, she sank into a lethargy which made it difficult for her to get out of bed in the morning or to get through routine tasks of the day. Nonetheless, her work as a therapist, by her account, did not appear to suffer. "The only time *I* felt OK," Martha said, "was when I was working with a kid on *his* problems." She maintained that the same was true now; her anxiety or obsessive ruminations subsided only when she was working with others—an apparent anomaly which would be clarified later as we worked more deeply with her mirroring issues in the second stage of therapy.

For now, Martha began to understand her internal dialogues with Mark in a way that fits in well with Sartre's description of the "conflict of consciousnesses" and the attempt to use the other person to create a self. As we looked more carefully at these dialogues, the first thing that became apparent was that they centered around a desire to absolve herself of guilt in Mark's eyes. The problem was that as Martha began to imagine Mark's reactions to her, she could only imagine condemnation. For example, she imagined with excruciating pain what he must be telling his new lover about his relationship with her. Or she invented words for the slight smile of contempt she thought she saw on his lips when they met. A poem Martha wrote around this time expressed her feelings: In it she describes a woman who feels fixed like an insect at the end of a pin by her lover's hostile gaze. Obviously, what Martha was experiencing was the hostile Look of an Other who is beyond her influence—the Look which cannot be looked at, transforming her into an object which she does not wish to be but which she in some respects recognizes as herself. After all, Martha *had* subjected Mark to her obsessive self-ruminations, and it was she who had put her hand through the window in a masochistic rage over his indifference. She therefore felt that the Look of her lover which she carried within her was an irremediable judgment that she *was* this monster whom she had, as we later came to learn, spent a lifetime trying not to be.

At this time, some of the roots of Martha's pain over being this object which she imagined she was for Mark began to emerge. In her family of origin, the worst sin appears to have been "selfishness"—which was apparently defined as any attentiveness to one's own needs and interests. Martha's mother was herself a self-styled martyr whose worst accusation was the terrible pronouncement: "You only care about yourself." Martha, it seems, had always feared that this judgment, which she tried valiantly to disprove by being "unselfish," was the real truth about herself. It was against this accusation that her "understanding nature" had in part evolved as a counterposition. Her behavior with Mark therefore seemed to validate her deepest fears: She was, undeniably and irremediably, this self-centered person she had early on been accused of being. Her mother was right in her initial judgment of Martha. Her counteridentity as the helpful, other-oriented child had finally been exposed for the ruse she had always suspected it was.

Yet as Martha began to see all this, she began to see something else as well: The needs/desires which she as a child had worked so hard not to feel were really not so horrific after all. She was beginning to get some insight into how she had, by accepting her parents' mislabelings, begun to live them as hexis rather than as praxis. And though she did not yet appreciate how deeply these distortions went, she began at this time to feel anger and grief over the counteridentity which had evolved at such a sacrifice of spontaneity and authentic relatedness—so that she could now only grope in the dark to find what she really wanted and needed and to express this.

There was, however, more to Martha's reaction to her breakup with Mark than the fear of being the selfish and unacceptable object which she felt she was in his eyes and which she had always feared she would become in the eyes of her mother. Although she hated and feared the misery of being forever fixed as an object beneath his imagined gaze, there was nonetheless, as we began to discover, something she feared even more than this. Worse than the hostile Look is the indifferent Look. A question I asked Martha one day in therapy initiated this theme. I said something such as this: "You know, you keep imagining that Mark is thinking this or that about you, and you see that this continues to torment you. But the truth is that you don't really *know* what he's thinking at all. He might be thinking what you imagine, he might be thinking something else, or he might not be thinking anything at all. I wonder what it does for you to keep imagining that he's judging you in this way." Martha's response was a gasp followed by an explosion of tears which surprised me. "The *worst*," she proclaimed vehemently, "would be if he's not thinking anything at all. How can he *not think anything* when *I'm* so miserable? I *hate* him if he's not thinking anything at all."

This, it seems, was Martha's greatest fear—not being regarded at all. But what, she began to wonder, were its roots? After all, had she not been firmly established as the confidante of every member of her family? Surely she was not ignored when her mother spent hours discussing with Martha the difficulties with her husband and her mother-in-law (who had lived in the household since Martha's younger brother was born when she was two and a half); when her father discussed with her his business plans and difficulties and made her his "playmate"; and when even her grandmother and her two younger brothers confided their unhappinesses to her. Yet Martha now began to remember as well the lonely hours she had spent worrying over things, feeling isolated from schoolmates, and feeling that she had no one she could talk to about her own difficulties. It seemed that her family wanted to be with her when *she* was there for them, but that for some reason she did not expect them to be there for *her*.

At this point, Martha began to question her mother's "goodness" and her father's "strength," qualities she had previously taken for granted. If her mother was too harassed and busy to be there for her daughter and yet took full advantage of her daughter's willingness to be there for her, who was the "selfish" person in this family? Also, she remembered how her father's need to have her be a "happy" child had left her with a feeling of unreality about herself. She began to question who this child was who had been her adored father's favorite (for Martha was sure she had been her father's favorite child). After all, it was becoming increasingly apparent that this "happiness" which he had ascribed to her and which she had playacted for him had not been real. Also, Martha's father had been erratic in his attention to her— picking her up and putting her down (as she now realized) "like a toy which was there only for his amusement."

As Martha allowed herself to reexperience the loneliness of being a child in her family, she started to recall the bitter tears shed alone in her room, the taunts by schoolmates which could be shared with no one, and the unreality of being a child in a family where one's real needs and feelings were simply not acknowledged. Ultimately, her suspicion had been this: If I weren't there for them, would they care about me at all? Deep inside herself, she believed that they did not.

This suspicion that no one really cared, kept carefully at bay in most of Martha's relationships, was, of course, behind her outburst over the notion that Mark might not be thinking about her at all. She now began to understand that part of her motive for holding so tenaciously to the idea that Mark was criticizing her had been the terrible thought that he might simply be no longer concerned with her. Certainly, she hated and suffered from her obsessive fantasies, but this suffering warded off an even deeper suffering—the suffering of the person who is not even important enough to be judged. As she had done with her mother before him, Martha latched onto the idea that the reason she was being rejected was that she was "selfish" and "bad." The contrary idea that her mother was simply too preoccupied with her own difficulties to pay much attention to Martha was much more threatening—as was the idea that Mark might *not* be talking to his new lover about her.

In terms of the future-directed side of her project, Martha continued to hold onto the idea of her "badness" both as a way of having a self and as a means to believing that she might somehow become a "better" self at some time in the future. In other words, this strategy had evolved as a way of avoiding the despair of realizing that she was simply not deeply significant to either of her parents—or probably, in the present, to Mark. Only when she fully understood both sides of the motives for her unhappy internal dialogues—her desire to hold onto the negative Look of the Other in order to try to counter it and her desire to hold onto the negative Look of the Other in order to counter the deeper fear of not being important at all—was Martha able to let go of this relationship. This letting go constituted the end of what I have designated as the first stage of Martha's therapy.

Stage Two. The work of the second stage of Martha's therapy centered around her taking a deeper look at her present difficulties, at her family dynamics, and at the primitive underpinnings of her fundamental project—that is, at the infantile experiences which underlay her contemporary choice of a way of being in the world. This second stage was inaugurated by a shift in Martha's interactions with me during the therapy hour. Where before she had been a kind of fountain overflowing with misery, Martha now became hesitant and silent, complaining of feeling uncomfortably "on the spot" as she began each session. It appeared that I had begun to occupy the position of source of the disquieting Look—except that Martha now seemed to wish to escape my Look rather than to use it as a means to self-validation. Instead of pleading with me to see her accurately, she attempted to divert my attention elsewhere. She began, for example, to try to discuss general therapeutic issues with me or to ask me questions about myself—suggesting that knowing me better might lead to an increased trust which would facilitate the movement of her therapy.

I was suspicious of this request, especially since it was accompanied by a shift in Martha's relations with people outside the therapy room. She reported feeling that her "old self" had returned—the self she had been more comfortable with for most of her life. Despite the work we had done with the "selfishness" theme in her family, Martha was obviously quite relieved by this shift. She felt, as she put it, that she had become "less self-absorbed and more open to others." The question, of course, was whether she was sufficiently open to herself. Martha also became very absorbed in her work at this time, remarking that she approached it with a new energy and enthusiasm. I commented that she seemed to be more comfortable in the role of therapist than in that of client—with listening rather than being listened to—and she agreed. The question was why she should continue to prefer to be there for others at the expense of her own needs/desires.

About two months into this phase of therapy, Martha became briefly involved in a relationship with a rather narcissistic man which provided some keys to understanding these issues. "Harry" felt completely comfortable with Martha's attempts to draw him out and to place his interests and ideas in the limelight. Martha herself also felt comfortable with this arrangement, especially as it seemed to counter her suspicions about the "craziness" she had displayed in her relationship with Mark. Indeed, the position Martha took in this relationship felt more like the norm for her adult relationships. It signaled the return of the Martha she had known in her friendships, in her relations with clients, even in her marriage and previous love relationships. Martha's newfound satisfaction with Harry, however, was short-lived. As she began to want more from the relationship, she was clearly aware that Harry was not a person who could offer her genuine intimacy. Yet her attraction to Harry confirmed something she had vehemently denied up to this point—that Martha herself, and not only the men with whom she became involved, was responsible for the lack of closeness she had experienced in most of her love relationships. What was most difficult for Martha in all of this was to see how her assumption of the role of the "good" reflective mirror for others distanced people and attracted the very narcissistic men who would later disappoint her.

As Martha began to understand how this might be so, she also started to question why she might be so fixated on this role. And as she began to observe how she insisted on maintaining the mirroring position in most of her relationships, she became aware that it was not only in therapy with me that she felt uncomfortably spotlighted when attention turned to her. A simple question from a stranger at a party, "Why don't you tell me about yourself?" provoked momentary panic. Even with friends, she found herself diverting attention from questions about herself to questions about the other person. As for public situations in which she was required to give a speech or make a presentation, these simply sent her into paroxysms of anguish. Asked by her university to teach a training course during this time, Martha found herself in total agony before and during each of the lectures she gave. As she stood before the class, she wished for nothing so ardently as to "be invisible." Only by eventually redirecting the attention from herself to discussion of her students' difficulties, thereby (as she put it) turning her class into "group therapy," was Martha able to begin to feel effective in her teaching.

During this time, Martha also began to see how disabling her desire for anonymity had been—not simply in her personal relationships but in her professional life as well. For one thing, it had made it extremely unlikely that she would be able to realize her dream of going into private practice since she felt unable to promote herself in any way or even to receive the credit she deserved from her colleagues and her institution. Furthermore, Martha began to glimpse the limitations of positive mirroring as a sole therapeutic tool. Although she often remarked on her effectiveness as an individual therapist, she now recognized that there were certain situations where the Rogerian techniques she preferred simply did not appear to work. For one thing, she found it difficult to work with groups or with couples using only reflective paraphrasing and unconditional positive regard. For another, certain clients seemed to respond adversely to her offer of positive mirroring.

These limitations became especially apparent in Martha's work with a very disturbed client who eventually began to display both suicidal and homicidal tendencies. In working with this client, Martha discovered to her dismay that she seemed to be getting more and more caught up in a delusional system in which she also started to feel "crazy." By the time she turned this case over to another therapist, she had recognized that what appeared to be positive mirroring in this situation may have amounted to collusion rather than useful therapeutic intervention. And though this client would undoubtedly have been hard for most therapists to work with, Martha could see that her own limitations—the rigidity of her role as the perfect mirror—had made this even more difficult for her. She was greatly disturbed by this experience, not only because of the apparent danger to her client, herself, and others but also because it challenged some of her own most cherished beliefs about the nature of the therapeutic process—beliefs which reinforced her own project of "being the perfect mirror."

Shortly after the termination of her work with this client about the middle of the second phase of her own therapy, Martha had another experience which provoked her to get more deeply in touch with some of the primitive roots of her present difficulties. This incident involved an experience of "identity diffusion" which she had while attending a professional conference in a distant location. Usually reluctant to travel alone, Martha had originally planned to attend this conference with a colleague. When her friend backed out, she decided to go alone. Arriving late one evening, she felt a definite sense of foreboding and fear as she bedded down in an unfamiliar room at the conference center. When she arrived at the dining hall for breakfast the next morning, she felt "completely lost" as she was greeted by a "sea of strange faces." For most of the morning, she "felt as though I didn't exist—as though a ghost were floating around and no one saw her." By her own account, Martha experienced "complete and utter panic."

When I asked if this was at all like the severe anxiety she had felt after her breakup with Mark, she agreed that it was—"except that this was more pure." What Martha did with her panic was to latch onto a fellow conference member during the middle of the first day and begin to draw her out. "The more *she* talked," Martha said, "the more real *I* felt." I suggested that in order to be a mirror, one must have something to reflect; otherwise, one has no "identity." Martha was profoundly shaken by this experience, which she described as "suddenly falling into the abyss." She could see that her response to the situation was not a "reasonable adult reaction"—and she and I both began to wonder if it might have its origins in some kind of preverbal trauma or traumas. It felt, as she put it, "primitive and hard to get hold of."

At this time, Martha began a series of conversations with her mother in which she asked questions about those earliest years. Fortunately, her mother was willing to share her memories with Martha. First of all, Martha's mother described how difficult the birth of her only daughter, which had followed three miscarriages, had been. Also, though her mother had initially nursed Martha, her milk had dried up after about four months and she had found it difficult at that time to switch the baby to the bottle. Finally, her mother's account of Martha's response to the feeding schedule on which she had placed her on the advice of her doctor proved especially revealing. According to her mother, Martha had "cried furiously for hours" between feedings. Asked why she thought Martha did that, Martha's mother replied, "I guess it was because you wanted your own way." Here it was then—a mother who regarded her infant daughter's needs for holding and nourishment as "demanding" and "bad." Martha the adult therapist was shocked.

This early deprivation of physical/emotional nourishment and holding apparently led Martha, by her mother's account, to become a shy and fearful toddler. The world, to use Margaret Mahler's terminology, was definitely not her "oyster." Indeed, rather than triumphing over her abilities at upright locomotion, Martha had developed a phobia about "bugs" that caused her to demand hysterically that her parents pick her up and carry her whenever they went outside. Perhaps in this way she had tried to compensate for the deprivation of her needs for secure holding in infancy. Yet this need to remain a baby was in some ways contradicted by Martha's otherwise precocious development. Not only did she walk early, she also talked early and (according to her mother) was toilet trained by fifteen months. Perhaps she felt pushed to please a mother who regarded her as a burden—or perhaps she simply decided that she had better learn to do these things for herself since her original others were unreliable.

Martha's mother also reported that Martha had experienced severe stranger anxiety up until after she started school—and that this had made it very difficult for her paternal grandmother (who was virtually a stranger at this time) to look after her when she took over her care when Martha's mother was hospitalized for six months after the birth of her second child. As for the illness itself, Martha's mother was vague about what it was—though Martha herself remembered hearing something about a "nervous breakdown" when she was a child. Also interesting was Martha's mother's account of Martha's reaction to her mother's homecoming and to her new brother. At first Martha refused to talk to her mother and displayed anger toward the baby. Then, about six months later, when she was three, Martha became extremely protective of "my baby"—carrying him about like a doll and dressing and feeding him. She also developed at this time a strong attachment to her grandmother.

All of this, of course, provides a picture of a little girl who had been severely deprived of the valorizing looks, touches, and words which might have helped her develop a secure sense of self. As a result, she had come to substitute "goodness" or conformity for spontaneity and authenticity in her interactions with the important people in her life. It is easy to see from this account how Martha's needs had, from a Sartrean perspective, been socialized as "guilty needs" and consequently how she had come to regard with suspicion the emergence of desires which were genuinely her own.

Martha, as she began to understand this and to give up certain habitual tactics for reinforcing her mirror identity, began to experience in a deeply physical way the hunger for holding and support which had been lacking since infancy. Deep breathing in one session provoked the reemergence of the "skin hunger" which she had reported feeling with Mark, as Martha began to actively and poignantly long for the security of a calm breast on which to lay her head and for loving arms to hold her. She remarked also on her continuing temerity about touching, as she began to understand how her avoidance of physical contact in most situations kept this hunger in check at the same time that it helped her to avoid the anticipated rejection. At this time, Martha began to reexperience a rage similar to the rage which had so disconcerted her in her relationship with Mark and to connect this with the infantile deprivation which she had obviously suffered. Her lack of valorization, she could now clearly see, went far deeper than the remembered childhood experiences to which she had hitherto attributed it.

Martha now began to put together strands from the various periods of her personal history and to see how later childhood (her personalization) and her family ethos allowed her to find ways to compensate for and deal with her earliest deprivations (her protohistory). Obviously, Martha's early lack of valorization had left her with a "mirror hunger" which is often displayed by clients with so-called narcissistic issues. Yet Martha did not become a classical narcissist. Instead, her fundamental project was not to *get* the missing mirroring, but to *be* the mirror for others. This choice, it seems, fit in well with the family situation which she discovered in early childhood. The truth was that Martha's developing capacity for empathic resonance both filled an apparent hole in the lives of her family members and gave her a sense of self-worth and (pseudo)contact which would otherwise have been missing in her life. It also fit in with the family "ethos" of centering on father and his business goals/difficulties and developing the capacity for "unselfishness"—which were the criteria for belonging, the structures of fraternity-terror, in Martha's family.

Each member of Martha's family, it seems, was peculiarly suited to respond to her offer of empathic mirroring. Martha's mother had come to her marriage with an apparent lack of self-esteem which may in part have explained why she chose to marry "beneath herself" in the sense of choosing a man from a family with considerably less social and financial status than her own. The middle child in a family where her older sister was reputed to have all the brains and her younger sister all the beauty, Martha's mother's pride was almost entirely in her well-connected and upwardly mobile family rather than in herself. As a wife and mother, she showered all her attention on a husband who seemed to look elsewhere for satisfaction—to his daughter or to several mistresses (a suspicion Martha confirmed by talking with her mother about this during therapy). Only on those occasions when he felt "down" and "needy" did he turn to his wife.

This "lack" in Martha's mother's relationship with her husband, which further confirmed the feelings of inferiority and worthlessness she had brought into the marriage, no doubt led her to feel that she had little real emotional support to give to her children—a feeling which was masked by the adoption of the role of harassed wife and mother, the martyr whom Martha simultaneously pitied and rejected as a role model. Part of Martha's mother's martyrdom, by her mother's account, consisted of the interferences of her mother-in-law in the household. And, indeed, Martha's mother, in the endless complaints which she shared with her daughter, blamed this strong-willed old woman for all of the difficulties in the family from her husband's declining interest in her to her children's misdeeds or difficulties. Martha, who listened to complaints from both sides, felt caught between them.

Less obvious to Martha initially was the fact that she was also caught in a second family "triangle"—one in which she was made the third party in a struggle between her mother and her father. Martha's father, it seems, brought with him into his marriage extreme feelings of deprivation from a childhood spent in relative poverty after the death of his father when he was three. Martha herself had as a child felt great empathy for the unhappy child her father had been. She had even now in her mind a very clear image of him trudging to school in hand-me-down clothes and accepting the taunts of other children because his mother worked as a maid. In comparison, she had as a child felt that her own vague unhappiness was totally unjustified; it was simply nullified by the events of her prehistory which related to her father's disadvantaged childhood. Martha's father reinforced this idea by his constant insistence that *his* children were happy and well cared for in a way that he had not been—a point of honor with him which seemed to have been a source of combined pride and resentment. Even now, although she was experiencing considerable difficulties and although her youngest brother had had a psychotic breakdown in high school from which he had never fully recovered, Martha found it hard to shake the idea that she and her brothers had somehow been exceptionally "fortunate." According to her father's perceptions, they were.

Perhaps because of his own early deprivation, Martha's father required great loyalty and support from his family—which he attempted to repay with the material advantages which his growing business empire afforded them. Dinner table conversations, as Martha remembered them, all centered around her father and what his day had been like rather than around other family members. Martha's father was especially reliant on his daughter, who seemed increasingly to replace her mother as his chief confidante and playmate. In addition to listening to his concerns about his business, Martha also shared his interest in the various sports which he took pride in teaching her. And it was Martha whom he took for rides in the fast cars which were his endless delight and to Martha that he confided some of his dissatisfactions with his wife.

As for Martha, she realized now that she had never shared with her father her own unhappiness and self-doubts—since these were things he apparently despised in a woman and considered unthinkable in his children. At the same time that Martha's father was entertaining and fun, however, he was also rather distant and cold physically—literally keeping her at arm's length. Only once, at the age of thirteen, did she remember feeling a kind of warmth edged with physical seductiveness coming from him—and this had sent her, when they returned home from a drive, to the bathroom in a paroxysm of vomiting. Nonetheless, as Martha now began to see, she had felt considerable guilt toward her mother about her father's attentions to her—guilt which was uncomfortably laced with feelings of superiority over her mother, fear of her mother's jealousy, and pity for her mother's pain. Perhaps this was why, Martha now began to see, she had always been so uncomfortable with the idea of competition with other women—and why in part she had yet to form a successful relationship with a man which would have allowed her to have the family of her own which she felt was long overdue.

Martha's solution to her earliest feelings of emotional deprivation, then, had been to become the empathic mirror in a family where everyone else's feelings of deficiency made them susceptible to valuing her for her abilities in this direction. Not that this was openly acknowledged, but rather that Martha increasingly found that her family members (her brothers and her grandmother, as well as her mother and father) showed their regard for her by using her as a listening post. Perhaps this was not genuine contact since Martha's own needs/desires got pushed into the background, but it appeared to be the next best thing in a family where genuine intimacy appeared impossible. Also, Martha found a great deal of vicarious satisfaction for her own repressed needs for mirroring in providing other people with the empathic mirroring she lacked. So far, her solution would appear to be totally benign with respect to others, though it might not be fully satisfactory for herself. This, however, as we learned, was not all there was to Martha's assumption of the role of the perfect mirror. It had its hidden vindictive side as well.

This became apparent in a series of therapy sessions which also helped to elucidate Martha's extreme discomfort with sharing herself with me in the beginning of the second phase of therapy. Martha, as she began to explore the mirroring theme, became increasingly aware that she found it very difficult to let go of her identity as a mirror. As she confronted this fact, it became clear that part of what was behind her reluctance was a distrust of other people—including me as her therapist. "I will not allow other people to mirror me," she finally said, "because I know they will do it badly and I don't want to be disappointed." This statement was followed by much weeping.

When I asked how she knew this since she so rarely shared herself, Martha announced in a voice that sounded both angry and proud, "No one is as good a mirror as I am. They simply cannot do it. I am the world's most perfect mirror." When I remarked on the grandiosity of this statement, Martha ironically dubbed herself "Martha the marvelous mirror"—a designation which indicated that she was beginning to distance herself slightly from this identity. Still, it seemed that she was much invested in her superior mirroring talents.

Gradually, Martha was able to grasp the anger in her assumption of this role. It was as though, in impersonating the perfect mirror, she was able to say to her parents, "Look how miserably you have failed me and how well I am able to do what you could not do." In insisting on being the mirror, Martha was also assuming the role of subject before whom her parents and others whom she mirrored were objects. This allowed her a kind of triumph over them at the same time that it served to protect her from the narcissistic wounds which their insensitivity had inflicted/might inflict on her. Consequently, in most situations where Martha found herself the center of attention (as she did as a client in therapy), she felt small and weak from two perspectives: First, she felt like the small weak child who had never received the empathic mirroring she needed and, second, she imagined that the other person felt a superiority similar to that which she herself secretly felt when she took the position of mirror.

Indeed, as it turned out, it was Martha's attribution of this feeling of superiority to me at the beginning of this phase of therapy which had caused her to fall silent. She had felt that she was "one down" and that I was "one up" in the relationship. As she was now able to tell me, it was my response that I could understand how difficult it was to exchange the position of therapist for that of client which had allowed her to break this impasse—since my remark seemed to imply that I understood her dilemma and might even share her vulnerability in this respect. Obviously, it was a Sartrean perspective on the implications of the subject-object alternation in therapy that had allowed me to be sensitive to her feeling put down by my presence as a witness—though I did not understand at the time why she had been so sensitive to this. How her discomfort in assuming the position of object tied in with her past and with her own fundamental project would not become clear until the later sessions.

Obviously, my intuitive feeling that self-revelation was not what was needed in the earlier session had been correct. What had been needed instead was the lengthy work through which Martha eventually came to understand the way in which her demand that I reveal myself to her related to her own mirroring issues. Certainly, there was a real present circumstance which provoked this: I did not deny that I *was* in the position of witness and she in the position of the object of that witnessing. But the reason why this was so difficult for Martha was that she was projecting onto me an attitude of superiority similar to the one which had long served to bolster her own fragile sense of self-esteem.

In the end, what I did reveal to Martha was my own surprised delight as she began to face all of the complex twists and turns of her fundamental project and to move beyond her previous sense of identity as the "marvelous mirror." As the second phase of therapy came to a close, Martha was thoroughly convinced that she did not wish to continue to live her life as a mirror. Her work on these issues had been deeply affecting at a "gut level." It had touched her in her being. She had wept, she had raged, she had resisted knowing what she was really about, and she had finally confronted the project she had constructed/was constructing for herself of impersonating the valorizing mirror which had been so lacking for her as an infant and young child. Eventually, Martha came to feel great compassion for the small child who had given up her own needs/desires for the impossible project of giving what she never got and thereby becoming a substantial self (the ego as object).

This, however, was not the conclusion of therapy. Martha was now faced with the difficult task of allowing those long disallowed needs and desires to emerge and of communicating with others in a way that might allow for the positive reciprocity and intimacy which she had until now only dimly suspected was possible—or else had convinced herself was already there in her attempt to merge with others through acting the perfect mirror. The task of the third stage of therapy would therefore be a confrontation with the void which Martha now found at the heart of her experience as she began to let go of the old mirror identity.

Stage Three. Up until now, Martha had examined the regressive and progressive aspects of her project as they formed a connection between past, present, and future. In the third stage of therapy, she would largely confront the task of making a new choice of being. And as might be expected, this provoked extreme anxiety. Martha did not, in making such a new choice, cease to have the past which she had; she merely began to live it differently by projecting herself toward a different future. Hence her anxiety at letting go of an "identity" that had never really jelled in the sense of providing her with the security she desired was perhaps more extreme than a similar letting go might have been for a person with a more solid sense of self. Nonetheless, Martha did take this step. In doing so, she experienced an existential anguish of almost overwhelming proportions. But she experienced good moments as well.

On the positive side, Martha began to share herself more often with others and found at times that she enjoyed doing so. She gave a talk at a professional conference and delighted in the positive feedback she received. She told a funny story at a party, she became exuberant during a night out with friends, or she allowed herself to enjoy the spotlight she was given in therapy. Of course, she sometimes retreated into her old patterns, suffering agonies of remorse as she imagined some silent person across the room judging her "self-centeredness." By and large, however, Martha was developing a new vulnerability and aliveness which had not been present before—a vitality which showed in her eyes and in her walk, as well as in the things she did and said.

During this time, I encouraged Martha to do things which challenged her old identity—to in a sense court the "identity diffusion" which had previously caused her so much trouble and which had brought her into therapy in the first place. As she did so, she experienced greater pleasure and more distress. Often she found it hard to share herself in a conversation for the simple reason that she was unsure whom she was trying to share. Living her own needs as hexis for so long made it difficult to get in touch with them; her desires, it seems, had been muted before they ever had the chance to see the light of day and for this reason would require much coaxing to do so. Now that she wished to allow them to emerge, she found herself frustrated by the inner emptiness she felt instead.

When Martha did manage to allow herself more spontaneity, the consequences were often even more difficult to bear. She experienced deep feelings of longing and isolation—an isolation which had, of course, in a sense been present all her life, but which she could only now feel in its devastating immediacy. She felt a grief which seemed endless and which would not leave her for days, as she mourned the years of lost life she had spent as the "marvelous mirror" with no needs of her own. She developed psychosomatic symptoms—migraine headaches, heart palpitations, nervous stomach, and a variety of hypochondriacal illnesses which she was half-convinced would kill her. She "felt like an utter fool." And she awoke nightly from horrible dreams, reminiscent of Lacan's *corps morcelé* dreams, in which body parts were strewn about rooms. I interpreted these symptoms as a reaction to the dissolution of her ego in the Sartrean sense—that is, of her image of herself as the perfect mirror. It was this image which was experiencing its death throes. Fortunately for Martha, the "marvelous mirror" had cracked and a new agent with authentic needs and desires of her own was beginning to emerge from behind it.

Just before she completed therapy, Martha began dating a man who seemed to be capable of the reciprocal intimacy which she was coming more and more to desire. Although "Jack's" genuine interest in her was frightening to her at times and although she was disappointed at other times by his lack of perfect empathy, even to the point of retreating into her old position of mirroring to avoid intimacy, Martha was able to catch herself and to work toward a genuinely reciprocal sharing. "After all," she said, "if he doesn't love *me*, then what difference does it make if he likes what I can *do* for him?" Gradually, Martha began to be able to accept the inevitable failures in understanding which occur even in the closest of relationships—and thereby to come to terms with the separation of consciousnesses which her project of believing in the possibility of perfect mirroring had in a sense denied.

At the same time, she began to note a new potency in her work as a therapist. She was now able not only to mirror but to confront, to interpret, to refuse to participate, or even to share herself if this seemed appropriate. She shared her feelings and thoughts easily in her own therapy sessions. And she was able to recognize and accept the fact that she had no fixed self in the substantive sense. As she phrased this, "I find it scary to realize how fluid I am, but I guess that's what being alive is all about." From a living death as the perfect mirror, Martha had resurrected herself into a life where reciprocal sharing means not perfect selfless understanding but a respect for her own and the Other's freedom. Even Rogerian "unconditional positive regard" seemed less appealing to her now than before.

My Response. As we come to the end of Martha's story, I think it only fair (and I believe it will be useful) to briefly discuss my own responses to her work with me in therapy. First of all, I should note that Martha's "issues" resonated with some of my own and that I found myself changed by witnessing and facilitating her struggle with them. For one thing, as Alice Miller has accurately observed in *The Drama of the Gifted Child* (1979), narcissistically used children who learn to meet their parents' needs for mirroring often grow up to be therapists—since it is exactly these talents which are needed in the work of therapy. I am no exception.

Also, as I came to see very clearly with Martha, being a therapist is one place where one may indulge one's needs to mirror without being expected to reveal oneself as a person in return. Naturally, I began to question my own "use" of the therapeutic process to this end. And, indeed, it was at this time that I saw more clearly the meaning of the incident of the man with the tape recorder and the grandiosity of the therapist who insists on playing the "unlooked-at Looker." I was even uncomfortably aware, as I listened to Martha talk about her difficulties in the classroom, that I myself also experienced some of this same discomfort with being "in the spotlight"—and I wondered whether I might at times have turned my own classes into something resembling group therapy in order to avoid this discomfort.

Martha's struggles with existential anxiety also affected me deeply. It was impossible to watch her go through this without having some of my own identity issues surface and to question the comfortable roles behind which I sometimes hide from myself the fact that I too have no substantial self. My own anxiety surfaced as hers grew stronger. Also, there were times, especially when Martha was at the height of her second experience of "disintegration anxiety" during the third year of therapy, when I questioned whether I was indeed helping her. Perhaps, I thought, the traditional psychoanalysts were right in attempting to build ego structure in the psyche. Perhaps Martha would become psychotic. Most of the time, however, I simply felt the power of the struggle in which she was engaging and admired her courage in sticking with it. Her emerging vulnerability and spontaneity affected me deeply.

I was also aware of confronting some of my own limitations in working with Martha on her desire to have me enact the perfect mirror. I was, for example, aware at times of being tempted to play the role which she seemed so badly to want to assign to me—to be the "good guy" rather than the "bad guy" in this situation. Yet I was at the same time aware that this was probably not what Martha needed from me. Certainly, my own discomfort was considerable as I confronted her on the meaning of her desires to give or receive perfect mirroring and received her angry remonstrances. Happily, I later discovered that this was exactly the kind of intervention which provoked her to move (I was afraid, of course, that it might send her out the door). I believe that in thus challenging Martha to move past her stuck points as a therapist and a person, I was challenging some of those same stuck points in myself. Hence when, at the end of her therapy, I felt that Martha was a more genuine person with me, I felt that I was in some ways a more genuine person with her as well. And though I did not often directly discuss my personal difficulties and challenges with Martha, I believe that she was aware from my responses and interpretations that I was there with her as a person and not simply as a mirror or neutral observer to her heartfelt struggle. In the end, I shared with her my admiration for the way in which she had been able to stay with and work through some very difficult issues in therapy—and how deeply her work had touched me as a person.

Comparing the Sartrean Approach with More Traditional Psychoanalytic Approaches. Obviously, I believe that Sartrean attention to the existential dilemma of fear of change as such, together with a careful examination of the roots of Martha's dilemma in the original failed mirroring which led her to distrust the Other as subject, contributed to a favorable outcome of her therapy. Certainly, Martha's own courage in facing what seemed at times to be unbearable anxiety over the disintegration of the only self (the "marvelous mirror") she had ever known was the deciding factor. But I believe that it was fortuitous that this courage was allowed to manifest itself in a therapeutic context in which I recognized her so-called disintegration anxiety as a sign not of the failure to achieve an adequately structured ego but of the failure to cope with the ontological dilemma of being human. Empathic resonance along Kohutian (or Rogerian) lines in the early part of Martha's therapy undoubtedly paved the way for her to develop the capacity to tolerate the existential anguish of the final seven or eight months. But empathic resonance alone, without the challenge to seek out and face the ontological dilemma that all of us lack an ego or self in the substantive sense, might not have prepared the way for that release of spontaneity which Martha experienced at the conclusion of therapy. A more traditional psychoanalytic approach would certainly have taken her partway there, but it would have been difficult to go the whole journey with her if one took the perspective that the sole aim of therapy was either to concentrate on the Oedipal struggle (classical psychoanalysis) or to build ego structure in the psyche (post-Freudian psychoanalysis).

In emphasizing the Sartrean themes in Martha's therapy, I do not mean to imply, however, that the regressive part of our investigation was altogether different from work she might have done either with a classical or post-

Freudian analyst. For example, there certainly emerged in Martha's therapy themes which might have been designated Oedipal by a classical analyst. Her loyalty to her father, for instance, was so persistent at times as to make it difficult to look at the flaws in their relationship. And there is no question that a so-called Oedipal triangle existed between Martha, her father, and her mother—though in looking at this I would, with Alice Miller (1984), question whether the suppressed sexual desire did not exist more on the side of the father than on the side of the child. In other words, I believe that what Martha desired from her father was physical warmth and love, not specifically sexual attention. It is also certainly true that Martha feared her mother's jealousy, had difficulty identifying with her mother as a role model (while worrying that she might be like her mother), and both desired and feared her father's attention—all traditional Freudian themes. And it is true that Martha repeated many aspects of her relationship with her parents in her later love relationships—a phenomenon Freud would attribute to transference and the repetition compulsion.

We have also seen how projection of her own motives onto her therapist and denial or repression of certain motives were issues which Martha had to work through in therapy. No doubt Martha's guilt over having needs/ desires of her own could also have found its place in a classical Freudian analysis—though I am sure that the idea of repressed libidinal impulses and unconscious conflicts would have played a part in a classical interpretation of these difficulties that it did not play in my own work with Martha.

Also, despite these classical themes in Martha's therapy, I believe that even most traditional post-Freudian psychoanalytic theorists would agree that the crux of her difficulties was not Oedipal. They would rather see them, as I myself do in part, as lying in the failure of her parents to provide early relational needs for a holding, mirroring, and empathic resonance which might have led to the development of a firm and coherent sense of self. Certainly, the issues that arose most persistently in Martha's therapy were "narcissistic" ones deriving from failed mirroring. On the other hand, as I have said, Martha's issues were not those of a classical narcissist. Perhaps they more closely resembled those of the "closet narcissist" described in passing by James Masterson (1981).

According to Masterson, narcissists (either classical or closet) are stuck in the "practicing subphase" of early infancy as described by Mahler. To a narcissist, other people are not real separate others but extensions of the self. Hence comes the classical narcissist's lack of genuine sensitivity to others combined with his or her feelings of entitlement and needs for attention and praise. Like the practicing subphase infant, the classical narcissist cannot hear too much applause. Narcissism is a pathological condition not only because such grandiosity is unrealistic, but also because beneath the narcissist's "false grandiose self" lives an empty, devalued self which the grandiosity is intended to camouflage.

The closet narcissist shares this sense of deep emptiness and devaluation, but instead of needing to be applauded and praised, he or she appears to need to applaud and praise and thereby to participate in the other person's grandeur. Like the classical narcissist, the closet narcissist is caught up in a "partially fused self-object unit" which is basically intrapsychic but which is projected interpersonally.[3] In such a unit, the grandiosity of one of the members is reflected by the other. It is just that the closet narcissist's needs for mirroring and idealization are more deeply buried than the classical narcissist's—or perhaps the closet narcissist is more in touch with the original lack of adequate mirroring. Hence, as Richard Fisher of the Masterson Group notes, the closet narcissist "does not display overt exhibitionistic behavior and may even present as humble, anxious, inhibited or shy" (in Masterson and Klein, 1989, p. 70). The truth is, however, that grandiosity is not absent in the closet narcissist. The false grandiose self of the closet narcissist is simply projected onto the other person rather than lived directly. Indeed, as Fisher also notes, in certain situations the closet narcissist's defenses against manifest grandiosity may break down and a more classical pattern of seeking mirroring and idealization may emerge.

Kohut believes that therapy with narcissists is largely a matter of providing failed mirroring while Masterson considers interpretation of narcissistic injury to be the technique of choice. The aim of such therapy, according to both Masterson and Kohut, is to repair defective development and allow the establishment of a separate self which can fully relate to a separate other. Kohut believes, as we have seen, that such repair happens through "transmuting internalization" of the therapeutic relationship. Masterson adds that the therapist must promote the development of the "real self" as opposed to the "false grandiose self"—an idea which he obviously borrows from Winnicott. In Mahler's terms, the goal of therapy with such patients would be the achievement of "self and object constancy." Other post-Freudian theorists, such as Kernberg, would say it is the repair of defective ego structure.

Clearly, many of Martha's difficulties can be explained in terms of the phenomenon which post-Freudian theorists refer to as the "narcissistic wound"—and her solution to these difficulties as being in many ways similar to the solution of the closet narcissist as described by Masterson. Masterson would probably view Martha as either a high-functioning narcissist or as a neurotic with strong narcissistic issues. Like Masterson's closet narcissist, Martha attempted to repair the defective mirroring she received in infancy and early childhood by taking the position of the mirror for others. Also, Martha in her relationship with Mark had experienced the reemergence of mirror hunger and with it the breakthrough of manifest grandiosity, which Fisher describes as characteristic of closet narcissists in special circumstances. Furthermore, in the course of therapy, Martha experienced the emptiness and lack of a sense of value which are said to underlie the narcissist's grandiosity. And she both practiced (in the form of Rogerian nondirectional therapy) and demanded of me as her therapist that very empathic resonance which Kohut prescribes as the treatment of choice for narcissists. When she did not receive this, like the narcissists described by many post-Freudian theorists, she unleashed her fury on me and threatened to discontinue therapy.

Yet the reader has probably already noted that it was only in part that I offered Martha empathic mirroring. I also confronted her on the meaning of her needs to mirror and to be mirrored. My practice with her in this regard points to a fundamentally different conceptualization of her difficulties and to a different idea of the aims of her therapy than those discussed by the post-Freudian theorists. Indeed, I attributed the grandiosity in Martha's project not to her wish to recover a lost omnipotent selfobject unit but rather to her fantasy that she could give perfect mirroring and thereby absorb into herself the Other as object. A part of this grandiosity also involved her attempt to assume the (vengeful) position of only subject reflecting the others as objects—thereby creating for herself a sense of superiority based on a kind of ontological fantasy that she could obliterate the pain involved in her original awareness of her Being-for-others by making the others into perpetual objects. In this respect, her position is similar to Sartre's account of the "sadistic" position in his description of the "conflict of consciousnesses"—though Martha's sadistic strain was subtle and secret. It also led to much suffering for herself.

Thus while I did, in fact, agree with the post-Freudian theorists that Martha's "pathology" derived from her attempt to use mirroring/being mirrored to create a union of self and Other, I did not view this desire as representing a regressive pull to a *real* earlier state of development. Rather, I viewed it as referring to Martha's painful discovery that the original others were unable to give her the sense of the valorization she needed in order to develop a viable project—a situation which led to her subsequent attempts to create such a self by any means she could. From this perspective, the narcissist's lack of regard for the Other as separate from self is a prospective fantasy rather than a regression to an earlier stage of life—a move designed to create the illusion of substantive freedom by absorbing the Other's Look into oneself or oneself into the Other.

Because I was working with Martha from a Sartrean perspective, I did not view her as a defective self or ego in need of structuring or restructuring. Nor did I see her problem as lying in a failure to achieve a self or object constancy which the rest of us more "normal" souls somehow have. Rather, I saw her historical dilemma as being that of an unvalorized child who had come up with a very elegant solution to her lack of valorization—a solution to the "problem of being" which allowed her to deal with many aspects of the ontological dilemma of creating a self as value within a family context which seemed antagonistic to viewing her as genuinely valuable.

Indeed, it was amazing to me how many sides this assumption of the position of the perfect mirror had as a solution to Martha's childhood difficulties. It allowed her to experience a vicarious satisfaction of her own denied needs for mirroring; to believe in the possibility of having a secure substantialized self; to uphold the family "pledge" of centering on father and being "unselfish"; to get revenge on her family for their failure to mirror her by assuming the position of the "superior" perfect mirror; to avoid her own feelings of hurt and disappointment about not being genuinely noticed and regarded by the important people in her life; and to cling to a semblance of contact and personal belonging in a family that did not offer real relatedness. Holding onto this idea of herself as the perfect mirror also allowed Martha to avoid looking at the unstable nature of this solution to the problem of Being and—except in the moments when she experienced identity diffusion—to escape the intolerable anxiety of recognizing that she did not have a substantial self. And it helped her to avoid the terrible grief which she later felt over a life lived without genuine intimacy and spontaneity.

I did not, of course, regard it as my task as Martha's therapist to aid her in continuing to avoid the hurts and emotional deprivations of her childhood. But neither did I see the aim of her therapy as being the creation of a structured ego or self which had hitherto been lacking. Indeed, from a Sartrean perspective, there is something slightly askew about the views of psychoanalytic theorists that the aim of therapy is to repair the ego, find and develop a real self, or coach one's client to finally develop self and object constancy. This is so because from a Sartrean perspective the real self, the ego as a seat of personality organization, and the notion that one carries about inside oneself internalized objects are all illusions in that they fail to recognize the fundamental translucidity of consciousness.

Hence I did not follow the traditional post-Freudian theorists in regarding Martha as a simple case of arrested psychological development. Obviously, Martha had not become developmentally fixated in the sense of remaining an infant, despite her carrying with her certain difficulties which originated in her protohistory and which she continually detotalized and retotalized as part of the givens of her future-directed project. The later turns of the spiral which was Martha's life project—for example, her discovery that her ability to mirror made her valuable to her parents and other family members and her later application of this ability to her profession—were not merely reducible to earlier life problems. Martha the Rogerian therapist was by no means exactly equivalent to Martha the unvalorized infant.

Hence while I was well aware that the disintegration anxiety which Martha experienced so dramatically at various stages of her therapy did indeed refer to her lack of valorization as an infant and young child, I was equally convinced that her anxiety resembled in kind—even if it was more intense— the anguish which we all must face in confronting the fact that we cannot become substantive selves. Certainly, this was more difficult for Martha, who had never experienced herself as the recipient of parental adoration and regard, but it was not an anguish from which I could save her by helping her (as many post-Freudian theorists would insist that I should) to build a more solid ego structure or to discover a substantial true self beneath the disguised false self she had hitherto displayed.

Instead, I saw my function in working with Martha as not only to explore with her the past sources of those terrible feelings of personality disintegration which she experienced, but also to promote that very disintegration of the ego (in the Sartrean sense) which she so deeply feared. In other words, I believed that a large part of Martha's difficulty was the tenacity with which she clung to the illusion that she could, in fact, be a person as a table is a table—that she could *be* the perfect mirror. When she was able to give up this ultimately quixotic quest, she experienced a release of spontaneity, an ability to experience her own needs/desires, and a growing capacity for genuinely reciprocal relations which only an acceptance of and respect for her own and others' freedom could have allowed. I believe that a Sartrean conceptualization of her issues was in part responsible for this positive outcome.

In coming to the end of Martha's story, I am aware that it takes more than one case history to demonstrate a clinical theory. My hope is that this longer example, together with the shorter vignettes and the suggestions for therapeutic application which are scattered throughout this book, have given the reader a sense of the difference which a Sartrean perspective can make to the practice of psychotherapy. Further clinical illustrations will have to await a later book, as will a detailed discussion of technique from an existentialist perspective—though I might add that my own techniques in working with Martha included empathic mirroring, interpretation, confrontation, body-oriented psychotherapy, and Gestalt role playing. At times, I simply shared my own thoughts and feelings directly with her. Later work will have to describe more precisely how these and other techniques come to be modified by an existentialist conceptualization of therapeutic issues. In this account, however, I wanted to concentrate on the existential/ontological concerns which are the focus of the present book.

Some Directions for Future Inquiry

In coming to the close of this last chapter, I am aware of numerous preliminary thoughts and discarded notes on topics and subtopics relating to existentialist therapy which did not seem to fit within the scope of this book. For one thing, the focus on Sartrean metatheory as it relates to Freud and the post-Freudian psychoanalytic theorists precluded the pursuit of many side issues which I found both intriguing and significant for the practice of psychotherapy. In the interest of suggesting some directions for future inquiry, I will share some of those discarded paths and ideas with the reader.

First, I found myself with more to say about Sartre's theories of the emotions, the imagination, and sexuality as these relate to clinical practice. After all, Sartre himself wrote books on the first two, and his treatment of the third not only in a major section of *Being and Nothingness* but also in the psychobiographies is extensive and careful. With respect to sexuality, it seems to me that more needs to be done, both theoretically and in terms of case examples, with relating sexual difficulties to the fundamental project, as Sartre has done in the psychobiographies.[3] If this connection holds, I think it would be particularly useful to show how one's sexual relations change as the fundamental project shifts. Also, more work could be done to describe precisely the ontological structure of various sexual deviations—from those which are close to the norm to those which are bizarre and even sinister.

With respect to the imagination, it seems to me that the suggestions made in Chapter 6 about the possibilities for using the capacity to imagine (or refusing to use this capacity) in the interest of a project lived in bad faith need to be much extended. Perhaps various forms of "psychopathology" could be redescribed by noting a person's overuse or failure to make adequate use of the capacity to imagine. For example, psychotic hallucinations might be regarded as the substitution of an imaginary future for a seemingly impossible real one or certain neuroses as a refusal to allow oneself to imagine a different future. Furthermore, it seems to me that more needs to be done in the direction of precisely defining and distinguishing between dreams and hallucinations as two forms of what Sartre refers to as "capture" by the imaginary. After all, the former seems to be a necessary condition of health, whereas the latter is usually associated with extreme psychopathology.

Furthermore, my own suggestion in Chapter 6 that transference is at least in part a matter of living one's relationships in the imaginary needs to be more precisely worked out, especially that aspect of it where memory, imagination, and the hope for a different future seem to intersect in explaining a particular interpersonal strategy based on a particular view of self/world. Furthermore, the idea that there is an imaginary self as well as a real self with the consequences of this idea for such things as body image needs further exploration. Perhaps it might help to explain, among other things, how schizophrenics, anorexics, and others come to have such distorted body images.

As for Sartre's theory of the emotions, this is one place where I find myself balking at what Sartre himself refers to as the overly rationalist strain in his early philosophical thinking. But though I do not believe that emotion is a purely magical changing of self in a situation where one feels frustrated with the world (I agree that emotion *may* be magical just as rationality itself may serve the purpose of a magical release from the constraints of the real), I do accept Sartre's idea that feeling is something one does rather than something one undergoes or suffers—that it is a particular way of (prereflectively) choosing one's world-consciousness. Future inquiry might reopen Sartre's question about the ontological significance of emotionality in general and of particular emotions, as well as try to account from a Sartrean perspective for the phenomenon of "repressed affect," which is well known to all depth therapy.

Perhaps repressed affect could in part be accounted for by considering a second topic which, although I have pursued it only tangentially in this book, interests me greatly. This is Sartre's idea that consciousness lives the world bodily—that "Being-for-itself must be wholly body and it must be wholly consciousness; it cannot be [a separately existing consciousness which is] *united* with a body" (BN, p. 305). From this perspective, it would seem that repressed affects would not be feelings which are repressed once and for all into the unconscious, but rather feelings which are constantly being held back through muscular constrictions in the body as part of a fundamental project in which I live these particular feelings as (reflectively) denied. I believe from my experience as a therapist that, despite the numbness which accompanies certain habitual holding patterns, this "repressed material" is available to reflective comprehension.[4] Nor do such holding patterns relate merely to the past, for, as Sartre has shown with regard to the similar issue of somatization in the case of Flaubert's hysterico-epilepsy, psychophysical symptomatology can only be fully deciphered in terms of strategies for solving present problems in the direction of a particular future which this person is attempting to bring into being.[5]

From this perspective, it would seem that an existentialist reconsideration of psychosomatic illnesses and the bodily manifestations of "psychopathology" would need to include the future as meaning as well as the past as ground for these particular symptoms. It would also need to include the interpersonal meaning of those same symptoms, since the body exists not simply for-itself but also for-others. Indeed, it is my body which is the recipient of the Look through which I discover the Other as another consciousness. And it is with respect to myself as embodied consciousness that I experience the shame, the fear, and the pride which Sartre associates with my awareness of my Being-for-others. In this respect, the questions arise: For whom is this bodily repressed affect or frozen attitude repressed or frozen, and to what end? Looked at in this way, the "character armor" which Wilhelm Reich (1945, 1948) associates with past traumas leading to the repression of orgasmic potency would have to be reconceptualized as having both an interpersonal and a future-oriented dimension. The dissolution of character armor would also be expected to reveal an ontological significance to human existence beyond the release of the capacity for satisfactory orgasm which Reich seems to regard as the sole aim of life.

This observation does not mean that Sartre, who was interested in Kretschmer's studies in character and body structure, would deny that "character is identical with the body" (BN, p. 350). But when Sartre speaks of character and the body, he is referring to my character as read in my body for-others; it has a relevance to my fundamental project, but this relevance is to that project as a transcendence transcended. I believe that a Sartrean recasting of Reichean-bioenergetic therapy, which I have found enormously useful in certain aspects of my own clinical practice, would need to take into account the future and the interpersonal dimensions of character armor, as well as the ontological significance of the various holding patterns which Reich and his follower Alexander Lowen (1967a, 1967b, 1980, 1983) ignore.

Obviously, traditional psychoanalysis, since Reich's defection from Freud, has defined itself more and more exclusively as a purely "talking cure." But since the body also "talks," I see no reason why depth therapy should ignore what it is saying. I also think, however, that Reich's literalization of Freud's concept of the libido[6] needs to be superseded in the direction of exploring the ontological/existential issues which are locked within particular bodily holding patterns. Furthermore, from an existentialist perspective, one needs to consider the meaning of habitual movements, facial expressions, intonations, and gestures as they relate to a person's fundamental project as well as the habitual muscular contractions which seem to be the focus of Reichean and bioenergetic therapy. All of this, however, will need to be worked out more precisely in future studies.

A third area which seems to me to be particularly promising for future theoretical and clinical exploration is Sartre's idea that the for-itself is temporalizing and spatializing. For Sartre, as we have seen, time and space are to be discovered neither out there in the world nor in here in the psyche but rather in the intersection between the two. They are operations of the for-itself on the world rather than static givens. Thus it would seem to be important from a clinical perspective to conceptualize an individual's way of temporalizing and spatializing self/world.

All of us are aware, of course, that subjective time frequently has little relevance to clock time—as is evidenced by such statements as, "This afternoon disappeared before I knew what was happening," or, "This has been the longest month of my life." There is also little doubt that subjectively lived space differs from person to person and situation to situation. Both my awareness of the closeness and distance of objects and people and my sense of what is figure and what is ground differ from yours and from my own in other situations and at other times. As Sartre himself notes, space is always "hodological space"—that is, it always consists of paths to and away from objects which figure in my fundamental project. Furthermore, my awareness of my own body in space—for example, my trying to take up much or little or no space—will vary with the character of my project.

In the case of severe psychopathology, these differences are, of course, much more obvious. For example, the schizophrenic (like Roquentin in Sartre's novel *Nausea*) seems to lose a so-called normal awareness of time and space.[7] The world may seem two-dimensional or things may appear to intrude relentlessly and meaninglessly into one's consciousness; one's bodily orientation in space may be severely distorted; and the ordinary awareness of succession may be replaced by a kind of timelessness in which a truncated future gives way to an imaginary present. Yet even in cases involving less severe difficulties, attention should be given to the spatial and temporal dimensions of a client's project—and case studies illustrating the ontological significance of temporalizing or spatializing oneself/one's world in this way or that should be attempted.

For example, with respect to temporalization, the therapist might consider the significance of a project in which a client is always feeling overwhelmed by the past at the expense of the future as contrasted with one in which a client perpetually denies the past in favor of a future which seems unrealistically "open to anything." One also wonders if human development might not be partially conceptualized in terms of stages of learning to spatialize and temporalize, as Piaget's studies (see Piaget and Inhelder, 1948) seem to indicate—though from a Sartrean perspective one would want to grasp the ontological and interpersonal significance of such development.

Temporalization seems especially relevant to the experience of psychotherapy, which may itself be defined as a client's remaking the past as he or she comes to *pro-ject* a different future. The present, as simple "presence to being" (BN, p. 208), allows the psychological instant of reorientation to occur. Of course, in saying that one can remake the past, we are really saying that one reorients oneself toward it. There is an aspect of the past which is pure in-itself—or, in Sartre's later conceptualization, pure practico-inert—and which remains simply and immovably *there* as the "unalterable background-depth of all my thoughts and all my feelings" (BN, p. 141). This past is "irremediable" in the sense that I cannot change its pure facticity or refuse in good faith to be a person with this particular past (BN, p. 496). But since "it is fairly impossible for me to distinguish the unchangeable brute existence from the variable meaning which it includes" (BN, p. 498), it will remain true that the past is changeable in the sense that its "urgency" and "illumination" come from the future (BN, pp. 498–99).

In this connection, all depth therapists are probably aware of those moments in therapy when the past takes on a shockingly new character as a client's present/future project changes. As Rollo May observes, therapists often find "that a patient cannot recall what was vital and significant in his past until he is ready to make a decision with regard to the future" (1983, p. 167). Also, the therapy session itself is often experienced as an odd sort of time, and clients frequently remark on the unusual rapidity or slowness of the therapy hour. This and other aspects of "therapeutic time" need to be explored further from a Sartrean perspective.

A fourth area of inquiry might involve developing more exact descriptions of the client-therapist relationship in existentialist therapy, together with clinical illustrations of how the existentialist therapist deals with the traditional Freudian issues of transference, resistance, and the defenses. Obviously, Sartre would recast these as choices rather than as mechanisms. But beyond this, detailed case histories demonstrating the handling of transference and other relationship issues in existentially oriented psychotherapy need to be written.

Also, I suspect that the defenses need to be precisely formulated as strategies in bad faith for living what originally seemed like an unhappy or even intolerable life situation. Sartre discusses projection in the Genet biography, where he views Genet as the recipient of the disowned wishes and impulses of ordinary "good citizens." But there projection has sociopolitical as well as personal implications, a point which could perhaps be made about the other defense strategies as well. I also think that the defenses, like other aspects of one's project, are lived bodily and not just psychically. For example, denial is associated with a certain way of "not looking" as reality which has physical components. Furthermore, I believe that the defenses were originally developed as strategies for dealing with the reflective implications of one's interpersonal relations—and that they therefore always involve both reflective and prereflective components. But all this will need to be worked out more precisely in further studies.

Finally, I am aware that Sartre's later social philosophy can be more thoroughly mined for its rich theoretical and clinical implications. In *Being and Nothingness*, Sartre suggests a "psychoanalysis of things" which might help to illuminate the meaning of an individual's tastes and material preferences. The significance of one's way of living the exigencies inscribed in the practico-inert could be added to this investigation. Furthermore, case studies investigating the social shaping of need as desire could be undertaken with the aim of describing the ontological structures of various "pathological" projects.

As for serial alterity, other-direction, and groups as ternary relations, the implications of these concepts for existentialist therapy need to be explored in more detail. In particular, the connection between the dyadic relations of earliest infancy and an individual's insertion into the ternary relations of the family group needs to be explored in individual case histories—an endeavor Sartre himself initiates in the Flaubert biography. Further studies dealing with the intersections between individual projects, class-being, and the Objective Mind of a generation need to be undertaken. And the effects of serial alterity on contemporary psychopathology need to be explored in more detail. It might even be possible, combining the insights of Sartre's early philosophy with his later social philosophy, to develop a specifically Sartrean approach to family and group therapy.

Needless to say, Sartre's later philosophy also has far-reaching implications for social psychology—and for therapeutic work with socially disadvantaged individuals, families, and groups. Social workers, in particular, might find Sartre's concepts of scarcity, the power of the practico-inert, serial alterity, other direction and the demands of an inhuman work world useful. Certainly, the ways in which particular individuals have been induced from childhood to live their needs/desires more as hexis than as praxis have special poignancy when one is dealing with situations in which racism, sexism, and social disadvantage play a significant role in the alienation/exclusion of specific individuals and groups from the larger society.

Attention to the effects of prejudice as "idea hexis," a topic Sartre discusses in the *Critique* (pp. 300–306n), on the individuals and groups against which such prejudice is directed (and perhaps also on those who engage in such prejudice) might prove particularly relevant here. Even the problems of the homeless, which have currently received so much focus both from psychological and sociological perspectives, could be investigated from the Sartrean perspective of attempting to understand the ways in which a society "chooses" its disadvantaged and its disfranchised, or, in this case, its unhoused—and the ways in which the individuals in question are induced to cooperate with these choices.

Ultimately, as we know, Sartre in his later philosophy views individual and social difficulties as being inextricably interlinked—not just for the disadvantaged but for all of us. Thus a social psychology operating from a Sartrean perspective would be activist rather than merely descriptive in its interactions with its objects of study—who would, of course, be recognized as other human subjects. The aim of such a "dialectical" social psychology would be not only to elucidate contemporary social interactions but also to help facilitate the development of an authentic future society—the "true intersubjective community" in which Sartre hopes that the only "real relations" will be those between people (CDR, p. 307n). A place to begin would obviously be the development of techniques for community building in both advantaged and disadvantaged groups—a community building which has as its objective the dissolution of hexis and serial alterity in favor of the development of group praxes in which other individuals and other groups appear not as my "demonic double" but as "another self" (CDR, p. 132) whose oppression/oppressiveness affects me in my being. Clearly, such a social psychology would also recognize that individual praxis is the creative force behind all social relations, whether positive or negative; it would therefore refuse to sacrifice the individual to the group, either conceptually or practically, although it would certainly recognize the significance of groups and series in shaping individual praxis.

All of these topics, as I have said, could provide fruitful directions for future inquiry into the value of Sartre's philosophy for the practice of psychotherapy or existentially oriented social projects. In the meantime, my hopes for this book will have been fulfilled if it succeeds in encouraging depth therapists and others to reconsider the therapeutic issues which I believe Sartre's metatheory can aid us in conceptualizing more adequately than other depth approaches—including classical psychoanalysis and the various "schools" of contemporary post-Freudian psychoanalysis. Chief among those issues, as I have emphasized throughout these chapters, is a Sartrean approach to change in therapy and to the existential anguish which accompanies a radical reorientation of one's fundamental project of being. If a therapist does not encourage a client to confront and deal with fear of change as such, as I have said, exploring the past can become a new source of self-reification rather than an instrument of release. Indeed, without learning something like the Sartrean technique of "pure reflection," a client's "stuckness" in old patterns might conceivably increase rather than decrease as he or she investigates the regressive but not the progressive aspects of his or her fundamental project—its past "pastness" but not its past or contemporary future-directedness.

Sartre's ideas can also be extremely useful, as I have noted, to depth therapists attempting to understand the nature of the interpersonal needs and conflicts which form the core of most unhappy life projects. Particularly important here, of course, will be an investigation of the ways in which the looks, touches, and words of the original others have affected a client's fundamental project, in both its reflective and prereflective dimensions, and the ways in which the interpersonal/intrapersonal aspects of that project have been carried forward (and changed/modified/augmented) in the present. Sartre can also aid depth therapists in clarifying those "identity" issues which inevitably arise in therapy—issues relating to confusions about the nature of the self as agent, the self as object, and the self as aim or value which derive from the structures of bad faith described in these chapters. And, finally, the later Sartre can add to depth therapy an appreciation of the sociomaterial aspect of a client's difficulties which is missing in most individually oriented psychotherapy. In these ways, whether or not one accepts all of Sartre's ideas, I believe that an appreciation of Sartrean existentialist metatheory can add a new and valuable dimension to the practice of depth psychotherapy.

Notes

Chapter 2. Sartre versus Freud:
Two Approaches to Metapsychology

1. Actually, although Sartre credits Lefebvre with the discovery of the progressive-regressive method, Sartre had already sketched its outline in his discussion of how the fundamental project becomes explicable in existential psychoanalysis in *Being and Nothingness*. He says that this comprehension of the fundamental project "is effected in two opposed senses: by a regressive psychoanalysis one ascends back from the considered act to my ultimate possible [original choice]; and by a synthetic progression one redescends from this ultimate possible to the considered act and grasps its integration in the total form" (BN, p. 460).

2. Freud actually presents the formation of the superego in a more complex fashion than this. For one thing, since all of us originally have bisexual tendencies, the boy loves as well as hates his father. For another, there is a secret connection between the id and the superego that the ego does not share. Thus a particularly harsh superego may not indicate that a person has had particularly harsh parents, but rather that he or she has very strong aggressive instincts, which are now (through this connection between the id and the superego) placed in the service of the superego. One turns what might have been aggression toward the parents for mild disappointments into aggression against the self, thereby satisfying this id impulse through superego attacks on the ego. Finally, what is most often introjected as a superego is not the actual parent but the parent's superego (Freud, 1933, pp. 61–69).

3. Freud did not always describe primary narcissism as a withdrawal from the world. For example, in *Civilization and Its Discontents*, he describes an original state in which the "ego includes everything," only later separating "off an external world from itself. Our present ego-feeling is, therefore, only a shrunken residue of a much more inclusive—indeed, an all-embracing—feeling which corresponded to a more intimate bond between the ego and the world around it" (1930, p. 68). This "oceanic feeling," Freud thinks, is the origin of much religious sentiment (1930, p. 64). The "symbiotic stage" described by many post-Freudian theorists might be considered, from a Sartrean perspective, to be the stage of prereflective consciousness relating directly to the world before the advent of a truly reflective awareness. In a way, Roquentin's horrific "ecstacy" in Sartre's novel *Nausea* is a fictional description of how disturbing such a state would be to an adult. It is in-

teresting how closely this description resembles the description of psychotic states by some psychotics (see Keen, 1970, pp. 211–31). Obviously, mystical experiences of oneness, as Freud notes, also resemble this state. The point is, however, that such an original and basic connectedness between consciousness and the world fits more adequately with Sartre's phenomenological view than with Freudian drive theory.

4. *Reason and Violence* is a description of Sartre's later works—*Saint Genet, Search for a Method*, and *Critique of Dialectical Reason*—but not the Flaubert biography (which had not yet been published). It is an example of the continuing influence of Sartre on Laing, though this letter indicates a kind of counterinfluence of Laing on Sartre.

5. An interesting development since the gay rights movement is the number of male homosexual clients who assert that their sexual preference is biologically determined. What this seems to give them is a sense of justification—of *being* a homosexual as a tree is a tree. Asked if it would be all right if being gay represented some kind of fundamental choice and this choice were okay to make, one client replied, "Yes, I see what you mean. That would be *wonderful*." Lesbian clients, by contrast, frequently represent their homosexual lifestyle as a political choice; however, one suspects that it is a much more fundamental and basic choice with roots in childhood experiences.

*Chapter 3. Sartre and the Post-Freudian Drive
Theorists: A Crisis in Psychoanalytic Metatheory*

1. Mahler, of course, was European- rather than American-born—in the small Hungarian town of Sopron near the Austrian border. Although she was later a part of the Viennese psychoanalytic circle (Helen Deutsch conducted an unsuccessful analysis with her, and Mahler was part of Anna Freud's child analysis seminar), Mahler by her own admission did not feel comfortable enough working in the shadow of the giants to develop her own path in child studies (Mahler and Stepansky, 1988). Thus her really original work followed her immigration to the United States after the rise of Hitler. Interestingly, Mahler did a (this time successful) analysis with Edith Jacobson after immigrating to this country. Her earlier contacts included the circle surrounding Carl Jaspers, who also influenced Sartre.

2. Greenberg and Mitchell, in an amusing example, note the extremes to which Mahler is willing to go to retain the orthodox language of Freud or, in this case, Hartmann. In an early paper, she describes the parents of a young child with a variety of psychosomatic and psychological symptoms with the following periphrasis: "The environment, extremely overanxious, consulted one doctor after another" (quoted by Greenberg and Mitchell, 1983, p. 282).

3. Sartre discusses the way in which the appearance of a third person unites a duo into an "us object." The original two become a unit beneath the Look of the third. It is for this reason that people falling in love often wish to avoid the company of others (BN, pp. 415–23). I might also add that once lovers become a "couple," arguments often arise because of the way in which each perceives that the other makes him or her "look" in the eyes of others.

4. In other words, it might well be conceivable from a Sartrean perspective—indeed, it would appear that this is the case from Sartre's description of infant development in *The Family Idiot*—that the Other would not all at once present himself or herself in his or her full power as a Look. That is, there might be a developing recognition of the power of the Other as a subject. It is entirely possible that at the very beginning the Other is not fully distinguished from other objects in the world—though recent infant studies have sug-

gested that babies recognize their mothers almost from birth. Still, as Mahler's studies suggest, there is growing awareness of the power of the Other, which is greatly augmented by the appearance of language—a fact that makes perfectly good sense from a Sartrean perspective.

5. George Klein (1976) comes very close to an existentialist perspective on sexuality while maintaining that he is simply following Freud's emphasis on psychosexuality. For Klein, who proposes that his is a purely "clinical" (as opposed to metatheoretical) orientation, the central organizing principle of the personality is the creation of a unified self. We might argue that Klein has not so much escaped from a metatheoretical orientation as shifted that orientation from metaphysics to ontology. In doing so, he recognizes that sexuality, like other human experiences, refers to this goal of creating a unified self. Having "excised" the "energy model" from his thinking (1976, p. 7), Klein goes on to redefine the Freudian pleasure principle to include such things as "benign messages of acceptance and affirmation, communicated through bodily responses of pleasure" (1976, p. 222) and as pleasure in being able to "affirm and be affirmed by others" (1976, p. 229). Like Sartre, Klein believes that sensual/sexual experience provides a microcosm of one's way of living one's life in the world, one's fundamental project in Sartre's language; and like Sartre, Klein insists that sensual/sexual experience "always involves . . . value meaning to the self" (1976, p. 97).

6. Recent critics have, I think, been unnecessarily hard on the Beauvoir-Sartre relationship—perhaps as a consequence of its having been held up for so long as a kind of ideal love between two well-known intellectuals. I think much of this criticism is uncalled for. Certainly, some of it is merely silly, as when John Weightman, in a review of several recent books about Sartre (including Cohen-Solal's and Hayman's biographies), states that if Sartre had "ever proposed marriage to [Beauvoir]—as he did to various other women, but only halfheartedly and for tactical reasons—it seems obvious that she would have accepted him" (Weightman, 1987, p. 43). Anyone familiar with the volumes of Beauvoir's autobiography knows that Sartre *did* propose marriage to her—on the occasion of their being otherwise separated by their teaching posts—and that she declined. But Weightman's vision of the Sartre-Beauvoir relationship is undoubtedly gained from reading Hayman, who also seems bent on disparaging this relationship while playing up Sartre's "contingent loves."

I think that Hazel Barnes's (1982, 1985) assessment of this relationship is much more balanced than Weightman's or Hayman's. In her discussion of Beauvoir's final tribute to Sartre in *Adieu* (Barnes, 1985), she notes that the respect the two had for each other and the centrality of the relationship remains obvious both in the narrative account of the last ten years of Sartre's life and in the "Conversations" with Sartre that Beauvoir records there. And even though it is clear from Beauvoir's own account that there were times when the "contingent loves" (his if not hers) caused pain in their relationship, it is also true that the respect, openness, loyalty, and love between them is apparent from Sartre's statements and letters, as well as from Beauvoir's autobiographical writings. After fifty years together, Sartre's last significant words to her were, "I love you very much, my dear Castor" ("Je vous aime beaucoup, mon petit Castor") (Beauvoir, 1981, p. 123).

7. Sartre himself has said that the sequel to *Search for a Method* is the Flaubert biography.

8. Hazel Barnes points out to me that Sartre's idea of the "melodious child" is strikingly different from Freud's concept of the infant as a bundle of instinctual (sexual and aggressive) drives which must be tamed by interaction with the (civilized) world and the acquisition of a superego.

9. I want to distinguish this natural acquisition of empathy for the parents with the

enforced empathy at the expense of the child's own needs and desires which is frequently demanded of children of narcissistic parents. Alice Miller describes this situation with great clarity and eloquence in *The Drama of the Gifted Child* (1979).

Chapter 4. Sartre and the Post-Freudian Relational
Theorists: Toward a Psychoanalytic Theory of the Self

1. I want to be clear about my use of the term "self." What I am calling the "self as agent" is really not a self in the usual sense. Rather, it is a "for-itself," a self-in-the-making. But because Being-for-itself includes "nonpositional self-consciousness," I think we can refer to it as a self as agent so long as we understand that this does not imply substantiality or content.

2. Actually, for Hartmann (1939), the self is the whole of the psychophysiological organism and therefore not a psychological concept at all. The "self-representation" is a set of images of oneself similar to the set of images one has of objects. Post-Freudian theorists such as Jacobson have shortened "self-representation" to "self," even where they follow Hartmann's traditional line of thinking.

3. Despite these theoretical confusions, Masterson is often very helpful when he discusses practical techniques for dealing with borderline and/or narcissistic patients (Masterson, 1976, 1981, 1983; Masterson and Klein, 1989).

4. Sullivan is also uniquely modern in recognizing that the "mothering one" does not necessarily have to be the infant's mother—he might, for instance, just as easily be the child's father.

5. Sullivan derives "parataxic" from the Greek term *paratassein*, "to lay side by side." By this, he means distorted perceptions, judgments, and relational experiences resulting from a distortion of new interpersonal relations based on an expectation that they will be like the old childhood relationships. The corresponding "parataxic mode" refers to the normally subjective, autistic interpretation of experience and events characteristic of very young children. "Syntaxic" by contrast, refers to "being with" others in the sense of consensual validation, the development of rational thought, reality orientation, and the expression of ideas in a commonly accepted language. The "syntaxic mode" is the highest stage of development; where an individual has not reached it, the goal of therapy is to promote its development. The "prototaxic mode," by contrast, refers to the chaotic, undifferentiated, and incommunicable mental states that occur in infancy when self-awareness and concepts of time and space are lacking. Not all personal experience can be or should be translatable into the syntaxic mode, although excessive indulgence in prototaxic or parataxic distortion is characteristic of mental illness.

6. Sartre says at one point in *Being and Nothingness*, "If bad faith is possible, it is because it is an immediate, permanent threat to every project of the human being; it is because consciousness conceals in its being a permanent risk of bad faith. The origin of this risk is the fact that the nature of consciousness simultaneously is to be what it is not and not to be what it is" (BN, p. 70). In another part of the book, he says that "most of the time we flee anguish in bad faith" (BN, p. 556). Nonetheless, Sartre proposes toward the end of *Being and Nothingness* that the purpose of existential psychoanalysis is to present the possibility of authentic living, to use its techniques as a "means of deliverance and salvation" which would mean a full acceptance of oneself as the being by whom values come to exist—a validation of oneself as freedom (BN, pp. 626–27).

Chapter 5. *Sartre's Later Philosophy and the Sociomaterial World: A New Dimension for Existential Psychoanalysis*

1. Although the term "dialectic" is as old as Plato and Aristotle and was used by Kant, Sartre's usage derives immediately from Hegel and Marx, who conceive of the dialectic as a dynamic process of interpenetration of opposites. According to this view, change is the distinguishing feature of reality. For Hegel, the Aristotelian principle of contradiction no longer obtains in the realm of the dialectic; in its place, Hegel would put the principle of contrariety, with the dialectic being equivalent to the resolution of contrarieties. Hence Hegel believes that history moves not by means of simple laws of cause and effect but by means of the dynamics of the dialectic: A thesis confronted by an antithesis leads to a synthesis. The "dialectical materialism" of Marx differs from Hegelian idealism in making the material world primary and in considering the world of ideas to be secondary or epiphenomenological; at the same time, Marx's philosophy differs from older (mechanistic) materialism in emphasizing movement through interpenetration of opposites rather than simple cause and effect. Because Marx believes that all existences are complexes of opposing elements and forces with the character of a changing unity, he can speak of "contradictions" (note the new usage of the term) as producing movement.

2. Nominalism, in scholastic philosophy, is the theory that abstract or general terms (universals) represent no objective real existents, but rather are mere words or names which exist *post res* rather than *ante res*—that is, they follow rather than precede the concrete existence of things in the world. Its obverse, realism, which we would now identify with idealism, is the theory that universals exist *ante res*.

3. Sartre defines process as "a development which, though orientated, is caused by a force of exteriority which has the result of actualising the series as the temporalisation of a multiplicity in the fleeting unity of a violence of impotence" (CDR, p. 304n). A process is something which happens as the result of the work of individuals on the sociomaterial world, but it lacks the goal-directed unity of individual or group praxis. On the other hand, to view praxis as process, as analytical social science is fond of doing (Sartre particularly cites American sociologists Kurt Lewin, A. Kardiner, and J. Moreno), is to make human affairs incomprehensible (CDR, pp. 551–52).

4. When Sartre, in *Search for a Method*, says that Marxism is the philosophy of our age and that existentialism is merely an "ideology" (or minor application of major ideas) within the philosophical domain of Marxism, he is referring to the Hegelian-Marxist notion that each age has a dominant philosophy in the sense that a particular philosophy encapsulates the awarenesses and struggles of that period. Sartre concludes that Marxism is the philosophy of our age because it is "one with the movement of society" (SM, p. 7). When the class conflicts and conditions of scarcity which Marxism addresses have been overcome, Sartre goes on to say, than a "philosophy of freedom will take its place," though we at present have "no means, no intellectual instrument, no concrete experience which allows us to conceive of this freedom or this philosophy" (SM, p. 34).

Later, Sartre questions the wisdom of insisting that the *Critique* is Marxist. In an interview in 1975, for instance, he admits that he used the word "Marxist" "a bit lightly then." "At that time," he continues, "I considered the *Critique* to be Marxist; I was convinced of it. But I have changed my mind since then. Today I think that, in certain areas, the *Critique* is close to Marxism, but it is *not* a Marxist work." And this is so, Sartre says, precisely because his "idea of freedom" makes of existentialism a "separate philosophy" (Sartre in Schilpp, 1981, p. 20). Sartre, of course, does not mean that he has turned his back on class conflicts or the human misery which derives from scarcity, but he does realize that to call his philosophy Marxist is to confuse those readers who equate Marxism with materialist determinism—as Marx himself did.

5. See, for example, Flynn (1984) and Aronson (1980, 1987).

6. Hazel Barnes reminds me that the umlaut in *ëxis* renders the English equivalent hexis rather than exis, as it appears in Sheridan-Smith's translation of the *Critique*.

7. "Praxis" in Aristotle is activity which has its goal within itself and, as such, is distinguished from "*poiesis*," which is production aimed at bringing into existence something distinct from the activity itself. Praxis is also "practice" as distinguished from "theory." Sartre's usage of the term in the *Critique* does not signal an ontological shift, but it does indicate the greater emphasis in his later philosophy on action in the world as opposed to consciousness. Still, we must remember that the intentionality of the for-itself had always implied action—that world-consciousness is world-involvement and world-transcendence.

8. The section on need and desire is part of 589 pages of unorganized notes from the mid-1960s, which is in the Bibliothèque Nationale. This manuscript is also discussed by Robert Stone and Elizabeth A. Bowman in an article soon to be published in *Sartre Alive*, ed. Ronald Aronson and Adrian Van den Hoven (Detroit: Wayne State University Press) and by Juliet Simont in "*Morale esthétique, morale militante: Au delà de la 'faribole'?*" *Revue philosophique de Louvain* 87 (1989). The paraphrase here is my own and is based on the original manuscript.

9. Contemporary work on anorexia does not contradict Sartre's thesis. Hilde Brüch (1988), for instance, notes that though the typical anorexic comes from an upper-middle-class, seemingly successful family, the underlying problems are problems of emptiness and despair arising from a disturbance in self-concept. Such children were early on too compliant, too "good." Presumably, they gave up their own needs for the desires of their parents. Perhaps, in doing so, they at the same time presented the anorexic symptom as a metaphor for what had happened. They cannot "eat," cannot partake of life, because they have learned that their needs are (in Sartrean terms) guilty needs. For a Heideggerian interpretation of a case involving anorexia nervosa, see Ludwig Binswanger's "The Case of Ellen West" (in May, Angel, and Ellenberger, 1958, pp. 237–364).

10. In the following passage, Sartre pictures at random some of the "hundreds of exigencies" by means of which the practico-inert shapes the everyday life of the Parisian citizen: "The field exists: in short, it is what surrounds and conditions us. I need only glance out of the window: I will be able to see cars which are men and drivers who are cars, a policeman who is directing traffic at the corner of the street and, a little further on, the same traffic being controlled by red and green lights: *hundreds of exigencies* rise up towards me: pedestrian crossings, notices, and prohibitions; collectives (a branch of the Crédit Lyonnais, a café, a church, blocks of flats, and also a visible seriality: people queueing up in front of a shop); and instruments (pavements, a thoroughfare, a taxi rank, a bus stop, etc., proclaiming with their frozen voices how they should be used). These beings—neither thing nor man, but practical unities made up of man and inert things—these appeals, and these exigencies do not yet concern me directly. Later, I will do down into the street and become *their thing*" (CDR, p. 323).

11. Sartre uses the volcano which destroyed Herculaneum as an example of the fact that simple matter, pure Being-in-itself, "does not appear anywhere in human experience": "At any moment in History things are human precisely to the extent that men are things. A volcanic eruption destroys Herculaneum; in a way, this is man destroying himself by the volcano. It is the social and material unity of the town and its inhabitants which, within the human world, confers the unity of an event on something which with-

out men would perhaps dissolve into an indefinite process without meaning" (CDR, p. 180).

12. Sartre, however, notes that the brace, bit, and monkey wrench address him as a petty-bourgeois intellectual in a purely abstract, general way as dead possibilities since he will not, like the skilled worker, actually use them to ply his trade (CDR, p. 186).

13. For a fuller description and evaluation of both the brilliance and the occasional flaws of Sartre's socioliterary analysis in the third volume of the Flaubert biography, see Hazel Barnes's *Sartre and Flaubert* (1981), pp. 245–309, and Douglas Collins's *Sartre as Biographer* (1980), pp. 151–83.

14. I have rendered *group-en-fusion* as "group-in-fusion" rather than as "fused group," which is the term used in Sheridan-Smith's translation of Sartre's *Critique*, because the more literal translation seems to capture more accurately the dynamic quality of this kind of group.

15. In the following passage, Sartre notes the lack of chronological order in the emergence of groups: "I will recall here that . . . there is no formal law to compel [groups] to pass through the succession of different statutes described above [the movement from group-in-fusion to institution]. A fused group [group-in-fusion] may either dissolve instantaneously or be the beginning of a long development which will eventually lead to sovereignty; and in the complex world glimpsed here, the sovereign group itself may arise directly from the collective itself (or rather from its sector of other-direction). . . . But in itself this should come as no surprise, and only the whole historical complex can determine whether the group will emerge *already half-petrified*, since in concrete reality, this is to say, in every moment of temporalisation, *all statutes of all groups*, whether alive or dead, and *all types of seriality* . . . are given together as a tangle of strict relations and as the dispersed raw material of the developing totalisation" (CDR, p. 676).

16. Actually, R. D. Laing (1969; Laing and Esterson, 1964) has begun this exploration of the family as series and group along Sartrean lines; in an interview, Laing explicitly cites Sartre's later philosophy as an influence on his work (Laing in Charlesworth, 1980–81).

17. Sartre cites many clues to the "autosuggestability" which he maintains fashioned Flaubert's hysterico-epilepsy—including his childhood impersonation of an epileptic beggar which Flaubert mentions in a letter as being extremely satisfying. Not that Sartre suggests that Flaubert is playacting the nervous crisis which made him an invalid until his father died two years later, thereby relieving the son of fulfilling the father's vocational plans for him. Rather, Sartre sees in Flaubert's epilepsy a somatization representing a repressed dual desire for suicide and parricide as well as a perfect passive-aggressive solution to an impossible dilemma.

18. Wallerstein's work should not be used, as she herself did not intend it to be used, to persuade people to stay in bad marriages. On the other hand, I do think it is worthwhile to look into the ways in which the dissolution of a family may have far-reaching effects on children's lives—effects which are perhaps more understandable if we accept the Sartrean premise that the family as a group is more than a collection of individuals. Hence even if both parents remain in contact with the children, the grief of losing the security of the experience of being grouped (and the damage this does to the child's trust in groups) may have to be faced as well.

19. For example, Martin Grotjahn's *The Art and Technique of Analytic Group Therapy* (1977) summarizes much of the wisdom of conducting groups in a psychoanalytic mode. My own favorite book on group therapy is Irvin D. Yalom's *The Theory and Practice of Group Psychotherapy* (1970).

Chapter 6. A Challenge to Existential Psychoanalysis:
Ego, Mirror, and Aggressivity in Sartre and Lacan

1. The translation of *Wunsch* as "desire" rather than "wish" may have done much to spur a philosophical orientation in French psychoanalytic theory which finds its culmination in Lacan. As Marion Michel Oilner says concerning Lacanian desire, it "lacks the specificity of aim, source, or object associated with the drives" in traditional Freudian metatheory (1988, p. 122).

2. For a sketch of Lacan's quarrel with the International Psychoanalytic Association and the splits that developed in the French psychoanalytic community over the IPA's treatment of Lacan, see David Macey (1988, pp. 222–57) and Marion Michel Oliner (1988, pp. 40–58).

3. See Howard Davies's *Sartre and Les Temps Modernes* (1987) for an excellent account of the interactions between structuralists and existentialists within the pages and behind the scenes of Sartre's own journal.

4. Kojévè (1947) taught Hegel to a generation of French intellectuals. In addition to Sartre and Lacan, Raymond Queneau (who later published the lectures), Maurice Merleau-Ponty, E. Weil, Emmanuel Levinas, and Alexandre Koyré were to be found among those attending Kojévè's lectures. They were the core of a group with whom Kojévè continued the discussion over coffee and beer in a local café after adjourning class (Samuel Cherniak and John Heckman in the introduction to Hyppolite, 1946, p. xxiii). Kojévè's reading of Hegel, which preceded the French translation of *The Phenomenology of Mind*, is careful and detailed. It also stresses a view of the Hegelian Absolute which is nonreligious in making humanity the focus of a developing dialectic at the center of which lies the master-slave relationship. For Kojévè, Hegel's philosophy definitely points in the direction of Marx and Heidegger. There is no doubt that Kojévè's "left-Hegelian" perspective influenced both Sartre and Lacan.

5. In addition to the slave's devaluation as an inessential consciousness, there is a second instability in the master-slave relationship as described by Hegel. While the slave remains the truth of the master, the slave begins to discover his own truth through another avenue—through the labor by which he initially serves the master but through which he discovers in worked objects his own objectification. The master does not have this avenue to truth. Instead, his relationship with things is one of pure consumption, pure negativity. Thus the slave has an objective truth which the master does not have. Obedience and servitude have led to a kind of freedom, which will indeed be freedom if the slave can overcome the master. The slave will then have both his freedom and the objective truth of his labor—as, for example, the medieval master craftsman does.

6. Hegel, like Lacan, links language with law and authority: "In the world of ethical order, in *law* and *command*, and in the actual world, in *counsel* only, language has the *essence* for its content and is the form of that content; but here it has for its content the form itself, the form which language itself is, and is authoritative as *language*." On the other hand, Hegel goes on to suggest a view of language which is more Sartrean when he notes that "in speech, self-consciousness . . . comes as such into existence so that it exists *for others*" (Hegel, 1807, p. 308).

7. Hazel Barnes's discussion of the positive side of the ego occurs in "The Role of the Ego in Reciprocity," in *Sartre Alive*, ed. Ronald Aronson and Adrian Van

den Hoven (Detroit: Wayne State University Press, forthcoming), and in "Sartre's Ontology Reconsidered: The Reality and Role of the Ego," a paper presented at the meeting of the Pacific Division of the American Philosophical Association in the spring of 1988.

8. It is possible that Flaubert (as he is presented by Sartre), with his inability to relate to others as other persons, his avoidance of intimate relationships with women, his passivity, and his preoccupation with mirrors, would be regarded by modern psychoanalysts as a high functioning character disorder (probably narcissistic) rather than as a neurotic personality.

9. In *The Prime of Life* (1960), Simone de Beauvoir tells the story of Sartre's experience with mescaline, which took place in February 1935 at Sainte-Anne's Hospital, where Lagache was a psychiatric intern. Sartre experienced visual hallucinations ranging from an umbrella which appeared to be a vulture to an attack by devilfish. Flashbacks precipitated a deep depression in which Sartre feared he might be entering an incurable "chronic hallucinatory psychosis." One of his hallucinations involved a lobster (one remembers Sartre's distaste for crustaceans as symbolic of the in-itself) that followed him on a hiking tour he took with Beauvoir in the summer of 1935.

Sartre's obsessional preoccupation with Olga Kosakiewicz, who is the model for Xavière in Simone de Beauvoir's novel *She Came to Stay*, also dates from this period. Sartre apparently tried to exchange the madness of hallucinations for the madness of love. Finally, one evening on a crowded bus he announced that he was tired of being mad and thereafter recovered. Beauvoir attributes Sartre's psychological difficulties during this period, including the unhealthy attachment to Olga (the three later became separate friends), to resistance to accepting the passage of youth. In any case, Sartre makes use of the mescaline experience both in his discussion of hallucinations in *The Psychology of Imagination* and in his description of Roquentin's horrific experience in *Nausea*.

10. These quotes are from two tape-recorded interviews which took place on July 27 and August 24, 1987. I am grateful to Joanne Greenberg for permission to quote from them. The passage quoted here is from the July 27 interview.

11. Interview, August 24, 1987.

Chapter 7. Sartre and Lacan on the Nature of Language: Existentialist versus Structuralist Metatheory

1. Lacan insists that *manque à être* be translated into English as "want to be." I have sometimes used the more usual "lack of being," with the French following it in parentheses to let the reader know that I am using Lacan's usual term.

2. Freud defines "primal repression" as the first (archaic) phase of repression, which forms nuclei that constantly attract those contents of consciousness which are due to be repressed (Freud, 1911, 1915c, 1915d, 1926).

3. Freud's famous remark that "biology is destiny," together with other statements about feminine sexuality, have led many feminists to regard him as sexist. Feminists of the Lacanian persuasion, such as Juliet Mitchell (1974), have on the other hand argued that Freud's theory is not implicitly sexist since it indicates that gender identity is created rather than biologically given.

4. I have considered this issue of the influence of the mother's role as first witness on the subsequent "need" to denigrate women in "Sartre, Transcendence, and Education for Equality," in *Men's and Women's Liberation: Testimonies of Spirit*, ed. Haim Gordon, Leonard Grob, and Riffat Hasan (Westport, Conn.: Greenwood Press, forthcoming).

5. For a fuller discussion of Flaubert and the Knights of Nothingness, see Barnes, 1981, pp. 268–77, and Collins, 1980, pp. 151–83.

6. For example, it is acceptable in contemporary scholarship to use "he or she," as I have chosen to do in the present book, rather than the generic "he." But the substitution is often awkward and usually less than elegant. Other solutions, alternating between the generic "he" and the generic "she" or using s/he, are perhaps even more problematic. In any case, there is nothing automatic in this changing area. One does not simply write the generic pronoun—one thinks about it and chooses what to do.

7. Sartre says that the poets in *Black Orpheus*, by wrenching French words away from their normal meaning, are "stripping them of their white underclothes" and thereby forcing them to serve revolutionary praxis (quoted in Barnes, 1981, p. 392).

Chapter 8. Clinical Implications: Sartrean Revolutionary Praxis versus Lacanian Amor Fati

1. Lacan explains this paucity of clinical examples by noting that he wishes to protect the privacy of his analysands—an admirable sentiment, but one which often leaves the reader at sea with respect to picturing concretely how his insights might be used in the practice of psychotherapy.

2. Lacan, for example, praises Melanie Klein's intuitive ability to bring a client ("Little Dick") into the symbolic order—despite her inadequate conceptualization of what she is doing (Lacan, 1975, pp. 68–70).

3. Lacan's controversy with the Société Psychanalytique de Paris (SPP), of which he was a member, over his use of short sessions in training analyses dates back to the 1950s. Lacan was elected president of the SPP in 1953; six months later, a vote of no confidence forced his resignation. At this time, a number of well-known French analysts (including Sartre's friend Lagache) resigned over the SPP's treatment of Lacan and formed the Société Française de Psychanalyse (SFP). The International Psychoanalytic Association then entered the controversy, making Lacan's exclusion as a training analyst a condition for recognizing the SFP. When the SFP made the decision to exclude him from its teaching program in 1964, Lacan formed his own school, the Ecole Freudienne de Paris (EFP). The EFP continued to draw important members of the French psychoanalytic community until Lacan dissolved it shortly before his death in 1980 (see Macey, 1988, pp. 222–57; Oliner, 1988, pp. 40–58).

4. Moustapha Safouan provides a Lacanian critique of Kohut in an article in Stuart Schneiderman's collection (1980, pp. 160–64).

5. Lacan, on the other hand, jokingly suggests that the goal of analysis is to restore to the analysand the illusory freedom of Humpty Dumpty: "But we analysts have to deal with slaves who think they are masters, and who find in a language whose mission is universal the support of their servitude, and the bonds of its ambiguity. So much so that, as one might humorously put it, our goal is to restore in them the sovereign freedom displayed by Humpty Dumpty when he reminds Alice that after all he is the master of the signifier, even if he isn't the master of the signified in which his being took on its form" (1966, p. 81).

6. Lacan contemptuously rejects contemporary psychoanalytic practice which is affec-

tively oriented: "Our experience is not that of affective smoochy-woochy. We don't have to elicit in the subject the return of more or less evanescent, confused experience, in which would consist all the magic of psychoanalysis" (1975, p. 55).

Chapter 9. Conclusion: Toward a Sartrean Clinical Practice

1. What Pontalis actually says is that Sartre, who "projects" into this transcript "the antagonistic couples of which he is so fond," demonstrates by his call for an equalization of the analytic relationship "a fundamental misunderstanding of the *whole* of psychoanalysis" (BEM, p. 220).

2. Masterson believes that his own approach does involve technical neutrality, though he is certainly willing to go further than purely classical analysts in noting that to interpretation must be added mirroring, communicative matching, and confrontation—depending on the nature of a client's psychopathological difficulties. Masterson, like Kohut, is also aware of the curative power of empathic understanding. Other analysts—Harold Searles (1979), for example—will go much further in insisting that it is the humanness, and the willingness to risk oneself, on the part of the analyst which aids his or her patients in curing themselves.

3. The theoretical base for the Masterson Group is British object relations theory combined with Mahler's account of early childhood development. Masterson (1981; Masterson and Klein, 1989) conceives of actual internalized self and object representations which inhabit a person's psyche. In the case of borderline patients, whose developmental impasse Masterson believes occurred at the rapprochement crisis, the object relations unit is split—consisting of a rewarding maternal part object which offers approval for regressive and clinging behavior linked with a good, passive child over against a withdrawing maternal part object which withdraws or is angry and critical of efforts toward separation-individuation linked with an inadequate, empty, bad self.

In the case of narcissistic patients, who are supposedly arrested at the practicing subphase, there are two fused object relations units. The first is a grandiose self-object with a sense of specialness supported by an omnipotent, powerful, and perfect object; it covers an aggressive or empty object relations unit consisting of an attacking and punitive object and a humiliated, shamed, and empty self. Although a Sartrean perspective would deny the existence of objects within the self or even the idea that it is the Other as an object (rather than the Other as a subject) who is at issue, it is nonetheless true that the desire to create a substantive self can motivate many of the clinical phenomena Masterson describes.

4. Asking a client to notice or breathe into habitual body patterns will often bring the so-called repressed material to light—which seems to indicate that it is prereflectively lived rather than unconscious.

5. In Flaubert's case, of course, the present impasse was his desire to escape the law career which his father was attempting to impose on him. Sartre throughout a masterly narrative demonstrates the significance not only of this present impasse but also of the roots of Flaubert's ability to somatize—and to catch himself in the psychosomatic symptom he had created.

6. It seems to me that Reich's (1951a, 1951b) later dubious experiments with orgone boxes and the like demonstrate *ad absurdum* the fallacies in Freud's own insistence on psychobiological and psychophysical metaphors for the workings of the psyche. Reich

himself, though brilliant in analyzing character structure, falls prey to this literalization to the point of believing that he can quantify and measure libido. Eventually, he ends up with a metaphysical principle—universal visually perceptible orgone energy dancing its way through the universe.

7. Other writers (Kaplan, 1964; Keen, 1970) have noted the similarities between Roquentin's "horrible ecstasy" (N, p. 176) and the experience of psychotics. What Sartre wishes to present is an experience of the world without the addition of human meaning, including temporalization and spatialization. In such a world, things seem to overwhelm. Keen (1964, p. 228) compares Roquentin's experience with the chestnut tree to the experience of meaninglessness and being overwhelmed by things recounted in Marguerite Sechehaye's *Autobiography of a Schizophrenic Girl* (1951).

Like Roquentin, Renée (the schizophrenic girl) feels overwhelmed by objects which seem to take on a life of their own in a world where they have lost their names, their functions, and their meanings. Again like Roquentin, Renée attempts to stave off her terror by counting, naming, and thereby reintroducing human meaning to the world where things have assumed the character of pure Being-in-itself. As Roquentin says, "In vain I tried to *count* the chestnut trees, to *locate* them by their relation to the Velleda, to compare their height with the height of the plane trees: each of them escaped the relationship in which I tried to enclose it, isolated itself, and overflowed" (N, p. 173).

Roquentin's and Renée's experiences remind me of the schizophrenic patient of a colleague, who meticulously catalogued the happenings in the daily newspaper in a desperate attempt to hold onto a sense of succession which otherwise escaped him. In an effort to ward off the terrible feeling of lacking a viable personal future, he became obsessed with the external passage of time. Eugene Minkowski similarly analyzes the paranoid schizophrenic delusions of another patient in terms of an experience of loss of temporalizing potency: "There was no action or desire which, emanating from the present, reached out to the future, spanning the dull similar days. As a result, each day kept an unusual independence, failing to be immersed in the perception of any life continuity; each day life began anew, like a solitary island in a gray sea of passing time" (Minkowski in May, Angel, and Ellenberger, 1958, pp. 132–33). This man also experienced being overwhelmed by things once time had stopped.

In all of these cases, the point is that once a viable future, one's ability to *pro-ject* oneself, has been truncated, objects in the world take on a strange, almost "surreal" quality in which spatial relations seem altered or distorted. The point is not, as some critics have thought of *Nausea*, that such experiences should be regarded as more "authentic" than our everyday experiences, but that this is how the world might be experienced without the addition of human meaning—a condition which most of us would regard as pathological if it persisted for any period of time.

Bibliography

Dates in brackets indicate original publication dates.

Aron, Raymond. 1969. *Marxism and the Existentialists*. New York, Evanston, and London: Harper and Row.

Aronson, Ronald. 1980. *Jean-Paul Sartre: Philosophy in the World*. London: NLB.

_____. 1987. *Sartre's Second Critique*. Chicago and London: University of Chicago Press.

Balint, Michael. 1969. *Primary Love and Psycho-analytic Techniques*. New York: Basic Books.

Barnes, Hazel E. [1967]. *An Existentialist Ethics*. Chicago and London: University of Chicago Press, 1978.

_____. 1974. *Sartre*. London: Quartet Books.

_____. 1981. *Sartre and Flaubert*. Chicago and London: University of Chicago Press.

_____. 1982. "Simone de Beauvoir's Autobiography as a Biography of Sartre." *French Review* 55 (Summer): 79–99.

_____. 1983. "Sartre's Concept of the Self." *Review of Existential Psychology and Psychiatry* 27: 41–65.

_____. 1985. "Beauvoir and Sartre: The Forms of Farewell." *Philosophy and Literature* 9: 21–40.

_____. 1988. "Sartre's Ontology Reconsidered: The Reality and Role of the Ego." Paper presented at the American Philosophical Association, Western Division, Oakland, Calif., Spring.

_____. 1989. "Sartre's Scenario for Freud," *L'Esprit Créateur*, special ed., "Writing Lives: Sartre, Beauvoir and (Auto)Biography" 29, 4 (Winter): 52–64.

_____. Forthcoming. "The Role of the Ego in Reciprocity." In *Sartre Alive*, ed. Ronald Aronson and Adrian Van den Hoven. Detroit: Wayne State University Press.

Beauvoir, Simone de. [1949]. *The Second Sex*. Trans. H. M. Parshley. New York, Toronto, and London: Bantam Books, 1970.

_____. [1960]. *The Prime of Life*. Trans. Peter Green.

New York: World Publishing Company, 1969.

————. [1981]. *Adieux: A Farewell to Sartre*. Trans. Patrick O'Brian. New York: Pantheon Books, 1984.

Benvenuto, Bice, and Roger Kennedy. 1986. *The Works of Jacques Lacan: An Introduction*. New York: St. Martin's Press.

Bettelheim, Bruno. [1982]. *Freud and Man's Soul*. New York: Random House, 1984.

Binswanger, Ludwig. 1963. *Being in the World*. Trans. Jacob Needleman, with critical commentary. New York and London: Basic Books.

Boss, Medard. 1957. *The Analysis of Dreams*. London: Ryder.

————. 1963. *Psychoanalysis and Daseinsanalysis*. Trans. Ludwig B. Lefebre. New York and London: Basic Books.

Bowlby, John. 1969. *Attachment*. New York: Basic Books.

————. 1980. *Loss: Sadness and Depression*. New York: Basic Books.

Brüch, Hilde. 1988. *Conversations with Anorexics*. Ed. Danita Czyzewski and Melanie A. Suhr. New York: Basic Books.

Bugental, James F. [1965]. *The Search for Authenticity: An Existential-Analytic Approach to Psychotherapy*. New York: Irvington, 1989.

Cannon, Betty. 1985. "The Death of the Objective Observer: Sartre's Dialectical Reason as an Epistemology for the Social Sciences." *Man and World* 18: 269–93.

————. 1985b. "Sartre's Idea of Community." In *Hypatia: Essays in Classics, Comparative Literature, and Philosophy Presented to Hazel E. Barnes on Her Seventieth Birthday*, ed. William M. Calder III, Ulrich K. Goldsmith, and Phyllis B. Kenevan. Boulder, Colo.: Colorado Associated University Press.

————. Forthcoming. "Sartre, Transcendence, and Education for Equality." In *Men's and Women's Liberation: Testimonies of Spirit*, ed. Haim Gordon, Leonard Grob, and Riffat Hassan. Westport, Conn.: Greenwood Press.

Catalano, Joseph S. [1974]. *A Commentary on Jean-Paul Sartre's Being and Nothingness*. Chicago and London: University of Chicago Press, 1980.

Charlesworth, Max. 1980–81. "Sartre, Laing, and Freud." *Review of Existential Psychology and Psychiatry* 17, 1: 23–39.

Cohen-Solal, Annie. [1985]. *Sartre*. Ed. Norman Macafee and trans. Anna Cancogni. New York: Pantheon Books, 1987.

Collins, Douglas. 1980. *Sartre as Biographer*. Cambridge, Mass., and London: Harvard University Press.

Contat, Michel, and Michel Rybalka. 1974. *The Writings of Jean-Paul Sartre: A Bibliographical Life*. Vol. 1. Evanston, Ill.: Northwestern University Press.

————. 1974b. *The Writings of Jean-Paul Sartre: Selected Prose*. Vol. 2. Evanston, Ill.: Northwestern University Press.

Culler, Jonathan. 1975. *Structuralist Poetics: Structuralism, Linguistics, and the Study of Literature*. Ithaca, N. Y.: Cornell University Press.

Davies, Howard. 1987. *Sartre and Les Temps Modernes*. Cambridge, Mass.: Cambridge University Press.

Dilman, Ilham. 1984. *Freud and the Mind*. Oxford: Basil Blackwell.

Eagle, Morris N. 1984. *Recent Developments in Psychoanalysis*. New York: McGraw-Hill Book Company.

Erikson, Erik. 1959. *Identity and the Life Cycle*. New York: International Universities Press.

————. 1968. *Identity: Youth and Crisis*. London: Faber and Faber.

Fairbairn, W. Ronald D. [1952]. *Psychoanalytic Studies of the Personality*. London, Henley, Eng., and Boston: Routledge & Kegan Paul, 1984.

Fell, Joseph P. 1979. *Heidegger and Sartre: An Essay on Being and Place*. New York: Columbia University Press.

Flynn, Thomas R. 1984. *Sartre and Marxist Existentialism*. Chicago and London: University of Chicago Press.

Frankl, Viktor E. [1955]. *The Doctor and the Soul: From Psychotherapy to Logotherapy*. 2d rev. ed. New York: Vintage Books, 1986.

_____. [1959]. *Man's Search for Meaning: An Introduction to Logotherapy*. New York: Pocket Books, 1985.

_____. [1967] *Psychotherapy and Existentialism: Selected Papers on Logotherapy*. New York: Washington Square Press, 1985.

_____. [1969]. *The Will to Meaning: Foundations and Applications of Logotherapy*. New York: New American Library, 1981.

Freud, Anna. [1937]. *The Ego and the Mechanisms of Defense*. New York: International Universities Press, 1985.

Freud, Sigmund. *The Standard Edition of the Complete Psychological Works of Sigmund Freud*. 24 vols. Trans. James Strachey. London: Hogarth Press, 1953–1974. Hereafter cited as SE.

_____. [1895]. *Studies on Hysteria*. Vol. 2 in SE.

_____. [1896]. "The Aetiology of Hysteria." Vol. 3 in SE.

_____. [1900]. *The Interpretation of Dreams*. Vols. 4 and 5 in SE.

_____. [1901]. *The Psychopathology of Everyday Life*. Vol. 6 in SE.

_____. [1905a]. *Three Essays on the Theory of Sexuality*. Vol. 7 in SE.

_____. [1905b]. "Fragment of an Analysis of a Case of Hysteria." Vol. 7 in SE.

_____. [1909]. "Notes upon a Case of Obsessional Neurosis." Vol. 10 in SE.

_____. [1910]. "Five Lectures on Psycho-Analysis." Vol. 11 in SE.

_____. [1911]. "Psycho-Analytic Notes on an Autobiographical Account of a Case of Paranoia (Dementia Paranoides)." Vol. 12 in SE.

_____. [1912a]. "A Note on the Unconscious in Psycho-Analysis." Vol. 12 in SE.

_____. [1912b]. "The Dynamics of the Transference." Vol. 12 in SE.

_____. [1912–13]. *Totem and Taboo*. Vol. 13 in SE.

_____. [1913]. "The Disposition to Obsessional Neurosis." Vol. 12 in SE.

_____. [1914a]. "On Narcissism: An Introduction." Vol. 14 in SE.

_____. [1914b]. "On the History of the Psycho-Analytic Movement." Vol. 14 in SE.

_____. [1914c]. "Remembering, Repeating, and Working-Through." Vol. 12 in SE.

_____. [1915a]. "Instincts and Their Vicissitudes." Vol. 14 in SE.

_____. [1915b]. "Observations on Transference-Love." Vol. 12 in SE.

_____. [1915c]. "The Unconscious." Vol. 14 in SE.

_____. [1915d]. "Repression." Vol. 14 in SE.

_____. [1916–17]. *Introductory Lectures on Psycho-Analysis*. Vols. 15 and 16 in SE.

_____. [1917]. "Mourning and Melancholia." Vol. 14 in SE.

_____. [1920a]. *Beyond the Pleasure Principle*. Vol. 18 in SE.

_____. [1920b]. "The Psychogenesis of a Case of Female Homosexuality." Vol. 18 in SE.

_____. [1921]. *Group Psychology and the Analysis of the Ego*. Vol. 18 in SE.

_____. [1923]. *The Ego and the Id*. Vol. 19 in SE.

_____. [1926]. *Inhibitions, Symptoms, and Anxiety*. Vol. 20 in SE.

_____. [1928]. "Dostoevsky and Parricide." Vol. 21 in SE.

_____. [1930]. *Civilization and Its Discontents*. Vol. 21 in SE.

_____. [1933]. *New Introductory Lectures on Psycho-Analysis*. Vol. 22 in SE.

_____. [1937]. "Analysis Terminable and Interminable." Vol. 23 in SE.

_____. [1940]. "Splitting of the Ego in the Process of Defense." Vol. 23 in SE.

————. [1950]. *A Project for a Scientific Psychology.* Vol. 1 in *SE.*

————. 1954. *The Origins of Psychoanalysis. Letters to Wilhelm Fliess, Drafts and Notes: 1887–1902.* Ed. Marie Bonaparte et al. and trans. E. Mosbacher and E. Kris. New York: Basic Books.

Fromm-Reichmann, Frieda. 1950. *Principles of Intensive Psychotherapy.* Chicago and London: University of Chicago Press.

Genet, Jean. [1952]. *The Maids and Deathwatch.* Trans. Bernard Frechtman. New York: Grove Press, 1962.

Giovacchini, Peter L. 1984. *Character Disorders and Adaptative Mechanisms.* New York and London: Jason Aronson.

Greenberg, Jay R., and Stephen A. Mitchell. 1983. *Object Relations in Psychoanalytic Theory.* Cambridge, Mass., and London: Harvard University Press.

Greenberg, Joanne [Hannah Green]. 1964. *I Never Promised You a Rose Garden.* New York: New American Library.

Grotjahn, Martin. 1977. *The Art and Technique of Analytic Group Therapy.* New York: Jason Aronson.

Guntrip, Harry. [1969]. *Schizoid Phenomena, Object-Relations and the Self.* New York: International Universities Press, 1985.

————. [1971]. *Psychoanalytic Theory, Therapy, and the Self.* New York: Basic Books, 1973.

Hartmann, Heinz. 1939. *Ego Psychology and the Problem of Adaptation.* New York: International Universities Press.

Hayman, Ronald. 1987. *Sartre: A Life.* New York: Simon and Schuster.

Hegel, G. W. F. [1807]. *The Phenomenology of Spirit.* Trans. A. V. Miller, with foreword by J. N. Findlay. Oxford, New York, Toronto, and Melbourne: Oxford University Press, 1977.

Heidegger, Martin. [1927]. *Being and Time.* Trans. John Macquarrie and Edward Robinson. London: SCM Press, 1962.

Husserl, Edmund. [1913]. *Ideas.* Trans. W. R. Boyce Gibson. New York and London: Collier Books, 1967.

Hyppolite, Jean. [1946]. *Genesis and Structure of Hegel's Phenomenology of Spirit.* Trans. Samuel Cherniak and John Heckman. Evanston, Ill.: Northwestern University Press, 1974.

Izenberg, Gerald N. 1976. *The Existentialist Critique of Freud.* Princeton, N. J.: Princeton University Press.

Jacobson, Edith. [1964]. *The Self and the Object World.* Madison, Conn.: International Universities Press, 1986.

Jacobson, Roman. 1987. *Language in Literature,* ed. Krystyna Pomorska and Stephen Rudy. Cambridge, Mass., and London: Harvard University Press.

Jacobson, Roman, and M. Halle. 1956. *Fundamentals of Language.* The Hague: Mouton.

Jones, Ernest. [1953]. *The Life and Work of Sigmund Freud.* Ed. and abr. Lionel Trilling and Steven Marcus. New York: Basic Books, 1961.

Kaplan, B. 1964. *The Inner World of Mental Illness.* New York: Harper and Row.

Keen, Ernest. 1970. *Three Faces of Being: Toward an Existential Clinical Psychology.* New York: Meredith Corp.

Kernberg, Otto F. [1975]. *Borderline Conditions and Pathological Narcissism.* New York: Jason Aronson, 1985.

————. 1976. *Object Relations Theory and Clinical Psychoanalysis.* New York: Jason Aronson.

Kirsner, Douglas. 1977. *The Schizoid World of Jean-Paul Sartre and R. D. Laing.* Atlantic Highlands, N. J.: Humanities Press.

Klein, George. 1976. *Psychoanalytic Theory*. New York: International Universities Press.

Klein, Melanie. 1964. *Contributions to Psychoanalysis, 1921–1945*. New York: McGraw-Hill. Hereafter cited as CP.

_____. 1975. *Envy and Gratitude and Other Works, 1946–1963*. New York: Delacorte Press. Hereafter cited as EG.

_____. [1923]. "The Role of the School in the Libidinal Development of the Child." CP.

_____. [1928]. "Early Stages of the Oedipus Complex." CP.

_____. [1930]. "The Importance of Symbol-Formation in the Development of the Ego." CP.

_____. [1948]. "On the Theory of Anxiety and Guilt." EG.

_____. [1957]. "Envy and Gratitude." EG.

Klein, Melanie, and J. Riviere. 1964. *Love, Hate, and Reparation*. New York: W. W. Norton.

Kockelmans, Joseph. 1967. *Edmund Husserl's Phenomenological Psychology*. Pittsburgh: Duquesne University Press.

Kohut, Heinz. 1977. *The Restoration of Self*. New York: International Universities Press.

_____. 1978. *The Search for the Self: Selected Writings of Heinz Kohut: 1950–1978*. 2 vols. ed. Paul H. Ornstein. New York: International Universities Press.

_____. 1984. *How Does Analysis Cure?* Ed. Arnold Goldberg. Chicago and London: University of Chicago Press.

Kojève, Alexandre. [1947]. *Introduction to the Reading of Hegel*. Trans. James H. Nichols, Jr., and ed. Allan Bloom. New York: Basic Books, 1969.

Lacan, Jacques. [1966]. *Écrits*. Trans. Alan Sheridan. New York and London: W. W. Norton and Company, 1977.

_____. 1968. *Speech and Language in Psychoanalysis*. Trans. Anthony Wilden. Baltimore and London: Johns Hopkins University Press.

_____. [1973]. *The Four Fundamental Concepts of Psychoanalysis*. Trans. Alan Sheridan and ed. Jacques-Alain Miller. New York and London: W. W. Norton and Company, 1978.

_____. [1975]. *The Seminar of Jacques Lacan: Book I—Freud's Papers on Technique, 1953–54*. Trans. John Forester and ed. Jacques-Alain Miller. New York and London: W. W. Norton and Company, 1988.

_____. [1978]. *The Seminar of Jacques Lacan: Book II—The Ego in Freud's Theory and in the Technique of Psychoanalysis, 1954–55*. Trans. Sylvana Tomaselli, with notes by John Forrester, and ed. Jacques-Alain Miller. New York and London: W. W. Norton and Company, 1988.

_____. 1985. *Feminine Sexuality*. Trans. Jacqueline Rose and ed. Juliet Mitchell and Jacqueline Rose. New York and London: W. W. Norton and Company.

LaCapra, Dominick. 1978. *A Preface to Sartre*. Ithaca, N. Y.: Cornell University Press.

Laing, R. D. [1959a]. *The Divided Self*. New York: Penguin Books, 1979.

_____. [1959b]. *Do You Love Me?* New York: Pantheon Books, 1976.

_____. [1961]. *Self and Others*. New York and London: Penguin Books, 1987.

_____. [1969]. *The Politics of the Family and Other Essays*. New York: Vintage Books, 1972.

_____. [1970]. *Knots*. New York: Vintage Books, 1971.

Laing, R. D., and D. G. Cooper. [1964]. *Reason and Violence*. New York: Vintage Books, 1971.

Laing, R. D., and David Esterson. 1964. *Sanity, Madness, and the Family*. London: Tavistock Publications.

Laplanche, J., and J.-B. Pontalis. 1973. *The Language of Psycho-Analysis.* Trans. Donald Nicholson-Smith. New York and London: W. W. Norton and Company.

Lévi-Strauss, Claude. [1958]. *Structural Anthropology.* Garden City, N. Y.: Anchor Books, 1967.

————. [1962]. *The Savage Mind.* Chicago and London: University of Chicago Press, 1966.

————. [1964]. *The Raw and the Cooked.* Trans. John Weightman and Doreen Weightman. New York: Harper and Row, 1970.

Lowen, Alexander. 1967a. *The Betrayal of the Body.* New York: Collier Books.

————. 1967b. *Love and Orgasm.* New York: Collier Books.

————. 1980. *Fear of Life.* New York: Collier Books.

————. 1983. *Narcissism: Denial of the True Self.* New York: Collier Books.

Macey, David. 1988. *Lacan in Contexts.* London and New York: Verso.

Mahler, Margaret S. 1979. *The Selected Papers of Margaret S. Mahler.* 2 vols. New York and London: Jason Aronson.

Mahler, Margaret S., Fred Pine, and Anni Bergman. 1975. *The Psychological Birth of the Human Infant.* New York: Basic Books.

Mahler, Margaret S., and Paul E. Stepansky. 1988. *The Memoirs of Margaret S. Mahler.* New York: Free Press.

Marks, Elaine, and Isabelle de Courtivron, eds. 1981. *New French Feminisms.* New York: Schocken Books.

Masterson, James. 1976. *Psychotherapy of the Borderline Adult: A Developmental Approach.* New York: Brunner/Mazel.

————. 1981. *The Narcissistic and Borderline Disorders: An Integrated Developmental Approach.* New York: Brunner/Mazel.

————. 1983. *Countertransference and Psychotherapeutic Technique.* New York: Brunner/ Mazel.

————. 1985. *The Real Self: A Developmental, Self, and Object Relations Approach.* New York: Brunner/Mazel.

Masterson, James, and Ralph Klein, eds. 1989. *Psychotherapy of the Disorders of the Self.* New York: Brunner/Mazel.

May, Rollo. 1950. *The Meaning of Anxiety.* New York: Ronald Press.

————. [1953]. *Man's Search for Himself.* New York: Signet, 1967.

————. 1983. *The Discovery of Being: Writings in Existential Psychology.* New York and London: W. W. Norton and Company.

May, Rollo, Ernest Angel, and Henri F. Ellenberger, eds. 1958. *Existence.* New York: Simon and Schuster.

Miller, Alice. [1979]. *The Drama of the Gifted Child.* Trans. Ruth Ward. New York: Basic Books, 1981.

————. [1981]. *Thou Shalt Not Be Aware: Society's Betrayal of the Child.* New York: Farrar, Straus, and Giroux, 1984.

Mitchell, Juliet. [1974]. *Psychoanalysis and Feminism: Freud, Reich, Laing, and Women.* New York: Vintage Books, 1975.

Modell, A. 1975. "The Ego and the Id: Fifty Years Later." *International Journal of Psychoanalysis* 56: 57–68.

————. 1981. "Does Metapsychology Still Exist?" *International Journal of Psychoanalysis* 62: 391–401.

Moi, Toril, ed. 1987. *French Feminist Thought: A Reader.* New York: Basil Blackwell.

Muller, John P., and William J. Richardson. 1982. *Lacan and Language: A Reader's Guide to Écrits.* New York: International Universities Press.

Murdoch, Iris. [1953]. *Sartre: Romantic Rationalist*. New York: Viking, 1987.

Oliner, Marion Michel. 1988. *Cultivating Freud's Garden in France*. Northvale, N. J., and London: Jason Aronson.

Peterfreund, E. 1978. "Some Critical Comments on Psychoanalytic Conceptualizations of Infancy." *International Journal of Psychoanalysis*, 59: 427–41.

Piaget, Jean, and Barbel Inhelder. [1948]. *The Child's Conception of Space*. New York: W. W. Norton and Company, 1967.

Pine, Fred. 1985. *Developmental Theory and Clinical Process*. New Haven, Conn., and London: Yale University Press.

Pribrim, G., and M. Gill. 1976. *Freud's 'Project' Reassessed*. New York: Basic Books.

Ragland-Sullivan, Ellie. 1986. *Jacques Lacan and the Philosophy of Psychoanalysis*. Urbana and Chicago: University of Illinois Press.

Reich, Wilhelm. [1945]. *Character Analysis*. Trans. Vincent R. Carfagno. New York: Farrar, Straus, and Giroux, 1972.

———. [1948]. *The Function of the Orgasm*. New York: Farrar, Strauss, and Giroux, 1972.

———. 1951a. *Cosmic Superimposition*. Rangeley, Me.: Wilhelm Reich Foundation.

———. 1951b. *The Orgone Energy Accumulator*. Rangeley, Me.: Orgone Energy Institute Press.

Ricoeur, Paul. 1970. *Freud and Philosophy*. Trans. Denis Savage. New Haven, Conn., and London: Yale University Press.

Riesman, David. 1950. *The Lonely Crowd*. New Haven, Conn.: Yale University Press.

Sartre, Jean-Paul. [1936]. *Imagination: A Psychological Critique [L'Imagination]*. Trans. Forrest Williams. Ann Arbor: University of Michigan Press, 1962.

———. [1937]. *The Transcendence of the Ego [La Transcendance de l'Ego]*. Trans. Robert Kirkpatrick and Forrest Williams. New York: Farrar, Strauss, and Giroux, 1957.

———. [1938]. *Nausea [La Nausée]*. Trans. Lloyd Alexander. New York: New Directions Publishing Corp., 1964.

———. [1939]. *The Emotions: Outline of a Theory [Esquisse d'une théorie des émotions]*. Trans. Bernard Frechtman. New York: Philosophical Library, 1975.

———. [1940]. *The Psychology of Imagination [L'Imaginaire]*. Trans. Bernard Frechtman. New York: Washington Square Press, 1966.

———. [1943]. *Being and Nothingness: An Essay on Phenomenological Ontology [L'Etre et le Néant: Essai d'ontologie phénoménologique]*. Trans. Hazel E. Barnes. New York: Philosophical Library, 1956.

———. [1944]. *No Exit [Huis clos]*. Trans. Stuart Gilbert. New York: Vintage Books, 1955.

———. [1946a]. *Baudelaire*. Trans. Martin Turnell. New York: New Directions, 1950.

———. [1946b]. "Preface" to *Black Orpheus [Orphée noir]*. Ed. Leopold Sedar Senghor and trans. S. W. Allen. Paris: Présence Africaine, 1963.

———. [1946c]. *Existentialism [L'Existentialisme est un humanisme]*. Trans. Bernard Frechtman. New York: Philosophical Library, 1947.

———. [1948]. *Dirty Hands [Les Mains sales]*. Trans. Lionel Abel. New York: Vintage Books, 1955.

———. [1952]. *Saint Genet: Actor and Martyr [Saint Genet, comédien et martyr]*. Trans. Bernard Frechtman. New York: George Braziller, 1963.

———. [1959]. *The Condemned of Altona [Les Sequéstrés d'Altona]*. Trans. Silvia Leeson and George Leeson. New York: Knopf, 1961.

———. [1960a]. *Critique of Dialectical Reason [Critique de la raison dialectique]*. Ed. Jonathan Ree and trans. Alan Sheridan-Smith. London: Verso/NLB, 1982.

———. [1960b]. *Search for a Method [Questions de méthode]*. Trans. Hazel E. Barnes. New York: Vintage Books, 1968.

————. [1963]. *The Words* [*Les Mots*]. Trans. Bernard Frechtman. New York: George Braziller, 1964.

————. [1971]. *The Family Idiot* [*L'Idiot de la famille*]. 2 vols. Trans. Carol Cosman. Chicago and London: University of Chicago Press, 1981 (vol. 1), 1987 (vol. 2).

————. [1972b]. *L'Idiot de la famille*. Vol. 3. Paris: Gallimard.

————. [1972a]. *Between Existentialism and Marxism* [*Situations VIII* and *Situations IX*]. Trans. John Mathews. New York: Morrow Quill Paperbacks, 1979.

————. [1975]. *Life/Situations* [*Situations X*]. Trans. Paul Auster and Lydia Davis. New York: Pantheon Books, 1977.

————. 1983. *Cahiers pour une morale*. Paris: Gallimard.

————. 1984. *The Freud Scenario* [*Le Scénario Freud*]. Ed. J.-B. Pontalis and trans. Quintin Hoare. Chicago: University of Chicago Press, 1986.

————. 1985. *Critique de la raison dialectique*. Vol. 2. Paris: Gallimard.

Saussure, Ferdinand de. [1915]. *Course in General Linguistics*. Trans. Wade Baskin and ed. Charles Bally and Albert Sechehaye. New York: Philosophical Library, 1959.

Schafer, Roy. 1976. *A New Language for Psychoanalysis*. New Haven, Conn., and London: Yale University Press.

Schilpp, Paul Arthur, ed. 1981. *The Philosophy of Jean-Paul Sartre*. La Salle, Ill.: Open Court Publishing Co.

Schneiderman, Stuart. 1983. *Jacques Lacan: The Death of an Intellectual Hero*. Cambridge, Mass., and London: Harvard University Press.

————, trans. and ed. 1980. *Returning to Freud: Clinical Psychoanalysis in the School of Lacan*. New Haven, Conn., and London: Yale University Press.

Searles, Harold E. 1979. *Countertransference and Related Subjects*. New York: International Universities Press.

Sechehaye, Marguerite. [1951]. *Autobiography of a Schizophrenic Girl*. Trans. Frank Conroy. New York: Signet Books, 1979.

Simont, Juliet. 1989. "Morale esthétique, morale militante: Au delà de la 'faribole'?" Revue Philosophique de Louvain 87: 23–58.

Skinner, B. F. [1971]. *Beyond Freedom and Dignity*. New York: Bantam Books, 1980.

Smith, Joseph H., and William Kerrigan, eds. 1983. *Interpreting Lacan*. New Haven, Conn., and London: Yale University Press.

Spitz, René. [1945]. *Psychoanalytic Study of the Child*. Vol. 1: 53–73.

————. 1946. *Psychoanalytic Study of the Child*. Vol. 2: 313–342.

————. 1965. *The First Year of Life*. New York: International Universities Press.

Stern, Daniel N. 1985. *The Interpersonal World of the Infant*. New York: Basic Books.

Stone, Robert, in collaboration with Elizabeth Bowman. 1986. "Dialectical Ethics: A First Look at Sartre's Unpublished 1964 Rome Lecture Notes." *Social Texts* 13, 4: 195–215.

Stone, Robert, and Elizabeth A. Bowman. Forthcoming. "Sartre's 'Morality' and 'History': A First Look at the Notes for the Unpublished 1965 Cornell Lectures." In *Sartre Alive*, ed. Ronald Aronson and Adrian Van den Hoven. Detroit: Wayne State University Press.

Sturrock, John, ed. 1979. *Structuralism and Since: From Lévi-Strauss to Derrida*. Oxford, New York, Toronto, and Melbourne: Oxford University Press.

Sullivan, Harry Stack. [1940]. *Conceptions of Modern Psychiatry*. New York: W. W. Norton and Company, 1953.

————. 1953. *The Interpersonal Theory of Psychiatry*. New York and London: W. W. Norton and Company.

————. 1956. *Clinical Studies in Psychiatry*. New York: W. W. Norton and Company.

_____. 1964. *The Fusion of Psychiatry and Social Science.* New York: W. W. Norton and Company.

_____. 1974. *Schizophrenia as a Human Process.* New York: W. W. Norton and Company.

Sulloway, Frank J. 1979. *Freud, Biologist of the Mind.* New York: Basic Books.

Thompson, M. Guy. 1985. *The Death of Desire: A Study in Psychopathology.* New York and London: New York University Press.

Van Kaam, Adrian. 1969. *Existential Foundations of Psychology.* Garden City, N. Y.: Doubleday and Co.

Van den Berg, J. H. 1955. *The Phenomenological Approach to Psychiatry.* Springfield, Ill.: Charles C. Thomas.

Wallerstein, Judith S., and Sandra Blakeslee. 1989. *Second Chances: Men, Women, and Children a Decade after Divorce.* New York: Ticknor and Fields.

Weightman, John, 1987. "Summing Up Sartre." *New York Review of Books,* April 13, pp. 42–46.

Winnicott, D. W. 1958. *Through Pediatrics to Psychoanalysis.* London: Hogarth Press.

_____. 1965a. *The Family and Individual Development.* London and New York: Tavistock Publications.

_____. 1965b. *The Maturational Process and the Facilitating Environment.* New York: International Universities Press.

_____. [1971]. *Playing and Reality.* London and New York: Tavistock Publications, 1985.

Yalom, Irvin D. 1970. *The Theory and Practice of Group Psychotherapy.* New York: Basic Books.

_____. 1980. *Existential Psychotherapy.* New York: Basic Books.

_____. 1989. *Love's Executioner and Other Tales of Psychotherapy.* New York: Basic Books.

Yeats, W. B. [1956]. *The Collected Poems of W. B. Yeats.* New York: Macmillan Company, 1963.

Index